A POLITE EXCHANGE OF BULLETS

The Duel and the English Gentleman 1750–1850

A POLITE EXCHANGE OF BULLETS

The Duel and the English Gentleman 1750–1850

Stephen Banks

THE BOYDELL PRESS

The right of Stephen Banks to be identified as
the author of this work has been asserted in accordance with
sections 77 and 78 of the Copyright, Designs and Patents Act 1988

First published 2010
The Boydell Press, Woodbridge

ISBN 978 1 84383 571 4

The Boydell Press is an imprint of Boydell & Brewer Ltd
PO Box 9, Woodbridge, Suffolk IP12 3DF, UK
and of Boydell & Brewer Inc.
668 Mount Hope Ave, Rochester, NY 14620, USA
website: www.boydellandbrewer.com

A CIP catalogue record for this book is available
from the British Library

Produced by Toynbee Editorial Services Ltd

The publisher has no responsibility for the continued existence or accuracy of URLs for external or
third-party internet websites referred to in this book, and does not guarantee that any content on
such websites is, or will remain, accurate or appropriate.

This publication is printed on acid-free paper

Printed in Great Britain by
CPI Antony Rowe, Chippenham and Eastbourne

Cover illustration
The Point of Honour Decided or the Leaden Argument of a Love Affair by Robert Cruikshank.
Taken from *The English Spy* by Bernard Blackmantle (London: Sherwood, Gilbert and Piper, 1826)
© The British Library Board 1023910.951.

Contents

Illustrations

Acknowledgments

A book such as this goes to press with more debts than can ever be fully repaid. My many friends and colleagues from the schools of law at Birkbeck College and then the University of Reading should all be acknowledged but in particular the insights, patience and generosity of Anton Schütz, Linda Mulcahy, Charlotte Smith and Lawrence McNamara have kept this project on track. I have profited much from the splendid work of scholars such as Donna Andrew, Ute Frevert and Robert Shoemaker but in particular from conversations with Antony Simpson whose views, not just on the subject of duelling, I have always found invigorating.

Some of the material contained within chapters four and chapters seven has previously been published in my articles in the *Journal of British Studies* and the *Kings Law Journal* and I am grateful for permission to reproduce it here. I would also like to thank the librarians and archivists of the many public institutions who dealt so patiently and professionally with my enquiries. As ever the staff of the British Library, the British Newspaper Library at Colindale and the National Archives were indispensible. The special collections at University College London and within the Museum of English Rural Life at Reading provided much of interest and in addition I was always grateful for the resources (and the coffee) of the Institute of Historical Research. The many unsung heroes of the public record offices at Norwich, Maidstone, Reading and elsewhere must be mentioned. Thanks also to Melissa Nelson who has tackled with manuscript with her own special breed of courage, the remaining eccentricities and errors being entirely of my own making.

Finally, the greatest debt of all that I owe is of course to Sanjeeda Ahmed my wife. She has coped not only with the difficulty of trying to explain to our young children exactly what it is that their father does for a living but has also grown inured to the sight of me wandering up and down the house mumbling to myself about footnotes at the most unlikely times of day and night. Thanks indeed.

Introduction

This is a study of one particular aspect of English society during a period of the most astonishing transformation. In 1750, a foreign-born king, who had not long before defeated an attempt to unseat him, presided over the affairs of a largely agrarian country. A constitutional settlement had limited his powers, but he still claimed the right to make and unmake administrations at will. Science had progressed, but until as recently as 1736 one could still be condemned for the offence of witchcraft. Travel remained a precarious endeavour limited to the speed of the horse and vulnerable to the predations of the highwaymen who infested the doubtfully maintained turnpikes. Education for most was rudimentary. By 1850, by contrast, men were flying over London in balloons for mere pleasure, hurrying about their affairs upon the paved and lighted streets or else journeying through the kingdom at hitherto unimaginable speeds of locomotion. A thriving middle class had begun to emerge, literate, rationally minded and politically enfranchised. By the time at which this study concludes its examination, Great Britain was on the threshold of the Great Exhibition.

Yet the period in between was often traumatic: abroad the nation spent much time and blood engaged in a deadly struggle with an old rival, while at home domestic conflict seemed scarcely less dramatic. By 1850, the institutions of power had successfully met and defeated challenges to public order, along the way introducing new modes of law enforcement and penalisation. For a long time, though, many supposed that the very existence of the society that they recognised was in doubt as Radicals, Deists, Frame-Breakers, Chartists and others appealed to an increasingly resistive and radicalised population to challenge the legitimacy of existing laws, customs, creeds and practices. The later eighteenth and early nineteenth centuries were a time of contending spirits and ideals, of new and widespread popular movements and anxious governmental responses.

This being so, some might think that studying duelling, out of the many rich opportunities for research apparent in the eighteenth and nineteenth centuries, represents a somewhat quixotic choice. One might be forgiven for supposing that observing the manner in which some few gentlemen resolved their personal, often petty, differences can tell us little about eighteenth- and nineteenth-century England. This assumption, however, would be mistaken. Although it will soon become apparent that duelling was not a very common phenomenon, this does not mean that it was a marginalised act of peripheral interest. Rather, this study will assert that as a phenomenon duelling was embedded in a broader language of violence, a language which, for good or ill, played an important role in constructing and sustaining the social structure. More specifically, the potential for this form of mannered violence – occasionally realised – both ordered the relations of gentlemen with each other and conditioned the way in which they perceived and were perceived by the rest of society. As such, I shall argue, the duel can tell us much about the more general nature of Georgian England. Similarly, the demise of the duel, during the early years of the reign of Victoria, can be seen to signal the most profound changes in the social fabric on the road to modernity.

That the ability to receive or to inflict certain forms of violence is a powerful mode of social delineation and a signifier of social status is not a new discovery, and at the risk of indeed seeming somewhat quixotic, I shall begin with a story told by the Greek Herodotus in the fifth century BC. In Book IV of his *Histories*, he relates that the Scythian people once invaded the country of Media. The army was away for twenty-eight years, and during this time their wives, who had been left behind at home, interbred with their household slaves. By the time they returned, the Scythians thus found that their country was now occupied by a new race, descended from the slaves and from their own wives. They promptly sought to oust them, but could not prevail in battle. Until, that is, one of the soldiers observed:

> My counsel is that we drop our spears and bows, and go to meet them each with his horse-whip in hand. As long as they saw us armed, they thought themselves to be our peers and the sons of our peers; let them see us with whips and no weapons of war, and they will perceive that they are our slaves; and taking this to heart they will not abide our attack.[1]

The plan, we are told, was put into effect and was immediately successful. At the sight of the whips these descendants of slaves forgot that they were soldiers and fled.

The story, like so much of Herodotus, is of course fictional and based on an obviously erroneous theory of natural slavery, but it is no less instructive for that. What we learn from it is that types of violence cannot be measured simply by the degrees of harm they engender. Violence is nuanced and in its different forms has appropriate and inappropriate, natural and unnatural facets. Violence speaks in different ways, and the ability to inflict and the duty to receive certain types of violence has historically played an important role in creating one's personal identity as well as classifying one's social status. The slaves in the Herodotean story were not afraid of finding death on the battlefield; indeed, the act of engaging in combat sustained them as the equals of their would-be masters. It was only when equality was denied and a different, symbolic, form of violence was substituted that they recalled their slave identity. The imposition of a particular form of violence or, conversely, the adoption by mutual consent of a very particular form of violence can then be what Pierre Bourdieu describes as:

> An act of communication, but of a particular kind: it signifies to someone what his identity is, but in a way that both expresses it to him and imposes it on him by expressing

---

1   Herodotus, *The Histories*, Book IV. 3, trans. A. D. Godley (London: Loeb, 1921).

it in front of everyone (kategorein, meaning originally, to accuse publicly) and thus informing him in an authoritative manner of what he is and what he must be.[2]

The nuances of violence serve as one of those devices through which, again quoting Bourdieu, 'social magic always manages to produce discontinuity out of continuity'. Historically, the passing through the boundaries of social groups has meant losing or gaining the capacity to receive, as well as to inflict, diverse types of violence. For example, the attainment of majority may mark the end of a period in which one may be lawfully beaten. The duel, in turn, represented a very formalised pursuit of violence, one in which ritual behaviours were adopted that seemed to deny the existence of the very emotions normally expressed when two parties seek to do harm to each other. Indeed, once the pistol had become the instrument of preference, the combat itself was often reduced to a single mechanical act that briefly, albeit sometimes fatally, interrupted a discourse of utmost civility. The right to demand satisfaction from a fellow gentleman legitimated a very particular view of society and of the role of the gentleman within it. As such, then, when the duel was no more, something very important had happened to the relationships between gentlemen and those between them and their inferiors.

Why the duel disappeared in England a full half century or so before its demise on the Continent is the question that will occupy the final portion of this book. The greater part of it will, however, be devoted to the study of duels themselves, to a consideration of their actual distribution socially and geographically through late eighteenth- and early nineteenth-century society and to an investigation of the causes of duelling and the significance, customs and mores of the practice. The limits of the endeavour should be acknowledged from the first. This is predominately a study of duels in England, and although it contains comparative material regarding duels in Europe and duels in the colonial possessions, I have for reasons of brevity chosen not to extend the study to a consideration of duelling in Ireland, where there is a rich independent tradition, or to Scotland. Similarly, this is not a moral study; while the copious literature produced by anti-duelling campaigners will naturally feature to some degree, the focus will remain predominantly upon the attitudes and attributes of the duellists themselves. Duelling, though, was not a native English custom. Although some English apologists were later to claim the duel for their own and to contrast domestic honour with foreign perfidy, the duel in fact arrived from Italy towards the end of the sixteenth century. Before considering the duel in its later manifestations, then, it will be helpful to first consider the arrival of honour culture in England and to sketch out something of its subsequent history up to the point where my period proper begins.

---

2   P. Bourdieu, *Language and Symbolic Power*, ed. J. B. Thompson, trans. G. Raymond and M. Adamson (Cambridge: Polity, 1992), p. 121.

1

Setting the Scene:
The Arrival of the Duel and
a Brief History to 1750

On 29 June 1612 Robert Creighton, Lord Sanquhar was hanged on a gibbet erected outside Westminster Hall for the offence of procuring the murder of a fencing master, John Turner. Although Sanquhar's rank alone would have been enough to make the execution memorable, it was the peculiar circumstances leading to the murder that lent the affair a particular notoriety. In brief, Sanquhar had some seven years before affronted and then challenged Mr Turner to a fencing match – seemingly wishing to demonstrate his prowess with the blade. In the encounter, however, Turner had prevailed, accidentally blinding Sanquhar in one eye. To all intents and appearances, though, Sanquhar appeared to have accepted the loss equably and to have forgiven his opponent. Until, that is, some years later, when the lord had found himself at the court of Henry IV and the King had inquired as to how he had lost his eye. Sanquhar had recounted the incident whereupon, as one observer reported, 'The king replie[d], Doth the man live? And that question gave an end to the discourse but was the beginner of a strange confusion in his working fancy, which neither time nor distance could compose.'[1] Unable to shake the conviction that it was shameful not to have requited the injury, but equally unable, both because of his social station and his disability, to challenge Turner to a duel, Sanquhar had then hired assassins to kill Turner. Although the fencing master had been shot in his house, the assassins had been captured and had confessed all.

At his trial Sanquhar had professed his guilt, expressed his remorse and appealed for clemency. However, he had nevertheless sought some justification for his conduct in reference to a particular system of values that had induced him to behave as he had. 'I considered not my wrongs upon terms of Christianity, for then I should have sought for other satisfaction, but being trained up in the courts of princes and in arms,

---

1   T. B. Howell, ed., *A Complete Collection of State Trials*, 33 vols (London: R. Bagshaw, 1809–1826), vol. ii, col. 745.

I stood upon the terms of honour.'[2] He declared, 'I confess I was never willing to put up a wrong, where upon terms of honour I might right myself, nor never willing to pardon where I had a power to revenge.' Of course, an unwillingness to finally forgive was no great novelty in human affairs. The intuition that requiting a wrong is an absolute, one might almost say ethical, imperative, the absence of which diminishes the self, is one that I shall often have cause to allude to in the following pages. One suspects that such a sentiment has always been embedded in human society, although its impact upon the conduct of human affairs perhaps waxes and wanes. In Christian-ised English society, however, such a sentiment was clearly inimical to the teachings of the Church; it might be felt, perhaps, but not decently expressed. Sanquhar, however, did so, and he did so because in the latter part of the sixteenth century a new wave of mores and manners had arrived in England which sought to recast reputation no longer in terms of Christian virtue but in terms of a very particular form of honour, a form of honour which legitimated, indeed prescribed, studied yet violent responses to transgression. It was by reference to these new mores that Sanquhar hoped to gain some sympathy for the predicament occasioned by being unable to requite a wrong done to him. Sir Francis Bacon, prosecuting as Solicitor General, was never-theless quick to identify their origin and to reject them: 'I must tell you plainly that I conceive you have sucked those affections of dwelling in malice rather out of Italy, and outlandish manners, where you have conversed, than out of any part of this island of England and Scotland.'[3]

The history of the affections and manners referred to – and connected with them the history of the Italian duel – can scarce be done justice here. In brief, however, the origins of the codes of honour that legitimated duelling are to be located with the Italian Renaissance theories of courtesy and civility that emerged in the fifteenth century and endured through the chaos of the Italian wars between 1495 and 1559. As the name suggests, courtesy was very much a quality deriving from life at court, where the ability to behave respectfully while concealing one's personal inclinations or views was a most useful attribute. As such, then, courtesy, as Markku Peltonen suggests, was rather more a mode of behaviour than a view of inner being: 'Whereas for Erasmus and others, courtesy was an outward sign of the soul, for Castiglione and his followers, it was largely a means to repress outward indications of feelings.'[4] Never-theless, closely tied to both courtesy and civility was the assertion that gentlemen by birth or deed held within them a reservoir of honour that they must keep inviolate by requiting any attempt to transgress upon it. Although both courtesy and civility

---

2 Ibid., col. 747.

3 Ibid., 751.

4 Markku Peltonen, 'Civilised with death: Civility, duelling and honour in Elizabethan England', in Richards, J., ed., *Early Modern Civil Discourses* (Basingstoke: Palgrave MacMillan, 2003), pp. 51–67 at 55.

might, by some, be approximated to dissembling and disingenuousness, in fact they served the dual functions of both preserving one's own honour and of enabling sociability between equals by recognising the honour of others. Where one's own honour was not acknowledged by a social equal, where one was affronted, the appropriate response according to courtesy literature was to reassert that honour, and to do so by means of a challenge to a duel. It was often asserted that the more vigorous the response to any transgression, the more punctilious one was in protecting one's reputation, then the greater indeed was one's honour. The consequence was that in some men the concept of honour grew so fetishised that they were always ready to perceive affront. The history of the duel is littered with instances of homicidal confrontations occasioned by the most minor, and sometimes entirely accidental, social slights.

The Church, of course, contested such new notions of courtesy and civility, but it was characteristic of the Renaissance that men became less afraid of combat with the Church in the realm of ideas. According to Peltonen, 'the extent to which the authors of civil courtesy and duelling were prepared to argue that some elements of their ideology were incompatible with the doctrines of Christianity is striking'.[5] From the end of the fifteenth century, a series of texts defended the duel as the legitimate response of gentlemen to specific affronts from their equals or betters. Girolamo Muzio's *Il Duello*, published in Venice in 1550, was to become an important duelling text, but the most influential of the more general courtesy books was undoubtedly Castiglione's *Libro del Cortegiano* (*Book of the Courtier*), published in 1528. The whole genre of Italian courtesy and conduct books espoused what Kiernan has described as, 'allegiance to that lodestar of Italian humanism, virtú: manliness, or the ideal of manly and courageous action, with overtones strongly aristocratic'.[6]

Not least among the attractions of courtesy literature was that it served not only to differentiate the well-born from the commoner, but also to create a certain rough equality within the ranks of the well-born: each within the order was to deploy civility and courtesy in the face of the other. When such was not observed, the privilege of the duel was, in Kiernan's terms, 'the sign and seal of a mystic equality between higher and lower, a fraternal bond uniting the whole multifarious class'.[7] That the duel disciplined social conduct and shielded the lesser gentlemen from oppression by their betters will be a claim that will reoccur throughout this work – allied to the assertion that far from encouraging interpersonal violence, duelling prevented indiscriminate social warfare. This was clearly a claim that many at the time and

5   Markku Peltonen, *The Duel in Early Modern England: Civility, Politeness and Honour* (Cambridge: Cambridge University Press, 2003), p. 78.

6   Victor G. Kiernan, *The Duel in European History: Honour and the Reign of Aristocracy* (Oxford: Oxford University Press, 1988), p. 48.

7   Ibid., p. 52.

thereafter accepted. According to Stone, the spread of civility and of duelling in Italy 'succeeded in diverting the nobility from faction warfare with armed gangs without leading to a dislocation of social intercourse by incessant fighting over trivial slights, real or imagined'.[8]

The routes by which these Italianate ideas of humanistic virtue found their way into English society were diverse. By means of courtesy literature certainly: Castiglione's *Courtier* was first translated into English in 1561 and soon inspired home-grown works such as Simon Robson's *The courte of ciuill courtesie* (1577), Annibale Romei's *The courtiers academie* (1598) and William Segar's *Honor military and ciuill* (1602), and by the beginning of the seventeenth century a series of English works devoted specifically to the duel were appearing.[9] Where words moved, so did people; English merchants and mercenaries travelled to the Italian cities and could hardly have failed to report upon the ideas that they found there. Italians, and other foreigners of course, returned the compliment. It is interesting that Cockburn, in his study of homicide in Kent, has suggested that 'the bulk of the (admittedly circumstantial) qualitative evidence suggests that after about 1620 most duels in Kent were occasioned by gentlemen or foreign sailors'.[10] Notwithstanding political difficulties and the turbulence of the times, English and Scottish aristocrats (such as Lord Sanquhar, of course) paid their visits to Italy and imbibed some of what they learned there.

In addition, towards the end of the sixteenth century there appeared in London a number of émigrés who did much to propagate the duel and honour culture. These were the Italian fencing masters, of which the most important early example was Rocco Bonetti, who arrived in London around 1569. Bonetti founded a college in Blackfriars for noblemen at the court, until, that is, he was himself killed by English swordsman Austin Bagger in 1587.[11] The death was far from accidental. The English masters had formed themselves into a corporation sometime before 1540 and in that year had acquired a commission from Henry VIII giving them the power to suppress unlicensed fencing schools.[12] Relations between these English masters and their unofficial Italian counterparts were far from cordial, and Bagger had deliberately sought out Bonetti and the fatal encounter. Nevertheless, the prestige

---

8 Lawrence Stone, *The Crisis of the Aristocracy, 1558–1641* (Oxford: Clarendon Press, 1965), p. 250.

9 For example, George Silver's *Paradoxes of defence* (1599) and John Selden's *The Duello or Single Combat* (London: J Helme, 1610).

10 J. S. Cockburn, 'Patterns of violence in English society: Homicide in Kent, 1560–1985', *Past and Present*, 130 (1991), pp. 70–106 at p. 84.

11 See J. P. Anglin, 'The schools of defense in Elizabethan London', *Renaissance Quarterly* 37:3 (1984), pp. 393–410.

12 J. S. Brewer, J. Gairdner and R. H. Brodie, eds, *Letters and Papers, Foreign and Domestic, of the Reign of Henry VIII*, 23 vols. (London: Longman, 1862–1910), vol. xv, p. 477.

of the Continental styles of swordsmanship – predicated upon the rapier as opposed to the broadsword – seems to have been undiminished by Bonetti's death. In 1589, Vincento Saviolo arrived and set up a thriving school. Many of the students were young lawyers who engaged fencing masters while studying at the Inns of Court.[13] Saviolo himself published a manual of his techniques, *Saviolo His Practise* (1595). A characteristic of the Continental styles of fencing, Anglin reports, is that they concentrated primarily upon attack. They were much more aggressive than the English system, which emphasised defence, and indeed the English master George Silver pointed out in his own *Paradoxes of Defence* (1599) that Continental systems were likely to lead to more violence.[14]

The contribution made by the Italian Renaissance to the spread of duelling and 'honour culture' in England is incontestable. This has led Peltonen to stress the novelty of duelling culture:

> The ideology of duelling (and thus the distinct notion of honour) not only emerged in England as part of a theory of courtesy and civility but throughout its history retained its central role in that theory. Far from being a remnant from medieval honour culture which a new humanist culture of civility replaced, the duel of honour came to England as part of the Italian Renaissance notion of the gentleman and courtier.[15]

Others before Peltonen have not always been quite so sure. One early authority, John Selden, in his *Duello* (1610), made little distinction between the old rites of trial by battle and the duel fought extra-judicially between private gentlemen. While he owned that 'the old Saxon laws of Alfred, Edward, Athelstan, Edmund, Edgar or others of those Times are silent of any such matter ... we admit that the Normans ... were the first authors of it in this their conquered kingdom'.[16] In truth, many of the early 'duels' resembled rather more the lawless chance-medleys fought with private retainers and long endured by society than the formal rule-bound encounters of later times. When Sir John Hollis fell out with the Shrewsbury family in the 1590s (a matter of a jilted daughter), the consequence was a clash between retainers in which one was killed. This was followed by a chance encounter between Hollis and a friend of the Shrewsbury family, Sir Gervase Markham, in which both drew swords and Markham was severely injured. Several commentators have regarded the latter encounter as a duel, but in truth later duellists would not have recognised it as such.

---

13 W. R. Prest, *The Inns of Court under Elizabeth I and the Early Stuarts, 1590–1640* (London: Longman, 1972), p. 24.

14 Anglin, 'The schools of defense', op. cit., pp. 408–409.

15 Peltonen, *The Duel in Early Modern England*, op. cit., p. 13.

16 Selden, *The Duello, or Single Combat*, op. cit., pp. 41–42.

Kiernan has described the duel as a 'vestigial survival of the early feudal right of private warfare' and gone on to make the rather grandiloquent statement that:

> Chivalry was part of the setting within which the early modern duel took shape, one of the siren songs that lured so many to soon forgotten graves. As often, a class unwilling to quit the stage of history could take refuge in fantasy or, more positively, hearten itself for its journey into the future by hugging the rags and tatters of the past.[17]

There is much here, however, to which I would object. Remarkable the rags and tatters that were to endure for the next three hundred years! The duel was a vibrant institution which transmitted itself to the new colonial worlds then opening up, which successfully crossed the barriers of social class, which survived industrialisation (for a time), descended the social classes and, as we shall see, long resisted all attempts to proscribe it. It cannot be usefully described as a remnant of a chivalric past, and if I am right in reading a certain pejorative judgement in Kiernan's use of the word 'fantasy', I would respond that there is a sense in which very many forms of successful social relations are rooted in imaginative orderings of the world that have no basis in objectively measurable reality.[18]

Perhaps the strongest reason for doubting that the duel should be primarily regarded as a vestigial remnant of chivalric ideals and private warfare is simply that it was not so perceived at the time. For instance, in 1613, James I declared, 'This bravery, was first borne and bred in Forraine parts; but after convaied over into this Island.'[19] Conversely, the duel could not have established itself so rapidly had its values not flattered existing predispositions among the aristocracy. The duel as we know it, with its elaborate honour theories, was a distinct product of the Renaissance and Renaissance Italy, but Anna Bryson is probably right to contend that the duel was able to establish itself in England because it appealed to ideologies left over from the late medieval world and to martial values that were entirely home grown. The connection between the peerage and the military was, and was to remain, close. Manning has shown that, in 1600, some 36 per cent of the living peers had held or were still holding military appointments and, by 1640, that percentage had risen to some 69 per cent. The numbers were to decline later in the century but even as late as 1700 nearly half, 49 per cent, of the peers were either serving or had served in the military.[20]

---

17 Kiernan, *The Duel in European History*, op. cit., p. 60.

18 Of course some of these fantastical constructions go by the name of 'religion' or, more fashionably, 'equality'.

19 James F. Larkin and Paul L. Hughes, eds, *Stuart Royal Proclamations*, 2 vols (Oxford: Clarendon Press, 1973), vol. i, p. 307.

20 Roger B. Manning, *Swordsmen: The Martial Ethos in the Three Kingdoms* (Oxford: Oxford University Press, 2003), Table 1.1 at p. 18.

During Elizabeth's reign there were a number of duels, and she actively intervened in 1597 to prevent duels at court between the Earl of Southampton and Lord Grey, and between Southampton again and the Earl of Northumberland. However, it was during the reign of James I that the vogue for duelling seems to have truly developed. Lawrence Stone found only five duels and challenges recorded in newsletters and correspondence from the period 1580–1589 but for 1610–1629 identified thirty-three, and there were probably many more.[21] Pressure, then, mounted upon the sovereign to forbid duelling and to penalise those who encouraged it or undertook it, even when no fatalities ensued. In October 1613, following the duel between Edward Sackville and Lord Bruce in which the parties had met ankle-deep in water in a meadow in the Netherlands and had hacked at each other until Lord Bruce was slain,[22] James I issued 'A proclamation prohibiting the publishing of any reports or writings of duels'.[23] He followed this with 'A proclamation against private challenges and combats' in February 1614.[24] Sir Francis Bacon had already declared that the Star Chamber would prosecute anyone who challenged another or who went abroad to fight, and he had carefully prepared specimen charges against two minor personages in January 1614.[25] James's 1614 edict was subsequently published as an expanded treatise penned by Henry Howard, Earl of Northampton, and contained within it what was to become something of a classic definition of the two species of offence that might engender honour disputes:

> Wrongs which are the grounds of Quarrels, are either Verball; that is, when one Gentleman accuseth another of some dishonest fact, or gives the Lye: or Reall; under which Head may bee comprised, Blowes, Stripes or Hurts in all degrees, though they differ in proportion; and beside all scornefull lookes, actes, or figures, that implie contempt.[26]

In 1614, the approved response to such provocations was to complain to an honour court, a commission fulfilling the office of the Earl Marshal, which would hear a gentleman's complaint and 'who shall right him in his Reputation, if they finde he be wronged'.[27] Peltonen has shown that Northampton, whose opinions were deeply

21   Stone, *The Crisis of the Aristocracy*, op. cit., p. 245.

22   Lorenzo Sabine, *Notes On Duels and Duelling, Alphabetically Arranged, With A Preliminary Histor-ical Essay* (Boston: Crosby and Nicholls, 1859), pp. 74–78.

23   Larkin and Hughes, *Stuart Royal Proclamations*, op. cit., vol. i, pp. 295–297.

24   Ibid., p. 304.

25   *The Charge of Sir Francis Bacon, knight, his majesties Attourney General, touching duells upon an information in the Star Chamber against Priest and Wright* (London, 1614).

26   *A publication of his majesty's edict, and severe censure against priuate combats and combatants* (London, 1613). Reproduced in Peltonen, 'The Jacobean Anti-Duelling Campaign', op. cit., pp. 1–2.

27   Larkin and Hughes, *Stuart Royal Proclamations*, op. cit., vol. i, p. 297.

influential in shaping the proclamation, was himself sympathetic to the values of civic courtesy and believed that insults to honour were egregious offences for which the common law offered no adequate remedy. An honour court, then, was necessary in order to avert the understandable responses of gentlemen who would otherwise have recourse to arms. Francis Bacon, however, was of different opinion and, as the Sanquhar trial was to demonstrate, entirely rejected the notions of Italianate courtesy and the associated theories of honour. Bacon, Peltonen has observed, 'held that the best and easiest remedy for these questions of honour was to ignore trifling insults and to harden one's sense of one's own reputation'.[28] Northampton accepted the premise of honour as proffered by civil courtesy but tried to avoid duelling as the natural consequence, whereas Bacon and other critics refused to accept the basic assumptions of this foreign fashion, refused to be dishonoured by trifles and invited others to feel the same. It seems that Bacon's views prevailed with the king. In 1618, Thomas Middleton penned *The Peacemaker* with royal approval, and this signalled what Peltonen has described as a volte-face in royal opinion since the document ridiculed the 'small things' that occasioned disputes, urged forbearance and made no mention of a court of honour.

Those who did not forbear risked prosecution, and between 1603 and 1625 there were about two hundred such cases heard in the Star Chamber.[29] Nevertheless, the very number of prosecutions is testimony to the ineffectiveness of the threat of prosecution in deterring would-be duellists. It is generally accepted, though, that duelling did decline somewhat after the reign of James I, less because of the effectiveness of the courts in proscribing it and more because of the spread of Puritanism opposed to it. Honour culture was inimical to Puritan piety – though it would be wrong to assert that Puritan gentlemen were wholly uninfluenced by it. The Articles of War on the parliamentary side specified that 'No Corporal, or other Officer commanding the Watch, shall willingly suffer a Soldier to go forth to a Duel or private Fight upon paine of Death.'[30] A Commons committee set up in 1651 proposed duellists should lose their right hand, and suffer confiscation and banishment.[31] Interestingly, in that same year duelling was still being cited as a new phenomenon; it was described by Hobbes in his *Leviathan* as 'a custome, not many years begun'.[32]

---

28 Peltonen, 'The Jacobean anti-duelling campaign', op. cit., p. 17.

29 Thomas G. Barnes, ed., *List and Index to the proceedings in Star Chamber for the reign of James I (1603–1625) in the Public Record Office, London, Class STAC8* (Chicago: The Foundation, 1975), pp. 159–163.

30 C. H. Firth, *Cromwell's Army* (London: Methuen 1902), pp. 418–419.

31 H. N. Brailsford, *The Levellers and the English Revolution* (London: Cresset Press, 1961), pp. 651–653.

32 Thomas Hobbes, *Leviathan* (1651), cited in Peltonen, *The Duel in Early Modern England*, op. cit., p. 13.

It is difficult to gauge how many duels there actually were during the civil war. It is possible that the ferocity of the conflict concentrated the minds upon matters at hand, leaving little time for concern about the punctilios of honour. It is equally possible however, that the fractures throughout better society led to more honour disputes, but ones which, in the bloody context of the times were scarcely remarked upon. Whichever is correct, by 1654, Cromwell had to issue a further proclamation providing for the imprisonment for six months of anyone sending, delivering or accepting a challenge. This did not prevent Philip Stanhope, second Earl of Chesterfield from wounding John Whalley in 1658 and being imprisoned that same year to prevent a duel with Lord St John.

After the Restoration in 1660, 'Duelling formed part of a popular royalist reaction, along with wild drinking and prostitution and the reopening of disorderly theatres.'[33] It is probably true that the return from exile of so many of the aristocracy keen to reassert their leadership of society led to conflict, but equally true that the end of war meant that duels were more likely to be newsworthy. Truman asserted that between May 1660 and February 1685 there were 196 duels with 75 fatalities, a death rate of some three per year.[34] Some of these were in all senses very much in the public eye, either because of the status of the participants or the location of the contest. In 1662, a fatal duel was fought in Pall Mall, St James between Mr Jermyn and Captain Thomas Howard and their two seconds. The Lord Chancellor himself, Clarendon, was challenged by Lord Ossory over a bill prohibiting the import of Irish cattle.[35] A duel in 1666 between Viscount Fauconberg and Sir Thomas Osborne led Sir Edward Thurlow to introduce a parliamentary bill whereby anyone who issued a challenge to another was liable to be imprisoned for life and to forfeit all his goods and estate. However, the second reading of the bill was deferred in the face of protests that forfeiture of goods would ruin whole families. The bill was directed to a committee appointed by Charles II to inquire into duelling, as was a second bill proposed in 1667.

In 1668, however, there was another scandalous duel, again involving the Shrewsbury family. Learning that the Duke of Buckingham had been wooing his wife, the Earl of Shrewsbury challenged. The king, learning of this, ordered Lord Abemarle to confine Buckingham and prevent the duel. This was not done, and the two combatants met at Barnes Elms assisted by two seconds, each from prominent families.

---

33 Kiernan, *The Duel in European History*, op. cit., p. 99.

34 Maj. B. C. Truman, *The Field of Honour: Being A Complete And Comprehensive History of Duelling In All Countries* (New York: Ford, Howard and Hulbert, 1884), p. 35.

35 J. G. Millingen, *The History Of Duelling Including Narratives Of The Most Remarkable Personal Encounters That Have Taken Place From The Earliest Period To The Present Time*, 2 vols (London: Richard Bentley, 1841), vol. ii, pp. 38–39.

As was still customary, all partiers engaged and 'the combat was long and desperate'.[36] One second, Sir J. Jenkins, was killed outright; Shrewsbury lingered for two months, and his widow promptly moved in with Buckingham, who seemingly ousted his own duchess. Notwithstanding the subsequent public proclamations against duelling, the true demeanour of the sovereign is best ascertained from the fact that Charles II promptly pardoned all those involved in the affair. He declared in April 1668, however, that he would no longer issue such pardons, 'The strict Course of Law shall take Place in all such Cases.'

This brings us to the question of what the strict course of the law was. Murder was a common-law offence, and the common-law position that a man who killed his opponent in a premeditated duel was guilty of murder was never formally questioned. The premeditated duel, however, was to be distinguished from those combats (also sometimes referred to as duels) occasioned by sudden quarrels and carried out in the heat of passion. These could be categorised as either chance-medleys or acts of manslaughter under provocation. Chance-medley was perhaps the older doctrine and, according to Horder, existed as an important species of voluntary manslaughter, separate from manslaughter under provocation, until the middle of the nineteenth century.[37]

For a homicide to fall under chance-medley, two conditions needed to be satisfied. First, the killing itself had to be carried out immediately and in anger before the blood had cooled. Thus, Crompton, in 1583. observed:

> Two men fall out suddenly in the town, and by agreement take the field, nearby, and there one kills the other, this is murder, for there was precedent malice ... But if they fought a combat suddenly without malice precedent, and paused a little in the combat, and then they took the field, and one killed the other, that would be manslaughter, because everything was done in the continuing heat of passion.[38]

Second, it was said that the parties must be equally and fairly combating. This requirement of the law was considered in depth in the case of *Mawgridge* in 1707. It was considered that if A.:

> Draws his sword, and then before he passes, B.'s sword is drawn, or A. bids him draw, and B. thereupon drawing, there happen to be mutual passes: If A. kills B. this will be but manslaughter because it was sudden; and A.'s design was not so absolutely to destroy B. to combat with him, whereby he run the hazard of his own life at the time.[39]

---

36 Ibid., pp. 42–45.

37 Jeremy Horder, *Provocation and Responsibility* (Oxford: Clarendon Press, 1992), p. 29.

38 Crompton, *Loffice et Aucthoritie de Justices de Peace* (1606 ed.), folio 23 b.

39 *R. v. Mawgridge*, 130–131.

Manslaughter on the basis of provocation was a much broader doctrine applicable in many different types of homicide. Unlike the doctrine of chance-medley it did not require evidence of equal combat; for instance, provocation might be pleaded by husbands who had murdered their wives. However, in the context of a dispute between two gentlemen, a defence of provocation was most unlikely to succeed unless there had been an equal combat. The defence required, as the name implies, the existence of some particular provoking act, but it was not enough to merely show that one had been provoked. As with chance-medley – no matter how severe the provocation – if the blood had cooled between the provoking act and the fatal combat then the defence was not available. Hence, Sir Matthew Hale's determination that:

> If A. challenge C. to meet in the field and C. decline it as much as he can, but is threatened by A. to be posted for a coward ... if he meet not; and Thereupon A. and B., his second, and C. and D. his second meet and fight, and C. kill A.; this is murder in C. and D. his second.[40]

Whether the blood had indeed cooled between the dispute and the subsequent homicide was determined by reference to the facts of the case and most particularly the time span between the quarrel and the homicide. Quoting once more:

> Two men fight suddenly without malice aforethought, and one breaks his sword, and goes into his house to fetch another sword, returns and, taking up the fight with his opponent again, kills him. This is murder if it appears that, as a result of the killer's intentional actions, his blood was able to cool before his return.[41]

It was an important aspect of the law of homicide that in cases of intentional homicide the burden was upon the defendant to show some evidence that the act had been committed in circumstances that either allowed for a complete defence (for example, legitimate self-defence) or a partial defence such as chance-medley, or provocation. In *Taverner's Case*[42] Sir Edward Coke declared, 'This is a plain case and without any question if one kill another in fight upon the provocation of him which is killed, this is murder.'[43] This was the presumption of the law; the exception was where it could be shown that the act was 'without malice express or implied',[44] which would make it

---

40 1 Hale's *Pleas of the Crown* 452.

41 Crompton, *Loffice et Auchtorite*, 26 a–b.

42 *Taverner's Case* (1616), 3 Bulstr. 171 at 172.

43 3 Bulstr. 172.

44 1 Hale, *Pleas of the Crown*, 166.

merely manslaughter. The law, though, implied malice where the killing was 'voluntary and of set purpose, though done upon sudden occasion, for if it be voluntary the law implieth malice'.[45] The defendant had then to show some evidence to suggest that the killing was not done of set purpose.

> In every charge of murder, the fact of killing being first proved, all the circumstances of Accident, Necessity, or Infirmity are to be satisfactorily proved by the prisoner, unless they arise out of the evidence produced against him: for the laws presumeth the fact to have been founded in malice, until the contrary appeareth.[46]

Furthermore, some courts weighed the gravity of any provocation; the defendant not only had to produce evidence that he had been provoked and had killed in hot blood, but also had to show that the provocation had been sufficient to justify his conduct. Thus in *Lord Morley's Case* (1666) it was said that it was murder to kill without provocation but similarly, 'if the provocation be slight and trivial, it is all one in law as if there be none'.[47] In *Mawgridge* (1707) it was declared that 'No words of reproach or infamy are sufficient to provoke another to such a degree of anger as to strike or assault the provoking party with a sword.'[48]

It should by now be apparent that the paradigmatic duel where parties set a date and a time for a meeting did not easily lend itself to an appeal to the defence of either chance-medley or provocation. Although both parties were at equal hazard, it had been declared conclusively in *Mawgridge* that 'if time was appointed to fight (suppose the next day) and accordingly they do fight; it is murder in him that kills the other'.[49] Judge Foster had been similarly explicit:

> In all possible cases deliberate homicide upon a principle of revenge is murder; for no man under the protection of the law is to be the avenger of his own wrongs ... deliberate duelling, if death ensueth is in the eye of the law murder; for duels are generally founded in deep revenge; and though a person should be drawn into a duel, not upon a motive so criminal, but merely upon the punctilio of what the swordsmen falsely call honour, that will not excuse.[50]

---

45 3 Coke's *Institutes*, c. 13.

46 Sir Michael Foster *A Report of Some Proceedings on the Commission for the Trial of the Rebels in the Year 1746, in the County of Surry; And of Other Crown Cases: to which are Added Discourses Upon a Few Branches of the Crown Law,* 3rd edn (London: E. and R. Brooke, 1792), p. 255.

47 *Lord Morley's Case* 1666 6. St. Tr. 770, 780.

48 *R. v. Mawgridge.*

49 Ibid.

50 Foster, *Crown Law,* op. cit., p. 296.

From the sixteenth century onwards, the common-law position was really quite simple then. Any pre-arranged duel in which one party was killed, be the combat ever so fairly conducted, was an act of murder on the part of the surviving combatant and also, it should be noted, upon the part of all who had assisted in the duel.

The rigour of the law in the seventeenth and eighteenth centuries was, however, entirely defeated by the insincerity of the sovereigns. Thomas Hobbes pointed out that obeying the law was no simple matter for ambitious young gentlemen. Although 'the Law condemneth Duells; the punishment is made capitall, yet, on the other; he that refuseth Duell, is subject to contempt and scorne, without remedy; and sometimes by the Soveraign himselfe thought unworthy to have any charge, or preferment in Warre.'[51] Faced with the prospect of leaving to the law personal favourites, or abandoning officers who might be of use, or resisting pressure from influential political supporters, the monarchs, themselves imbued with very particular notions of honour, often intervened to save duellists who had slain. James II, for example, ordered the Lord Justices in Ireland in 1685 to cashier all officers involved in duels, and then the following year reversed a decree of outlawry on David Stanier for killing Sir William Throckmorton in a duel. The Glorious Revolution did little to inhibit this practice. William III pardoned William Drummond in 1697 after a duel in Edinburgh with two fatalities, and in 1701 he reversed a decree of outlawry on John Young for killing William Carey.[52]

Perhaps the sovereigns felt that they could afford to be indulgent since, as Pelltonen and Kelly have argued, the number of duels was probably not very large at the end of the seventeenth century.[53] Cockburn has written that 'by and large enthusiasm for swordplay declined in the course of the seventeenth century',[54] and Peltonen notes that minor skirmishes were thought noteworthy precisely because they were rather rare and that by 1720 'nobody talk[ed] of anything but stocks and South Sea, and now and then a duel'.[55] However, it can still be asserted of eighteenth-century society that it 'was unusually, perhaps uniquely, conditioned to accept violent behaviour'.[56] The extreme physicality and, it seems, the ill temper and ill discipline of the aristocracy of the late seventeenth and early eighteenth centuries are difficult to convey today. This was a time when young aristocrats might terrorise parts of London and be labelled

---

51 Thomas Hobbes, *Leviathan*, cited in Peltonen, *The Duel in Early Modern England*, op. cit., p. 211.

52 James Kelly, *That Damn'd Thing Called Honour: Duelling in Ireland 1570–1860* (Cork: Cork University Press, 1995), p. 46.

53 See generally, Peltonen, *The Duel in Early Modern England*, op. cit., pp. 205–206.

54 Cockburn, 'Patterns of violence', op. cit., p. 84

55 HMC, Portland Manuscripts (London, 1891–1931), vol. iv, p. 59, cited in Peltonen, *The Duel in Early Modern England,* op. cit., p. 205.

56 Cockburn, 'Patterns of violence', op. cit., p. 101.

Mohocks. When the Duke of Grafton, the grandson of Charles II, might beat his coachman in the middle of the street,[57] and when the Duke of Leeds might shoot his son's steward.[58] Some sense of the vigour of such men and some sense of the incapacity of the law to restrain them may, however, be gleaned from a brief examination of the lives and circumstances of two men who were to perish in a duel in 1712: Charles, the fourth Baron Mohun, and the Duke of Hamilton.

The fourth Baron Mohun might perhaps have been forgiven had he shied away from the duel, for his own father (also called Charles) had been killed in one in November 1676. The third baron and his friend Lord William Cavendish had quarrelled with John Power, an Irish officer in the service of Louis XIV, seemingly over matters of religion. Cavendish and Power had fought as principals, Mohun as Cavendish's second against his opposite number. The initial duel had been concluded with only minor injuries; however, Mohun had subsequently perished when he had quarrelled on the field with Power and swords had again been drawn.

The conduct of the fourth baron soon made it clear that he was nothing daunted by his family's history. According to Victor Stater, Mohun fought his first duel in 1692 at the age of fifteen, having quarrelled with the twenty-year-old Lord Kennedy. William III had heard of their quarrel prior to the meeting and had tried to prevent it by commanding both to remain confined to their houses. Both had disobeyed, and minor wounds had ensued on both sides. Significantly, neither party was punished thereafter for disobeying the royal command. The following year Mohun was brought to trial before his peers at Westminster Hall for murder. Richard Hill, a friend of Mohun, had persuaded him to take part in the kidnapping of an actress, Anne Bracegirdle. The attempt had failed, and Hill and Mohun had thereafter burst into the house of her lover, the actor William Mountford. Hill had fatally stabbed Mountford before he had had time to draw his sword. Fortunately, Mohun had not drawn his weapon, and his peers found that he had not been complicit in Mountford's death.

Undaunted, in October 1694, Mohun drew his sword upon the MP Francis Scobell, who had intervened to protect a coachman from his wrath. Mohun issued a challenge but the duel was never fought. In early 1697, however, he fought a duel with an army officer in St James Park, but the park keepers broke up the swordplay. Then, in September of that year Mohun stabbed to death an army officer called Hill in a drunken brawl in a tavern in Charing Cross. A trial was prepared, but the king pardoned him, seemingly so that, now twenty-one, he could take his place in the Lords as a Whig peer favourable to the government. Little more than a year later he was again being tried at Westminster Hall, on 29 March 1699, for assisting Lord

---

57 Henri Misson, *Memoirs and Observations of His Travels over England* (London, 1719), pp. 305–306.

58 Margaret Verney, ed., *Verney letters of the Eighteenth Century*, 2 vols (London, 1930), vol. i, p. 373.

Warwick in the murder of Captain Richard Coote in Leicester Square after a drinking party. He was acquitted, whereas Warwick was convicted and symbolically burned with cold iron.

By the time of his duel with James Douglas, fourth Duke of Hamilton, Mohun's life had, then, been distinguished by a catalogue of violence from which he had nevertheless always been exculpated. Hamilton could offer no illustrious pedigree of violence to match that of his eventual slayer. He had seemingly fought one duel with Lord Mordaunt sometime before 1700, with no lasting consequences. The reasons for the fateful confrontation in 1712 were numerous. Hamilton was a high Tory who had remained loyal to James II and Mohun a Whig; therefore, a natural antipathy between them was to be expected. Indeed, they had soon become bitter political rivals, but the deepest cause of their enmity seems to have been a complex property dispute. This was caused by the death in 1701 of the second Duke of Macclesfield, who had named his friend Lord Mohun as the heir to his estates. Hamilton had expected much of the property to pass to his own wife, she being the niece of the second duke. A series of legal suits had followed in respect of the property, at first to Mohun's advantage, but by 1712 the tide had begun to turn against him. Hamilton had acquired an important situation in Robert Harley's Tory administration after the Whigs had been routed in the elections of 1710. Mohun anticipated that he would lose a suit laid by Hamilton over the Macclesfield properties. Furthermore, the Tory government were seeking peace with France and Mohun, as a client of the Duke of Marlborough, was opposed to it. The prospect of losing his properties, the infuriating elevation of his rival and perhaps a desire to serve his patron led Mohun to issue a challenge in November 1712.

Hamilton accepted and selected a kinsman as his second; Mohun chose another Marlborough client, Gen. George Maccartney, who was also opposed to the forthcoming peace. Mohun and the Duke met in Hyde Park on 12 November 1712 and during the combat both were killed. The seconds, who had also been engaged in the fray, survived. Mohun died immediately, but Hamilton emerged before succumbing to blood loss from a sliced artery. Maccartney promptly fled after the duel but by contrast the second to the Duke of Hamilton, his kinsman Col. John Hamilton, promptly surrendered himself for trial. In parliament the Tories suggested that the affair had been got up as a Whig plot to derail the peace with France, and their fears were confirmed when Col. Hamilton gave evidence that Maccartney had treacherously and fatally stabbed the duke after the duke had laid his sword aside.[59] Maccartney, who had escaped to the Low Countries, produced a pamphlet in his own defence,[60]

---

59 HMC, Portland Manuscripts, vol. v, pp. 246–247, cited in Peltonen, *The Duel in Early Modern England,* op. cit.

60 *A Letter from Mr. Maccartney to a Friend of His in London* (London, 1713).

and partisans on both sides engaged in a war of pamphlets, press editorials and scurrilous letters. Col. Hamilton, meanwhile, was tried at the Old Bailey on 12 December 1712. He claimed that he did not know when he came to the field that a duel was in the offing. The jury affected to believe him, found him guilty of mere manslaughter, and after pleading clergy he was released.[61]

The duel is of particular interest to us for three reasons. First, it was conducted on the cusp of a change in duelling practice. On the field Mohun had suggested that the seconds should not be engaged in the combat itself, although Hamilton had demurred and Maccartney had indicated his enthusiasm for the match.[62] Henceforth, it was to become increasingly common for the seconds not to engage in combat – indeed, after the middle of the eighteenth century it was almost unknown, although I shall deal with this further in Chapter 6. Second, the duel had an avowedly political dimension but the use of duelling as a tool of political partisanship was slowly falling out of favour. The duels of John Wilkes are sometimes alleged to have had a political character, and remarks characterised as personal during the conduct of politics could engender combats; for example, Charles James Fox and William Adam duelled in 1779 under such circumstances. However, all sides in the later eighteenth century seemed to draw back from adopting duelling as a conscious and bloody strategy to advance political interests. Perhaps the temper of politics had simply cooled somewhat. The most celebrated 'political' duel of the nineteenth century was fought between members of the same administration.[63] Finally, of course, the whole career of Lord Mohun and the leniency extended to Colonel Hamilton are testimony to the bankruptcy of the previous attempts to prohibit duelling per se.

Superficially, at least, Parliament's failure to take a stand against the duel was not from want of activity. Following Charles II's declaration in 1668, a number of further but equally abortive attempts had again been made to proscribe the act of duelling. The Duke of York introduced a bill into the Lords in 1668 that proposed the forfeiture of the estates of all duellists whether or not a death had ensued. This, however, was buried in committee. A second committee established in 1675 continued to debate the preparation of an anti-duelling bill but had come to no conclusions by 1680 when Charles II delivered a new proclamation against duelling. Bills were actually proposed in the House of Commons in 1692 and 1699, but neither made progress. It was apparent that there was no great enthusiasm for the proscription of duelling in either of the houses, notwithstanding an

---

61 *A Particular Account of the Trial of John Hamilton, Esq.; for the Murder of Charles Lord Mohun and James Duke of Hamilton and Brandon* (London, 1712).

62 HMC, *Earl of Dartmouth's Manuscripts* (London, 1887), p. 313.

63 That between Castlereagh and Canning in 1809.

increasing number of publications deploring the practice.[64] The deaths of Mohun and Hamilton in 1712 reinvigorated the campaign against duelling, and Queen Anne condemned the practice at the opening of Parliament in April 1713. Two bills were introduced in consequence, but both came to nothing. A bill introduced in 1720 passed through the Commons only to fall in the Lords at the first reading.[65] Thereafter, the parliamentarians seem to have simply given up, and no further bill to prohibit duelling per se was laid until a further abortive effort in 1819.

It seems that in the final analysis there was no constituency prepared to take a consistent and principled stance against duelling. Numerous individuals wrote to deplore it, but no organised and effective opposition resulted. The churches might be thought to have been best placed to formulate a coherent campaign for effective prohibition, but as an institutional body, the established Church was curiously ambivalent. As Peltonen has pointed out:

> It seems obvious that Christianity did not play a very prominent role in the anti-duelling discourse in the late seventeenth and early eighteenth century. Certainly, the problem of duelling did not impinge on the anti-vice campaign of the Societies for Reformation of Manners in the 1690s and 1700s. It is indicative that during the most sustained parliamentary campaign against duelling one critic remarked that the divines remained curiously silent about the whole issue.[66]

By the nineteenth century, as we shall see, this was to change, and Church leaders were to play an important role in mobilising constituencies of opinion against duelling and even in threatening to oppose the re-election of politicians who had duelled. Not before, however, they themselves had succumbed in part to the attractions of honour culture: there were those in the late eighteenth century who sported clerical titles and yet who duelled, most notably the editor of the *Morning Chronicle* and sometime clergyman the Rev. Bate., who fought with Captain Stoney in 1777 and with many others besides.

The general temper of better society as the early eighteenth century progressed can be gleaned from Millingen's observation that not only duels but also general affrays between gentlemen were still common. For example, in 1717 a large party of gentlemen quarrelled at the Royal Chocolate house in St James Street. Swords were drawn and three gentlemen killed before a contingent of the Horse Guards restored

---

64 For example, Thomas Comber's, *A discourse of Duels* (London, 1687) and William Darrell's, *A Gentleman Instructed in the conduct of a virtuous and happy life* (London, 1704).

65 *Journals of the House of Commons*, xix, pp. 296, 313, 323, 326, 331, 339, 352; *Journal of the House of Lords*, xxi, pp. 314, 320.

66 Peltonen, *The Duel in Early Modern England*, op. cit., pp. 214–215.

order. In 1720 a hundred gentlemen were involved in an affray in Windmill Street. The watch summoned to quell the affair found themselves severely handled, and a detachment of Horse Guards had to plunge in to assist, killing several in the process.[67] The violence, fuelled by alcohol, was greatly facilitated by the wearing of swords. Yet already the practice of carrying of a sword was beginning to be in decline. Césare de Sassure in 1726 described the English gentleman as wearing 'little coats called "frocks," without facings and without pleats, with a short cape above. Almost all wear small, round wigs, plain hats, and carry canes in their hands, but no swords.'[68]

Swords were still available if required, however, for in that same year a Major Oneby and a Mr Gower quarrelled in a tavern during a game of hazard with a number of others. Oneby, objecting to some jest of Gower's, described him as 'impertinent', whereupon Gower responded by calling Oneby a 'rascal'. Oneby then flung a bottle at Gower, who responded with a flying candlestick. Their swords were sent for, but the rest of the company intervened and the two men sat down for an hour. Gower then attempted a reconciliation and offered his hand to Oneby, who, however, refused to take it and declared, 'No damn you I will have your blood.' Everyone hurriedly made to leave, but Oneby then contemptuously called Gower back and shut the door on the others. The two drew on each other. Gower was killed, although he did not die before being asked if he had received the fatal wound in a fair manner and declaring, 'I think I did.'[69] The encounter was typical of a species of duel that was to become more common from then on until the 1770s: duels where the parties combated alone in a closed room. For example, Mr Dalton and Mr Paul fought in this fashion in 1750, and Lord Bryon and Mr Chaworth in 1765. What was most unusual in this case, however, was that Oneby was brought to trial and subsequently convicted of murder. More remarkably still, no intention of respiting the sentence of execution was expressed. In the event, however, Oneby, despairing of any reprieve, cheated the hangman by committing suicide.

While it might be tempting to see the Oneby trial and conviction as indicative of an increasing impatience with duelling, this however, would almost certainly be an error. What this affair demonstrates is nothing more than that there were occasions upon which the courts were prepared to penalise homicides that were both outside the law and at the same time outside the normal conventions of honour. Here it counted very much that the parties sat calmly together for an hour before the final confrontation. Where the blood had cooled and the homicide was the product of a deliberate act, the offence was clearly that of murder. Now, duellists were rarely

---

67 Millingen, *History of Duelling*, op. cit., vol. ii, pp. 50–51.

68 Césare de Sassure, *A Foreign View of England in 1725–1729*, trans. Madame Van Muyden (London: John Murray, 1902), p. 113. Letter of February 1726.

69 Millingen, *History of Duelling*, op. cit., vol. ii, pp. 52–55.

convicted of offences merely because they had actually committed them. However, there were additional elements to the affair that seemed to render Oneby's conduct particularly dishonourable. First, it seems that it was he who was responsible for the original quarrel. Second, he thereafter refused a generous attempt to reconcile the parties. Third, as a matter of principle gentlemen were expected to fight according to the dictates of honour, but without espousing any personal animosity towards their opponent. According to Millingen, 'The main point then, on which the judgment turned ... was the evidence of *express malice*, after the interposition of the company.'[70] It counted very much with the court that 'he had made use of that bitter and deliberate expression, "That he would have his blood".'[71] Oneby was an experienced swordsman who might be expected to prevail, and:

> Calling back the deceased by the contemptuous appellation of 'young man' on pretence of having something to say to say to him, altogether showed such strong proof of deliberation and coolness, as precluded the presumption of passion having continued down to the time of the mortal stroke, and there was no doubt but that he had compelled Gower to defend himself.[72]

The Oneby affair is to be viewed as very particular; indeed, it resembles nothing so much as the duel between Major Campbell and Captain Boyd in 1807, to which I shall return to as the only instance in the nineteenth century in which the sentence of execution was actually carried out upon a duellist. Similar elements were present in both cases: Campbell too refused all offers of reconciliation, overbore his opponent's reluctance to fight, declared his malice and conducted the affair without witnesses to ensure fair play.

Where combat was perceived as both fair and honourable, duellists were not left to the mercies of the law, notwithstanding professions of abhorrence for the duel. For example, a series of duels among naval officers culminated in a fatal meeting on 12 March 1750 between Captains Innes and Clarke. The quarrel had been caused by an encounter in October 1748 between a British fleet in the West Indies under Admiral Knowles and a Spanish fleet under Vice Admiral Reggio. Criticism of the subsequent conduct of battle had led to Knowles being impeached. Some captains, including Clarke, supported him against others who had complained of his conduct to the Admiralty, Innes among them. In the duel Innes was slain, and, after a trial at the Old Bailey Clarke, was convicted of his murder. This had been no unequal or dishonourable combat though, and George II

---

70 Ibid., p. 54

71 Ibid.

72 Ibid., pp. 54–55.

promptly pardoned him. Indeed, shortly afterwards he was promoted to the captaincy of a larger vessel.[73]

By 1750, under the eyes of intermittently hostile but more often indulgent sovereigns, the honour culture that propagated duelling had spread through the virile peerage and among the officers' messes of both army and navy. However, honour theorists were never able to vanquish an opposition that was grounded in theology and Christian morality. Many gentlemen, of whom Bacon and Northampton were but two, were opposed to the duel from the very moment of its arrival in England. Speeches were made, sermons were preached and pamphlets appeared at regular intervals denouncing duelling. Since we cannot know how many disagreements would have otherwise proceeded to a duel, we cannot truly assess the effect that such anti-duelling activity had, but it is hard to believe that so many appeals to law and conscience operated to no effect.

It is often pointed out, and I shall do the same, that the laws against duelling were frequently thwarted. From another prospective, though, duellists and their apologists did not succeed in amending the law, which, doctrinally at least, held true to its position. While there were those, perhaps many, within the judiciary prepared to tolerate duelling, there were none avowedly seeking to legalise it. By the eighteenth century, however, the duel appeared to have successfully subverted the actual operation of the criminal justice system. Similarly, it had, for the moment, prevailed against the tenets of religion. The Church as an institution had no stomach for a fight with powerful interests. Again, though, that is not to say that most of the clergy and the laity were ever convinced of the legitimacy of duelling but rather that on a personal level many, not all, felt obliged to turn a blind eye to it. In short, by the eighteenth century there were groups of powerful, active men operating under a common ethos who were able to propagate in public a vigorous, noisy and even romantic honour culture, able to ignore moral sanction and turn aside legal retribution. Even if most of society did not share their values, a respectable portion of those that mattered did. Opposition was strident but, in the absence of coherent leadership, fragmented and uncertain. Those who adhered to the codes of honour in the eighteenth century could scarcely have predicted then that it would be their opponents who would ultimately win on the battlefield of ideas.

---

73 John Charnock, *Biographa Navalis: Or Impartial Memoirs of the Lives and Characters of Officers of the Navy of Great Britain, from the year 1660 to the Present Time*, 6 vols (London: R. Faulder, 1798), vol. v, p. 475.

2

Fashion and Physicality

As we have seen, neither the somewhat insincere disapprobation of the sovereigns and their ministers, nor the operation of the courts, nor the appeals of the pious, sufficed to prevent influential members of the court and aristocracy from becoming infused with the values of the duel during the late sixteenth and the seventeenth centuries. Numerically though, this represented but a small constituency, the strength of honour culture in the eighteenth, and continuing into the nineteenth, centuries was to lie in its transmission out from the court into the much broader, if ill-defined, classes of gentility. In Chapter 3 I shall consider the norms of behaviour and of honourable conduct that came to be expected by honourable gentlemen in the eighteenth century, norms the violation of which might lead to fatal consequences. However, the particular concepts of honour with which we are concerned could not have embedded themselves within society had that society not been configured in such a way as to prove susceptible to their arguments. As we shall see, in the complex web of violent relations that did so much to constitute national culture, the duel was able to find a home – so much so that some gentlemen came to quickly regard this European import as emblematic of very particular English martial virtues.

By way of explanation, one might first observe that the English society of the seventeenth and indeed later centuries was animated by a spirit of extraordinary competitiveness. Competition within the court and within the developing political establishment naturally focused not only upon placements and perquisites but also upon the need to catch the eye and to cultivate that careful self-regard fitted for the well born. Thomas Hobbes was the man who most powerfully expressed the seventeenth-century conviction that all life was a matter of self-assertion, a matter of prevailing over the interests of others. According to Hobbes, 'Because the power of one man resisteth and hindreth the effects of the power of another: power is no more, but the excess of power of one above that of another.'[1] In such a society, reputation served as a form of cultural capital, a form of social power, and the Hobbesian view that the natural state of being was but 'a chaos of violence' encouraged men to be

---

1 Thomas Hobbes, *The Elements of Law, Natural and Politic*, ed. F. Tonnies (London: Frank Cass, 1969), p. 34.

vigorous in asserting their interests when they came into conflict with the interests of others.

However, although society applauded personal aggrandisement, along with the evolution of politeness there developed from the seventeenth century onwards a compensatory sense that all those of a certain station were entitled to an equal protection of interest and reputation. This extended not merely to the scions of the aristocracy but to all those who might truly style themselves gentlemen. Such men were qualified to appeal to the shared values of their social group when seeking protection against the transgressions of others. Members of the social elite were, in brief, in competition with each other, but united in the need to differentiate themselves from those below. Thus, while many duels were caused by the competitive nature of elite society, the institution itself became, in the eyes of its apologists, a rational strategy for maintaining the coherence of the social group and restraining the more destructive impulses of the competitive ethos. The duel, those apologists argued, was a controlled, rule-bound mode of dispute resolution absent which men would war indiscriminately upon one another with far more deleterious consequences. Indeed, the existence of duelling and the latent potential of all gentlemen to hold others to account upon the field, they were to argue, prevented much social conflict for it served as a putative sanction which deterred men from unwarranted trespasses. Social intercourse was, in other words, lubricated by the fear of what might follow should one not observe social norms. To illustrate, Bernard Mandeville's fictional Col. Worthy observed in the *Female Tatler* of 1709 that he could not conceive how civil conversation could be maintained if duelling was abolished.[2] Samuel Stanton in 1790 reiterated what had by then become a commonplace argument: that the duel upheld the interests of lesser gentlemen in the face of the greater.

> Was it not from the fear of being called on for redress in this manner, many persons whose fortunes and interest are large, would without scruple, injure and oppress their inferiors in those respects ... Money will carry through any thing; power and interest will work similar effects; but, happy is it, neither will turn a pistol ball, nor ward off the thrust of a rapier; otherwise gentlemen who are deficient in riches, would be subject to continual injuries and insults.[3]

The argument that the existence of the duel helped to prevent indiscriminate violence in higher society has a certain cogency when one observes that the formal duel which

---

2   *The Female Tatler*, 52, 4 Nov. 1709.

3   Samuel Stanton, *The Principles of Duelling with Rules to be Observed In Every Particular Respecting it* (London: Hookham, 1790), pp. 21–23.

had fully developed by circa 1770 served to displace the former chance medley in which protagonists and their supporters rushed upon each other and inflicted random injury. Similarly, the difficulty that Sanquhar had faced had been that his injury had been inflicted by a man too lowly to be included within the penumbra of the duel. Had this not been the case, a duel between the two would surely have restored his honour, perhaps without any fatality.

One could counter, however, and detractors did, with the argument that the duel itself legitimated violence in society. Furthermore, its existence as a final test of honour and courage both impelled some to seek it out as a test of their manhood and compelled others to accept challenges they would otherwise have declined but for the fear of the consequences. Men were driven to combat not only by fear of the disapprobation of society but also, it seems, by fear that unless they so acted, they could not be the men they had considered themselves to be. According to Piotr Hoffman, the message of Hobbes was that:

> I come to know both myself and the other – to know the qualities of myself and of the man I confront – by facing up to the threat of the other. As long as I don't measure myself against such a threat, I will live in an imaginary world where the qualities I attribute to myself may very well be unrealistic or fictitious.[4]

Michael Roper and John Tosh have observed that 'Masculinity is never fully possessed, but must be perpetually achieved, asserted and renegotiated.'[5] For some men it seemed that the only way to feel appropriately masculine was to prevail over others constantly and demonstrably through restless action. Many disputes seem to have been provoked by such men, who immediately and aggressively asserted their interest in contexts where even a modicum of conciliation would have enabled a resolution. Nevertheless, the duel in general could not have been sustained had it not been that the broader class of men who claimed it shared a particular sensitivity in respect of reputations, and had it not been that they were ready to contemplate the commission of violent acts. A goodly number of the duellists, it will be observed, were hardened by war, inured to violence and its consequences, but this was by no means true of all. Where, then, did the duellists of our period acquire both their acute sensitivity in matters of reputation and their ability to act swiftly and violently to defend it?

To no small degree, I believe the answer lies in the fact that the European social elites were inured to the receipt and delivery of violence during the course of their early

---

4   Piotr Hoffman, *The Quest for Power: Hobbes, Descartes and the Emergence of Modernity* (New Jersey: Prometheus, 1996), p. 9.

5   Michael Roper and John Tosh, 'Introduction: Historians and the Politics of Masculinity', in M. Roper and J. Tosh, eds, *Manful Assertions: Masculinities in Britain since 1800* (London, Routledge, 1991), pp. 1–24 at p. 18.

upbringing and education. Dostoevsky wrote, 'In our country, everything began with perversion. The sense of chivalric honor was beaten in with a stick.'[6] Like his Russian counterpart, the young English gentleman experienced the infliction of physical chastisement from infancy to late adolescence. Punishment, allied with deprivation, inculcated both a physical hardiness and an understanding that personal assertiveness was a necessary requisite for survival in the society of equals. This insistence upon the equality of gentlemen imposed itself upon even the aristocracy, although they might later be disposed to forget it.

> Many young gentlemen of Eton and Westminster, are eager to make a young Lord know that he is their equal by nature ... the good effects, however, of this ardour, soon wears off. Repeated and thorough drubbings, without the walls of the school, will never make one of our young nobility behave like a man for life. In his mature years he will always treat an inferior as if he was a being of a different species.[7]

At Eton the Scholars were left to the mercies of each other, locked in the Long Chamber and unsupervised from 8 p.m. until 7 a.m. Incarcerated, they passed their time in fighting, bullying, drinking and gaming. The consequence was not a society in which learning and contemplation were prized above vigour or even active, spirited cruelty. Rather, to maintain one's place in the hierarchy of schoolboy society, one was required to display fortitude, resolution and courage. To fail to maintain one's place was to be subject to indignity, insult and worse. There was, as yet, little institutional interest in correcting the many brutalities that occurred. The process was viewed as a lesson in the development of spirit, what one might now call a Darwinian education. To the well-heeled pupils of Eton, those poorer boys who had entered through scholarships were known simply as the Tugs because those who tugged less succeeded in eating less.

In the case of Eton, reform was muted by the end of the eighteenth century, and was given some further impetus in 1825 when the son of Lord Shaftesbury was killed in a bare-knuckle boxing match. Even then, however, the reaction of the headmaster Dr Keate, is instructive. He declared that this was regrettable, but that the boys must know how to defend themselves.[8] Spirit, rather than obedience to form, rule and

---

6 Fedor Dostoevsky, 1875–1876 *Notebook*, cited in Irina Reyfman, 'The Emergence of the Duel in Russia: Corporal Punishment and the Honor Code', *The Russian Review* 54:1 (1995), pp. 26–43 at p. 26.

7 Percival Stockdale, *The Memoirs of the Life and Writing of Percival Stockdale*, 2 vols (London, 1809), vol. ii, pp. 416–417.

8 Lord Malmesbury, *Memoirs of an Ex-Minister* (Leipzig, 1885), cited in Victor. G. Kiernan, *The Duel in European History: Honour and the Reign of Aristocracy* (Oxford: Oxford University Press, 1988), p. 214.

order, remained the priority of this education. Individual acts of violence were tolerated, and collective acts of violence were positively institutionalised. Boys were constantly competing among themselves, but at the same time they generated their own rules of conduct and could display a common solidarity in the face of challenges from those outside.

It is difficult to ascertain how far this outcome was consciously conceived. During the triennial celebration, the Ad Montem, Eton boys were dispatched to prey upon those in the surrounding countryside, almost like the Spartan youths, the Neanioi, were dispatched to steal. The festivities comprised two elements. First, there was a procession up the Salt Hill by boys, a procession which, until 1778, concluded with the dirtiest boy being kicked down again. Second, two senior boys entitled Salt Bearers, and each attended by twelve boys called Servitors, were dispatched to block the bridges over the Thames and the roads of South Buckinghamshire. Led by the Salt Bearers, the boys would stop all passers-by and demand from them 'salt' money before they would allow them to proceed. This was no quaint token ritual: the boys were supplemented by thugs hired for the occasion and acting in earnest. The boys themselves were armed with staves bearing legends such as *mos pro lege* (custom instead of law), and those who attempted to pass without meeting the exaction were liable to acquire a cracked head. Such confrontations were not infrequent, but those who paid were given tickets in receipt, which would protect them against ambush by the other band of boys. During a typical Ad Montem a substantial sum would be collected, and the Salt Bearers would pass a bounty of between £600 and £1,200 to the Captain of Montem.[9] The brutality occasioned during Ad Montem led to its suppression in 1847, but until then it remained a sanctioned, collective but extralegal act practised by those initiated into its rituals, and one designed to express a common identity that violently imposed itself upon those inhabiting the surroundings.

The extensive use of corporal punishment was of course a general European phenomenon, but it surprised foreign commentators that in England's system of education the same corporal punishments were applied to adolescents as to younger children. One passed abruptly, as it were, from the status of one who might be punished with impunity to that of the gentleman entitled to respond to such affronts with ferocity. In 1821, Christian Gottlieb Goede noted:

> A stripling is never invested with the dignity of a man, and no difference obtains in the penal laws of the higher and lower classes. A scholar of the first form at Eton, who already indulges himself with fond hopes of running a brilliant career at Cambridge or

---

9   T. A. J. Burnett, *The Rise and Fall of a Regency Dandy: The Life and Times of Scrope Berdmore Davies* (London: John Murray, 1981), pp. 24–25.

Oxford, receives the chastisement of the rod for any transgression, as certainly as the naughty boy of eight years old.[10]

The product of this system of education was a young gentleman who, although trained in the arts of courtesy, could nevertheless both endure violence and inflict it. Having come of age, a young man was naturally keen to assert that he was now to be immune from such well-remembered forms of physical humiliation.

Had the assertive qualities that such an education inculcated not been of use in adult life, then perhaps educational reform would have come earlier, but in the seventeenth, eighteenth and early nineteenth centuries there were sound reasons for regarding pugnacity as a necessary attribute for a gentleman. Such was clearly the case for those going on to military service, but such an attribute was also of great utility for any gentleman who had to move through public urban space. In the metropolis in particular, the dignities and entitlements of gentlemen were quite likely to be challenged by a populace endowed with their own independent and feisty labouring tradition. In time there were lighted pavements, elite residential districts and policemen to turn to for aid, but in the crowded metropolis of these centuries the interests of gentlemen were not yet institutionally recognised and secured. Gentlemen were forced to struggle to assert their privileges against the claims of the broader society.

In the middle of the eighteenth century, when our period proper begins, this had in fact begun to change as the interests of the better classes began to be vigorously prioritised and promoted, while those of others were conversely denigrated and suppressed. For example, London's residential squares began to be enclosed and dedicated to the private needs of the few – Grosvenor Square, for example, was enclosed in 1774. However, this process was resisted, and in much of London and for much of the period under consideration the segregation of the classes had not yet been achieved. Squares, rather:

> Were in effect commons to which prior residents had old rights of access for productive activities and for non-productive purposes ... They were not entirely private places under the control of the landlord or of the estate tenants who resided around them.[11]

In the nineteenth century, legislation such as the Highways Act 1830 was to affirm a segregation of the city that money had in fact largely already accomplished, but until

10 C. A. Gottlieb Goede, *A Foreigner's Opinion of England, Englishmen, Englishwomen ... and a variety of other interesting subjects, including memorials of art and nature*, 3 vols, Thomas Horne trans. (London, 1821), vol. i, p. 237.

11 Henry W. Lawrence, 'The Greening of the Squares of London: Transformation of Urban Landscapes and Ideals', *Annals of the Association of American Geographers* 83 (1993), pp. 90–118 at p. 97.

then the interests of the gentlemanly classes of London could not yet be presumed to always prevail against the rights of the hawkers, beggars, prostitutes and others in London's streets and squares.

The difficulty in making the streets safe for gentility is admirably illustrated by many of the works of Hogarth. In *Night* (1738), for example, a gentleman's carriage is portrayed. It has crashed into a bonfire in the street, but it is doubtful that it could have proceeded further because the road is obstructed by an enormous barrel outside a tavern. In the foreground two revellers receive the contents of a chamber pot emptied from above, while under a window a group huddle together for warmth. Hogarth's work reminds us of the intense struggle to appropriate undifferentiated space for so long as is necessary to accomplish one's purpose. Mandeville could not conceive that things could be otherwise, declaring, 'it is impossible that London should be more cleanly before it is less prosperous'.[12] In this city the forces of order were inadequate and parochial and they exerted a somewhat superficial control. The poor conducted the pleasures of life and death under the windows of the rich and deposited their ordure on their pavements and, occasionally, on the heads of their betters. In such a city the gentleman was constantly exposed to the potential of affront from the common populace. He simply could not avoid them, and they were notorious for their lack of deference to their social betters.

Writing of life in the 1820s, Grantley Berkeley claimed:

> Though nothing was said then of 'muscular Christianity', the art of self-defence was considered to be as necessary to the education of a gentleman as dancing a minuet or speaking French. It was a rough time, when, if a dispute arose, a word and a blow became a matter of course – the last not infrequently coming first – and men of rank who could rely on their 'science' as it was termed, did not shrink from displaying it at the expense of their inferiors, when the latter were insolently aggressive.[13]

Such a competence, however, was as useful in offence as defence. Lord Lennox reflected that the training of young men in self-defence resulted in 'the disgraceful fights that constantly took place in the streets'.[14] What strikes one is the ease with which gentlemen were able to move between a world of polite society and the world of popular living, and the dexterity they exhibited in both. It was in the context of performance and, in particular, in the context of violence that the move from the

---

12 John Mandeville, *The Fable of the Bees Or Private Vices Public Benefits*, ed. E. J. Hundert (Indianapolis: Hackett, 1997), p. 22.

13 Hon. Grantley Berkeley, *My Life and Recollections*, 4 vols (London: Hurst & Blackett, 1865), vol. i, p. 105.

14 Lord William Pitt Lennox, *Fashion Then and Now: Illustrated By Anecdotes, Social, Political, Military, Dramatic and Sporting*, 2 vols (London: Chapman and Hall, 1878), vol. ii, pp. 187–188.

former to the latter was accomplished. De Sassure, in *A Foreign View of England*, was astonished at the willingness of the nobility to resort to personal combat:

> Noblemen of rank, almost beside themselves with anger at the arrogance of a carter or person of that sort, have been seen to throw off their coats, wigs and swords in order to use their fists. This sort of adventure often befell the Duke of Leeds and he even made it into an amusement. My Lord Herbert, who is a very strong and robust man, recently fought a porter and punished him well.[15]

The willingness to combat with a porter does not necessarily signify an absence of distain for the lower orders. Egan, in his *Life in London*, describes a noble as a man who if a commoner touches him responds, 'Damn you, who are you?'[16] The behaviour of Herbert, however, indicates an inability or reluctance to retreat into a sanctuary built by social position. The magistrate is not summoned; neither are the servants instructed to chastise nor a weapon drawn. For his part the porter is not overawed, for, as Gottlieb Goede observes, 'even the indigent mechanic will infallibly pass sentence upon the nobility according to his criterion, and will not hesitate to degrade an unmannerly and illiberal nobleman by the coarse epithet of a vulgar fellow'.[17]

Patricia Mann has pointed out that streets can be the setting for countless acts of micro-politics, wherein individuals adopt acquiescent or repudiatory strategies when faced with the claims of authority.[18] Many of the conflicts between the orders were played out upon the streets of eighteenth-century England particularly in London where apprentices and labourers had a long and independent tradition. A sense of the rightness of acts and rightness of place that was to become a feature of Victorian society had not yet become embedded, and encounters of interest had not yet become scripted in ways that so certainly suggested whose interest would and should prevail. When passing through the city streets, then, the gentleman had to anticipate the possibility of challenge and prepare for it. One consequence was that even the most cultivated of men displayed a pre-modern capacity to move quickly and smoothly from studied courtesy to violence, even extreme violence, and then with equal assurance back to courtesy.

The life of the dandy Scrope Berdmore Davies here provides a suitable case study. A close friend of Byron since meeting him at Trinity College in 1807, Scrope Davies

---

15 Sassure, *A Foreign View of England*, op. cit., p. 181.

16 Pierce Egan, *Life in London or the Day and Night Scenes of Jerry Hawthorn Esq. and his elegant friend Corinthian Tom, accompanied by Bob Logic, the Oxonian, in their Rambles and Sprees through the Metropolis* (London, 1820), p. 67.

17 Gottlieb Goede, *A Foreigner's Opinion*, op. cit., vol. ii, p. 63.

18 Patricia S. Mann, *Micro-Politics: Agency in a Postfeminist Era* (Minneapolis: University of Minneapolis Press, 1994).

was one of the most prominent of the Regency Dandies. Captain Gronow said of him that 'his manners and appearance were of the true Brummell type; there was nothing showy in his exterior. He was quiet and reserved in ordinary company but he was the life and soul of those who relished learning and wit.'[19]He was described by Byron as a small, thin man, inoffensive in his manners and entirely without the abrasive characteristics of men such as Lord Camelford or Captain Aston. The painter James Holmes, however, recounted an anecdote of Davies's life that concerned a visit to a Thames wharf:

> Some of the coal-heavers and others about the wharf, seeing the dapper little gentleman got up in the most dandified manner, began to make fun of him. Davies replied, and from the bandying of words there soon came threats ... he found himself confronted by a big broad shouldered fellow, squaring up to him in lusty anticipation of soon putting him 'hors de combat'. 'I knew', said Davies, 'that a blow from his big fist could do for me, and took my precautions accordingly. He made a lunge at me, which I warded, and then let him have one with all my might ... He instantly fell in a heap'.[20]

Davies was equally robust in responding to affronts from social equals. In 1813, after Davies had challenged Lord Foley, Byron accommodated the matter but remarked that Davies was, 'though very mild, not fearful and so dead a shot that although the other is the thinnest of men, he would have split him like a cane'.[21]

Davies was not a man who seems ever to have actively instigated violence. The same, however, could not be said of his equals and contemporaries who sometimes resorted to violence merely in order to dispel boredom. In a class denied the release of productive employment boredom was always a problem. Dandyism, Barbey D'Aurevilly had declared, sprang from the unending struggle between propriety and boredom, and gentlemen of energy were driven to challenge orthodoxy as much for diversion as from conviction. For some, a certain pleasure was to be extracted from the notoriety acquired by the Infidels Club and, later, the Hellfire Club. Some chose simple, even juvenile, transgressive acts. Of his youth, Lord Lennox recalled that:

> wrenching knockers, pulling off bell handles, breaking lamps, smashing chemist's huge coloured bottles, carrying off golden canisters, barber's poles, red boots, cocked hats ... flooring Charleys (as the guardians of the night were called) and upsetting their boxes were the fashion of the days that I refer to.[22]

---

19 Burnet, *Life of Scrope*, op. cit., p. 51.

20 Ibid., pp. 66–67.

21 Ibid., p. 64.

22 Lennox, *Fashion Then and Now*, op. cit., vol. i. p. 183.

In Pierce Egan's *Life in London* Jerry Hawthorn, Corinthian Tom and Bob Logic tour Hyde Park. While visiting a coffee house, they are assailed by a group determined to provoke them. They fight and are arrested. Freed, they visit the boxer Gentleman Jackson and spar. Then they attend a dogfight, and finally, to conclude the entertainment, they creep up behind a watchman's box and overturn it, trapping the watchman. The passage of the day, it seems, is from one form of violence to another, but at its conclusion Bob Logic declares that 'the Lower Orders really know to enjoy life, whereas the rich go out night after night, to kill time, and what is worse, dissatisfied with almost everything that crosses their paths from the dullness of repetition'.[23]

At times feckless young men formed into street gangs, such as the Mohocks, could be very threatening; on the whole, however, society at large was remarkably tolerant of the excesses of the well born. Alexandra Shephard notes that:

> in many instances antipatriarchal or resistant behaviour by men was not deemed inherently threatening to the social order. Young men's misrule was often written off as sport and its potential for conflict thus diffused and minimised.[24]

Such disruptive behaviour can only be fully understood in the context of the broader culture of performance in society, a culture of which the gentlemen were a part, though by turns they denied it. Naturally, the rhetoric of gentlemen was wont to assert that they were set apart from the many. However, this did not prevent them arrogating to themselves the positions of figureheads for the many, espousing what were declared to be common values, particularly in the context of patriotic speaking. There was, in fact, a dialogue between the top and the bottom, dependent to a degree upon the propagation of common values and the adoption of common positions. This was no mere happy correlation of views. As E. P. Thompson suggests:

> The price which aristocracy and gentry paid for a limited monarchy and a weak state was, perforce, the licence of the crowd. This is the central structural context of the reciprocity of relations between the rulers and the ruled.[25]

Thompson argues that the weakness of the authority of the Church by the mid eighteenth century had made possible the resurgence of a vigorous plebeian culture.

---

23 Egan's *Life in London*, cited in John C. Reid, *Bucks and Bruisers: Pierce Egan and Regency England* (London: Routledge & Kegan Paul, 1971), p. 64.

24 Alexandra Shephard, 'From anxious patriarchs to refined gentlemen? Manhood in Britain, circa 1500–1700', *Journal of British Studies*, 44 (2005), pp. 281–295 at p. 292.

25 Edward P. Thompson, 'Eighteenth century English society: class struggle without class', *Social History*, 3 (1978), pp. 133–65 at p. 145.

In such a context and with the state weak, relations between gentry and the plebs could not but possess a certain reciprocal character. The gentry were required to extend a toleration or flattery to plebeian culture and to maintain their hegemony through appealing theatrically to the crowd. For their part the common people were 'aware of the reciprocity of gentry-crowd relations, watchful for points to exert for their own advantage'.[26]

This was a society in which, according to Gillian Russell, performance, display and spectatorship were essential components of the social mechanism.[27] Of the nobleman, Gottlieb Goede observed the following:

> The nation narrowly watches his motions, his conduct, his ostensible and his retired life, are the topics of common discourse. The newspapers publish the secret history of his occupations ... It is announced what parties he has had ... all his sumptuous entertainments, all his illustrious visitors, are detailed by the inquisitive journalists.[28]

In a censorious society such attention would likely result in a restraint in conduct, or at least a concealment of vice. But eighteenth- and early-nineteenth-century society was lived with an expectation of appetite; the great were expected to display great appetites, and their pugnacity was not generally reproved so long as it could be fitted within the model of what I shall call 'honest British violence'. John Broughton, advertising the opening of his boxing academy, declared thus:

> Britons then who boast themselves Inheritors of Greek and Roman Virtues, should follow their example, and by encouraging Conflicts of this Magnanimous Kind, endeavour to eradicate that foreign Effeminacy which has so fatally insinuated itself amongst us, and almost destroyed that glorious spirit of British Championism, which was wont to be once the Terror and Disgrace of our enemies.[29]

Linda Colley has said that British culture has largely defined itself through fighting.[30] What is apparent is that by the mid eighteenth century national vigour had become conflated with notions of interpersonal combat to construct a national identity whose purported superiority to that of other nations was expressed by the

26 Ibid., p. 158.

27 Gillian Russell, *The Theatres of War: Performance, Politics and Society 1793–1815* (Oxford: Oxford University Press, 1995).

28 Gottleib Goede, *A Foreigner's View*, op. cit. pp. 101–102.

29 Handbill in the Bodleian Library (Douce G 548), cited in Christopher Johnson, 'British championism: early pugilism and the works of Fielding', *The Review of English Studies*, 47 (1996), pp. 331–351 at p. 331.

30 Linda Colley, *Britons: Forging the Nation 1707–1837* (Yale: Yale University Press, 1992), p. 9.

habitual resort of the British (English) man to bounded fair and manly violence. This was to be contrasted to the inhumane, indiscriminate and, above all, cowardly violence allegedly practised abroad.

Two caricatures by John Collet engraved for the *Oxford Magazine* illustrate the sentiments expressed. In *Frenchman at Market* we see a London street. Outside his shop a portly butcher assaults a gaunt Frenchman, hitting him in the belly. Behind them a chimney sweep is mounted on another and drops a mouse into the Frenchman's wig, while a patriotic dog fouls his leg. The engraving illustrated a letter allegedly sent to the editor:

> Passing one day through a street near Clare-market, I saw a very curious encounter between an English butcher and a French Valet de Chambre. The Butcher happened to rub against Monsieur, which greatly enraged him – 'Vat you mean, said he, to rub your greasy coat against my person.' The Butcher like a true bulldog, put himself into a posture of attack, gave the Frenchman two or three blows, and obliged him to ask pardon.[31]

The engraving is companion to another by Collet, *The Frenchman in London*. A street similar to that above is portrayed, and again a butcher is offering to fight a Frenchman with his fists. The Frenchman puts up his hands helplessly and turns away, while two harlots laugh at him. Over a window in the background is written '*Foreign Gentleman Taught English*'. Two attributes of supposed British character are on display here: first, open manly violence; the Frenchman is simply unable to respond to the direct pugnacity of the butcher. Second, in England insult is not swallowed by those in any station. The valet, a gentleman of sorts, does not expect a resort to fisticuffs when he upbraids a mere butcher for contacting his person; he is expecting apology and deference. The violence on display here, then, is both open and, in a sense, democratic. What the caricature presents is a counterpart to the physicality, and to an extent the ideology, of the gentlemanly class as enunciated by Goede. Lord Herbert does not disdain from fisticuffs with a porter, but equally, the porter is not prevented by fear or deference from trading blows with the Lord. The exchange of blows becomes, then, an expression of a certain type of liberty, a freedom from social repression, and a method of common communication. The parties are far apart socially yet both acknowledge and respond to the same notions of fairness and manliness, exult in violent contest and endure its consequences.

Erving Goffman, in his study of contemporary interaction rituals, identifies what he describes as a crucial distinction between class groups in respect of their perception

---

31 *Oxford Magazine*, v (1770), p. 108.

of risk. Middle-class men, he asserts, are prepared to run risks if necessary, but the taking of the risk has no value in itself, whereas:

> For the working man, a physical confrontation provides the setting for the possible achievement of status. He subscribes to character definitions that are situational, and to a notion of status as something to be won or lost in the swift action of moments, rather than in the effort of years ... The participant is in a situation in which he will be judged and rated according to how he handles levels of danger that are incalculable, and have at that moment become inescapable. Heroism is not achieved by demonstration of ability, but by the exhibition of calm in the face of the possibly unmanageable.[32]

Goffman's comments about confrontation and the attitudes of some contemporary workingmen could aptly have been applied to the young gentlemen of the eighteenth and early nineteenth centuries. Both the top and the bottom of society during that period were connected by common attitudes to violence. As yet little distinction had been made between the education of gentlemen in the art of fencing and the unmannered practices of popular violent recreation. Fencing and boxing were often associated; when Jack Broughton opened his amphitheatre in the Haymarket in 1743 audiences came to see both, as well as cudgelling and single stick. All were taught side by side.

Pierce Egan, in his *Boxiania*, made the claim that Britain was:

> a country where the stiletto is not known – where trifling quarrels do not produce assassination, and where revenge is not finished by murder. Boxing removes these dreadful calamities; the contest is soon decided, and scarcely ever the frame sustains material injury ... In Holland the long knife decides too frequently; scarcely any person in Italy is without the stiletto; and France and Germany are not particular in using sticks, stones, etc. to gratify revenge; but in England only the fist is used ... The fight done the hand is given in token of peace ... As a national trait, we feel no hesitation in declaring that it is wholly-British![33]

Note the similarity of Egan's rhetoric to that of the duelling apologists. Both the fist fight and the duel were said to be absent the malice that characterises disputes elsewhere: both were bound by rules of natural justice, and both were corrective of vices that flourish where such principles are not acknowledged. Egan's writing to a degree idealised the pursuit of violence. However, there is independent evidence that in some measure his comments reflected a certain social reality, that rules and limits

---

32 Erving Goffman, *Interaction Rituals: Essays in Face to Face Behaviour* (New York: Pantheon edn., 1983), pp. 106–108.

33 Reid, *Bucks and Bruisers*, op. cit., p. 20.

upon modes of combat were actually acknowledged and obeyed by rough society. De Sassure noted:

> Should two men of the lower class have a disagreement which they cannot end up amicably, they retire into some quiet place and strip from their waist upwards ... The two champions shake hands before commencing, and then attack each other courageously with their fists.[34]

Gentleman Jackson's boxing school claimed Byron as its most illustrious pupil, and Lord Lennox could remember three other schools in the early nineteenth century to which the nobility flocked: the Fives Court in St Martin's street; the Tennis Court in the Haymarket; and Daniel Mendoza's school in City Road.[35]

V. G. Keirnan suggests that the regulations governing duelling derived from an awareness on the part of the gentleman that the man in the street had definite, if rough-and-ready, standards of fair play.[36] Duelling and boxing articulated common assumptions about fair and manly violence. Pugilism reached its zenith around 1815 when John Jackson organised a display for the allied monarchs in London to sign the peace, and it was he and fellow boxers who, dressed as ushers, provided the monarch's protection at the crowning of George IV in 1821.[37] Jeremy Bentham's Society for Mutual Improvement met in 1820 to ask whether magistrates were worthy of censure for negligent execution of the laws against pugilistic contests or, conversely, of approbation for their prudence in not too violently opposing public taste. The society voted overwhelmingly for the latter.

Relationships of mutual respect and even some intimacy were possible between orders, although these should not be mistaken for assumptions of social equality. In their patronage of pugilism, and in particular in their practice as enthusiastic amateurs, gentlemen were imbibing values that were abroad in wider society. They were, it seems, able to communicate with that society through a reciprocal appreciation of the nuanced violent act. During the Old Price Riots, the well-heeled theatregoers in their boxes joined in with the demands of the pit for fair prices, and equally in the fisticuffs that followed. They had at their disposal both the equipment to participant in the fighting and the rhetoric with which to whip up those notions of liberty that served to preserve their hegemony.

---

34 C. de Sassure, *A Foreign View of England in 1725–1729*, trans. and ed. Madame van Muyden 1902 (London: Caliban, 1995), cited in Robert Shoemaker, 'Male honour and the decline of public violence in eighteenth-century London', *Social History*, 26:2 (2001), pp. 190–208 at fn 21.

35 Lennox, *Fashion, Then and Now*, op. cit., pp. 187–188.

36 Kiernan, *The Duel*, op. cit., p. 215.

37 M. H. Downs, *Pugilistica: The History of British Boxing*, 3 vols (Edinburgh: John Grant, 1906), vol. i, p. 100.

The ability of gentlemen to deploy different facets of their personalities selectively did much to sustain the relationship between the orders of society. Among equals gentlemen generally observed the rules of politeness. Yet the urban gentleman was equally adept at abandoning such formality in order to speak Flash and adopt a manner appropriate to the common cant of the streets. Parker wrote in 1791 that the extremes of society 'border close on each other; and the manners and languages of the ragged rabble differ in only a few instances (and those merely circumstantial) from the vulgar in lace and fringe'.[38]

To no small degree, this was a temporary act of rebellion against stifling formality. Helen Berry notes:

> Rakes who by definition did not abide by prevailing codes of normative behaviour were at liberty to engage in flash talk at the coffee houses since they were sufficiently secure in their status to flaunt linguistic conventions as a mark of their general disregard of prevailing social mores.[39]

Gatrell reports that rakes and half-pay officers and bucks 'flirted with the rough trade in conviviality'.[40] The lower orders were aware, naturally, that they were being patronised, but as yet this did not necessarily carry pejorative overtones. For Lennox, Camelford and others, though, such escapades were but a temporary diversion from the demands of their position. They were merely asking to be excused while they exited for a moment to indulge their natures.

This intimacy with the many returns us to the earlier remarks about the undifferentiated nature of space and the absence of private life. The discrete segregation between rich and poor was as yet undeveloped. Indeed, Lord Lennox described the aristocratic amusement, which prevailed in his youth, of seeking out the poor to share drink and entertainment.[41] The rich had their amusement, but the poor their entertainment. As Thompson puts it: 'The Poor interposed on the rich some of the duties and functions of paternalism, just as much as deference was in turn imposed upon them. Both parties to the equation were constrained within a common field of force.'[42]

---

38 G. Parker, *A View of Society and Manners in High and Low Life*, x vols (London, 1781), vol. i, p. 9.

39 Helen Berry, 'Rethinking politeness in eighteenth century England: Moll King's coffee house and the significance of flash talk', *Royal Hist. Soc. Transactions*, 11 (2001), pp. 65–81 at p. 80.

40 V. A. C. Gatrell, *The Hanging Tree: Execution and the English People* (Oxford: Oxford University Press, 1994), p. 129.

41 Lennox, *Fashion Then and Now*, op. cit., p. 185.

42 Thompson, 'Eighteenth century English society', op. cit., p. 163.

The preface to a dictionary of cant published in 1699 declared that it was useful for people, foreigners in particular, 'to secure their Money and Preserve their Lives'.[43] Communication required tact, understanding and intuition, and above all, perhaps, experience. These skills were lacking in a valet who did not know how to address a butcher or, more dangerously, in a rich man who did not know how to conduct himself in a London rookery. It was this ability to communicate with the commons that was on display when Lord George Gordon inspired the London mob. John Wilkes possessed it too, but he was a rather more temperate and judicious judge of changes in society than Gordon. When a group of French sympathisers smashed the windows of his house in 1789, he refused to prosecute the culprits, saying, 'They are only some old pupils of mine ... set up in business for themselves.'[44] There was always a danger that the mob would overwhelm the bounds set by their masters, and to control them it was necessary to astound them, entertain them, intoxicate them and, of course, suppress them.

Relations with fellow gentlemen were equally tricky. In the early modern period, Anna Bryson has observed, one identified a social equal not merely by dress or language but by deportment. Young noblemen often carried themselves in physically expansive postures seemingly expressive of incontinence or arrogance.[45] Jennifer Low has suggested that it was their skill in fencing that impelled gentlemen to adopt such expansive postures. The fencer, she suggests, developed 'extended corporeal parameters that structured his behaviour in relation both to the opposite sex and the men lower on the social scale'.[46] The fencer attempted in a contest to invade his opponent's space, pressing him closer and closer and thus gaining both practical and psychological advantage. The opponent, in response, attempted to defend that space. Accepting Hall's contention that the boundaries of the self extend beyond the body,[47] Low concludes that the body space of the fencer eventually ceased to be delineated by the reach of the outstretched arm and instead became extended to the tip of the rapier:

> The fencer manifested a physical expansiveness denied to women and to men untaught in fencing – essentially making this proxemic behaviour a class marker. Over time

---

43 'A New Dictionary of the Terms Ancient and Modern of the Canting Crew, in its several Tribes of the Gypsies, Beggars, Thieves, Cheats etc.', cited in Helen Berry, 'Rethinking politeness', op. cit., p. 77.

44 See Thomas A. Critchley, *The Conquest of Violence* (London: Constable, 1970), p. 91.

45 Anna Bryson, 'The rhetoric of status: gesture, demeanour and the image of the gentleman in sixteenth- and seventeenth-century England', in L. Gent and N. Llewellyn, eds, Renaissance *Bodies: The Human Figure in English Culture c. 1540–1660* (London: Reaktion Books, 1990), pp. 136–53.

46 Jennifer Low, *Manhood and the Duel: Masculinity in Early Modern Drama* (New York: Palgrave Macmillan, 2003), p. 44.

47 Edward T. Hall, *The Hidden Dimension* (New York: Doubleday, 1966), p. 46.

I would argue, the extended proxemic sense gained from fencing became part of how men of a certain rank conceived of their masculinity.[48]

The personal domain of the fencer became expanded such that to pass within it was an invasion that ignited physical reactions and sparked mental responses that were only partly conscious. The body sought to protect its intimate space and adopted the appropriate deportment:

> The physical carriage of the fencer, with its indication of an extended proxemic area, would not necessarily be consciously noted by every passer-by but it would have an effect.[49]

Low particularly contrasts the expanded proxemic area of men with the shrinking proxemic area accorded to the female sex. However, she also asserts that a similar contrast may be made between the extended proxemic space of the well born and the restricted space accorded to the low. Familiarity with a sword served to inculcate a particular type of sensitivity in respect of body space, one which, consciously or unconsciously, others observed and which denoted a certain social position. Low's study derives in the main from sixteenth- and seventeenth-century fencing manuals; by the end of the eighteenth century swordsmanship was no longer an essential attribute. However, it remained a marker of a sound education and also a necessary accomplishment for those in military service. Low asserts:

> For the Fencer, having one's space invaded was not only to be threatened but to be lessened as an autonomous individual. The physical carriage of the fencer literally embodied his assumptions about his place in the physical world.[50]

The gentleman, then, attempted to maintain his dignity by controlling the space around him as he moved through the metropolitan environment. The attempt was not, however, limited to the physical. Gentlemen sought, as per Hobbes, to impose their will upon others, and where the protagonists were social equals, there was always the possibility of engendering a duel. Lord Kilmaurs was wounded by a French officer in 1765 after having talked too loudly at the theatre. In 1790 Mr Stephen, a secretary to the Admiralty, was killed after a dispute over the shutting of a window in a public room. Lt Rennell was prosecuted in 1812 for having challenged a surgeon who had complained about his arriving late at the theatre and disturbing his party while trying to take his seat. An all too familiar species of traffic dispute led to the

---

48 Low, *Manhood and the Duel*, op. cit., p. 44.

49 Ibid., p. 60.

50 Ibid., p. 92.

duel in 1792 between the Earl of Lonsdale and a Capt. Cuthbert. Cuthbert had ordered a street to be shut off to traffic, and the Earl had insisted upon his right to pass down it, calling out, 'You rascal do you know I am a peer of the realm?' To which the harassed Cuthbert had responded, 'I don't know that you are a peer, but I know that you are a scoundrel for applying such a term to an officer on duty; and I will make you answer for it.'[51]

To summarise, then, the duel found its place among a broader and violent performative culture and among an elite who had in no small part been educated to regard individual assertiveness, and even truculence, as a manifestation of both spirit and character. The menace of the artless social bore, portrayed by William Hazlitt, was apparent:

> The fine gentleman at the play enters the box with a menacing air, as if prepared to force his way through some obstacle, which he habitually anticipates and resents beforehand. A true Englishman, on coming into a coffee house looks round to see if the company are good enough for him, to know if his place is not taken, or if he cannot easily turn others out of theirs ... There is always much internal oath, preparatory knitting of the brows, implied clenching of the fists, and imaginary shouldering of affronts and grievances going on in the mind of an unsophisticated Englishman.[52]

If the portrait contains a measure of truth, there will, however, be more to say later for there were many contradictory forces at work. Gentlemen were also schooled in moderation, in religion, in conscience and in pity. There were many countervailing qualities possessed, in varying degrees, by gentlemen. Indeed, the emotional and moral flexibility of such men was considerable. Their lives had a performative quality, and as they moved through space, particularly public space, they changed, exposing different facets of their personality and adjusting their expectations. The dexterity with which this was accomplished explains in part why many, probably most, gentlemen passed their lives without recourse to the pistol or the street brawl. Nevertheless, even the most conciliatory of gentlemen seem to have possessed the ability, if truly necessary, to move seamlessly into the performance of violent acts, an ability that largely eludes their modern counterparts. They were not so inhibited, nor, it appears, were they so prone to interpose between their emotions and their actions, the rational calculations of interest that so govern the conduct of the 'modern man'.

The memoirs of Col. Bayley, to whose life upon campaign in the Sikh Wars I shall return, contain an illustration of this final point. In 1800 he fought a duel at St Helena

---

51 *The Times*, 11 Jun. 1792, p. 2, col. d.

52 J. Cook, ed., *William Hazlitt: Selected Writings* (Oxford: Oxford University Press, 1991), pp. 156–157.

in consequence of a quarrel during the passage there. A fellow diner aboard ship had downed a glass of wine that Bayley had ordered for himself:

> Irritated at the imagined insult, I rose from the table, descended to the great cabin and prepared swords ... Bryant soon appeared; I handed him a sword, but he prudently declined the combat malgre all my taunting expressions ... However at my landing at St Helena ... a meeting was arranged for satisfactory explanations ... I took deliberate aim, but a better feeling prevailed, and I elevated the muzzle of the pistol so that the ball passed far over my adversary's head ... he instantly discharged his pistol, the contents of which flew innocently wide of the mark; I then approached him, exclaiming, 'Bryant, I have acted like a foolish, thoughtless boy throughout the whole of this affair, and I hope the friendly intimacy that has hitherto existed between us may be once more renewed ...' How strange that men possessed of the most amiable generous feelings should sometimes, by an unaccountable fatality, be involved in such disgraceful dilemmas! Not a mortal existing is certain of his line of conduct for the ensuing twenty four hours, some sudden impulse or capricious emanation from the brain hurries him on to the commission of absurd and even criminal actions, repugnant to his very nature.[53]

Bayley's conscience would not, of course, have had an opportunity to intervene to prevent bloodshed had not Lt Bryant resisted all attempts at provocation. Bayley was not alone in his surrender to sudden impulse; it was one of the characteristics of the gentlemen of his age.

---

53 Col. Bayley, *Diary of Colonel Bayley, 12th Regiment, 1796–1803* (London: Army and Navy Cooperative Society, 1896), pp. 118–119.

3

Politeness, Interest and Transgression: Social Interaction and the Causes of Duelling

Although, Col. Bayley had given way to the 'capricious emanations' from his brain, it nevertheless caused him to consider his own conduct both foolish and regretful (see previous chapter). Despite the latent potential for violence lying within the breast of many a gentleman, it will soon become apparent that most – the overwhelming majority, I will suggest – of gentlemen conducted their lives without resort to so serious a hazard as a duel. The instinct for self-preservation was not still-born in the English gentleman and although I have referred to the tensions that existed when gentlemen vied for attention or sought to impose themselves upon public space, nevertheless it is self-evident that even the most trying of social gatherings did not engender a blood bath. In truth, reference to the obligations of honour was rarely made save where the norms of gentlemanly behaviour had been so violated that no equable resolution was possible.

In the seventeenth century the norms of behaviour had been established by the values of courtliness; but by 1700, courtliness had given way to politeness, as espoused by Addison and Steele and the *Spectator*. Politeness, according to Klein:

> was situated in company, in the realm of social interaction and exchange, where it governed the relationship of the self to others. While allowing for differences among selves, politeness, was concerned with coordinating, reconciling or integrating them.[1]

Politeness was not a value-free step towards general civility, rather, as Langford asserts, the new values of politeness marked a claim, even a demand, on the part of

---

1 Lawrence. E. Klein, *Shaftesbury and the Culture of Politeness: Moral Discourse and Cultural Politics in Early Eighteenth Century England*, (Cambridge: Cambridge University Press, 1994), p. 4.

the relatively well placed to be acknowledged and accommodated. The politeness of the turn of the seventeenth and eighteenth centuries helped to provide, 'a means of escape on the part of the well born from the trammels of the even better born'.[2] Politeness had a ready appeal to those excluded by primogeniture from their father's titles, to those sons of knights who had descended to the commons and to the lesser relations clustered around nobility but reduced to an inferior station.

Politeness, then, operated among gentlemen with a certain levelling effect. It emerged and displaced courtliness at a time when both the Court and the Church were 'declining as centres of discursive and cultural production'.[3] The authority of the early Hanoverian court was rather weak, and gentlemen no longer had to fear social extinction at the hands of the king. In place of a dominant court, a society had formed that was 'post courtly and post godly'.[4] Religion was not scorned but confined within its place, and so too the court. Within the space thus opened up there had formed, by the early eighteenth century, a polite culture, which Shaftesbury attempted to inform dedicated to the art of pleasing in company.[5]

One key component of politeness was the recognition of interests. That is to say that the polite gentleman recognised the interests of others around him in society and acknowledged those interests by adopting pleasing demeanour and modes of conciliation in social interaction. To Shaftesbury there was a relationship between the free society of gentlemen and polite discourse based upon the fact that the interactions that comprised politeness did themselves constitute a form of liberty. In a sense, conversation itself here became a paradigmatic mode of liberty, and thus, liberty was assimilated into the notion of culture itself.[6]

Upon such an understanding, the failure to adopt modes of politeness indicated a failure to recognise the estate and interests of other parties, and an attempt to engage in an unequal form of social discourse. As Klein puts it, 'A gentleman in England had to have a public standing and be seen to exist as a gentleman in the eyes of others, it required a substantial social dimension.'[7] However, one was not necessarily reduced by all forms of unequal discourse. One did not expect to be treated as an equal by the king, although even here there were limits to what could be tolerated. When, though, unequal communication was attempted in inappropriate contexts one was indeed reduced, one's honour was impugned.

---

2   Paul Langford, 'The uses of eighteenth century politeness', *Transactions of the Royal Historical Society*, 12 (2002), pp. 311–331, at p. 312.

3   Klein, *Shaftesbury*, op. cit., p. 10.

4   Ibid., p. 9.

5   Ibid., p. 3.

6   Ibid., p. 197.

7   Ibid., p. 79.

If politeness generally prevailed, there were nevertheless views abroad in society that doubted its sincerity and utility. As Michele Cohen writes:

> Politeness and conversation, though necessary to the fashioning of the gentleman, were thought to be effeminising not just because they could be achieved only in the company of women, but because they were modelled upon the French. The question was whether men could be at once polite whilst at the same time manly.[8]

She writes that the answer, according to the Bishop of Worcester, was, at least in part, no. In his imaginary dialogue between John Locke and Lord Shaftesbury it was said:

> No great man was ever what the world calls, perfectly polite. Men of that stamp cannot afford such attention to little things ... It tends to cramp their faculties, effeminate the temper and break that force and vigour of mind that is requisite in a man of business for the discharge of his duty, in this free country.[9]

John Andrews claimed that through refinement France had 'lost in strength what it had gained in politeness' and that French manners induced men to 'substitute politeness in place of truth'.[10] The Dane Ludvig Holberg observed that whereas the French respected their superiors, the English respected themselves.[11] Part of that respect seems to have been constructed around a fear of being unduly deferential, of surrendering too much of gentlemanly equality.

Shaftesbury, in his writings, attempted to sever the connection between French society and politeness, characterising French political society as imbued with an obsequiousness and a servility that were in fact the opposite of the values which he espoused:

> In making these points, Shaftesbury contradicted expectations, according to which, France and politeness were naturally associated. The aim of course was partly to expand

---

8 Michele Cohen, 'Manliness, effeminacy and the French: gender and the construction of the national character in eighteenth-century England', in T. Hitchcock and M. Cohen, eds, *English Masculinities 1660–1800* (London: Addison Wesley, 1999), pp. 44–62, at p. 47.

9 Richard Hurd, Lord Bishop of Worcester, *Dialogues on the Uses of Foreign Travel as a Part of an English Gentleman's Education: Between Lord Shaftesbury and Mr Locke* (1764), pp. 114–115, cited in Cohen, 'Manliness', op. cit., at p. 53.

10 John Andrews, *A Comparative View of the French and English Nations in their Manners. Politics and Literature* (London, 1785), p. 185, cited in Michele Cohen *Fashioning Masculinity: National Identity and Language in the Eighteenth Century* (London: Routledge, 1996), p. 3.

11 S. E. Fraser (ed.), *Ludvig Holberg's Memoirs: An Eighteenth Century Danish Contribution to International Understanding* (Leiden: Brill, 1970), p. 232.

into the cultural realm the means for vilifying France and partly to set terms for a program of British cultural improvement.[12]

However, this was a project at best only partially successful. The identification of what (in the eye of the beholder) was deemed excessive politeness with foreign effeminacy remained. Against such effeminacy one could speak with the abruptness of authentic patriotism or adopt the tone of high-minded liberty, in opposition to the servility of placemen. An unease, occasionally even a contempt, endured for the demands of courtesy. A constituency appreciated Johnson's remark that the accommodating politeness of Chesterfieldism was merely schooling in 'the morals of a whore and the manners of a dancing master'.[13] Assertive, even patriotic, rudeness was a cause of many of the meetings, especially since it was allied to the notions of national manliness that sanctioned immediate recourse to violence.

After the mid-eighteenth century politeness was joined by sensibility. Harvey links the development of sensibility to the publication of the Earl of Chesterfield's letters to his son in the mid-1770s, which revealed how politeness could be entirely manufactured and divorced from inner morals. For its advocates, she asserts, sensibility was a more authentic alternative and unlike politeness linked inner virtues with outward performance.[14] Neither can be said to have entirely prevailed, and towards the end of the eighteenth century Harvey detects a cyclical pattern which:

> seems to have brought a revival of older types of manhood, suggesting that the dominance of politeness was relatively short-lived, sandwiched between early modern and nineteenth century ideals that had much in common ... Certainly some things have endured through the move from manhood to masculinity, including a core notion of self-discipline and an (often specifically English) roughness that remained while codes of manners waxed and waned.[15]

English roughness did indeed endure in forms of frank speaking or in behaviours such as those exhibited by Hazlitt's truculent bore; furthermore, in some sections of gentlemanly society such behaviours were actually becoming more legitimate:

> Since the middle of the eighteenth century, a counter-image of the gentleman, the Ancient Briton had been emerging, and a specific vocabulary was used to imagine him: a 'manly ... ancient nobility and gentry', with plain, rough and bold manners.[16]

---

12 Klein, *Shaftesbury*, op. cit., pp. 192–3.

13 James Boswell, *The Life of Samuel Johnson 1791*, ed. A. Glover (London: J. M. Dent and Sons, 1925), vol. i, p. 170.

14 Karen Harvey, 'The history of masculinity, circa 1650–1800', *Journal of British Studies*, 44 (2005), pp. 296–311, at p. 311.

15 Ibid., p. 311

16 Cohen, 'Manners Make the Man', op. cit., pp. 312–29, at p. 325.

Michele Cohen asserts that by the end of the eighteenth century politeness was ceasing to be the dominant ideal; it was rather to become domesticated and feminised, such that by the early 1800s it came to be seen as a characteristic of femininity. In its place came a new system of manners, inspired by the Gothic revival and based upon a notion of chivalry. One facet of the new chivalry was a veneration for women, but one which, although it resembled politeness, operated to different effect. Politeness had placed women at the centre of society, whereas chivalry operated to marginalise women and identify them as in need of protection.

Cohen employs Austen's novel *Emma* (1816) to illustrate this new man; as embodied by one of Emma's acquaintances, Mr Knightly. Mr Knightly never flatters. He is plain spoken, always speaks the truth and does so in a simple way. He is quite prepared to reproach Emma when he feels it to be necessary. By contrast the a second acquaintance, Mr Churchill, strives to be universally agreeable. He endeavours to please everyone but all his emotions are shallow and insubstantial. A third, Mr Elton, is politeness personified; he performs the obligations of society impeccably, but has no virtue in himself being entirely venial. To Cohen, Mr Knightly embodies:

> What chivalry seems to have provided, a solution to the problems of politeness, especially the tensions surrounding its uneasy relation to authenticity and its association with effeminacy, tensions which even sensibility, could not resolve.[17]

The characters of the novel are of course devices of artifice, as are all constructions of masculinity that seek to define the moment when one form of behaviour shades into another. What interests is that all three forms of behaviour co-exist within the social setting and it would be impossible to describe any single mode as representing the opinion of society and the mode of normative behaviour. That is to say that each of the characters is operating within the range of common social norms. Each solution to the problem of life in society is in varying degrees acceptable. There were references available that legitimated obsequiousness or plain speaking, points of view that approbated frankness and points of view that appreciated delicacy and circumlocution. That is not to say that I believe there was absolute unanimity as to what was within the range of acceptable norms, but I believe there was broad consensus. Gentlemen were, after all, usually able to interact with each other upon a daily basis without recourse to any form of dispute or violence. The difficulty came, though, when men went beyond the norm in unduly asserting their interest or in failing to recognise the interests of others. It also came when some men, for reasons of their own, chose to take very particular exception to behaviour

---

17 Ibid., p. 328.

that most fellow gentlemen would have regarded as no more than unfortunate or mildly irritating.

> So stringent were the laws of honour, that no one occupying the position of gentleman could refuse to give satisfaction ... an accidental collision in the streets ... an undesigned push in a crowded room, or a chance shove at a levee were considered sufficient provocation for a challenge.[18]

Yet, gentlemen were actually rather more accommodating and pragmatic than the romantic memoires of such as Lord Lennnox might suggest – else indeed normal social intercourse would barely have been possible. Gentlemen met at the theatre, at the races or the hunt and, as the evidence in the next chapter will suggest, it was in fact only rarely that they embarked upon a deadly quarrel. Gentlemen, most gentlemen, were perfectly capable of understanding that things were said when drunk that would not be meant when sober, that interests had to be compromised and apologies made and accepted. The duel existed as a present possibility between gentlemen, and it was important that that was so. However, that should not be taken to imply that that possibility was at the forefront of the minds of the parties during normal social interaction. At the same time, however, there were certain offences against the dignity of a gentleman that, if they were committed, were regarded to be so heinous that it was difficult for the recipient to retain his place in society unless he took steps to requite them.

One of those offences was to declare or even imply that a fellow gentleman was a liar. It was said in the seventeenth century that it was so great a shame to be so regarded that:

> Any other injury is cancelled by giving the lie, and he that receiveth it standeth so charged in his honour and reputation, that he cannot disburden himself of that imputation, but by the striking of him that hath so given it, or by chalenging [sic] him the combat.[19]

But if *The Spectator* is correct, it was not the allegation of having uttered a falsehood that wounded the honour of the accused, but rather the implication of a lack of courage:

> The great Violation of the Point of Honour from Man to Man is the giving the Lie. One may tell another he whores, drinks, blasphemes and it may pass unresented; but

---

18 Lennox, *Fashion Then and Now*, op. cit., vol. ii., pp. 185–186.

19 L. Bryskett, *A Discourse of Civill Life* (London: 1606), cited in Robert Baldick, *The Duel: A History of Duelling* (London: Chapman and Hall, 1965), p. 33.

to say he lies, tho' but in jest is an Affront that nothing but Blood can expiate. The Reason may perhaps be, because no other Vice implies a Want of Courage so much as the making of a Lie.[20]

When Mr Howorth played while with Lord Barrymore, the latter asserted that a remark Howorth had made about the cards was false. Howorth instantly struck him in the face, and a duel was the natural consequence.[21] A Lt W. was killed in 1804 after suggesting to Lt H. that he had given false evidence at a court-martial. Lt H. had not immediately responded. However, after the circulation of a report saying he had not resented Lt W.'s remarks like a gentlemen, he had been advised by friends that it was absolutely necessary to issue a challenge.[22] In 1839 Capts Younghusband and Berkeley, both members of a committee, fought after one had used the word false in respect of a remark of the other.[23]

However, here too there were gentlemen who swallowed insults, or traded them in return without seeking recourse to the field. An even more egregious offence, however, was committed when one gentleman lost his temper sufficiently to actually strike another. Richard Hey asserted in 1784 that:

> A modern European gentleman resents a blow not for the pain which it gives him, nor in order to prevent the disorders in society which would follow from such violence being suffered to go unpunished, but because a Blow dishonours him.

A polluting blow was a form of violence out of place; it existed where it had no right to exist, and the consequence of its passage remained until it was expunged. Hey, though, was not speaking of any blow but rather of a blow from a social equal. Gentlemen, as we have seen, could and did consent to receive blows in the course of pugilism or country sports. Furthermore, they might also exchange non-consensual blows in combats with the lower orders, and they did not feel dishonoured in consequence. The offence, then, lay not in the blow per se, but in the significance attributed to a blow given by a fellow gentleman. To receive such a blow was to be diminished not only in the eyes of society but also in the eyes of oneself.

A dispute chronicled in Samuel Pepys's diary admirably illustrates the acute sensitivities involved in the protection of bodily autonomy. Two friends, Sir Henry Belasye and Tom Parker were drinking amicably in a tavern, but Belasye was speaking rather loudly and in consequence was asked if the two of them were quarrelling. Belasye

---

20 *The Spectator*, II, 99, 1794.

21 Sir Herbert Maxwell, ed., *The Creevey Papers: A Selection from the Correspondence and Diaries of the Late Thomas Creevey M.P.* (London: John Murray, 1912), pp. 78–79.

22 *The Times* 18 Jun. 1804, p. 2, col. d.

23 *The Times* 29 Jul. 1837, p. 5, col. f.

responded, 'No, I never quarrel but I strike!' Although the remark was not addressed to him, Parker could not but notice the implication that Belasye was asserting the possibility of striking him and so responded, 'Strike, I would I could see that man in England that durst give me a blow!' Belasye in return could not but see this as a suggestion that Belasye would not have the courage to give him a blow, and so he boxed Parker's ear. Parker resolved upon a duel as soon as possible, not because of anger but because he was afraid they would be friends again the next day, and that therefore the blow would rest upon him. He did not fear being traduced in society by his friend if he did not respond; he was scarcely concerned with Belasye at all. The imperative was internal: to expunge the stain left by the blow and restore his self.[24]

It is not always easy to disentangle the desire to eradicate a stain from simple vindictiveness. Sometimes a sense of offence or indeed of malice was maintained over a prolonged period, and men did not seem abashed to declare that this was so. To illustrate, when a naval captain, Augustus Hervey, chose to record in his diary an affront given to him in 1747 he did so in such terms as to suggest that his own capacity to maintain a sense of grievance for years afterwards was evidence of his high honour. The circumstances in brief were that while his ship was in a Portsmouth dockyard one of the dockyard clerks, Mr Blankely, had, allegedly, been insolent to him. Hervey had threatened to beat him, 'yet he never took any notice of it'.[25] As a putative gentleman, the clerk had obviously mulled the matter over however for some three days later he had turned up drunk at Hervey's lodgings. Blankely had declared that he had been ill-used and had demanded satisfaction. Hervey had responded that he would receive it in the morning whereupon the drunken man had aimed an ineffectual blow with his stick. Hervey had given the man a very good drubbing in return. The following day he had gone to the man's house to give satisfaction only to discover that the man had fled. Hervey had then responded by blackening the clerk's name in the dockyard and writing to the commander of the local regiment to spread the news of the man's cowardice.

One might suppose that having beaten and socially humiliated the clerk that would have sufficed; not so. For five and a half years thereafter, military service kept Hervey away from England. However, he followed the fortunes of Mr Blankely and heard that he had been posted to Gibraltar. In October 1752 Hervey's ship berthed there:

> Having long resolved wherever I met Mr Blankely to call him to account for his behaviour at Portsmouth ... I desired Captain Morgan, a friend of mine, and an officer of

---

24 *The Diaries of Samuel Pepys*, 11 vols (London, 1970–1983), vol. 8, pp. 363–364, cited in Shoemaker, 'Male honour', op. cit., pp. 190–208, at p. 195.

25 Entry of 11 April 1747, David Erskine and William Kimber (eds), *Augustus Hervey's Journal: Being The Intimate Account Of The Life Of A Captain In The Royal Navy Ashore and Afloat 1746–1759* (London: William Kember, 1953), p. 50.

the garrison, to go to that fellow and tell that I desired he would immediately give me satisfaction for his conduct and that we must meet with sword and pistol on neutral ground. He send word by Captain Morgan he desired to ask my pardon publickly in any manner I pleased, upon which Captain Morgan and Lord Robert Manners, whom I had sent to, told me surely it was sufficient, let his offence have been what it would. And so he came with his friend, and asked me pardon before these gentlemen, all in humblest manner.[26]

Hervey's account is a healthy corrective to those unduly attracted to the values of honour, for it provides us with a rare insight into the condition of those persons who, although neither wounded nor killed, were in their own way also victims of the duel. These were simply men who either could not face a challenge or, for other reasons (dependent families for example), were forced to forebear. Such men are no more considered in the modern studies than in the duelling chronicles. What we get a glimpse of in Hervey's journal is the fate of the subjugated, the fate of those in a theoretically equal, but in fact highly competitive, gentlemanly society, who could not maintain themselves on a par with their fellows.

Charles Cameron, in his critique of duelling, put the matter most aptly:

> The man who is constitutionally timid, the weakness of whose individual character most especially requires the protection of the public, is delivered up prey to his oppressor; while the man of ferocious courage, and skill at his weapon, is invested with power over the destinies of his fellow creatures.[27]

Blankely was four times humiliated. First, he failed to resent the threat to beat him. Second, when he summoned up courage, he was thrashed with contempt. Third, when courage failed, he had to flee. Finally, years later, he was again abjectly humiliated in front of his peers. To understand why men of normal apprehensions forced themselves to face the possibility of violent death over seemingly trivial matters, it is absolutely necessary to understand the humiliation of Blankely and the possible consequences of a failure of martial nerve: dismissal, disgrace, even disinheritance. Matthew Clarkson remarked after the Burr–Hamilton duel of 1804, 'If we were truly brave we should not accept a challenge, but we are all cowards.'[28] There were those afraid to fight and those afraid not to; both, in different ways, were victims of honour.

---

26 Entry of 10 Oct. 1752, *Hervey's* Journal, p. 12.

27 Charles H. Cameron, *Two Essays On The Sublime And Beautiful, And On Duelling* (London: Ibotson and Palmer, 1834), p. 79.

28 Joanna B. Freeman, 'Dueling as politics: reinterpreting the Burr–Hamilton duel', *William and Mary Quarterly*, 3rd series, 53:2 (1996), pp. 289–318, at p. 316.

It would be interesting to know what became of Blankely. He was not protected by wealth and lineage like the Earl of Pomfret, of whom it was said that he often had issued challenges and many men had in response gotten him to Hyde Park Corner but none had ever induced him to go beyond. Blankely's humiliation at Portsmouth did not prevent him securing a military appointment. However, Hervey's account may not be trustworthy; perhaps his humiliation was not in fact as abject as suggested. Furthermore, chance had favoured Blankely in so far as Hervey had had to sail almost immediately after the dispute. Who knows what version of events Blankely had told in Hervey's absence and what was being said about Hervey in the Portsmouth dockyards. Furthermore, society was broadly dispersed, in colonies, at sea and so forth. Not all humiliations might come to public notice, although Hervey did his best to make sure that Blankely's did.

That someone reading his journal might regard his conduct with disapprobation did not occur to Hervey. Forgiveness was seemingly not a quality easily separable from cowardice in his eyes. Nor was the domination of others to be the subject of censure; rather, it was a token of manly spirit, as indeed was the capacity to preserve afresh a grievance and extract reparation from the culpable. Hervey was careful to record that it was not he who deemed that the final humiliation heaped upon Blankely was adequate reparation, but rather two reputable witnesses. When writing, then, he did have in mind the judgment of others. There must be no suggestion of compromise with the clerk, no doubt that the dictates of honour had been observed. The dictates of pity are nowhere apparent, and this tells us much about Hervey. More importantly, it tells us a good deal about how he viewed his peers.

Greenberg, considering modes of expressing contempt in Southern American states, comments that to pull someone's nose was to 'communicate a complex set of meanings to an antagonist and an audience'.[29] It was, he alleges, 'an extreme expression of disdain for a man's projected mask'.[30] Much of the previous chapter was concerned with performance, with the need to perform the acts of a gentleman and so acquire gentlemanly attributes in the face of a critical audience of equals and inferiors. That a gentleman might endure blows was a necessary constituent of his gentility; a gentleman could be many things, but he could not be a coward. Similarly, when violence was inflicted upon the gentleman from outside the circle of gentility, it seems there was no danger that in consequence he would be expelled from that circle – so long as he displayed the requisite fortitude. To respond otherwise would be to subvert the structures of social power upon which the very notion of gentility was predicated. If Lord Herbert had

---

29 Kenneth S. Greenberg, 'The nose, the lie and the duel in the Antibellum South', *American Historical Review*, 95:1 (1990), pp. 57–74, at p. 57.

30 Ibid., p. 68.

been dishonoured by a blow from a porter, the power to confer the honourable state of gentleman, or at least the power to remove that state, would have been conferred upon one outside it. The group would no longer be the determinant of its own status.

A blow from within the group, however, represented a strategy that could lead to the expulsion of the recipient from the group. By his response, the recipient had to demonstrate that he was worthy to remain. However, the very fact of the blow could, to some, suggest that the recipient had failed to project himself as a gentleman. Men whom everyone knows it is impossible to getting away with striking are not struck. When, therefore, a man is indeed struck by another gentleman, he must in some way have suggested that he might be so struck. The dishonour of the blow, then, to a man who exists within and accepts this culture of honour is not merely to be viewed as an external consequence, a matter of the lowering of one's status in the eyes of a social audience. The blow questions the masculinity of the recipient; it challenges his self-view and exacerbates his own apprehensions. Men are profoundly disturbed by such a blow even if it is neither witnessed nor publicised; they may repress its consequences, but they can scarcely avoid its implications.

Those implications were further reinforced by the common adoption of a particularly symbolic form of violence against the person. Gentleman fought, lashed out with their fists and feet, struck with their walking canes. However, when they premeditatively set out to dishonour another or wished to ensure that the other was provoked to a duel, they seem almost invariably to have had recourse to one instrument to accomplish their purpose – the horsewhip. When an Irish barrister in 1809 wished to visit vengeance upon the solicitor general, he took a horsewhip to his house. The solicitor general was not at home, but the King's Bench viewed the presence of the horsewhip as evidence of an intention to provoke a duel and bound the barrister over.[31] When a clerk in the army commissariat wished to chastise a lieutenant colonel for dalliance with his wife, he met the colonel with a horsewhip, which he had brought along for the purpose, and belaboured him.[32] In 1829 Lt Crowther applied to join a pigeon shooting club in Boulogne, but he was blackballed by a Col. Helsham because the colonel believed that Crowther had been horsewhipped by a gentleman in England and had not resented it has he should have done. Crowther rehabilitated his reputation by issuing a prompt challenge.[33]

The whip served as an instrument of social placing. Who might be whipped? A beast might be whipped, a felon might be whipped and a slave might be whipped.

---

31 *The Times* 18 Feb. 1809, p. 1, col. d.

32 *The Times* 5 Nov. 1816, p. 2, col. e.

33 Millingen, *History of Duelling*, op. cit, vol. ii., pp. 304–309.

Greenberg describes the effect the scars of a whip had upon the perception of abolitionists and men of honour in the American South:

> Abolitionists read for meaning beneath and beyond the surface. They found it important to imagine the scene behind the scar ... But men of honour did not linger over the scene that gave rise to the scar, it was irrelevant. The scar in a sense spoke for itself – or rather spoke about the man to whom it was attached – regardless of the process or the larger set of relations that brought it into existence.[34]

When a man, a former gentleman, had received such chastisement it was in vain to plead circumstance in mitigation, to argue one's conscience in the face of such an enormity. However, the English gentleman was not irrevocably placed, as was the slave, in the sense that he could be rehabilitated through a determined act of courage. The outraged party could also restore himself by a symbolic equalisation of relations with the person who had committed the act. At the very least he had to show a determined attempt to confront the aggressor and obtain satisfaction. In 1829 Crowther asserted that he had done everything possible to obtain reparation from the man who had assaulted him in England. His accuser Col. Helsham responded by stating that he would be satisfied by evidence that this was so. Crowther, though, could produce no witnesses to this effect. Challenged to produce the paper with which he claimed he had 'posted' his opponent at Peel's Coffee House, he at first assented, but then, unable to produce it and presumably realising the impossibility of his position, he challenged Helsham instead.[35]

The symbolic meaning of implements of chastisement, but of the whip in particular, was such that the actual infliction of the blow came to be superfluous to the act of dishonouring another. In 1813 a Lt Hudson was court-martialled for having waved a horsewhip over the head of Lt Scott 'with the intention to provoke a duel'.[36] In *R. v Cooke* 1817, Cooke was charged with the murder in a duel of William White. The court was told that White's second had offered, on the field, a compromise between the parties. The second of Cook had, however, replied that it was impossible since 'a horsewhip had been shaken over his friends head'.[37] In 1818 a criminal information was laid by Mr Floyer against William Peel, the son of Sir Robert. Peel had challenged Floyer, who had declined. Peel had challenged again, and Floyer had expressed the intention to lay the challenge before the King's Bench whereupon:

> Mr Peel, accompanied by Mr Dawson, paraded in front of Mr Floyer's house, with his horsewhip in his hand. On Sunday ... when Mr Floyer and his family, among whom

---

34 Greenberg, 'The nose, the lie', op. cit., p. 68.

35 *The Times* 20 Apr. 1829, p. 3, col. b.

36 *The Times* 16 Aug. 1813, p. 3, col. b.

37 *The Times* 12 Apr. 1812, p. 3, col. c.

were several ladies, were going to church, Mr Peel and Mr Dawson came from behind a wall, the former with a horsewhip in his hand, appearing to be very much agitated, and uttered something the whole of which Mr Floyer did not hear, but he heard him say that he must consider himself as horsewhipped – no blow in fact being struck. Mr Floyer smiled and said, 'very well'.[38]

An American reviewer of Jonah Barrington's *Recollections* envisaged himself as a primitive in order to imagine how such a person would understand 'the strange mode of valuation wherein, while you sometimes kill a man for jostling you at play, you think you sufficiently punish him for propagating against you the vilest slanders, by lightly laying a whip across his shoulders'.[39] A primitive, of course, would fail to appreciate the significance of the act.

When Hamilton in his *Royal Code* (1805) attempted to address the question of how a dispute might be resolved where a gentleman had actually been assaulted, he claimed that no gentleman who valued his honour in such a circumstance would refuse to accept as reparation for a blow, 'an apology with the usual accompaniment'. The usual accompaniment is explained in the caveat that follows:

> The handing of a horsewhip, to a person who has been assaulted, may be dispensed with, at the solicitation of the offending party, and upon the written plea of his hazarding his commission, rank, pay or family expectance.[40]

The offended party might be given a horsewhip in the presence of the offender and lightly touch him to expunge the blows received. Yet, where the consequences might be the forfeit of military rank or the loss of inheritance, a written plea of extenuation should be accepted instead. The humiliation of the touch is apparent. In 1808 Baron Hompeach accidentally bumped into a Mr Richardson who was walking with two ladies in a London street. Richardson interpreted this as a deliberate insult and knocked the baron down. They met at Blackheath and each missed at the first salvo. Richardson then proposed a compromise:

> This was refused by the Baron, unless Mr Richardson would permit him to lay a cane gently upon his shoulder. This being declined by Mr Richardson, they again took their ground, and fired a second time without any serious effect. Being again furnished with fresh pistols, the Baron shot Mr Richardson through the body.[41]

---

38 *The Times* 16 Nov. 1818, p. 3, col. b.

39 Anon. 'Jonah Barrington's recollections', *American Historical Review*, 32:2 (1828), pp. 498–514.

40 Joseph Hamilton, *The Royal Code of Honor, For the Regulation of Duelling: As it was Respectfully Submitted To The European Sovereigns* (Dublin: Alexander Thom, 1805), p. 8.

41 *The Times* 22 Sept. 1806, p. 2, col. d.

One wonders if, once the equilibrium between gentlemen had been disturbed, it could ever be perfectly restored. To assault another in a moment of anger was wrong, but understandable and forgivable. However, to permit oneself to suffer a symbolic violation while in full possession of one's faculty might, to some, suggest a certain lack of spirit. Such nuances, graduations of honour, were not the subject of social rules that can be formally transcribed. Some parties were more vulnerable than others to the whispers of society; in some notions of honour were honed more finely. To Richardson and others like him the laying of the cane upon his shoulder was intolerable; to others to refuse this harmless recompense was inexcusable.

A mode of thinking that insisted upon impeccable politeness but which also valued plain speaking, which attributed the gravest offence to the smallest physical trespass and yet which operated within the context of the hurly-burly of the Georgian city was to a degree always vulnerable. That is to say that it was liable to collapse due to its own elaboration of standards that were impossible to maintain. What is striking about the values displayed by Mr Richardson was that they cast a gentleman into a state of uncertainty. Who could be sure that they would not bump into someone in the street? Richard Hey noted the process which led to an ever more extreme fetishisation of honour:

> The punctilious nicety of Honour which the duellist takes for his guide is apt to refine itself perpetually by framing new distinctions. If it indeed be a Virtue or a Mark of a virtuous mind, to take Offence at every unjust Imputation, at every instance of Neglect or Contempt; a person may feel a stronger consciousness of Virtue in proportion as he finds himself more easily offended. Hence every person who does not disapprove of duelling will rather be inclined to add something to the niceties of the fashionable honour; and no one ... will dare to think of retrenching its influence. [42]

Hey's conclusion was that left to its own devices, the institution of duelling would grow ever more vigorous – as it became ever more difficult not to fall foul of the demands of honour. Absent any balances to check this process, though, the system itself might have eventually collapsed in the face of its own impossible demands. However, even among men of honour there existed a counter-weighing resistance to the tendency to seek restitution for mere trifles. Opinion could be critical of those constantly demanding recourse to the field. The price of the fame of the inveterate duellist was often to be shunned by men of their own society, for reasons of morality and self-preservation. In a letter to the army in 1757 it was asserted, 'A man who has drawn his sword more than once in defence of his honour is looked upon as a quarrelsome ill-natured fellow and is avoided as a dangerous companion.'[43]

---

42 Hey, Richard, *A Dissertation on Duelling* (Cambridge: Magdalen College, 1784), p. 7.

43 Anon., *A Letter to the Gentlemen of the Army* (London: R. Griffiths, 1757), p. 9.

Two parodies by Addison and Steele published in *The Tatler* in 1710 suggest that there were indeed men who constructed ever more elaborate systems of courtesy and found offence in ever more trivial transgressions. However, *The Tatler* also attests that there was by contrast a constituency in society prepared simply to ridicule such pretensions and to subject them to the most damning criticism possible by inflicting upon them the sound of laughter. Both parodies take the form of mock court scenes wherein defendants are indicted for breaching contemporary etiquette. On 28 November 1710 Peter Plumb is indicted for having put on his hat two seconds before the Honourable Thomas Gules and having 'feloniously stole the wall of him'.[44] Plumb protests that he had motioned with his hat to indicate to the prosecutor that he should put on his hat. The jury, however, finds that the motions were in fact tokens of superiority in conversation, for which offence against courtesy he should be 'whipped through to the lungs'. The jury then move on to consider the case of Mr Richard Newman, indicted for having said in conversation to a Maj. Punto, 'Perhaps it may be so', thus suggesting that perhaps it may not be so and therefore giving the lie. Henceforth, the word 'perhaps' is to be banned by edict of the court.

On 19 December 1710 Harry Heedless is indicted by Col. Touchy for assault and battery. His offence was that he had removed a feather from the colonel's shoulder with a stick:

> The prosecutor did not think himself injured till a few days after the aforesaid blow was given him; but that, having ruminated with himself for several days, and conferred upon it with other officers of militia, he concluded, that he had in effect been cudgelled by Mr Heedless and that he ought to resent it accordingly.[45]

The court orders the prosecutor to beat some dust off of the defendant's cloak so that if the defendant is tempted to boast of having cudgelled the prosecutor he in return can boast of having brushed his jacket. Benjamin Busy then appears, indicted by Jasper Tattle for having looked at his watch three times while Tattle was accounting the funeral of his first wife. Finally, Sir Paul Swash is indicted by Peter Double for failing to return a bow.

The society that laughed at these parodies contained men with a robust cynicism towards and disapprobation of those who had continual recourse to their honour. These were men who, while prepared to sanction duelling as a legitimate response to grave offence, were unwilling to construe their honour as bound up in every petty breach of courtesy or incidental trespass, men who refused to be dishonoured by trifles. There was a widespread understanding of the symbolic importance of the

---

44 *The Tatler*, 256, 28 Nov. 1710.
45 *The Tatler*, 265, 19 Dec. 1710.

blow, and the necessity of courteous conduct, but just as society contained men like the young William Peel who simply displayed a whip and declared its meaning, so too there were men like Floyer who merely smiled indulgently in return.

There is some evidence though that even that indulgence was strained when the dispute in question related to behaviour towards a woman. The protection of women, or, to put it less generously, the extension of a proprietary interest over women, reoccurs as a theme throughout the history of English duelling. The Vauxhall Affray of 1773 was occasioned by a group of young men who ogled a Mrs Hartley while she was dining with the Reverend Bate and culminated in three or four duels.[46] In 1796 a gentleman who had persisted in being troublesome to a lady while attending the Haymarket theatre was wounded by the naval officer under whose protection she had attended.[47] In 1805 two captains wounded each other in a dispute engendered by the indecorous remarks made by one of them, at a function, about a young lady acquainted with the other.[48] In 1812 a militia lieutenant challenged a man who struck him at the theatre when he attempted to pass through some ladies to take his seat. In 1840 Capt. Fleetwood had to fight Mr Brocksopp after his dog shook himself over two ladies with whom his opponent was walking.[49]

However, while it would be true to say that duels consequent upon attempts at emotional or sexual conquest were occurring during the period in question, considered against the totality of English duels, such were not the preponderant cause of meetings. It is particularly significant that one finds little evidence of challenges being issued by men to protect women over whom they had not customary social control or interest. There were very many more duels fought by men over seemingly trivial inconveniences offered to the women whom social convention had placed under their protection than there were fought by men who had interposed themselves to prevent serious harm to women over whom they had no social claim. One might react aggressively when one's theatre companion was obliged to rise from her seat by a latecomer; one did not react if from one's townhouse one could hear one's neighbour beating his wife. The difference, of course, between one's companion being inconvenienced and one's neighbour's wife being beaten was that in the former instance one's own honour was engaged. The inconvenience was to the woman, but in consequence of his relationship to her at that time, the affront was to the man accompanying. It lay in the suggestion that he was unable to protect her interest. That is not to say that duellists never displayed disinterested instincts of chivalry, but rather to observe that there were two sets of sensibilities operating that often prove difficult to disentangle.

---

46 *The Morning Chronicle*, 27 Jul. 1773.

47 *The Times*, 13 Sept. 1796, p. 2, col. d.

48 *The Times*, 26 Nov. 1812, p. 3, col. c.

49 *The Times*, 8 Apr. 1840, p. 7, col. e.

Did the man whose wife was affronted act upon her behalf, in anger and empathy? Or did he act predominately because of a sense of shame that someone had felt able to affront her despite his own interest? In many cases it was impossible to disentangle the two sentiments. What is clear is that society was divided by zones of male interest over women, but when those zones were violated men conventionally defended them by reference to the interests of the women themselves.

Proprietorial attitudes to a woman could arise from something as simple as escorting an acquaintance at a social function, naturally however, it was during the process of sexual competition that men were most likely and most fiercely to defend their actual or putative interests.[50] Taking the field might prove persuasive in a courtship. In 1772 Richard Brinsley Sheridan succeeded in procuring the approbation of the parents of Miss Linley after his desperate duel with rival suitor Mr Matthews.[51] In 1777 a Capt. Stoney fought with Mr Bate, the editor of the *Morning Post*, in consequence of some remarks in the paper referring derogatively to Lady Strathmore. The following Saturday Capt. Stoney secured the hand of the Lady.[52] In August 1811 Lord Kilworth and Mr Wellesley-Pole met in consequence of verses written by Kilworth about a Miss Tylney Long. Wellesley-Pole announced his engagement to Miss Long three months later.[53]

This of course begs a question as to the role of women themselves in sustaining honour culture. Shame in the eyes of women has always proved a strong motivator and more specifically, the duels occasioned by sexual competition referred to above, could perhaps not have occurred had the prize in question expressed her strong disapprobation. As Hester Stanhope suggested, men of violent honour such as the remarkable Thomas Pitt, Lord Camelford, were sexually attractive to women. She recalled, 'His taking me one evening to a party, and it was quite a scene to notice how the men shuffled away, and the women stared at him.'[54] After John Wilkes had duelled, he wrote triumphantly to Charles Churchill, 'A sweet girl, whom I have sighed for unsuccessfully these four months, now tells me she will trust her honour to a man who takes so much care of his own'.[55] Following the Duke of Wellington's duel with Lord Winchilsea, John Russell wrote to Henry Brougham, 'All the Ladies are

---

50 University College London, the Brougham Papers HB/38138. Letter of John Russell to Henry Brougham, 25 March 1829.

51 Maxwell, *The Creevey Papers*, op. cit., p. 54.

52 Ibid., pp. 101–102.

53 *European Magazine*, 60, p. 148.

54 Cited in N. Tolstoy, *The Half-Mad Lord: Thomas Pitt, 2nd Baron Camelford* (New York: Holt and Rinehart and Winston, 1978), p. 91.

55 Edward Wetherley, ed., *The Correspondence of John Wilkes and Charles Churchill* (New York: Columbia Press, 1954), p. 19.

in Heaven about the Duke's duel – such flummery you never heard.' An Edinburgh essayist observed in 1790 that:

> the most amiable and tender hearted part of the human race, have not always the horror that we might expect at those cruel men, who deprive the wife of her dear husband, the mother of her darling son ... they esteem and favour those who, they imagine, are endowed with valour ... duels are seldom fought on account of women possessed of virtuous characters, it is from quarrels occasioned by those who disgrace their sex, that these bloody conflicts commonly take their rise.[56]

The prevailing mores of the time meant that women were to be portrayed as entirely passive onlookers protected by the rules of honour and little reference was made to their potential role in the instigation of disputes. Yet they could be more active in provoking confrontations than was conventionally acknowledged. For example, the duel between Capt. Thomas Best and Lord Camelford in 1804, which led to the demise of the latter, was to no small degree engineered by Ms Fanny Simmonds; a woman who had been under the protection of both. She had formerly been a lover of Best, but had moved on in 1801 to Lord Camelford. The men, however, had continued to be the best of friends until Ms Simmonds falsely reported to Camelford that Best had made insulting suggestions to her at the opera. Although Camelford's enquiry through his seconds suggested that accusation was false, nevertheless for the sake of his own honour he felt obliged both to challenge and to fight.

Unfortunately, the language of interests was not so clear cut, the course of correct conduct so clear, that honourable men could not be set at variance with each other. Not infrequently one can observe other men interposing between two men in order to provoke a meeting. Rather more rare, however, is the type of evidence that can be gleaned from the Walpole Papers of a woman manipulating the language of honour in order to set two parties in contention. Generally, men knew that one did not act improperly with another's wife, one behaved courteously to the women of the house and so forth. Even so, difficulties might arise for a man of manners if a boorish or over-possessive husband chose to interpret any extension of customary courtesy to a wife (or a daughter or a sister) as a potential trespass. Sometimes the very validity of a proprietary interest was uncertain and claims of interest competed with general social custom in such a way that no proper conduct was suggested.

The duel between Mr Dalton and Mr Paul, as described in the Walpole Papers, arose out of just such a difficulty. Mr Dalton had become engaged to Miss Mary Green, the younger of two eligible sisters. Shortly thereafter a Mr Paul paid a visit to the sisters accompanied by his own sisters. Mr Dalton chanced to be present, and he

---

56   Anon., *Reflections upon Duelling and on the most Effectual Means for Preventing it* (Edinburgh: W. Creech, 1790), p. 48.

and Mr Paul were amicably acquainted. There was no hint of rivalry in love between them. Shortly before the day in question, however, a minor dispute had occurred between Dalton and Mary Green. Mary's older sister had complained to Dalton that Mary had become accustomed to taking too much snuff. In response, Dalton had taken Mary's snuffbox from her. During Mr Paul's visit Mr Dalton took out Mary's snuffbox and took for himself a pinch. When Mary then requested some, he refused to give it to her. She soon after asked Mr Paul for some snuff, which he gave her:

> At this trifling circumstance the then present Company perceived Mr Dalton to be somewhat Affected but neither of the Miss Greens took any notice of it. The Youngest Sister said She thought that Mr Paul's Snuff not so good as her own which Occasioned Mr Paul to desire he might taste the Snuff in Mr Dalton's Box upon which Mr Dalton gave the Box to Mr Paul. Whilst the Box was in Mr Paul's hands the Youngest Sister desired Mr Paul as he had then got her Box that he would keep it and give it her again, the whole Company thereby understanding her meaning to be that she might recover Possession of her Box so as not to be debarred the liberty of taking Snuff when she pleased. Upon this Mr Dalton instantly said he was sure Mr Paul would take care and give it to the Person from whom he had it. Mr Paul made Answer that he should obey the Lady's Command and would put it in his Pocket or Words to that Effect and was seemingly going to do so Whereupon Mr Dalton sprung up from his Chair with great Anger in his Looks and seized Mr Paul very roughly as he sat in his Chair and struggled with him some time till Mr Paul quitted the Box at the request of the Lady to Mr Dalton and told him at the same Time if he made so serious an Affair of it he gave it up.[57]

Paul left, acquired a sword and then went to Dalton's house. There were no other witnesses to what followed, but in a letter of 29 May Paul gave his account:

> As Mr Dalton came into the Room they Embraced, Mr Dalton instantly expressed a concern for the occasion of their Meeting and said he knew it must come to that for it could not be avoided. The parties debated whether they should fire pistols or draw swords. The latter was decided upon and after another embrace they set to. During the contest the candles in the room were extinguished, so they paused whilst Dalton fetched another. They embraced again and in the next pass Dalton was mortally wounded. Mr Paul ran for the surgeons, and remained until Dalton had expired. Thereafter he fled to France, but not before declaring to a friend that he, never had any dispute or Quarrell or Jealousy with or on account of Mr Dalton till that very afternoon, nor did he pretend to have ever received the least Encouragement from the Lady or that she was in any Degree to blame in the Affair.

---

57 For the account of the affair and the statement of Mr Paul see British Library Add. 74087, Walpole Papers vol. cccxviii, f. 17.

Mr Paul's chivalrous declaration does not dispel the impression that responsibility for the encounter lay in no small part with Miss Green. Knowing nothing of the history of the dispute between the parties, he was requested by a lady, one of his hosts, to return property to her that was hers. Conversely, he was also aware of Mr Dalton's proprietary interest, actual and impending. In the presence of the ladies of the house and those of his own family, it is difficult to conceive that a gentleman could have acted other than as he did without creating the impression that he was intimidated by the demands of Mr Dalton.

In respect of Mr Dalton, he too was in difficulty. Having established an authority over his intended (which according to the customs and mores of the time he was unquestionably entitled to do), to have his future wife subvert that authority with the assistance of another man and in the presence of other ladies would have been an acute affront to his dignity. Both, it seems, empathised with the situation of the other, but neither could see a way of avoiding the encounter. Recognition of honour, it was suggested, enabled gentlemen to communicate with each other upon a peaceable basis of mutual understanding. However, honour was a language that sometimes failed in its articulation; it spoke of modes of behaviour but was not competent to describe each social situation and prescribe appropriate conduct. Under such circumstances it became not a coherent system of reasoning but rather a contradictory series of assertions, necessarily set in opposition to each other and available for exploitation. From the moment that Miss Green, possessing the knowledge that she did, chose to request return of her snuffbox, the parties had either to set themselves at hazard or to accept one of those small dishonours that gentleman so often in fact found intolerable.

4

Controversies and Calculations: The Incidence and Distribution of Duelling

Thus far I have considered the physicality of gentlemanly society, and those species of quarrel that were most likely to conclude in an actual duel. However, I have also suggested that there were many countervailing considerations that induced gentlemen to compromise with each other; the absence of which would have made society very precarious indeed. Two questions then fall to be answered in this and Chapter 5. First, how common a phenomenon actually was the duel during the period under consideration? Second, were duellists distributed evenly throughout gentlemanly society or were there particular species of gentlemen who were more prone than others to resort to combat?

Unfortunately, assessing both the general incidence of duelling and the authenticity of individual accounts of duels has always been difficult. Early on the duel captured the popular imagination, and periodicals did not refrain from presenting, as authentic, accounts of duels which appear, upon investigation, to have been entirely fictional. Such accounts reflected a range of contemporary social prejudices and narrative practices, as did those others which, while containing a historical core, were nevertheless clearly embellished, either to lampoon or to lionise. The researcher quickly becomes aware that in the history of the duel fact and fiction are closely intertwined and that while the historical fact of the duel served to fuel its fictional history, the continual production of the duel in the realm of the imagination also served to propagate the institution in the realm of the real.

The bald statements contained in memoirs or conduct books are quite unreliable. There are, for example, numerous contemporary statements and assertions attesting to the propensity of Irishmen to duel, as though duelling were a daily and ubiquitous affair in Ireland. However, a recent study of Irish duelling presents a much more sober picture.[1] Occasional statistics as to the incidence of the duel may be found in duelling histories and newspapers, but their authority is in fact illusory. Donna

---

1   Kelly, *That Damn'd Thing Called Honour*, op. cit.

Andrew has correctly described these statistics as 'hopelessly inconclusive, unscientific and perhaps contradictory'.[2] *The Times*, for example, asserted in 1844 that there had been only 200 duels fought between 1760 and 1837, whereas in fact the newspaper had itself reported more than 800 encounters since 1785 alone. Perhaps wisely, Andrew does not commit herself to a view of the frequency of duelling other than to conclude that it was not a very common occurrence.

Andrew nevertheless asserts that the duel showed 'signs of increase in the last decades of the eighteenth century and first decade of the nineteenth'.[3] She suggests, however, that this enthusiasm quickly ebbed away and that by the 1830s the symbolic value of the duel had been weakened. By the end of that decade 'a duel which resulted in death was no longer usual, but was an extraordinary happening and a spectacular public show'.[4] Her interpretation, then, seems to provide a straightforward chronology, with a rise until about 1810 and then a clear decline after 1830. She additionally suggests that duelling became less fashionable with the upper classes, in consequence of the fact that 'some of the less enlightened of the lower orders had themselves begun to duel ... This fact, as much as anything must account for the increasing unfashion-ableness and infrequency of duelling'.[5] To support this contention Andrew cites a magazine report from 1810 and a remark of Lord Ellenborough's from 1812, but it is left unclear whether she believes that the higher classes were beginning to eschew the duel as early as 1810. Finally, she remarks, 'It is ironic, though fitting, that the final discouragement to duelling should have come about through its increase in public popularity and participation!'[6]

There are, however, difficulties with this interpretation. Notably, if an increasing number of the 'lower orders' were participating in a declining number of encounters, this presupposes (though she does not explicitly say so) that the decline in the number of upper-class participants must have been quite dramatic in the years after 1810. However, as we shall see, many of the duellists of the later period, from Wellington to Cardigan, were indeed from the top drawer of society.

In an influential article, Antony Simpson subsequently concurred with Andrew that the social status of duellists declined as the institution neared its demise, a hypothesis that I will deal with in more detail when I come to consider the final demise of the duel. Simpson himself attempted to quantify the extent of the duelling phenomenon between the years 1785 and 1850 using the references to duelling contained within

---

2 Donna T. Andrew, 'The code of honour and its critics: the opposition to duelling in England 1700–1850', *Social History*, 5 (1980), 409–434, at p. 410, fn 6.

3 Ibid., p. 423.

4 Ibid., p. 432.

5 Ibid., p. 433.

6 Ibid,, p. 433.

Palmer Index to The Times and four collections of duelling accounts.[7] He did not attempt to distribute the duels geographically, but he did record those duellists who are known to have held military rank. He also reported the instances of known fatalities. This is all extremely useful, but unfortunately, there are difficulties in relying upon these sources alone to accurately portray the state of duelling during this period.

First, the collections of duelling reports are all rather late, and it is proper to stress that they are of noteworthy or sensational accounts rather than works of scholarship per se. True, Gilchrist's list of duels dates from 1821, but Millingen's work was not published until 1841, Sabine's not until 1855 and Truman's not until 1884. It would be surprising if the latter three were not better informed about duels in the 1840s and 1830s than about duels occurring in the 1780s and 1790s, especially in respect of those duels that were otherwise unremarkable and involved minor personages. The danger is therefore that as the quality of the reporting improves through time, a bogus trend emerges.

There should be some doubt as to the status of these collections as independent sources at all. None of them describe how they gathered their material; however, it is apparent that both Millingen and Sabine were heavily dependent upon *The Times* and repeat its reports verbatim. Truman, too, may have acquired much of his information from the most obvious resource for those seeking access to old newspaper reports, that is to say from *The Palmer Index*, which began publication in 1868. In reality, then, these are largely duplications of previously published material, derived from London newspapers and from *The Times* in particular. Furthermore, as aforementioned, the veracity of some of *The Times* reports must be challenged: some were but a recycling of old apocryphal tales; some were delivered in good faith but were based on mere gossip and were subsequently retracted. Above all, it may be doubted whether a single, albeit contemporaneous, source concerned with London society can be relied upon to provide an accurate picture of duelling in the counties or, indeed, out in the Empire.

Based upon his data, Simpson has concluded that Andrew was wrong in her belief that that the incidence of duelling declined during the period. Simpson argues that there was a steady average of about thirteen duels per year right up until 1843. It was only after 1843, when the government refused to grant a pension to the widow of a slain army officer, that duelling swiftly declined, becoming extinct in England by 1853. He also avers that the Napoleonic Wars had no influence upon the incidence of duelling and that duels neither increased nor decreased before or during the war.[8] It seems somewhat implausible that so momentous a conflict, which had so great an

---

7   Antony E. Simpson, 'Dandelions on the field of honor: dueling, the middle classes, and the law in nineteenth-century England', *Criminal Justice History*, 9 (1988), 99–155, at p. 106.

8   Ibid., p. 110.

impact upon the martial experience of a generation, could have had no impact upon this particular form of interpersonal violence. I shall argue that, on the contrary, there is strong evidence in the record that points to an upsurge in duels during that very period. Simpson however, agrees with Andrew in contending that the social context of the duel changed after the first decade of the nineteenth century. Indeed, at the very heart of his explanation of the reasons for the demise of the duel, to which I will return, is the contention that duelling became a bourgeois phenomenon and survived as long as it did as a monument to bourgeois ambition.[9] This, in his view, caused the elite to turn against duelling and induced them, in alliance with the respectable middle, to take steps to suppress it.

In terms of the frequency of duelling Robert Shoemaker has, in my view, struck an appropriate note of caution in declaring that 'One should not, therefore, conclude, from the fact that the duelling persisted for so long that it was universally or even very widely supported.'[10] Shoemaker locates the duel within the context of a general decline in the level of public violence committed by gentlemen by the end of the eighteenth century and asserts that by that time those who participated in duels were performing to an ever-shrinking audience.[11] For Shoemaker, then, the duel was very certainly in decline by 1800, the very middle of the period under consideration here. His is the very antithesis of the picture painted by Simpson. Furthermore, after a survey of the occupations of duellists, Shoemaker concludes – correctly, I will suggest – that the only evidence that the duel became bourgeois rests upon complaints made in the columns of *The Times*. In Shoemaker's view the duel was 'fatally undermined in the eighteenth century by changing understandings of the role of violence and honour in definitions of elite masculinity'.[12]

We have, then, three different views as to the nature of the duel during the period in question. In Simpson's model the duel is perceived as being in rude health until its very sudden demise in the 1840s. Although the numerical incidence of duelling does not increase, duelling attracts a broader class of participant in consequence of an embourgeoisement of the institution. Andrew, while having propounded the notion of embourgeoisement, which so clearly influenced Simpson, nevertheless seems to presume that the institution did begin to decline numerically after perhaps 1810 and certainly by 1830. Shoemaker, however, is sceptical as to the reality of this embourgeoisement. For him, the duel, at least in the metropolitan environment, was

---

9 Ibid., p. 115.

10 Robert B. Shoemaker, 'The taming of the duel: masculinity, honour and ritual violence in London, 1660–1800', *Historical Journal*, 45 (2002), pp. 525–545, at p. 539.

11 Ibid., p. 539.

12 Ibid., p. 545.

by the end of the eighteenth century a 'pale reflection of its former self' and 'fatally undermined'. I hope that the new data that I have gathered here will go some way towards resolving these issues.

It should be stressed at this point, however, that the incidence of duelling was not necessarily directly related to its significance. If, at the extreme, we were to find that during the period in question the duel was a common occurrence among gentlemen, a regular mode of conduct and consequent mortality, it would be difficult not to conclude that the institution played, as the duelling apologists suggested, a very important role in defining what it meant to a gentleman during that period. Yet if it were determined that duels were but unusual, exceptional occurrences, it does not necessarily follow that the converse was true and that they played but a small role in creating a sense of social identity. It is entirely possible for individuals to define themselves by potential powers that are rarely activated, by reference to acts that are, in fact, rarely performed.

Performance, though, if supported by other affirmations of commitment to acts, may serve as a guide to the relative adherence to classes of acts on the part of different groups within society. Although gentlemanly society was constituted by a core of collective assumptions and expectations, it nevertheless allowed for an order still diverse in its occupations, social situations, religious or philosophical inclinations and so on. As we shall see, there were particular groups within society who made particular reference to the codes of honour and who, therefore, were particularly likely to be involved in duels.

The Times contains much the most comprehensive contemporary series of duelling reports and so is the starting point in my own attempt to assess the true incidence of duelling during the period in question. Unfortunately, we know but a little about the day-to-day management of the newspaper. Newspapers were, and are, driven as much by felicities of chance, vagaries of opinion and the desire to titillate readers as by the need to supply a dispassionate social testament. They were and are, of course, greatly limited by their powers of discovery. However, on the positive side, the newspaper's ability to report duelling must have been greatly facilitated by the happy coincidence of interest between duellists and a press fascinated by the drama and controversy of the duel and the opportunity for homily that it afforded. For the duellist, in a society as yet very much orientated towards display and the search for public approbation, the press served as the medium through which he could publicly declare the erasure of a stain or the resolution of a dispute or could narrate an encounter which would (in the main) enhance the reputations of both of the participants. Indeed, a duel might be said to have often neither begun nor been concluded on the field, but rather to have commenced with a series of representations in print and to have been concluded with common declarations (or, occasionally, contending statements) placed in the press after the event. It required in short, no great labour upon the part of *The Times* to elicit information about most encounters.

The Times may have remained interested in duelling through until its demise, but that is not to say that the nature and quality of its reporting of duelling did not change. Until 1817 the newspaper did not have an editor, merely lead writers. This changed with the appointment of Thomas Barnes, who remained editor until 1841.[13] Barnes was a middle-class constitutionalist of reformist inclination, but his personal views on duelling are unknown. They are perhaps unlikely to have been overly sympathetic. What is clear is that under his editorship the newspaper slowly created a constituency of independent public opinion and also gradually gained confidence in leading it.

From the outset *The Times* was sporadically opposed to duelling. That is to say that it was opposed to duelling in much the same way that contemporary tabloids are opposed to vice. Whatever the moral stance of the moment was, duels were reported and dissected in such titillating detail as to suggest that the newspaper was entirely grateful for their existence. A generous interpretation would suggest that rather than adopting a coherent ethical approach, the newspaper was trying to reflect the confused and contradictory state of opinion in society, with a mild disposition to being hostile to the duel. *The Times* remained generally critical of the weaknesses in the law that drove men to seek unlawful restitution, and it occasionally advocated leniency to particular duellists. What seems to have changed under Barnes's editorship was that in the last two decades of the duel's existence the newspaper determined that it would no longer be used as the voice of the duellist. It more clearly conceived of itself as appealing to a different constituency of readers and began to refer to duellists as though they belonged to a section of society that operated outside of the sensibilities of its readership. In 1831 a distinct change in policy as to the placing of correspondence by duellists was announced. *The Times* reported a bloodless encounter but damned the parties by remarking, 'In future we shall require payment as for advertisements (except under extraordinary circumstances) for the insertion of paragraphs which are of no interest except to the parties concerned.'[14] *The Times* no longer felt obliged to print as free copy details of every meeting sent to it, although it was prepared to do so upon payment, and to waive that requirement in cases of particular interest. By 1841 the paper was by turns both reporting duels and condemning rival newspapers for doing the very same thing.[15]

As aforementioned not every duelling account that appears in *The Times* can be taken at face value. There existed a fictional genre of duelling report that owed its existence to the penchant for filling copy by repeating amusing and apocryphal stories as though they were true and had just occurred. For example, it was claimed in 1786

---

13 For a history of Thomas Barnes's editorship see Anon., *The Thunderer In The Making 1785–1841* (London: *The Times*, 1935), pp. 187–213.

14 *The Times,* 31 Dec. 1831, p. 2, col. f.

15 *The Times,* 20 Feb. 1841, p. 4, col. d–e.

that two tailors had just met in Hyde Park to settle a rivalry in love conceived at Vauxhall Gardens. However, the duel had not proceeded because the heroic snips were taken into custody.[16] Unfortunately, in September 1791 the same story reappeared, more or less identical save that the heroic snips had proposed to meet at the Kensington gravel pits.[17] Combative tailors were a favoured theme. Two were at odds in Kilkenny in 1788, fighting with sheers, until their fellows declared, 'As each of the brethren of the sheers had demonstrated more than a ninth part of manhood, they ought to be reconciled.'[18] Presented as fact, such stories are mere stock comic tales. The sources of the reports are not identified, nor, generally, are the names of the parties and although the duellists are sometimes said to have been brought before unnamed magistrates, their cases do not find their way into the law reports. Since this genre of lower-order duelling tale was designed to amuse and uphold the prejudice of the reader, some defect had to be related and satirised. When a florist met a quack in 1806, the pistols were loaded with blood and the bogus doctor was deluged. Terrified, he was carried to bed declaring he was a dead man.[19] Cowardice and fraud were again on display in the duel between a draper and a silversmith: 'each with trembling hand and shaking knees took the death-like weapon'.[20] Little did they know that the pistols were not loaded. Allegations that such vulgar parties invariably tipped off the police abounded;[21] at best, they might take the field with a display of unseemly fear.[22]

In the comedy *Where to Find a Friend* a leading protagonist is again a tailor. A caricature by George Cruickshank publicising a song from the performance shows the terrified tailor rushing off clutching his pistol and his shears, while his opponent, an Irish bruiser, mistakenly shoots a signpost.[23] Whether readers believed or merely purported to believe such amusements is unclear, but the newspaper was still, in 1829, citing as authentic a report from the *Cheltenham Chronicle* of an alleged meeting between a linen-draper and yet another tailor:

The belligerents sallied forth, accompanied by their seconds, to the field of martial glory ... bystanders were in a state of breathless expectation – when just at this awful

---

16 *The Times,* 30 Aug. 1786, p. 2, col. c.

17 *The Times,* 9 Sep. 1791, p. 2, col. b.

18 *The Times,* 5 Apr. 1788, p. 3, col. c.

19 *The Times,* 30 Jan. 1806, p. 3, col. a.

20 *The Times,* 18 Dec. 1829, p. 2, col. e.

21 *The Times,* 1 Nov. 1827, p. 3, col. e.

22 Note, for example, the comic coverage of the duel between two thespians, Mr Kemble and Mr Aikin in 1792, *The Times,* 3 Mar., p. 2, col. d.

23 I. R. Cruickshank, *The Irish Duel; Or, The Loves Of Paddy Wackmacruck and Mackirkcroft The Tailor* (London, 1816).

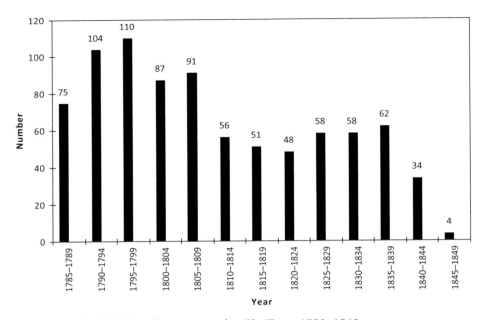

Figure 1 Duels of British subjects reported in *The Times,* 1785–1849

crisis, a constable, whom some one had very thoughtfully apprised of the circumstance, took one of the combatants into custody.[24]

Figure 1 then derives from *The Times* reports of duels either conducted upon British soil, or conducted abroad where at least one of the participants can be identified as a British subject. But it does however, exclude those duelling reports that I feel can be confidently regarded as apocryphal.

Simpson has contended that the duel did not increase during nor decline after the Napoleonic War.[25] However, *The Times* reports do seem to suggest that the incidence of duelling between 1790 and 1810 was rather higher than before. Later I will show that the process of enlistment, deployment and service during the war did indeed have an impact upon the locations in which duels were fought and upon their frequency. After the Napoleonic War, there appears to have been, if *The Times* can be taken to be a fair indicator, a decline in duelling. However, this was followed by a revival in the 1820s and 1830s, then by a swift decline after 1840.

The evidence from *The Times* is obviously in need of further corroboration and to begin with there seems to be some correlation between the data displayed in

24 *The Times,* 21 Feb. 1829, p. 3, col. e
25 Simpson, 'Dandelions', op. cit., p. 110.

Table 1 Percentage of homicides in Kent caused by
shooting, 1780–1849

Years	Percentage
1780–1789	28
1790–1799	21
1800–1809	26
1810–1819	11
1820–1829	16
1830–1839	17
1840–1849	2

figure one and related data gathered by Cockburn from the indictments and coroners inquests in the assize files for Kent.[26] Table 1 is derived from Cockburn's table two recording the percentage of homicides caused by shooting in the period that concerns us. Homicide by shooting in Kent significantly declined after 1810, revived somewhat about 1820, and then declined once more to become a very rare occurrence after 1840. Not all the incidents recorded by Cockburn were those in which death was occasioned by a duel, but it is interesting that the apparent decline in the use of firearms in Kent coincides with the decline in the frequency of duelling. Indeed, the incidence of such use declines to almost nothing at around the same time as the duel expires.

If we revisit *The Times* data but divide the reported duels geographically, as in my Table 2, we may draw interesting conclusions as to the distribution of the duel in society. Unfortunately, not all duels can be geographically located and so the sample size is less than previously reported. Column A includes the capital and the surrounding countryside for twenty miles. I have attached a hinterland to the metropolis because quarrels in London were commonly settled by riding outside the city. I accept, however, that there must be a degree of arbitrariness in the choice of a figure of twenty miles, although, in fact, I believe the results and their implications would not be substantially different if we were to increase this figure to thirty or to decrease it to ten. Column B includes the rest of England and Wales and the Channel Islands, with the exception of the port towns listed in column C.

Clearly as a geographical phenomenon duelling was most unevenly distributed. There were for example, few duels reported from Scotland. Perhaps this was because for much of the period under consideration Scottish regiments were in service elsewhere: in Ireland, of course, and in England and the Empire. It may also

---

26 Cockburn, 'Patterns of violence', op. cit., pp. 70–106, Table 2 at p. 81.

Table 2 Geographic distribution of duels as reported in *The Times*, 1785–1844

Years	A	B	C	D	E	F	G	H
1785–1789	28	5	3	22	2	1	6	67
1790–1794	25	14	12	35	5	6	4	101
1795–1799	29	30	8	20	4	1	11	103
1800–1804	16	17	7	31	1	0	13	85
1805–1809	25	28	8	10	4	1	12	88
1810–1814	15	12	4	8	1	4	11	55
1815–1819	5	5	3	14	0	12	10	49
1820–1824	22	5	0	12	2	4	3	48
1825–1829	13	7	1	13	4	7	11	56
1830–1834	11	11	0	17	2	11	6	58
1835–1839	15	11	1	11	0	10	10	58
1840–1844	9	5	2	2	2	5	6	31
Total	213	150	49	195	27	62	103	799

Notes:
A.　London and twenty miles around.
B.　England and Wales excluding column A. and column C.
C.　Twelve English ports, Bristol, Deal, Dover, Falmouth, Gosport, Harwich, Holyhead, Hull, Liverpool, Portsmouth (including Southsea), Plymouth and Southampton.
D.　Ireland.
E.　Scotland.
F.　Europe, excluding Gibraltar and Malta.
G.　Overseas possessions including Gibraltar and Malta.
H.　Total located duels.

be of some import that Scottish Presbyterianism adopted an uncompromising attitude to the duel, whereas the attitude of the Church of England was so ambivalent that a vicar might assist in provoking a duel[27] or even tear up his card and be ready to take the field.[28]

In total, more than half the duels in England and Wales reported in *The Times* were fought in the capital or environs although London in 1801 comprised only 11 per cent of the total population.[29] The number of duels outside the metropolitan area though, did increase noticeably during the wars with France. Civilians were still

---

27　*The Times,* 13 May 1806, p. 3, col. c.

28　*The Times,* 15 Jun. 1824, p. 3, col. e.

29　E. A. Wrigley, *People, Cities and Wealth: The Transformation of Traditional Society* (Oxford: Blackwell, 1987), p. 162, Table 7.2.

duelling and men on leave might settle long-standing quarrels, but many virile young men were now deployed outside the metropolis. Clearly, in normal times London life, with its complex interplays of competing interests, was much more productive of duelling disputes than rural life. Yet it is striking that few duels were reported from the ten largest towns outside London.[30] For example, Manchester, as the second largest city scarcely figures at all in duelling reports and neither does Birmingham, Leeds or Sheffield. However, there were a number of duels reported from the older coastal towns: Liverpool, Norwich, Bristol and Plymouth.

The data then from *The Times* would seem to rebut any assertion that duelling was becoming popular among the middling orders of either the smaller inland towns or the rapidly expanding centres of manufacture. Furthermore, studies of the social situations of duellists similarly suggest that duelling was rarely practised by the middle classes. Shoemaker has studied the social situations of more than 200 duellists prior to 1800 and believes that there is little evidence that the social status of duellists was changing as the eighteenth century came to its close. Only 6 per cent of his sampled duellists could be shown to be of middle-class occupation, and 16 per cent if lawyers and doctors were included.[31] Similarly, in the Irish context, James Kelly has suggested that duelling descended further down the social scale than in England, yet in his study of the status of 268 identified Irish duellists between 1790 and 1810 he identifies only 27, some 10 per cent, as being of the middle class or lower.[32]

I separated out twelve major ports in Table 2 (column C), because by doing so one can demonstrate their significance as places for duelling during the French wars. During that period there was a substantial increase in the number of duels reported on the coast, followed by a rapid decline at its conclusion. The increase is to be accounted for by the presence of large numbers of military officers in consequence of expanded fleets, garrisons and regiments embarking or disembarking. In 1805, for example, there were four military duels at ports. Two officers exchanged shots at Deal following a dispute at billiards,[33] and two others fought at the Shorncliffe barracks.[34] Two naval lieutenants were arrested at Falmouth after a duel, and a Capt. G. and Lt R. exchanged shots after a dispute over a dream about winning lottery numbers.[35]

---

30 Ibid. p. 160, these were Manchester, Liverpool, Birmingham, Bristol, Leeds, Sheffield, Plymouth, Newcastle, Norwich and Portsmouth.

31 Shoemaker, 'The taming of the duel', op. cit., p. 544.

32 Kelly, *That Damn'd Thing Called Honour*, op. cit., p. 213. The figure excludes lawyers.

33 *The Times*, 29 Oct. 1805, p. 3, col. a.

34 *The Times*, 3 Sep. 1805, p. 2, col. d.

35 *The Times*, 8 Jan. 1805, p. 3, col. d.

I have identified thirty-five duels at these ports between 1790 and 1809, yet only eight between 1810 and 1829.

During the period from 1815 to 1819 the army was quartered in France and this accounts for the significant increase in the number of British duels in Europe recorded in column F. Sieveking reports anecdotal evidence that after the occupation of Paris, French officers intent on a restoration of national honour would seek out British officers and provoke them into duels. Lt Gen. Charles F. Smith shot dead one such protagonist in 1815.[36] Capt. Gronow appears to be referring to the same officer when he reports that a Charles S. shot dead three French officers in Paris during this period.[37] Gronow records duels in 1815 between French and British officers in Paris, Lyon, Boulogne and Beauvais. With the return of the English forces the number of reported duels abroad declines, but it rises again towards the end of the duelling period. By the 1830s English authorities were readily interrupting duels and binding both parties over; this prompted an increasing resort to journeys outside their jurisdiction.

However, is *The Times* portrait valid? Might there not have been, for example, groups duelling within provincial towns whose encounters were not recorded by a national newspaper? My archival research suggests not, but in an attempt to adopt a more systematic approach to the question I have surveyed local newspapers from three locations: Portsmouth, Bristol and Manchester. The *Hampshire Telegraph* published in Portsmouth was soon revealed to be the most assiduous not only in terms of the number of duels that it reported but also in respect of the detail given. I began at 1800 and read the copy for that year, for 1805, 1810 and so on up until 1835 – unfortunately the 1840 editions are too damaged to be consulted. In total, sixty-three duels were reported, of which *The Times* noticed forty-one. The Figure 2 records those sixty-three duels, and it is interesting to note that although the data set is small, the incidence of reported duelling mirrors the pattern derived from *The Times*. That is to say that duelling was most prolific during the Napoleonic War, declined significantly thereafter, but then underwent a modest revival after 1830.

The duels that were omitted by *The Times* but reported by The *Hampshire Telegraph* were not necessarily trivial affairs. For example, the newspaper reports that an unknown army officer was killed near Haddington in 1810,[38] and that a Lt Mackglashen of the 60th Regiment was killed in 1815 in Jamaica.[39] There are the usual

---

36 A. Forbes Sieveking, 'Duelling and militarism', *Transactions of the Royal Historical Society*, 3rd series, 11 (Jan. 1917), pp. 165–184, at p. 167.

37 Capt. Gronow, *The Reminiscences and Recollections of Captain Gronow: Being Anecdotes of the Camp, Court and Society 1810–1860* (London: Bodley Head, 1964), p. 93.

38 *Hampshire Telegraph,* 10 Sep. 1810, p. 4, col. a.

39 *Hampshire Telegraph,* 24 Dec. 1810, p. 1 col. a.

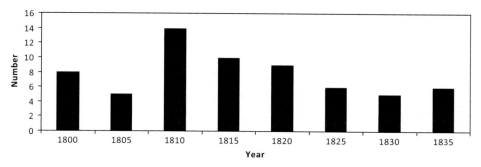

Figure 2 Duels reported in the *Hampshire Telegraph*, 1800–1835

difficulties about apocryphal stories but what is clear however is that the majority of duels known to the *Hampshire Telegraph* were reported in *The Times* although not all. This was the case notwithstanding the fact that the *Hampshire Telegraph* seems to have had a particular interest in duelling and ability to learn about it that is probably to be explained by its close connection to the military. Until 1802 the publication was alternatively titled *Mottley's Naval and Military Journal* and was distributed along the South Coast where the garrisons and the Home Fleet were concentrated. Of the twenty-two duels noticed by the *Hampshire Telegraph* but not *The Times*, seventeen involved at least one military officer. There are eight persons whose situation is unknown, so the total might be higher still. Only four of the duels omitted from *The Times* actually took place in Hampshire, but significantly, they all occurred within the period from 1800 to 1815. Two duels occurred near Portsmouth in 1800: one on Southsea Common[40] and one near Hilsea Barracks.[41] A duel occurred at Chichester in 1810,[42] and another again at Southsea Common in 1815.[43]

A close military connection did not impel the newspaper to defend duelling. Presumably this reflected the fact that, notwithstanding the assertions of duellists, not all military officers were in favour of the duel. Reporting the Chichester duel on New Year's Day 1810, the paper sarcastically declared it had been fought 'in honour of that sacred season, when peace was proclaimed on earth and goodwill towards men'. The newspaper also reported on attempts abroad to suppress duelling. In 1805 it noticed a memorial against duelling after the Hamilton–Burr duel. In 1810 it

---

40 *Hampshire Telegraph*, 22 Feb. 1800 p. 3, col. d.

41 *Hampshire Telegraph,* 11 Aug. 1800, p. 3, col. b.

42 *Hampshire Telegraph,* 8 Jan. 1810, p. 3, col. a.

43 *Hampshire Telegraph,* 6 Jan. 1815, p. 4, col. c.

noticed a motion barring duellists from public office in Richmond,[44] and in 1830 an edict against duels issued by the Elector of Hesse.[45]

By contrast, there were few duels reported within the pages of the *Manchester Mercury* and *Manchester Guardian*. Again I began in 1800 with the *Mercury* and proceeded as before until 1830. However, the *Mercury* is unavailable after 1830 and so I then substituted the *Manchester Guardian* for 1835 and 1840. Only twenty-four duels were reported over the nine years considered. Eighteen of those duels (75 per cent) were also noticed by *The Times*. Significantly, none of the duels reported took place in or near Manchester. The nearest took place at Liverpool between two local militia officers.[46] Of the six duels not reported in *The Times*, only one is said to have resulted in a serious wound.[47] Only one of the twelve protagonists is identified as a military officer.

To argue from an absence of material is problematic, but it seems reasonable to conclude that, as both the Manchester newspapers and *The Times* data suggest, there were very few duels occurring around the Manchester area throughout this period. The *Mercury* and the *Guardian* noticed some of the duels occurring in London, Ireland and abroad; it seems somewhat unlikely that editors would have decided to ignore reports of local encounters had they known of them. Furthermore, editorial policy alone did not determine the content of local and regional newspapers. Advertisements and submitted correspondence from personages of local importance formed a significant part of their content. As we shall see, local newspapers were the medium through which competing gentlemen both reported their respective views of disputes and, if matters came to a head, recorded the mode of their settlement. Editorial policy or priorities aside, one would expect to find principals or their seconds placing their accounts in the Manchester newspapers if there were encounters. However, I found only a single example of a publicly advertised honour dispute. In 1840 the paper published correspondence detailing the bloodless resolution of a dispute between a Mr J. Brotherton, MP for Salford, and Mr William Garnett.

Unfortunately, in respect of Bristol only eight editions of the *Bristol Gazette* survive from 1800. I chose to use that newspaper from 1805, however, because of its wide circulation throughout the South-West down as far as Cornwall and into the South of Wales. Once again, very few public honour disputes were reported and in terms of actual encounters, the publication listed only twenty-four duels. Almost none of these took place in the South West and each was also reported in *The Times*.

---

44   *Hampshire Telegraph,* 26 Mar. 1810, p. 3, col. e.

45   *Hampshire Telegraph,* 1 Feb. 1830, p. 3, col. b.

46   *Manchester Mercury,* 23 Oct. 1805, p. 4, col. f.

47   *Manchester Mercury,* 1 Nov. 1825, p. 2, col. b.

I would not wish to lay undue emphasis upon the results of an analysis of so small a number of newspapers. At the time few newspaper series were available digitally and clearly digitisation would now make a much more thorough survey practicable. However, my reading does suggest that the overwhelming majority of duels reported in regional newspapers did find their way into *The Times* and this supports the impression gained both from *The Times* itself and from literature and local archives that duels in the shires and counties were rather rare. Such a conclusion is further supported by a survey of the few and erratic series of indexes to local and regional newspapers available in the British Newspaper Library. The indexes to the *Hull Advertiser* from July 1794 until December 1845[48] record only a single attempt at a local duel that was prevented at Grimsby in 1832.[49] The indexes to the *Norwich Mercury* from 1770 to 1774 record no encounters in the Norwich area. The index to the *Durham County Advertiser* from January 1826 to December 1835 makes reference to a single affair of honour, which occurred at North Shields in 1827.[50] Finally, the indexes to the *Maidstone Journal* from 1830 to 1833 refer to a duel in Greenwich Park in 1832 but not to any encounters in the Maidstone area itself.[51]

I feel confident in asserting that further research, although it may well sharpen the picture, will not reveal substantial but hidden reservoirs of duellists that have hitherto escaped the attention of others as well as myself. The evidence thus far, then, suggests that most duels were fought in London and its environs and that where this was not the case, duels were particularly clustered around port and garrison towns. This leads on to the natural inference that such duels as there were in the counties and shires can be substantially attributed to the quarrels of military officers. There is a considerable body of evidence which supports this contention. Shoemaker, in a study of 206 duels fought in or around London between 1660 and 1800, identified 33 per cent of those who participated in the duels before 1775 as having possessed military rank.[52] For the period from 1775 to 1800 he found that this figure rose to 44 per cent. I have similarly attempted to identify officer duellists from *The Times* reports between 1785 and 1844. My findings are set out below in Figure 3.

Again one must be cautious about the data since these are the minimum percentages of duellists who can be identified as holding or having held military rank.

---

48 K. A. Mahon, *An index to the more important historical information contained in the files of the Hull Advertiser and Exchange Gazette 1794–1825* (Hull: University of Hull, 1955); D. Parry, *The Meadley Index to the Hull Advertiser 1826–1845* (Humberside: Humberside College, 1987).

49 *Hull Advertiser,* 3 Feb. 1832.

50 *Index to the Durham County Advertiser* (Durham: Durham City Reference Library, 1978), referring to the edition of 27 Oct. 1827.

51 J. Hilton, *Index to the Maidstone Journal* (Orkney: Kirkwall Press, n.d.).

52 Shoemaker, 'The taming of the duel', op. cit., p. 540.

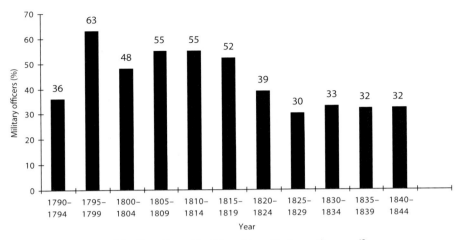

Figure 3 Percentage of duellists from *The Times* identified as military officers

As Shoemaker points out, the habit of referring to lower-ranking officers as simply 'Mr' means that some officers must remain unidentified. As can be observed above, there was a significant rise in the proportion of duellists holding military rank during the period of the Napoleonic Wars. This is not surprising given that by the end of the conflict as many as one in five of all men of military age in Great Britain had seen service.[53]

There is quite simply overwhelming anecdotal evidence that officers formed by far the largest contingent of duellists and that there were particular pressures upon military men to respond to affronts to honour is amply attested. For instance, when, in 1785, Capt. Bulkley of the Guards received an acrimonious letter from Capt. Brisco, he foolishly requested a court of enquiry. The result was that all the officers of the Guards voted to send him to Coventry. It was not until he had duelled with Brisco that the officers would again associate with him.[54] When Mr Riddell of the Horse Grenadiers challenged Mr Cunningham of the Scots Greys, Cunningham declined until the reproaches of his fellows forced him into the duel in which he was wounded and Riddell killed.[55]

---

53 Clive Elmsley, *British Society and the French Wars 1793–1815* (London: Macmillan, 1979), p. 133. Huw Bowen calculates that by 1809 the embodied militia and the army totalled some 300,000 men: H. V. Bowen, *War and British Society 1688–1815* (Cambridge: Cambridge University Press, 1998), p. 13.

54 *The Times,* 3 Feb. 1785, p. 3, col. a.

55 Millingen, *The History of Duelling,* op. cit, vol. ii, pp. 116–117.

The military atmosphere was sometimes so attuned to the nuances of honour that men unwittingly became entrapped by the unforeseen consequences of their actions or fell prey to the malice and misrepresentations of others. In 1810, for example, a naval officer chanced to enquire of a Lt Cecil if he knew of a Capt. Stackpole. Cecil replied that he did and thought of him as a brave officer, but he fatally added that he believed him capable of exaggeration. By chance the remark reached the ears of Stackpole's officers, who informed their captain. Stackpole declared that he would call Cecil to account. Four years passed, however, before Cecil's vessel happened to come into Port Royal, where Stackpole's ship was berthed. Stackpole immediately demanded that Cecil apologise for the slander or else meet him. Cecil could only respond that he could not remember the remark, but that if a fellow officer had said he had made it, then he could only avow that he had done so. His position was most difficult, for if he doubted he had made the remark, he would have in effect accused the officer who had reported it of lying and have invited a challenge from that quarter. Unfortunately, he also found it impossible to apologise:

> He wished Captain Stackpole to understand that under all the circumstances he should have no objection to apologise to any other officer in His Majesty's Navy, but to him it was impossible; the Captain being reputed throughout the Navy as a good shot.[56]

Cecil supposed that if he indeed apologised others would believe that he had been induced to do so by consideration of his personal safety. In consequence, Cecil fought a duel over a remark that he could not remember, with a man with whom he had no grievance and to whom, in other circumstances, he would gladly have apologised. Stackpole was killed in the encounter.

So strong was this sense of collective honour that officers sometimes volunteered to duel in the place of their colleagues and thus propagated running quarrels. At Gibraltar in 1819 garrison sentries detained a party of Americans who had contravened port regulations by travelling at night without a light. One, Mr Taylor, a merchantman captain, was drunk and abusive. The sentry officer, Mr Johnston, ordered him detained overnight. Upon release, Taylor departed with his ship. Thereafter, though, a rumour spread among American vessels that Taylor had challenged Johnston but that Johnston had declared that an American captain was beneath him. In consequence, Johnston then received a challenge from a Lt Browne of the American warship *Erie* demanding satisfaction on behalf of his countryman. Johnston wounded Browne, whereupon Browne's second stepped in. This second encounter was broken up by guards.[57] A whole series

---

56 *The Times*, 16 Jun. 1814, p. 3, col. b; 7 Jul. p. 2, col. e.

57 Millingen, *History of Duelling*, op. cit, vol. ii, pp. 235–240.

of challenges between officers of the *Erie* and officers of the garrison followed, and the cycle of violence was only broken when British authorities temporarily prohibited American warships from entering Gibraltar.[58]

Conflicts within regiments or ships could be equally fierce. Col. Bayley recorded that when his 12th Regiment arrived in Cape Town from England, the officers began to settle among themselves the quarrels that had arisen in consequence of the long and stressful voyage:

> The infernal practice of duelling was resorted to on the most trivial occasions, no less than eleven were fought in the Governor's gardens ... an order having been issued that no more duels should be fought in the Governor's gardens ... the place of rendezvous was subsequently changed, so that townspeople and officers could now walk there, [in the gardens] without fear of a stray shot.[59]

The propensity of officers to duel did not escape the attention of the civilian population. At a trial for a challenge in 1810 it was said that if a defendant had indeed offered the 'satisfaction of a gentleman and a soldier', as the prosecution asserted, then a duel had clearly been intended. If he had merely offered 'that of a gentleman', then this was not so certain.[60] The association endured. In 1842 a constable detained a man upon suspicion of being an army deserter; he had been struck by his military cap and manner. Questioning by the magistrate revealed the following:

> The prisoner was a plasterer and shop men who were allowed to wear a moustache or an imperial, passed as genuine military officers, keeping carefully out of the way of the military, (laughter). Mr Jeremy, the magistrate said. 'Well, those who do act so foolishly run the chance of being taken up as deserters, or perhaps of having to fight a duel.'[61]

When I come to consider the reasons for the demise of duelling, I shall return to the military in order to point out that, notwithstanding all that has gone before, there was a constituency within the army and navy that had long been opposed to the duel. However, during the latter part of the eighteenth century and the early nineteenth century those opposing voices did not prevail. Indeed, although the duel was never lawful, it still received no small degree of institutional support within the services and within military law through the operation of the so-called, 'Devil's Own Article': 'Whatsoever Commissioned Officer shall be convicted before a general Court Martial of behaving in a scandalous infamous manner, such as is unbecoming the character of

---

58 Sabine, *Notes On Duels,* op. cit., p. 165.

59 Bayley, *Diary of Colonel Bayley,* op. cit., p. 35.

60 *The Times,* 27 Aug. 1810, p. 3, col. b.

61 *The Times,* 28 Sep. 1842, p. 7, col. d.

an officer and a gentleman, shall be discharged from our service.'[62] Though the Articles of War (to which I shall return) contained fulsome provisions against duelling, their efficacy was undermined by the tendency to interpret a failure upon the part of an officer to respond to a slight or to accept a challenge as conduct unbecoming. In 1762 Lt Strode was court-martialled for failing to respond to an affront from a surgeon's mate.[63] In 1766 a Capt. Beilby was court-martialled in Minorca for having repeatedly received from Capt. Robinson 'language unbecoming the character of an officer and a gentleman without taking proper notice of it'.[64] The court suspended him from pay and duty for a year, and the governor of Minorca approved their decision. The judge advocate general pointed out the somewhat paradoxical position of the court and recommended that the conviction be reversed, saying, 'I do not conceive that the sentence of a Court of Justice can at any rate be supported which awards a punishment for neglecting to seek a method of redress forbidden as well by the military as the common law.'[65] The logic was impeccable, but as late as 1840 it was claimed that an officer who had failed to respond to an affront had been threatened with court martial.

The martial virtues required of an officer may in themselves go no small way towards explaining why such men were prone to duelling; acts of courage are always held in esteem within military institutions. In the case of the army, however, there may also be a further explanation. That is to say that army officers may have been taught to be particularly sensitive to matters of personal honour in consequence of the difficulties that they had historically experienced in becoming accepted in society as respectable gentlemen. In the late seventeenth and early eighteenth centuries there had developed a marked antipathy to the very notion of a standing army as being injurious to the liberties of the propertied classes – as evidenced for example in the works of the pamphleteer John Trenchard.[66] M. M. Goldsmith, in his study of Bernard Mandeville, describes this 'country ideology' as 'neo-Harringtonian and neo-Machiavellian'.[67] The proponents of such sentiments naturally held the army in low esteem, and they

---

62 *Rules and Articles for the Better Government of His Majesty's Horse and Foot Guards* (London, 1778), sec. xvi, art. xxii.

63 W.O. 71/71 cited in Arthur Gilbert, 'Law and honour amongst eighteenth century British army officers', *Historical Journal*, 19 (1976), pp. 75–87, at p. 83.

64 W.O. 71/50 cited in Gilbert, 'Law and honour', op. cit., p. 80

65 W.O. 81/111 cited in Gilbert, 'Law and honour', op. cit., p. 81.

66 John Trenchard, *An Argument, Shewing that a Standing Army is Inconsistent with a Free Government and Absolutely Destructive of the English Monarchy* (London, 1687).

67 M. M. Goldsmith, 'Public virtue and private vice: Bernard Mandeville and English political ideologies in the early eighteenth century', *Eighteenth Century Studies*, 9:4 (1976), pp. 477–510, at p. 479.

were influential in securing the reduction of William III's standing army from some 87,000 to just 7,000 during the years between 1697 and 1700. According to Goldsmith, during the eighteenth century, 'Machiavelli became an eighteenth-century English gentleman and Harrington an opposition ideologist.'[68] All institutions of centralised power were viewed with suspicion, and although the Napoleonic Wars were to mobilise national sentiment in support of military institutions, Lord Shelburne touched a raw nerve when he said in Parliament in 1780 that a Tory MP, Mr Fullarton, and his regiment were as ready to act against the liberties of England as against her enemies. A duel resulted.[69]

Nichols has argued that the charge of conduct unbecoming a gentleman emerged as a military offence between 1700 and 1765,[70] and it seems entirely plausible to suggest that the development of the very particular military sensitivity in matters of honour was a response to the general disapprobation (of the army in particular) expressed by sections of higher society. Officers, as it were, had to constitute themselves as an honourable body and establish their status among a society that was inclined to be sceptical of their claim to be gentlemen. Carl Philipp Moritz noted in 1782 that when officers in England on leave went out they did not wear their military uniforms but civilian clothes.[71] C. G. Kuttner reported in 1793 that the military enjoyed little respect among the general populace and were regarded as consisting of no particular estate. Punctiliousness in matters of honour was one way of obtaining from civilian gentlemen a respect that would not otherwise have been readily forthcoming.

Adherence to the dictates of honour culture then can be viewed as having been a strategy by which one asserted a claim to gentility that might otherwise have been disputed. This was true in contexts other than that of the military, for honour culture seems to have played a role in the development and the elevation of a number of professions, most notably those of the law. Beginning with the law one must note that until at least the end of the eighteenth century, many species of lawyer did not possess what we might call professional status. Wilfred Prest has pointed out that by 1750 barristers had ascended the social ladder and enjoyed a high degree of prestige but that:

> In some respects the professed lawyers of Hanoverian England were actually rather less 'professionalised' than under their Tudor and Stuart predecessors ... the decline of the

---

68 Ibid., p. 483.

69 Millingen, *History of Duelling*, op. cit., vol. ii, pp. 108–110.

70 D. B. Nichols, 'The devil's own article', *Military Law Review*, 12 (1963), 116–117.

71 *Reisen eines Deutschen in England im Jahr 1782* cited in Ute Frevert, 'Honour and middle class: the history of the duel in England and Germany', in J. Kocka and A. Mitchell, eds, *Bourgeois Society in Nineteenth Century Europe* (Oxford: Berg, 1993), pp. 207–240, at p. 224.

corporate life and educational functions of the Inns of Court and the Chancery had left a vacuum not yet filled by other forms of professional association and academic provision.[72]

Barristers at least had acquired gentlemanly status, but attorneys and solicitors were still struggling to do so. Regulation was to prove indispensable in the struggle to improve the status of lawyers and key to developing the internal culture and identity which characterises the modern professions of law. However, progress was slow. The Society of Gentleman Practisers in the Courts of Law and Equity was founded in 1740, but it was not until 1770 that a provincial society was formed in Bristol and not until 1792 that the whole was renamed The Law Society. Although the society campaigned successfully upon some issues, for instance, being granted a monopoly on conveyancing in 1804, it was not until the foundation of the London Law Institution as a joint stock company in 1825 and its sponsorship of the Solicitors Act 1843 that the profession became truly regulated. Barristers were even tardier, with the four inns forming the Council of Legal Education only in 1851. By 1851, of course, the professions presented a quite different appearance to that apparent in 1780. Penelope Corfield has estimated that there were only about 280 practising barristers in England and Wales in 1780 but that this number had grown to 730 by 1805 and 2,800 by 1851; the number of attorneys grew over the same period from about 4,000 to 11,000.[73]

There is a strong if anecdotal tradition that during this period of maturation lawyers were actively participating in the duel, and nowhere more so than in Ireland, where Jonah Barrington, himself a King's Counsel, asserted, 'In my time, the number of killed and wounded among the bar was very considerable. The other learned professions suffered much less.'[74] Lord Norbury, Chief Justice of the Common Pleas, was said to have commented of himself that he began the world with fifty pounds and a pair of hair-trigger pistols.[75] Accordingly, James Kelly has subjected the Irish duel to just such scrutiny, and in Figure 4 I have recorded the number of lawyers identified by him as having participated in duels in Ireland between 1760 and 1810.[76] Also shown are the number of members of the legal professions of England, Wales and Scotland that I myself have identified as having duelled between 1780 and 1840, including those in pupillage who had not yet been called to the Bar.

---

72 W. R. Prest, *The Professions in Early Modern England* (London: Croom Helm, 1987), p. 85.

73 Penelope Corfield, *Power and the Professions in Britain, 1700–1850* (London: Routledge, 1985), p. 91.

74 Jonah Barrington, *Personal Sketches of His Own Times* (New York: Redfield, 1858), p. 190.

75 Sabine, *Notes on Duels*, op. cit., p. 254.

76 Kelly, *That Damn'd Thing*, op. cit., Table 2.1 p. 80, Table 3.1 p. 118 and Table 5.1. p. 213.

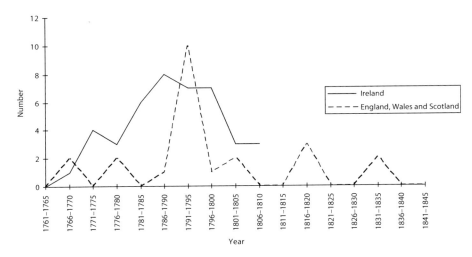

Figure 4 Members of the legal profession participating in duelling in England and Ireland, 1761–1845

Kelly's data does not go beyond 1810, but it suggests that the Irish legal professions conceived of a new fashion for duelling around 1780 and that that interest had waned somewhat by 1800. Some support for this view is given in an essay from Cork written by the Reverend William Odell in 1814:

> The dispensers of legal knowledge are often the first to violate its precepts ... However, this unwarrantable practice is on the decline; and that general detestation in which it is held by all ranks will, it is to be hoped, entirely banish this opprobrium of the Irish Bar.[77]

My data suggests that this fashion spread to England around 1790, and between 1791 and 1795 ten such duellists can be identified. Furthermore, the phenomenon seems to have spread across the common-law world around roughly the same time. In his study of American duelling, Root argues that American lawyers adopted the duel towards the very end of the eighteenth century, with Tennessee being the first state to react, in 1801, by requiring lawyers to swear an oath upon entry to the Bar that they would not duel.[78]

---

77   W. B. Odell, *Essay on Duelling In Which The Subject Is Morally And Historically Considered; And The Practice Deduced From The Earliest Times* (Cork: Odell and Laurent, 1814), pp. 9–10.

78   Roger Roots, 'When lawyers were serial killers: nineteenth century visions of good moral character', *Northern Illinois University Law Review*, 22 (2001), pp. 19–34, at p. 23.

Yet in England at least, the fashion seems to have been both short-lived and unable to penetrate the very highest ranks of the profession. After 1800 duels among active legal professionals in England and Wales seem to have been rather rare. With the exception of Lord Eldon, who was induced to duel while Solicitor General, most of the duellists in England and Scotland were undistinguished. Two were judges, but in colonial posts, and one of these duelled abroad in Minorca. The rest were mere pupils, pleaders, attorneys or largely unknown barristers. Both the limited incidence of duelling and the status of those who duelled suggest that duelling was not generally accepted as a suitable enterprise for members of the higher legal profession. When two barristers, Alley and Adolphus, travelled to France to duel in 1816, a scandal ensued, and when Adolphus was challenged again in 1819, he turned instead to law and prosecuted the offender.

It would be too much to assert that after 1820 the duel no longer held any attraction for legal professions; there were two such duels in the 1830s, and as late as 1841 a radical barrister challenged Disraeli to a duel, although nothing came of it. Furthermore, as we shall see when I come to judges' directions in duelling trials, some judges and barristers remained attracted to the values of the duel. The decline of lawyers as participants, however, seems to be related to the development of professional mentalities and identities. If we look at the biographies of judges in the nineteenth century we can observe that the number of judges who came from the landed classes was declining significantly.

Duman has identified some 45 per cent of judges during the period from 1727 to 1760 as major landowners, whereas by 1820 to 1850 this figure had shrunk to only 16 per cent. During this time the number of professionals on the bench had risen from 25 per cent to 52 per cent, and the number of merchants and proprietors from 7 per cent to 18 per cent.[79] Eighteenth-century judges had portrayed themselves primarily as gentlemen of leisure, classically trained and aspiring to be accepted in landed society. However, Duman charts the rise during the nineteenth century of a new model judge. Such a judge regarded himself as a skilled practitioner, with a high moral status supported by a rapidly evolving code of ethics. His aspirations were increasingly orientated towards accomplishment within the profession rather than the instrumental use of the profession to enter the landed class. Such men underwent an increasingly vigorous legal training. They considered themselves practical men upholding a functioning and rational system and were more constrained both in their ability or willingness to depart from legal norms. Duman notes:

These men consciously turned away from landed investments, thereby diminishing the likelihood that their eldest sons would be landed gentlemen ... The abjuration of

79 Daniel Duman, *The Judicial Bench in England, 1727–1875* (London: Royal Historical Society, 1982), p. 51.

allegiance to the standards of landed society becomes complete with the rejection of primogeniture. While this change is difficult to date with any precision it becomes significant by the years 1820–1850. With the weakening of the connection between the bar and bench, and the landed classes, the judges began to discard those behaviour patterns that they had inherited from their landed associations.[80]

Such men became less willing to adhere to the values of honour at the expense of rule-based systems of law. English judges never developed that penchant for duelling that can, to a degree, be evidenced from the Irish judiciary and Bar. Nor indeed did the duel become firmly ensconced within the English Bar; rather, it seems to have flourished as a passing fashion. As early as 1810, when Captain Best applied to be admitted to the Bar, the members of Lincoln's Inn rejected his application upon the grounds that he had been arrested for duelling.

It seems reasonably clear that by the 1820s the duel was no longer seen as a respectable activity for someone of the legal profession. When, in 1829, *The Times* presented a whimsical portrait of the modern duellist, he was not a lawyer but rather a medical student. Figure 5 illustrates the number of members of the medical profession, including medical students, reported as having taken part in duels. This gives the initial impression that duelling became fashionable among the medical profession around the same time as it gained favour with the lawyers, declined after 1820 and then underwent a modest revival after 1835.

This, however, needs to be heavily qualified by the observation that hardly any of the medical duellists identified before 1820 were in fact civilian practitioners. Almost all the medical duellists reported at the very beginning of the nineteenth century were military surgeons. For example, the exploits of eight medical duellists were reported between 1800 and 1804. In July 1801, Mr C., an assistant army staff surgeon, met a Lt B. in Waterford,[81] and another military surgeon met a gentleman in Dublin.[82] In 1803 a surgeon, Mr A., met a lieutenant in Hyde Park. It is not immediately clear whether Mr A. was a military officer, but it seems most likely since we are told that the duel arose from a dispute while both parties were in St Domingo in 1797.[83] In March 1804 yet another army surgeon met a Mr T. in Hyde Park,[84] and a Mr Kelly, attached to the Royal Artillery, met an officer in Dublin.[85] In St Vincent around May 1804, two garrison surgeons, Dr Warcup and Mr Sharpe, met a Mr Grant and Governor

---

80 Ibid., p. 182.

81 *The Times,* 14 Jul. 1801, p. 2, col. b.

82 *The Times,* 29 Jul. 1801, p. 3, col. b.

83 *The Times,* 29 Jan. 1803, p. 3, col. a.

84 *The Times,* 27 Mar. 1804, p. 3, col. c.

85 *The Times,* 13 Mar. 1804, p. 3, col. a.

Bentinck, respectively.[86] Finally, an unnamed surgeon was called out after an alleged criminal intercourse with his opponent's wife.[87] In short, seven of the eight can be readily identified as being in military service, while the status of the other is unknown. One can imagine that surgeons living in the messes of military gentlemen were obliged to conform to the same codes of behaviour as their compatriots, indeed, how else could they compel professional respect. With the decline of military activity at the conclusion of the Napoleonic War, the number of duelling surgeons naturally declined.

It does not appear that during the Napoleonic War or in its immediate aftermath the duel spread very far into the medical professions. Those professions, like those of the law, were expanding and indeed becoming 'professionalised'. In 1783 there had been only eighty hospitals and dispensaries in England, Wales, Scotland and Ireland, but by 1852 this number had grown to 785.[88] A number of new professional bodies appeared. In 1800, for example, the Company of Surgeons founded the Royal College, although not until 1843 was its membership and jurisdiction extended to cover all of England and Wales. In 1832 the Provincial Medical and Surgical Association was founded, which was to form the British Medical Association in 1855. At the same time, both a collective identity and an expanding base of empirically tested knowledge were being fostered by the establishment of learned journals such as the *Lancet*, which began publication in 1823. It was this rapid development that caused Corfield to declare that of all the professions, the early nineteenth century 'belonged to the doctor'.[89]

Despite this, there seems to have been an increase in interest in duelling among doctors towards the very end of the institution. The last duel *The Times* reported from Scotland, in 1842, was between two medical students in Edinburgh.[90] That same year a Scottish doctor and a surgeon exchanged shots over the right to claim credit for an anatomical discovery. *The Times* does not report if each had hoped to demonstrate their discovery upon the cadaver of the other.[91] Finally, in 1843 a surgeon, presumably also an army officer, fought a regimental captain in Mauritius.[92]

Military surgeons were of course dispersed with their regiments, but the majority of civilian English physicians, or at least those of the highest social status, were naturally situated in London; so, for obvious reasons, were the lawyers. Both lawyers and doctors

---

86 *The Times,* 18 May 1804, p. 2, col. c. Both duels are described together, but it is not clear by how long that of Warcup had preceded the Sharpe duel.

87 *The Times,* 17 Nov. 1804, p. 2, col. e.

88 Corfield, *Power and the Professions,* op. cit., p. 165.

89 Ibid., p. 137.

90 *The Times,* 10 Jan. 1842, p. 6, col. f. One party, Topp, was wounded, but the other party and his second were merely convicted of breach of the peace at the High Court of Justiciary.

91 *The Times,* 25 Feb. 1840, p. 6, col. c.

92 *The Times,* 11 Jan. 1843, p. 5, col. d.

then did something to swell the ranks of the London duellists. Subtract the metropolitan duellists and also those who were military officers and we can see again that the number of other gentlemen duelling in the shires and county towns must have been really rather small. In part I believe that this was because the disposition of social power in the countryside served to inhibit challenges, and to prevent many of the challenges that were issued from proceeding to actual combat. This notwithstanding the works of the honour theorists who asserted that all gentlemen were entitled to claim absolute equality with each other and that all must obey the unyielding rules of honour.

Understanding the disposition of social power is vital to understanding the nature and incidence of duelling for when one examines meetings between gentlemen, one observes that they were often occasioned by struggles over social image or induced by events which had called the status of one party into question. For a would-be gentleman there could finally come a point where the only way one could maintain one's social position, or restore one's respectability and impose oneself upon society, was by hazarding one's life. Duels, in short, were often fought for fear of the consequences of not fighting them. However, where an individual controlled the society around him, either individually or in collaboration with others, and where the challenger came from outside the penumbra of that society, the challenged party was often much better equipped to refuse an invitation to take to the field. Quite simply, in such circumstances the power of the challenger to damage his superior's social image was greatly reduced.

Now, outside large towns gentlemanly society was small and intimate, and local magnates were often able to exert a degree of control over their society far more comprehensive than that possible in London. Where power is obvious and overwhelming it is often unspoken, and where social rules are clear they may often go unchallenged. Thus for example, we do not find evidence of lords declining invitations from draymen to duel, because both parties knew that a meeting was not a social possibility. Similarly, despite what honour literature may have suggested, it is clear that those whose social position was secure did not feel the need to respond to challenges from every would-be gentleman who came along. There was, in effect, a hidden history within the culture of honour, a history of great gentlemen who knew that they could offend certain lesser gentlemen with impunity and lesser gentlemen who knew that there were certain persons to whom they could not respond. County magnates did not regard themselves as the mere equals of everyone in society who designated themselves gentlemen. Such men had the power to control the interpretations consequent upon acts and did not normally need to fear rival interpretations espoused by the disadvantaged unless their own social power was already in doubt. The country clerk whose demand for satisfaction had been contemptuously dismissed by the local magnate had little social power; he could not prevail in a contest of representation — unless, that is, his cause was taken up by others greater than himself.

There were, though, always some who refused to accept the realities of social power or were induced by desperation to try to overthrow them. A controversy at

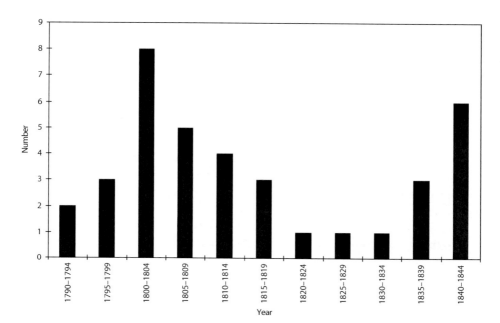

Figure 5 Medical duellists reported in *The Times*, 1790–1844

Queenborough in Kent in 1822 illustrates my point. The background to the affair was that sometime prior there had been a dispute over the oyster fishery between the Corporation of Queenborough and the free burgesses. The burgesses were dredger men whose livelihood depended upon their right to exploit the fishery. However, denying this right, the corporation had advertised the fishery for sale. The burgesses had appealed to the courts and the case was progressing when, on 15 April 1822, Thomas Greet JP, the mayor and head of the corporation, laid an information against John Jones, local burgess, for sending a letter challenging him to a duel. What was remarkable about Greet's complaint though, was that he himself had himself actually invited, indeed already issued a challenge to his opponents and was now complaining of their response:

> Sir, you say that there is not a man among the radicals, you say there is not one who will meet you with a brace of pistols but I will bid denial to your words as I, Jones the man, will meet you on Monday morning at seven o'clock on Rushenden hill.[93]

Greet's fellow JP, a Mr Marshall, promptly intervened, but not against both parties equally. Jones and a John Thompson (who had actually conveyed the letter) were immediately arrested. They were ordered to find recognisance of £200 each. The sums

93 Centre for Kentish Studies, Queensborough Borough Records Qb/JP/1 1814–28.

and the terms were especially onerous. The sureties were to be for a period of three years, and in their absence the men were to be jailed for two years. Fellow burgesses offered to stand surety until the next quarter sessions, when both men were to appear on a writ of habeas corpus, but bail was refused and the two were committed to jail. Their health swiftly deteriorated, and other burgesses then applied to the two magistrates, Marshall and Greet, for permission to supply them with better food but Greet persuaded his colleague against it. Now gravely ill, Jones was forced to declare that his response to Greet had been but a misunderstood joke, whereas Thompson held out and continued to maintain in an affidavit that it had been Greet who had first invited a duel. Greet seemingly never denied this, but neither man was released before their appearance before Mr Justice Bayley on 4 June. He displayed some sympathy for the men and reduced the sureties to £140. These were found and they were discharged.

The law, as embodied in Marshall and Greet, had taken an entirely partial view of the matter, and there was of course no other legal authority on hand to bind Greet over in consequence of his own conduct. By comparison with customary procedure the two unfortunates were treated with exceptional severity since even where a duel had actually occurred detention was rarely resorted to unless there had been a fatality. The sureties required of the men were onerous and none of the customary courtesies that gentlemen duellists might expect while awaiting trial were extended. Greet it seems emerged entirely unscathed from the affair. In the military, a strong tradition of equality might have forced a man such as Greet to live up to his boastful challenge. However, here, with his fellow magistrate supportive, Greet was under no great pressure to do so. In practice, whatever conduct books might say, for many marginal and would-be civilian gentlemen the possibility of challenging a social superior remained but a theoretical one, and one that if appealed too might have the most deleterious consequences.

Nevertheless, some gentlemen, those more nearly socially equal, were duelling in the counties, and when such duels are examined common themes frequently emerge. These are contests over borough politics, disputes over property and sporting rights, and arguments over the conduct of the local militia. To illustrate, in 1770 Thomas de Grey of the Manor of Merton and William Tooke, lord of the neighbouring Manor of Thompson, quarrelled. Tooke complained that de Grey grazed too many sheep upon the local common. He alleged that de Grey's plantation encroached upon the common and that he had constructed a sheep walk which intruded into Tooke's land.[94] De Grey responded in respect of the threatened prosecution in the matter of the sheep walk:

> Sir, you will consider, I am not only member for the county, but an Officer under Lord Townshend; whatever may be my own opinion upon this subject, I must not hear an

---

94 Norfolk County Records Office, Walshingham Merton Collection WLS/XLVI/8 f. 2. Letter of 7 Sep. 1770.

Insult. To your court I will not come ... I will not be bound by the Rabble, such as you treat at alehouses, and mix in society with them, and promise to cloath ... if you cast down the poles by violence, or hire the Mob, I will consider it as a personal Insult, and a Gentleman shall wait upon you for this purpose.[95]

Note that de Grey referred to his status as an officer of the militia when describing himself as one who must not hear an insult. Militia officers adhered to the same code of honour as their professional brethren, and their conflicts seem to have accounted for a good proportion of county duels. In 1779 a lieutenant of the militia was shot dead by a militia colonel who had accused him of inciting his men to mutiny.[96] In 1783 a Col. P. wounded a Capt. I. in a dispute over the Anglesey militia.[97] In 1795 there were duels fought over the management of both the Somerset militia and the North Lincoln militia.[98] Regular army officers accorded even junior militia officers the same rights of satisfaction. I have discovered no instance where a regular officer refused a challenge upon the basis of his opponent's status as a militia officer. For example, in 1797 a lieutenant of the Horse Guards met an ensign from the West Suffolk militia.[99]

De Grey had referred to Tooke's association with the rabble or mob, which presumably reflects a difference of political affiliation. Yet in view of the continual differences in matters of property, it seems unlikely that the challenge was politically motivated. Similarly, Thomas Greet had referred to the burgesses at Queenborough as radicals, but the challenge was in truth issued in the context of a bitter dispute over the rights of the burgesses. John Sainsbury has, somewhat unconvincingly to my mind, asserted that John Wilkes adopted the duel as a tool of political campaigning, but it seems at least clear that, thereafter, duelling was rarely resorted to as a calculated political act.[100] What one does observe is that in the hurly-burly of electioneering, the passion of campaigning did inspire challenges that were, in that sense, political. William Peel challenged the election agent of Sir Charles Townshend following the Tamworth election of 1818.[101] A Capt. Barrie challenged the Whig candidate at Preston in 1826,[102] and Sir Thomas Hastings challenged Richard

---

95 Ibid.

96 Millingen, *History of Duelling,* op. cit., vol. ii, pp. 103–104.

97 Ibid., pp. 118–119.

98 *The Times,* 30 Apr. 1795, p. 3, col. b. and *The Times,* 7 Jul. 1795, p. 3, col. d.

99 *The Times,* 3 Feb. 1797, p. 3, col. d.

100 John Sainsbury, '"Cool courage should always mark me": John Wilkes and duelling', *Journal of the Canadian Historical Association,* 7 (1996), 19–33.

101 *The Times,* 16 Nov. 1818, p. 3, col. b.

102 *The Times,* 29 June 1826, p. 2, col. a.

Cobden after a speech in Manchester in 1850.[103] Most of these challenges were ignored, but Sir James Egerton and Viscount Belgrave met after the Chester elections in 1818.[104]

In addition to political contests, disputes over game rights feature prominently. George Townshend challenged The Earl of Leicester in 1759 not only over remarks concerning the efficiency of the Norfolk militia but also over his instruction to his gamekeeper to kill all the foxes he could lay his hands on.[105] A dispute over game and a dispute between shooting parties occasioned the death of Mr Tythen in Buckinghamshire in 1806.[106] When Thomas Ritchie invoked antiquated Scottish law in 1818 against a Lt Rollo, it was because Ritchie had ordered Rollo's shooting party off his father's land and Rollo had challenged in return.[107] Added to this were also passions arising from gaming disputes at the races.[108] To repeat, though, contests between country landowners appear rather rare. Aside from the prominence, again, of military officers, duellists were generally men who had feet in both camps; that is to say, they were members of London society who held seats, familial or political, in the counties. They were most likely to come into conflict when leaving London to contest their traditional seats or to attend the races, and the men with whom they came into conflict were men like themselves.

Below the level of borough proprietors, militia colonels and politicians, there existed small groups of gentlemen in the traditional urban centres and prosperous, sometimes wealthy, independent farmers. It is noteworthy, though, that the latter are generally absent from the duelling record. In 1837 the *Hereford Times,* reporting a duel at Brecon, declared, 'It has caused a great sensation in this town, such a circumstance not having occurred for a great number of years'.[109] Not much duelling in Hereford or Brecon then. Nor among the substantial farmers of Bletchingley, who laid a complaint at the West Sussex assizes in 1810.[110] A regiment of dragoons was quartered there, and that had been accustomed to hunt over the farmers' lands in an unruly

---

103 Sabine, *Notes on Duels,* op. cit., p. 212.

104 *The Times,* 29 Oct. 1818, p. 2, col. c.

105 Norfolk County Records Office, The Ketton-Cremer of Felbrigg family papers WKC 7/58 f.1. Letter of Townshend to Leicester, 24 Jan. 1759.

106 *The Times,* 18 Sep. 1806, p. 2., col. b.

107 *The Times,* 7 Oct. 1818, p. 3., col. b.

108 Duels followed the Nantwich races (*The Times,* 1 Aug. 1791, p. 2, col. d.); the Ascot races (*The Times,* 20 Feb. 1796, p. 3, col. b.); the Portsmouth races (*The Times,* 13 Jul. 1818, p. 3, col. a.); and the St Leger (*The Times,* 25 Dec. 1839, p. 6, col. e.).

109 Cited in *The Times,* 2 May 1837, p. 5, col. a.

110 *The Times,* 27 Aug. 1810, p. 3, col. b.

fashion. In consequence the farmers had banned the officers from their land and had laid their complaint. The local magistrate, Mr Harben, was however, very friendly with the officers of the regiment and in reprisal he summoned the farmers to answer complaints from the officers about the state of the roads around their properties. The regimental officers attended the meeting and then abused the farmers, who replied in kind. Mr Harben at this point, invited the farmers' representative, Mr Hitchin, to withdraw with the regiment's colonel to another room, with the clear intent that the two should fight a duel. The response of the farmer, however, was entirely practical: he would have nothing to do with pistols as he had a wife and a family, but he was prepared to meet the colonel with a horsewhip or a stick. What interests is the clash of values represented by the two competing groups. The farmers had clearly been deemed competent to give satisfaction, but they had not responded to the insults heaped upon them. It seems that the duel did not speak to them in the same way that it did to their military opponents.

In summary, then, if we consider the social positions of those who duelled, it is clear that military officers supplied by far the largest proportion of duellists. Added to these were the riotous young bucks of the metropolis, sometimes former officers such as Lord Camelford, or in other cases the mere libertines whose activities were remembered years later in the diaries of Lord Lennox. Supplementing the ranks of the duellists were the parvenus, the aspiring lawyers and surgeons whose orders were intent on ascending the social ladder. For gentlemen in civilian life resident outside the metropolis, the possibility that they might duel, the privilege of duelling, remained an important social signifier, but it was by and large an extremely improbable occurrence. Such gentlemen as did duel in rural England were predominantly drawn from the county leaders, the magistrates and, most significantly, the officers of the militia. In fact, many of the duels in the counties and the small towns were the product of the London season, of the metropolitan elite travelling out to the racecourses at Ascot, Chester, Nantwich and elsewhere or arriving to compete at the hustings at election time.

There is little evidence to suggest that the duel successfully spread into the substantial farming class below the titled county leaders. Men like Mr Hitchen were more prosperous than most army officers; they could seek a place within the penumbra of the duel, but they rarely chose to do so. Non-commissioned officers duelled, as did apothecaries and even clerks, but not farmers. Perhaps most importantly of all, the duel did not gain much purchase in the newly emerging centres of manufacture. It was not unknown among the financial and mercantile interests of the city, but here too it was rather rare. When Mr Bell, a city merchant, was convicted for issuing a challenge in breach of the peace, Justice Le Blanc could remark that the high honour of London merchants had never caused any of the merchants to stand in a disgraceful situation on that floor to receive the judgement of the court.[111] If the duel, then, had indeed spread out from the court, its most significant success lay in colonising parts of the military, descending down the ranks of the aristocracy to the young untitled but well-born in the metropolis, and springing up for a time in the new professions. It was crucial, however, to its demise in the nineteenth century that in the eighteenth century the duel did not succeed in insinuating itself among the new manufacturing and managerial orders, nor indeed in winning to its side the solid and substantial independent farming classes. It remained indeed, as Shoemaker suggested, the property of a widely dispersed but in fact quite limited subculture.

---

111 *The Times,* 29 Nov. 1813, p. 2, col. e. Two merchants did in fact meet on Hampstead Heath in 1822, *The Times,* 2 Nov. 1822, p. 2, col. c. In 1826 a fatal duel ensued between a bank manager and a merchant; see James Landale, *Duel: A True Story of Death and Honour* (Edinburgh: Cannongate, 2005).

5

Guts and Governance: Honour Culture and Colonial Administration

As the previous chapter has demonstrated there were many sections of society into which the ideals of the duellists barely penetrated. Nevertheless honour culture was particularly entrenched within those very groups of gentlemen who were most likely to be tasked with service abroad, that is to say within the military and the political and administrative elite. Honour culture had an important role to play in the mentality of those administering His Majesty's colonial possessions, sustaining the homogeneity of a class over great distances and yet at the same time posing, as we shall see, constant threats to good governance. It was, of course, in the Americas that honour culture was most successfully implanted, but unfortunately, justice to the rich history of American duelling cannot be done here. Since revolution and independence came early within our period, I shall not pursue the American duel with vigour. Instead I have chosen to focus upon the remaining North American possession, Canada, and to compare duelling there with honour culture in an area of British dominion that was only later to become part of the empire, that is to say, those parts of India that were as yet still under the aegis of the East India Company.

Naturally, honourable conduct in each location was influenced by dynamics sometimes peculiar to the local situation; small gentlemanly societies picked up nuances of their own. Differences between Canadian society and that of the British in India are easy to observe. However, the empire was interconnected and facets of behaviour were sufficiently uniform that, as aforementioned, the different gentlemanly societies in each location nevertheless formed a single cultural whole. As we shall see, men, and their disputes and reputations, moved between communities: a Canadian barrister became a judge in Sierra Leone; a quarrel between Indian administrators resulted in a duel in London; a dispute at Portsmouth was played out before the garrison at Gibraltar; and so on. The language of honour that was spoken in such disputes served along with a common heritage of law, of history and of fealty to unite men in very varied situations. Honour culture was in no small part created by, and served to create, a particular type of mental trope: a particular species of personality the attibutes of which did much to condition the temper of the early empire for both good and ill. Just as British law, civil or military, travelled out into the empire and bound the disparate fragments together in allegiance to the mother country, the obligations and privileges of honour went out with such men and served to ensure them a cultural home in the community of gentlemen. As we shall see, the punctilious self-regard that was a necessary qualification for membership in that community was more vehemently advanced in colonial contexts, where civil society was small and undeveloped, than it was wont to be at home. The result was that there were particular tensions between the needs of sound administration and strategic planning and the obligations of personal honour.

Unfortunately, the imperfect survival of materials suggests that a goodly proportion of the duels occurring out in what I am somewhat imprecisely referring to as the empire must have eluded our attention. The problem, though, is further exacerbated by evidence that fatal duels were actively concealed upon foreign station. Reminiscing at the end of a long military career, William Douglas observed that it had been commonplace for officers to adopt absurd fictions in order to conceal the occurrence of duels, such as pretending that wounded officers not on parade had contracted a disease or had met with unfortunate accidents. He recalled one case from Poonah in 1842 where officers successfully persuaded the regimental doctor to forge the death certificate of a young ensign shot down in a duel in order to attribute the death to cholera.[1] In the diaries of his service with the 12th regiment between 1796 and 1803, Col. Bayley reported that on the way to India the regiment had stopped off for a time at Cape Town and that during that time at least eleven duels were fought.[2] The officers had taken the opportunity to settle the disputes that had arisen during the voyage, yet I can find no trace of any of them in the domestic press.

In the case of Canada, however, much remains which closely resembles the English material; that is to say that there are newspaper reports, family papers, biographies and so forth, and there have naturally been a series of detailed studies of North American duelling by Freeman, Halliday, Riddell, Root and still others. Such, however, is not the case for duelling in Company territories. The India Office Records in fact record only a few duels, which I have examined in some detail. Nevertheless, the material is rewarding in that it offers fresh perspectives on duelling and civil administration. Whereas much of the supposedly private correspondence concerning duels was actually written with an eye to publishing and the public domain, the India Office Records contain detailed confidential reports and private advice for government as well as long justificatory statements made by men reporting to distant superiors. They

---

1   William Douglas, *Duelling Days in the Army* (London, 1887), pp. 22–31.

2   Bayley, *Diary*, op. cit., p. 35.

offer a particular insight into the dilemmas faced by honourable men obliged to deal with the sensitivities of other honourable gentlemen – while at the same time trying to keep afloat the precarious ship of colonial administration.

Beginning, then, with Canada, one can usefully observe that of thirty-four duels fought in Upper and Lower Canada between 1782 and 1840 at least fourteen of the participants were regular or militia officers. Most probably the true proportion of duellists who held some military rank was very much higher – for the biographies of the participants are far from complete. No clear pattern emerges from the military duels other than the impression that they were often caused by trivial disputes, most probably engendered by the boredom of garrison duties and the limited opportunities for social diversion. To illustrate, in 1797 lieutenants billeted in the Quebec garrison quarrelled over the quality of the beer in their respective regiments. Lt Ogilvy was foolish enough to declare that the beer in his mess was better than that enjoyed by the other mess, and when Lt Evans denied it, Ogilvy declared him a 'lying scoundrel'. Evans despatched him at the first fire, and although he was tried, he was acquitted and seemingly retained his commission.[3] In situations in which female companionship might be somewhat restricted one can readily imagine that the attractions of such companions as there were might engender disputes. At least two duels were fought over the attentions allegedly paid to other men's wives. In 1795 Lt Samuel Holland was killed at Montreal by Capt. Lewis Thomas Shoedde following his advances to Shoedde's wife.[4] In 1838 a mistake in the delivery of a bouquet occasioned the death of Maj. Henry Warde. Warde had sent a bouquet to a French-Canadian lady, but it was delivered to the wife of Robert Sweeney, a former cavalry officer who was at that time working as an advocate. Sweeney promptly rode to Warde's mess and accused him of an affair with his wife. They met the next morning, and after Sweeney had despatched Warde he fled to the United States.[5]

British officers in Canada were operating in circumstances that were particular to them, for there was of course a French population with divided allegiances and with a vigorous honour culture of its own. However, Elinor Kyte chronicles the development of an entente cordiale between the upper ranks of French-Canadian society and the military establishment after the conquest. The sons of several prominent French-Canadian families joined the British army at the end of the eighteenth century, for example, Lt Col. Charles de Salaberry. The politics of Montreal during the period in question are too complex to explore here, but Kyte observes the careers

---

3   Hugh A. Halliday, *Murder Among Gentlemen: A History of Duelling in Canada* (Toronto: Robin Brass Studio, 1999), pp. 33–35.

4   Aegidius Fauteux, *Le Duel au Canada* (Montreal: Editions de Zodiaque, 1934), pp. 66–72.

5   Ibid., pp. 242–256.

of several officers who served the Crown then took up arms against it in 1837, but later affirmed their loyalty and enjoyed successful military and political careers. It seems, though, that there existed a prejudice against French-Canadian officers, since it is said that such officers were regularly taunted with their origins and had to be prepared to defend their honour in duels.[6] Yet these alleged duels do not find their way into the record.

The division between Loyalists and Patriots, however, did lead to one duel in 1837. This was occasioned by the attempt of two men to force their way past a garrison sentry. The sentry sought advice as to how to respond from Lt A. H. Ormsby, who instructed him to use his bayonet if necessary. At this point Edouard Rodier, one of the two men, challenged Ormsby. The following day the officers of the garrison debated the appropriate response. They concluded that Ormsby would have to respond but that he should be removed from the field after only one shot. A shot was duly exchanged, Ormsby withdrew and the garrison sent a message that no other officer would accept a challenge from the French-Canadian community.[7] The event, if not its consequences, recalls earlier events at Gibraltar in 1819, where the detention of a party of Americans by garrison sentries occasioned a series of duels between British officers and American seamen, each demanding satisfaction upon the part of fellow countrymen. In the case of Gibraltar the cycle of violence was broken only when the British authorities temporarily prohibited American warships from entering Gibraltar.[8] In Montreal, however, the considered conduct of the officers served to avert the possibility of such a confrontation between the communities.

Mention of the service of French Canadians brings me to the obvious point that as time went on the number of men within the armed services who were either recruited locally into British units or into forces recruited under the Crown that were specifically Canadian in origin grew. There were officers in the Crown forces, then, who had been born in Canada and who never thought to go elsewhere and also permanent professional forces whose next posting might be to India, or Gibraltar, or wherever. Of course, the honour culture within the Crown forces generally communicated itself to those coming into those forces, and, as we shall see in the context of the lawyers, gentlemanly education in North America served to inculcate such values at least as proficiently as the mother country. A goodly number of officers serving with either the militia or the regular forces were also deeply involved in the struggles over local politics and perquisites. Peter Clark, for example, the clerk to the Legislative Council, was killed at Kingston in Upper Canada in 1793 in consequence of a dispute with

6   National Archives of Canada, Bellingham Memoirs MG24/B25/11/140.

7   Laurent Olivier David, *Les Patriotes de 1837–1838* (Montreal, 1884), pp. 76–77.

8   Sabine, *Notes On Duels And Duelling*, op. cit., p. 165.

David Sutherland of the 25th Regiment of Foot, the cause being that Sutherland had applied for Clark's job.[9]

Personal grievances, boredom and the struggle for advantage were similarly responsible for military duels in India. In the Company's territories, however, disputes were exacerbated by the existence of parallel institutions vying for precedence. Officers of the British Army and Company forces viewed each other with suspicion, united perhaps only by their barely concealed contempt of civil administration. 'I have at the age of fifty, cheerfully dropt a bloody limb, while others at their ease are only dropping ink on their paper in black characters.'[10] So wrote Maj.-Gen. Stuart in 1784. He was at this time in dispute with Lord MacCartney, the governor of Madras. Although temporarily in the employ of the army of the East India Company, Stuart, as a King's officer, had refused to be bound by their commands.[11] The upshot was that he was eventually removed from his command and sent to England. He had his revenge, however, for when Lord MacCartney returned home Stuart immediately challenged and wounded him.

The conflicts between the Company and His Majesty's Army were exacerbated by contrasting conditions of service. Bayley wrote bitterly that a King's officer might retire after a career of up to forty years upon a pension of as little as £200 per annum, whereas a Company Officer 'In twenty or twenty-five years may return at volition upon full pay (of £800 per annum) independent of the little pickings accumulated.'[12] Actually, both sides perceived inequalities in their terms of service, and both resented it. In respect of Company ships and His Majesty's Navy, resentments arose as a consequence of occasional attempts by the navy to press-gang men from Company ships. In 1809, for example, an honour dispute erupted between Admiral Drury of the Royal Navy and the governor of Prince of Wales Island because officers from Company Indiamen had refused to drink to Drury's health.[13]

In 1807 a bitter dispute arose between the military authorities at Fort St George and the East India Company following the killing of the fifth mate of an East Indiaman by an army officer whose 14th Regiment was being transported to India.[14] The captain of the vessel had ordered the arrest of the duellist and his second. However, upon arrival

---

9 Cecelia Morgan, 'In search of the phantom misnamed honour: duelling in Upper Canada', *Canadian Historical Review*, 76: 4 (1995), 519–562.

10 Lord Macartney, *The Private Correspondence of Lord Macartney, Governor of Madras 1781–1785*, ed. C. Davies (London: Royal Historical Society, 1950), pp. x–xi.

11 Ibid.

12 Bayley, *The Diary of Colonel Bayley*, op. cit., p. 105.

13 P. Napier, *Part One of the Life of Captain Henry Napier RN 1789–1853*, 2 vols (London: Michael Russell, 1997), vol. i, p. 101.

14 The British Library, India Office Records IOR/f/4/292/635.

at Fort St George the senior army officer aboard had forcibly released both men and allowed them to disembark. This had prompted an angry complaint from the ship's captain to the governor about the 'subversion of [his] authority ... a total disregard of that subordination essentially necessary to be maintained onboard the Honourable Company's Ships'.[15] In response the governor had written to the commander of the army demanding an explanation and had received the robust reply that 'Maj. Miller was answerable to his Commanding Officer for the persons of these unfortunate men and he only performed his duty in landing them'.[16] Urgent consultations between the governor and the army followed. Upon this occasion it was the Company that prevailed. The army eventually conceded the jurisdiction of the civil authorities over the men, and they were indicted and tried before a civilian court for the murder of Matthews. The jury, however, acquitted them both.

Whether the commander of the army had been concerned to protect his men from the consequences of a civilian court (in the event unnecessary) or whether he was merely concerned to protect his sphere of authority is uncertain. What is clear, however, is that at the end of eighteenth century there was a powerful constituency of opinion within the military reluctant to see officers punished for adherence to the principles of honour. Indeed military authority was scarcely sufficiently established as to protect senior officers from the consequences of trying to discipline their subordinates. After an ensign, Mr Purefoy shot his former commanding officer Col. Roper following a dispute over an infraction of military discipline, it was Roper's own second who spoke up for him at his trial, declaring that he had 'entertained no malice against the deceased; he had been laid by a call of honour, or, more properly speaking, driven by the tyranny of custom, to an act which in early life had embittered his existence; but without which, he was taught to believe that he should lose all consideration which society could afford'.[17]

What strikes the modern and rather calculating mind as surprising about the conduct of these duels is that they were often carried through with very little regard given to the greater imperatives of the time. Sometimes, the refusal of officers and administrators to suborn their personal inclinations to quarrel, shoot and sometimes kill each other could not but put the achievement of broader military or political objectives in some jeopardy. In 1799, for example, the 12th Regiment found itself in India and about to take the field in a bloody campaign against Tipoo Sahib. However, this did not prevent the commander of the regiment, Col. Hervey Aston, from duelling with both his second in command and with the regimental paymaster. The

---

15 Ibid. Letter of Captain Charles Gribble to the Honourable Governor in Council, 5 Nov. 1807.

16 IOR/f/4/292/635 Letter of G. Strachey Secretary to Government, 9 Nov. 1807 and reply of Lt Gen. MacDonald Commander in Chief, 13 Nov. 1807.

17 Ibid.

first quarrel was caused by the second in command, Maj. Picton, calling a meeting of the officer's mess upon some minor administrative matter while Aston was absent. The second was prompted by Aston foolishly describing the paymaster, Maj. Allen, as an 'illiberal fellow'.[18] From such trifles came two duels, the second of which deprived the regiment of its commander on the very eve of a major campaign. No action was taken against Maj. Allen, who had killed Aston; he retained his commission but died later in the conflict.

One might suppose that the government at home was frustrated by such outbreaks of self-indulgence, but in truth its members too were either themselves so deeply implicated in the values of honour culture or so partisan as to be incapable of applying effective sanctions against duellists. The attitude of government can best be described as ambivalent. When it was forced to act, it did so in ways which demonstrated both its half-heartedness and its partiality. In 1804 the governor of St Vincent duelled with a member of the island council, Mr Sharp.[19] Lord Camden's response to the duel appeared decisive. He wrote to the Duke of Portland, 'A governor fighting a Duel in his own Government is so subversive of that Authority which he should maintain and so dangerous a precedent if he remains, that I shall think it my duty to advise his majesty to recall him and appoint another governor.'[20] Sharp, who had challenged the governor, was immediately removed from his position on the council.

The apparent impartiality of the government was however, entirely spurious, for it had already commissioned advice from Lincoln's Inn as to whether it might bring criminal proceedings against Sharp alone. However the opinion when it came pointed out that fighting a duel was, under any circumstances, an offence. Therefore, the barristers were 'of the opinion that it is impossible that any Criminal proceedings should be carried on with any degree of propriety, or without such manifest partiality against Mr Sharpe, without instituting a similar proceeding against the governor himself'.[21] The government was not prepared to treat both parties equally and quietly shelved the idea. Sharp's career was, one suspects, ruined, but the governor's patrons were already rehabilitating their man. Portland had during this time written to Camden, agreeing that Bentinck must be removed but praising 'the integrity and independent spirit which attended his character'.[22] Portland summoned up the common feeling by declaring, 'I cannot consider what has happened as an

18 Bayley, *The Diary of Colonel Bayley*, op. cit., pp. 61–67.

19 Centre for Kentish Studies, The Pratt Manuscripts, Sir John Jeffreys Pratt 2nd Earl and 1st Marquis Camden. U0840 0217/1. Letters upon the Sharp–Bentinck duel.

20 U080 0217/1/1. Lord Camden to the Duke of Portland, 7 Sep. 1804.

21 U0840 0217/1/5. Opinion of Mr Manners and Mr Perceval to Lord Camden, 1 Oct. 1804.

22 U0840 0217/1/2. Duke of Portland to Lord Camden, 24 Sep.1804.

appropriate disqualification of him for the Government of any other Island, less for any other mark of his Majesty's favour.'[23]

Senior officials and politicians did not wish to bar duellists from colonial appointments, still less did they wish to criminalise them, because, quite simply, they admired the spirit these men displayed. For some within government, the occasional crisis thrown up by men of honour was entirely preferable to an empire administered by clerks acting upon bureaucratic principles. One consequence of this, however, was that, by and large, men were left to their own devices when it came to setting their disputes. What was missing was that instinctive solidarity so evident in the operation of a modern bureaucracy. Colonial officials were largely left to fend for themselves, and while perhaps at times they relished this autonomy, at others this had grave implications for the performance of their office.

In 1812 the magistrate and chief judge of Malabar, Thomas Baber, complained to Fort St George that he had been challenged by a Lt Brown in consequence of his, Baber's, inquiry into the role of the lieutenant's father in the kidnapping and enslavement of children from neighbouring Travancore.[24] The lieutenant's complaint was that Baber had revealed the results of his investigations to the officers of the local garrison. At the time of the inquiry the advocate general had been full of praise for Baber's conduct, for his 'zeal and ability in tracing the infamous traffic and in restoring the children to their parents and liberty'.[25] However, Lt Brown had responded to the enquiry by demanding satisfaction, and Baber had declined.[26] What followed was a series of provocative attacks performed by the associates of Lt Brown with the avowed intention of goading Baber into taking up the challenge. Among other things they hindered the administration of justice by delaying payments to the police stations for which Baber was responsible and finally posted him as a liar and a coward.[27]

However, when Baber appealed to Fort St George for help, the advocate general declined to assist him upon the very nice ground that while all he had done during his investigation was approved, Baber's disclosing the results of the investigation to the military authorities had not been strictly within his remit:

> It is plain it was no necessary part of his duty as a Magistrate to shew the Records to strangers ... It is highly illegal to call any man to account for merely making known the

---

23 U0840 0217/1/4. Duke of Portland to Lord Camden, 2 Nov. 1804.

24 IOR F/4/406/10143.

25 IOR F/4/406/10143 ff. 53–61. Letter from the Advocate General A. Anstruther to the Secretary to the Government in the Judicial Department, 30 Oct. 1812.

26 IOR f/4/406/10143/ ff. 18–23. Affidavit to the Court by Mr Baber, 9 Oct. 1812.

27 IOR F/4/406/10143 ff. 37-38. Letter of Mr Baber to Mr H. Warden, Collector of Malabar, 15 Sep. 1812.

truth of what happened in the Court of Judicial Investigations – but it is not more so in the case of a Magistrate than of any other man. I do not therefore think that this is a case which calls of the interference of the government, and as a general proposition, I think that the aid of the Government ought not to be given except in cases clearly and exclusively respecting the public acts of its servants and entitling them as such to its protection. [28]

The government, in other words, would not assist in indicting men who were seeking to provoke a judge into the commission of a felony. This was so even though the provocation offered was both a consequence of a proper judicial inquiry by the judge and of the subsequent distribution of a government-approved report into a series of serious criminal acts. Baber was not to be easily fobbed off; he persisted in his complaints, and the government was finally induced to order the removal of all four of the protagonists from Tellicherry. However, one can only imagine what Baber thought of the concluding advice of the Advocate General that 'His conduct continued to be highly approved and that the Government agreed with him in thinking the case proper to be the subject of criminal prosecution ... but that ... the Government thought it proper that the prosecution should be carried on by himself.'[29]

Such equivocal support can hardly have induced confidence in those men who sought to avoid the implications of honour by having resort to civil and legal power. Furthermore, although gentlemen in the colonial environment were by nature tough minded and competitive, in matters of their reputation they were, I believe, peculiarly vulnerable. In England one might decline a challenge, lose one's reputation and yet not suffer a complete social extinction. That was especially so if one had a thick skin, an impeccable lineage or independent means. Lord George Sackville survived being cashiered in 1759 after his alleged cowardice at the battle of Minden; it took him some considerable time to rebuild his reputation but by 1766 he had largely rehabilitated himself. In the much more intimate and limited colonial society, the disapprobation of society was a fearsome consequence, especially since many men were dependent upon appointments and their perquisites rather than independent in property. In many places there was, almost literally, nowhere to hide from a bad name. Not all men who duelled were men of unimpeachable courage or men who agreed with the dictates of honour; some were simply impelled to it by fear of what might otherwise be the consequence.

Colonial society was often a very small society, where, in the never-ending round of monotony, honour might become fetishised and reputation a matter of public anxiety and profound personal introspection. As late as 1828 the population of York

---

28 IOR f/ 4/406/10143 ff. 125–133. Letter of Advocate General Mr Anstruther to the Chief Secretary to the Government, 5 Jan. 1813.

29 IOR f/4/406/10143 ff. 1–8. Extract from a judicial letter from Fort St George, 3 Mar. 1813.

(renamed Toronto in 1834) was only around 2,200. A gentleman in such a society knew almost every other. This posed a number of practical difficulties: one was forced to socialise with those whose politics one disagreed with, for example, and men without independent means were often forced to rely upon the patronage of a limited circle of others. Again, such a society could easily split into factions, and slights, once given, could scarcely be taken back. It was just such a division into petty factions that occasioned the death in 1800 of the attorney general of Upper Canada, Mr White, at the hands of Mr Small.

The roots of the quarrel between Mr White and Mr Small lay in a simple slight given by Mrs Small to Mrs White at a social event. Upon learning of this, Mr White 'was unfortunately impelled by the Violence of his Resentment to Communicate to Mr Smith, the Acting Surveyor General, some Circumstances to the Prejudice of Mrs Small's reputation which that Gentleman (thou in some degree authorised by Mr White), related to Mrs Emsley and the Chief Justice.'[30] Either Mrs Emsley or the chief justice (or indeed both) was indiscreet, and these detrimental remarks reached the ears of Mrs Small. Mrs Small in return, as it were, reached for her own husband and sent him off to the chief justice to elicit full details. The chief justice obliged, and Mr Small promptly challenged Mr White. They met the following day, with an army officer as second to Mr White and Sheriff O'Donnell as second to Mr Small. After the duel Small surrendered himself and was tried before Justice Henry Allcock and promptly acquitted.[31] So many of the leading gentlemen were seemingly complicit in the duel, the attorney general himself, the chief justice, the sheriff, an army officer and, seemingly, the surveyor general. It seems, though, that Small's act of courage did not suffice to rehabilitate the reputation of his wife. Six years later society was still not receiving her. When the new governor, Mr Gore, arrived in 1806, he tried in vain to heal the divisions in society by inviting all its members to a series of public functions. Unfortunately, he included Mrs Small in his invitations and this sparked a new storm in society. As Edith Firth has it, this was a society in which 'social slights were magnified beyond all significance and gossip was virulent', and 'the moralists of York were willing to divide and disrupt society rather than accept Mrs Small in their ranks'.[32] Unfortunately, for someone so ostracised it was almost impossible to withdraw from society and prosper.

The tensions created by a small, competitive and yet inward-looking, almost neurotic community can also be observed at work in India. In the case of the dispute in 1826 between the governor of Bombay, Mountstuart Elphinstone, and Sir Edward

---

30 Edith G. Firth, *The Town of York, 1793–1815: A Collection of Documents of Early Toronto* (Toronto: Champlain Society, 1962), document H. 14, pp. 233–234.

31 Ibid.

32 Ibid., p. lxxx.

West, the recorder and chief justice of Bombay, that tension manifested itself in the form of an obsessive concern for rank and courtesy. On 6 January 1826 Sir Edward West wrote to Elphinstone to record his astonishment at having received a challenge from him, West believing that he had been challenged by the governor at a dinner the previous night.[33] Elphinstone wrote back claiming that he thought that it had been West that had challenged him and that West had promised to waive his position as a judge should the governor choose to accept it. West wrote once more denying that he had done any such thing and stating, 'You must be quite aware that it is absolutely impossible for me in my situation as a judge to accept a challenge ... it would not only be a loss of my situation of Chief Justice, but an utter loss of my character.'[34] Elphinstone again replied, 'I understood you to have almost in plain terms challenged me.'[35] Further acrimonious correspondence followed, with both men casting the other as the originator of the demand for satisfaction. In the event, West refused to countenance a meeting. One suspects that both men had been drunk. What emerged from the correspondence, though, was a catalogue of the petty slights allegedly suffered by West at the hands of Elphinstone over the preceding three years. Each of these had been noted and nurtured. For example, West complained of insufficient attention paid to him at a formal dinner:

> You thought proper at a Dinner given at your own house to give Sir Ralph Rice the precedence before me ... You thought it proper upon rising from the table at your House to join the Ladies to walk from the Dining Room upstairs into the Drawing Room where half or more of Bombay was assembled with Mr Horton, leaving me, the first person of rank in your House, to follow in the crowd ... [you] assigned no Lady to me, nor said a single word to me, but left me to follow in the crowd of young men.[36]

The tyranny of society, wherein every nuance was noted, every discomfiture observed, provided the opportunity for the transmission of slights which, although perhaps insignificant in themselves, would, if unchallenged, eventually place the recipient in a position of subordination.

Sir Edward West claimed that his position as a judge made it impossible for him to accept a challenge, and Judge Baber as we have seen, similarly declined. It seems, though, that the judiciary were not united on this point; they too were split into factions of interest. In 1822 another magistrate, John MacAlister, complained to the East India Company, to the court of directors itself, that the Company and its officers

---

33 India Office Records, Papers of Sir Edward West, Recorder and Chief Justice of Bombay, 1823–1828 Mss. Eur. D/888/7 f.1.

34 Ibid. Letter from Sir Edward West to Mountstuart Elphinstone, 6 Jan. 1826.

35 Mss. Eur. D/888/7 f. 3.

36 Mss. Eur. D/888/7 ff. 5–8.

had failed to support him against an aggressor, a Maj. Monckton Coombs.[37] The two men had quarrelled over the distribution of perquisites on Prince of Wales Island, but when Coombs challenged MacAlister:

> The Governor did not, as was certainly due to the dignity and rank of his Colleague in Council, direct him to be put under arrest; nor did my brother Judge and Magistrate, the Recorder, in support of the dignity of the Bench and of the Magistracy, as was naturally and properly to have been expected, cause him to be apprehended and punished for contempt in sending a challenge to a member of the court.[38]

Quite the contrary, the Recorder, if MacAlister's account is to be believed, seems to have pressured him into accepting the challenge, which indeed he duly did. The parties met on 3 June outside Calcutta. The result was something of an anticlimax: Major Coombs fired at MacAlister but his priming did not ignite; in return MacAlister merely lowered his pistol. A full statement of this and the circumstances that followed was published by the seconds in the *Bengal Hurkaru* of 8 June 1822.

It would be hard to suggest that either policy or principle governed the attitudes of either the East India Company or the War and Colonial Office in London regarding the criminal activity of duelling. Partiality was the order of the day, and those without powerful patrons were obliged to act for themselves in order to either protect their interests or, if they were so minded, fulfil the obligations of their office. The higher authorities were not, of course, blind to their own interests, where a case could be made they might be badgered into reluctant action on behalf of others, but they were rather quicker to protect themselves. For example, that same year, 1822, the Company was being particularly irritated by the activities of James Buckingham, the editor of the *Calcutta Journal*. Buckingham had published a number of articles commenting unfavourably upon the distribution of perquisites in India. One article in particular, entitled 'Summary Pluralities',[39] noted unfavourably the career of a Dr James Jameson. The article asked how Jameson could possibly fill all four medical posts that connections had secured for him. Jameson demanded a retraction, but Buckingham refused to retract the article since this would be 'a virtual abandonment of the Liberty of the Press and an immunity no man in a public station has the right to ask'.[40] He declared his intention to publish further articles upon similar subjects. Jameson subsequently challenged, and they both exchanged two shots at twelve paces, which the newspaper

---

37 IOR f/4/666/18569.

38 IOR f/4/666/18569 ff. 23–52. Letter from MacAlister to the Court of Directors of the East India Company, Prince of Wales Island, 26 Oct. 1822.

39 IOR/H/532, 600–614.

40 Ibid., 602.

faithfully reported. The Company, however, mindful of Buckingham's numerous complaints against them, quickly stepped in and ordered his removal from its territories. For the most part, though, the Company adopted an attitude that might be characterised as *laissez-faire*. In the meantime, commanders of both Company and King's forces continued to conceal duels and judges and magistrates continued to allow them to go unpunished.

Duellists were perhaps no more likely to be punished in Canada than in India, given that a goodly proportion of such Canadian duellists were not merely lawyers but holders of important legal offices within the administration. At least twenty-five of the duellists who fought in thirty-four duels in Upper and Lower Canada between 1782 and 1840 were lawyers. Lawyers then made up the largest single occupational group among the Canadian duellists, and their participation in the enterprise has to be set in the context of a passion for duelling that seems to have gripped lawyers in the home country around 1790. Canadian lawyers, then, received the duel as something of a fashion that the home country would soon reject. To the south, however, lay a republic wherein the duel was to endure rather longer than in Britain and wherein lawyers were to remain even more prominent in the activity. Root has asserted, for example, that 90 per cent of duels fought in Tennessee were between attorneys.[41] The influence of Canada's southern neighbour accounts for the fact that the pattern of lawyerly duelling there was rather different from that discernible in Britain, that and the fact that Canadian lawyers had to be particularly assertive in order to be successful in their practice and secure in their reputation. To develop this further, however, it is necessary to make some brief observations about the situation of the Canadian lawyer.

The criminal law of England was introduced into the area subsequently known as Upper Canada by royal proclamation in 1763 and into the remainder of Canada by the Quebec Act 1774.[42] A further act in 1800 in respect of Upper Canada made the implications of the royal proclamation more explicit.[43] The administration of that law, however, devolved upon very few persons indeed. In Lower Canada two courts of King's Bench were established in 1793, one at Montreal and one at Quebec, each with three justices, a Chief Justice and three puisne judges.[44] After 1794 Upper Canada relied upon a single court of King's Bench with three judges.[45] In both cases, however, most criminal cases were heard before single judges upon circuit under a commission of Oyer and Terminer. These courts were initially serviced by only a very few lawyers. According to Riddell, 'When Upper Canada began her active provincial

---

41 Ibid.

42 14 Geo. III, c. 83 (L.C.).

43 40 Geo. III, c. 1. (U.C.).

44 34 Geo. III, c. 6. (L.C.).

45 34 Geo. III, c. 2 (U.C.)

career in 1792; there were only two regular certified lawyers in all her broad domain.'[46] These were the Attorneys General, John White and Walter Roe. In 1794, however, the legislature passed an act allowing the lieutenant governor to license not more than sixteen British subjects to act as advocates and attorneys, and only these were entitled to fees for appearing in court.[47] However, when the Law Society of Upper Canada was formed on 17 July 1797 it mustered only ten lawyers.[48]

Not only were there very few lawyers, then, but most of them were also very young. For example, one of the founders of the Law Society was Robert Isaac Del Gray, Upper Canada's first Solicitor General, who was only about twenty-two when he took up that office in October 1794. Some of the founders of the Law Society had been educated in England, whereas Del Gray had left at the age of four. However, English notions of personal honour had already found their place in the schoolrooms of the new world and through them into this new society of legal gentlemen. As Joanne B. Freeman has indicated, Chesterfieldism and its values were well represented in the North American schoolroom literature of the period. Indeed, it was said that duelling in general was on the increase in North America at the end of the eighteenth century precisely because of Chesterfield's influence.[49]

The tranquillity of legal society can hardly have been helped by the fact that a violent disposition or tempestuous temperament was no bar to entry. According to Rhodes, there were 'almost no instances of denial of admission on character-related grounds' to the North American legal profession in the nineteenth century.[50] Under such circumstances the distinction between professional adversarialism and personal animosity was but irregularly maintained. This was all the more so when political factionalism was added to the mix. When William Weekes opposed William Dickson in court in October 1806, the animosities were further aggravated by the fact that the former was an opponent of the current administration and the latter a supporter. During the court proceedings Weekes made an attack upon the government and Dickson rose to defend it and to attack Weekes in person. The presiding judge, Mr Justice Thorpe, was also a critic of the government and he met with Weekes thereafter to discuss the sending of a challenge to Dickson. Dickson accepted and both parties crossed the Niagara to American territory, where Weekes was killed. Since the duel had happened

---

46 William Renwick Riddell, *Upper Canada Sketches: Incidents in the Early Times of the Province* (Toronto: Carswell, 1922), p. 127.

47 34 Geo. III, c. 4 (U.C.)

48 Riddell, *Upper Canada Sketches*, op. cit., p. 130

49 See 'On the Increasing Prevalence of Duelling, No. II', *The Balance and Columbian Repository*, 18 Jan. 1803, cited in Freeman, 'Dueling as politics', op. cit., p. 299.

50 Deborah L. Rhodes, 'Moral character as a professional credential', *Yale Law Journal*, 94 (1985), pp. 491–585, at p. 497.

upon American territory, no prosecution followed and Dickson subsequently enjoyed a political career as a member of the Legislative Council of Upper Canada. Mr Justice Thorpe returned to England and was appointed Chief Justice of Sierra Leone. A further quarrel in the courtroom led to a duel in 1811 between John MacDonnell, the attorney general for Upper Canada, and William Baldwin. Baldwin was an English doctor who had taken up law upon arrival in Canada (an indication of the unregulated state of the profession). No injuries were occasioned. Nor were there any injuries when two other lawyers quarrelled in court and duelled near Montreal in 1819. The protagonists, Samuel Gale and James Stuart, both subsequently became judges.

So deeply were members of the legal establishment implicated in this species of illegal act that at times the consequences were almost risible. On 12 July 1817 Samuel Jarvis duelled with John Ridout following a petty dispute over the paying of a schoolgirl's bills. The seconds were men of impeccable legal credentials: Henry John Boulton, acting for Jarvis, was the son of the attorney general and later became the solicitor general of Upper Canada and, ultimately, the chief justice of Newfoundland. James Small, acting for Ridout, was also a practising lawyer and later a treasurer of the Law Society of Upper Canada. Ridout was killed in the encounter, and both seconds left York. Jarvis stood trial, but the jury took only a few minutes to acquit him. However, in 1828 Francis Collins, the editor of the *Canadian Freeman*, wrote an article criticising Henry Boulton, who was by then the solicitor general. Boulton indicted him for criminal libel. When the matter came to court, however, Collins promptly demanded that Boulton and Small (who was also appearing as counsel) be indicted as accessories to murder for their role in the duel. The grand jury found a true bill, and Boulton and Small were arrested, still clad in their court robes. They were tried but acquitted.[51]

Detailed accounts of Canadian duelling trials are rarely available. However, an account of the 1819 trial of Richard J. Uniacke Junior was subsequently published in pamphlet form by the *Acadian Recorder* and has been studied by Riddell. The pamphlet relates an event not without its theatricalities and absurdities in which the perversion of the law amply explains why so few Canadian duellists were ever convicted.[52] The cause of Uniacke's dispute with William Bowie was again words said in the context of trial advocacy. During an address to the jury on 19 July 1819 Uniacke made remarks that offended Bowie, Bowie being a defendant in the particular case. Immediately after the trial Bowie despatched a note demanding retraction of the remarks lest he be regarded as 'not a man of truth'. Uniacke replied robustly:

> As a barrister I had a right to draw any conclusions upon your conduct, from the evidence about to be produced, that I thought in the minds of the jury would promote

---

51 Riddell, *Upper Canada Sketches,* op. cit., pp. 25–32.

52 Ibid., pp. 75–81.

the interest of my client; as a proof those conclusions were not imaginary, the strongest testimonial I can offer is the verdict of the twelve men who tried you. However, Sir to conclude I have only to add that whatever expressions may fall from me at the bar, I consider myself as responsible for, as if said in private society.[53]

The parties met on 21 July 1819 near Richmond, and at the second fire Bowie was fatally wounded. Uniacke and his second Edwards MacSweeney were arrested, and on 27 July true bills were found against them for the murder of Bowie.

At the commencement of the trial, however, the solicitor general rose and told the court that he declined to act for the prosecution, partly because he had been a close friend of the deceased and partly because he was also closely acquainted with the father of Sweeney, the second defendant. A new King's counsel, Mr Archibold, took his place, and the defendants entered the court, accompanied by Mr R. J. Uniacke senior, the attorney general of Nova Scotia, and by Norman Uniacke, the defendant's older brother, who was at that time attorney general of Lower Canada. Mr Archibold then opened with some remarkable legal assertions:

> I find it is a rule of law, that the deliberate killing of another in a duel constitutes murder in the seconds, as well as in the principal; but where the Jury have been convinced of the fairness and correctness with which it was conducted, I know of no instance in their deciding on the case wherein they returned a verdict of murder – If then gentlemen, you find in this case a rancorous and malicious disposition, which has hurried the parties beyond the bounds of reason and the law, I hesitate not to say, you will have found what constitutes the crime of murder. If, on the other hand, you find no other malice accompanying this transaction, than what may be inferred from the circumstances of the case, you will be bound to acquit them of the crime.[54]

Archibold's assertion that the doctrine of implied malice did not apply in such a case was, as we shall see, quite contrary to authority. It was a perversion of the law, but one with which the presiding judge, Sir Brenton Halliburton, was happy to acquiesce.

The witnesses for the prosecution provided much of the requisite defence evidence. One testified to hearing the dying Bowie say that 'all was fair and honourable'; one that the deceased had declared, 'I forgive Mr. Uniacke and I hope he will pray for me.' When Uniacke himself came to speak to the jury, he denied all malice and made an interesting observation: 'You, gentlemen, have known me from childhood ... you have marked my progress through life ... you know my general character and you must be

---

53 G. Patterson, *More Studies in Nova Scotia History* (Halifax: Imperial Publishing Company, 1941), pp. 73–74.

54 Ibid., p. 76.

satisfied that I had no other motive than to defend my reputation and my honour.' Finally, Uniacke produced in his defence five barristers (no small proportion of the Bar in the province) to swear to his good character and mild disposition. The jury retired for half an hour before acquitting the defendants.

Occasionally, juries would return manslaughter verdicts in such cases, but the sentences imposed thereafter reflected a reluctance to recognise the duel as fully criminal. When Capt. David Sutherland was convicted of manslaughter in August 1793, having shot down Peter Clark of the Legislative Council of Upper Canada, he was merely fined thirteen shillings and four pence. John Norton might have felt himself unfortunate to be fined twenty-five pounds after an irregular duel with a Mohawk chief in 1823.[55] Furthermore, it does not seem that there were any professional sanctions applied against duellists. An affair of honour was no bar to further legal advancement, Indeed, Richard Uniacke Junior. was appointed to the bench in 1830.

Canadian lawyers were clearly much more likely to duel than their more numerous English counterparts. Furthermore, while in England lawyerly duels were sporadic and distinctly the product of isolated disputes, in Canada duels sometimes appear to have been the consequence of long-standing hostilities between interconnected groups. To illustrate, in June 1830 Thomas Radenhurst and James Boulton, both lawyers of Perth, duelled harmlessly upon an island in the St Lawrence. However, the background of both parties strongly suggests an antecedent hostility. James Boulton was the brother of Henry John Boulton, Henry being the second to Samuel Peters Jarvis, who had duelled with and killed John Ridout in 1817. On the opposite side, Thomas Radenhurst was married to the sister of the aforementioned John Ridout. Carrying the matter forward, in 1833 there was another duel near Perth, between John Wilson and Robert Lyon. The duel was ostensibly over the reputation of a woman, but it seems a remarkable coincidence that both were trainee attorneys, one apprenticed to James Boulton and one to Thomas Radenhurst.[56]

The life of the lawyer in early Toronto or Montreal was rather different to that of the lawyer in London, and different again from that of the colonial administrator in British India. Duelling culture, however, was flexible: it embraced them all. This was so because at its roots that culture depended not upon a similarity of circumstances but upon a similarity of dispositions. This, then, harks back to that which I said earlier about the education of young gentlemen and their consequent attributes. At Kingston in Canada, Peter Clark and David Sutherland quarrelled and fought over a lucrative public office; in India, MacAlister and Coombs, Jameson and Buckingham were set at loggerheads over the distribution of perquisites. The society of

55 *The Gleaner,* 20 Sept. 1823.

56 Halliday, *Murder Among Gentlemen,* op. cit., p. 183.

Elphinstone and West was as obsessed with gossip and trivia as that of Mr White and Mr Small. Men such as these were barely able to cope equably with any setbacks in either their personal or their professional capacities. When they were opposed or contradicted, such men nurtured grievances and reacted in ways which seem to modern eyes to display nothing so much as childish spite. When Marc-Pascal de Sales Laterrière was invited to a ball by the governor of Lower Canada, he simply could not forebear to notice that there was present a lawyer, Elzéar Bedard, who had represented an opponent of his brother in a lawsuit. He could not desist from stamping on Bedard's foot at the dance and so occasioning a duel.[57] Whether the early nineteenth-century gentleman indeed experienced emotions so different from that of the modern European man, I leave to others less cynical than myself to decide. What is apparent, however, is that by comparison to most of us today, such men displayed an absence of inhibitions such that the threat of violence was never far away. Such men often gave way to their emotions and were not ashamed of it; restraint, in their eyes, seemed all too close to servility or cowardice.

Courage may win an empire, yet it is scarcely sufficient in administering that empire, and still less in developing a successful civil society. The incapacity of duellists to suppress their personal feelings in the interests of furthering greater purposes is as striking as their seeming imperviousness to considerations of personal preservation. In Canada many lawyers seemed incapable of accepting that there was something that held a greater claim to their loyalty than personal inclination; lawyers, in other words, seemed incapable of obeying the law. Similarly, some colonial administrators were rather more concerned to safeguard their reputations than to safeguard the interests of the Crown. Col. Aston's conduct might be thought to have been reprehensible enough in respect of its lack of forethought about consequences but it was by no means unique. The island of Dominique was left without both a governor and a lieutenant governor in 1775, for the former had been shot by the latter.[58] The duel between Warren Hastings and Sir Phillip Francis on 17 August 1780 ended with the death of Francis, but had the reverse been the case, the consequences for the government of British India might have been severe.[59] This was not lost upon all; not all men were blinded by partiality or dazzled by spirit. After the duel between MacCartney and Stuart the *Universal Register* protested at the consequences for government: 'If men acting for the public good are to be dragged forth by every offended individual, to answer with their lives for the exercise of their duty, then there is an end to civil

---

57 Ibid., p. 119.

58 The Centre for Kentish Studies, The Amherst Manuscripts U1350/080/21. A letter from Lt Col. Christie to the effect that Governor Shirley had been killed in Dominique in a duel with Lt Governor Stewart, 2 May 1775.

59 The British Library, The Warren Hastings Papers, vol. viii, f. 33b.

society ... It is an offence spurning at authority, tending to create disorder in every department of the State.'[60]

Squeezing honour culture out of political life, out of the accepted framework of social relations, was a laborious task. I shall observe in later chapters that the duel was in decline in England after 1815. Military manliness became less important as a social virtue after the end of the Napoleonic War. Within the army and navy themselves men were beginning talk of 'military science' and to think of war as a careful bureaucratic endeavour. The press were increasingly swayed by a new middling constituency of 'public opinion', and both they and the judges and politicians were arguing that if society was to be delivered from radicalism and saved for the propertied interest, then it was necessary to demonstrate that all classes were equally subordinate to the law. Above all, new, calculating mentalities were emerging that were to subdue the arenas of politics, law and economics. Men possessed of such mentalities applied themselves methodically to the achievement of goals; they did indeed know how they would be behaving twenty-four hours hence, and they scorned the uninhibited and violent dispositions of men of honour.

However, in many colonial situations courage still commanded a particular premium. Canada, of course, remained under the influence of its southern neighbour, where duelling retained its vigour long after it had expired in England, but Canadian duelling was in terminal decline by 1840. That was similarly the case in India, although there is some evidence of military duelling there in the 1850s. In the real and the imaginary space of the empire, combat was to be remodelled and reconceptualised; it was to become a struggle between man and beast and between civilised and uncivilised. For good, or perhaps for ill, the empire was to fall under the sway of men of a rather different spirit.

---

60 *Universal Register*, 29 Apr. 1786, col. e.

6

Dangerous Friends:
Conciliation, Counsel and the
Conduct of English Duelling

Thus far I have surveyed the distribution of duels, both geographically and socially, and said something about the disputes which led to them. However, the time has come to, as it were, take a step backward and consider the means by which honour disputes were resolved – for very many honour disputes did not, in truth, conclude in a duel. Here, then, I will examine the ways in which quarrels might be resolved, but I will also conversely consider the manner in which, where a resolution could not be found, duels might actually be conducted. Resolving disputes and refereeing combats might well appear rather different enterprises but of course in the late eighteenth and early nineteenth centuries the duties of conciliating between the parties and, if necessary, conducting the actual duel were vested in the same persons, the seconds or friends of the protagonists. As we shall see, reconciling the rather different calls upon them required not a little delicacy upon their part.

The second is a much-neglected figure in modern studies of the duel, scarcely accorded more than a few brief lines in works that invariably concentrate upon the fact of the violent encounter and the conduct of the principal protagonists. Yet contemporaries placed great value on the role that they played. Samuel Stanton declared that 'Nothing with respect to duelling can be, or really is of more consequence than the choice of the second.'[1] Paolo Fambri was still contending in 1868 that 'it is neither the sword nor the bullet that kills duellists, but the seconds'.[2] Since they managed disputes and guided them towards peaceful resolution, or, alternatively, arranged the mechanics of duel where peaceful endeavours had failed, seconds played an absolutely indispensable role in configuring later honour culture. Without their intervention the relationship between disputants would have been irremediably altered. In discussing

---

1   Stanton, *The Principles of Duelling*, op. cit., p. 59.

2   P. Fambri, 'The free press and duelling in Italy, a lecture delivered before the Tribunal of Honour by Paolo Fambri, Questor of Deputies of the Kingdom of Italy', *North American Review*, Jan. (1869), p. 300.

the progress of honour disputes and the actual mechanics of meetings on the field in this chapter, then, it is the figure of the second who for a moment will loom even larger than that of his principal.

How many honour disputes there were that did not actually proceed to a duel, and how many owed this happy outcome to the labours of seconds, is unfortunately impossible to determine save to say that the evidence suggests that there were many more quarrels that were resolved before a duel than there were disputes that went on to an actual meeting. Byron acted as second twice for his friend Scrope Davies and succeeded on both occasions in preventing matters from proceeding further:

> I was called in the other day to mediate between two gentlemen bent upon carnage, and ... I got one to make an apology and the other to take it, and left them to live happily ever after. One was a peer, the other a friend untitled, and both fond of high play ... They both conducted themselves very well, and I put them out of pain as soon as I could.[3]

Abraham Bosquett claimed that he had been a second twenty-five times, adding, 'I have the greatest satisfaction in being able to aver, that life or honour were never lost in my hands; but I am confident it would have been otherwise on many occasions had I not been concerned.'[4] Some of the honour disputes that did not actually proceed to a duel can be followed in some detail, for such disputes, like the full-blown encounters themselves, necessarily had a public dimension. In resolving an honour dispute, it was important to demonstrate publicly that nothing had been done to achieve the resolution that might cast a stain upon the honour of the parties. Honour disputes began of course competitively with the parties seeking to convince a relevant constituency of opinion as to the appropriate nature of their conduct and the contrasting delinquency of their putative opponent. The opinion appealed to might be general, broad society addressed through the medium of the press, or it might be rather more narrow, the immediate companions in an officer's mess, for example. In all circumstances, however, there was the necessity of clearly stating one's case. Should a resolution be achieved, with or without a duel, the competing narratives were then usually merged into one via means of a mutually agreed statement formulated in order to present a common position amenable to both. However, in those instances where, for whatever reason, a resolution had not been achieved, the contest might continue, with the publication of contradictory statements and even the publication of private letters by the seconds.

---

3   T. A. J. Burnett, *The Life of Scrope*, op. cit., p. 64.

4   Abraham Bosquett, 'A treatise on duelling, together with the annals of chivalry, the ordeal trial and judicial combat from the earliest times', in A. J. Valpy, ed., *The Pamphleteer* (London, 1818), pp. 79–125, at p. 81.

The seconds of the latter half of the eighteenth century and beyond, it should be noted, were very different personages from those who accompanied disputants to the field in the seventeenth and early eighteenth centuries. In the earlier years the second had resembled nothing so much as a retainer, who, as in a chance medley, joined in with his principal and was entirely committed to his cause.[5] Thus, when the Duke of Buckingham and Lord Shrewsbury quarrelled in 1668, each brought two soldiers to the field with them and all six fought each other.[6] In 1712 when Lord Mohun and the Duke of Hamilton met, their respective seconds, Lt Gen. Maccartney and Col. Hamilton, drew their swords and fought each other. However, the use of such assistants was already declining at that point and seems to have ended entirely soon after.

Many of the duels during the period from around 1720 to 1770 were fought without any assistants and indeed without witnesses. When in 1726 Maj. Oneby quarrelled with Mr Gower while playing cards in a tavern, the rest of the company were shut out and the encounter was conducted in private. Similarly, when Mr Dalton and Mr Paul met around 1750, they did so alone in the lodgings of Mr Dalton. It was again in a tavern that Lord Byron and Mr Chaworth quarrelled in 1765 over the management of game; this dispute, too, was resolved by requesting a private room and drawing swords behind closed doors. By the 1760s, however, the second who acted not as a potential combatant but as an intermediary between parties was emerging. Thus, when John Wilkes quarrelled with Lord Talbot in 1762, Talbot responded by appointing a Col. Berkeley to write to Wilkes on his behalf. This, then, was something of an advance, although later commentators would have disapproved of the fact that Wilkes responded to Berkeley in person. Wilkes did, however, ask a Mr Harris to accompany him to a tavern at Bagshot, where, one way or another, the matter was to be resolved. When, at the tavern itself, it became clear that no peaceable resolution was possible, Berkeley at first proposed to leave the two men to settle the matter alone behind closed doors. Lord Talbot objected. The result was that the duel was actually carried through in the garden. The number of shots was determined by Lord Talbot (which would again have later been seen as inappropriate), but the assisting gentlemen stayed to witness the encounter and the discharge of pistols followed a signal given by one of them.[7]

Judged by the later conventions of honour, the affair was somewhat imperfectly conducted, yet Wilkes' duel marks an interesting and intermediate stage in the development of the position of second, a situation soon endowed with a distinctive character and obligations. By 1793 and the publication of the anonymous *General Rules and*

---

5   Peltonen, *The Duel in Early Modern England*, op. cit., p. 203.

6   *The Diaries of Samuel Pepys*, 11 vols (London, 1970–1983), ix, pp. 26–27, cited in Shoemaker, 'The taming of the duel', op. cit., p.531.

7   Millingen, *History of Duelling*, op. cit., vol. ii, pp. 66–76.

Instructions For All Seconds in Duels,[8] the role of the second had been formalised, such that the office assumed much the same appearance it held until the very end of the duel itself. The author of this pamphlet took it for granted that seconds would be appointed in any affair of honour between gentlemen and was clear what their obligations under such circumstances were. He had to admit, however, that seconds did not always measure up to that which was expected of them. The very reason for writing the pamphlet was because 'Most of the shocking accidents we read of are often owing to the Ignorance or Inattention of the SECONDS and it is my Duty to remark upon their frequent Misconduct and give them their Instructions.'[9] The very first and foremost duty of these seconds, as the author makes clear, was, if at all possible, to find a peaceful resolution to the dispute at issue.

In the German context, Ute Frevert has asserted that the very development of the office of the second was part of a broader, 'middle-class programme of socialization'.[10] The second emerged rather too early for that to be quite right in England, for the influence of the middle class in the 1760s and 1770s must not be exaggerated. It would perhaps be better to place the second in the context of Shoemaker's observation that throughout all levels of society one can observe a declining enthusiasm for violent acts in the later eighteenth century. Frevert is surely right, though, to have pointed out that the ability to appoint others to act for oneself, without impugning one's own honour, must have greatly reduced a gentleman's need to respond to a first insult. By withdrawing and appointing seconds, gentlemen allowed time for reflection and, no small matter this, time for the parties to sober up. The appointment of seconds, then, surely played a role in occasioning the final disappearance of the sudden and violent chance medleys of earlier times, although it must be owned that here much was owed to the fact that, the military aside, after the 1730s it was no longer customary to wear swords. By 1793 pistols were the preferred weapon and could be sent for and hired, but again the expectation that seconds would be employed to arrange affairs greatly reduced those occasions upon which gentlemen felt impelled to withdraw swiftly to some secluded spot or sequestered room to resolve their grievances.

In order to understand the role that seconds played in managing honour disputes, however, one has to understand that they were rarely endowed with a judgmental function, they did not adjudicate disputes and determine who was at fault. Rather they depended upon their persuasive powers and upon the goodwill of their opposing numbers and sought to find a resolution acceptable to each protagonist. Each second

---

8 Anon., *General Rules and Instructions for All Seconds in Duels: By a Late Captain in the Army* (Whitehaven: 1793).

9 Ibid., p. 17–18.

10 Ute Frevert, *Men of Honour: A Social and Cultural History of the Duel* (Cambridge: Cambridge University Press, 1995), p. 154.

was obliged to consider his own principal's interests first, but just as he did not bind his principal so he was not bound by his principal. The men accompanying duellists in the seventeenth century had often been mere retainers, but the seconds of the later eighteenth century were of a quite different species. That is to say that they were their own men. Although under normal circumstances they willingly acted for the gentlemen who had appointed them, they were no mere servants or delegates but rather social equals who had their own reputations to consider. Or so the honour theorists asserted. As ever there were some exceptions, and Joseph Hamilton in 1805 reserved his particular disapprobation for those 'melancholy instances upon record in which principals have converted seconds into mere automatons at their own command'.[11]

More common though were the circumstances in which a principal observed propriety and placed the dispute in question into the hands of his second and entrusted him with arranging a satisfactory resolution. Such trust indeed called for some courage and faith, and Kiernan has compared the relationship to that of a believer obeying his priest.[12] Thus it was that it was the seconds who by the end of the eighteenth century were routinely conducting all the negotiations between parties and proposing the terms of any resolution. Obedience, however, went only so far, for the final say as to whether the proposed compromise was acceptable lay with the principals. This, then, placed the second in a position that was somewhat contradictory. On the one hand, he had to maintain his independent character, in order to be able to vouchsafe to society that the matter had been honourably conducted. On the other hand, the second inevitably had some of the facets of an agent. The tensions between these apparently conflicting attributes were exposed by a question that was never entirely or unanimously resolved. If the second was tasked with settling the dispute in accordance with the principles of honour, to what extent, then, was he entitled to sit in judgement upon his principal's cause? Was a second who interested himself in acting for a principal who was clearly at fault himself acting honourably?

According to some conduct books the answer was no. Lt Stanton argued in 1790 that:

Every Gentleman requested to attend in this capacity has a most undoubted right to enquire into each minute particular respecting the commencement and cause of the quarrel: he ought also, if a stranger to, or not in some degree an intimate of, the party, to insist upon his committing the same to paper, with his signature annexed as under. He then cannot be deceived as to the propriety of his attendance.[13]

---

11 Hamilton, *The Royal Code of Honor*, op. cit., p. 17.

12 Kiernan, *The Duel in European History*, op. cit., p. 138.

13 Stanton, *Principles of Duelling*, op. cit., pp. 63–64.

It was declared in 1793 that a second must determine which of the parties was at fault, and if the fault was that of his principal, then he must impose conditions upon him:

> If however, it should happen that the Offence is of that Magnitude as to preclude any Explanation, he must then determine according to the Right or Wrong of the Party that applies – if it be the former he must readily attend him; but if the latter, it should be done with the utmost reluctance, and only on this one Condition: That having the Odium of being the flagrant Aggressor, he goes upon the Ground to make the proper Atonement, and Nothing more.[14]

Yet this was but a counsel of perfection, for there were considerable practical difficulties for any second who wished to set himself up as adjudicator of right and wrong.

Although a gentleman must pause to appoint a second, and although some time must be allotted between the offence and the meeting, this did not necessarily provide a second with an opportunity to investigate the circumstances of the quarrel. Col. Bayley recalled being dragged from his bed to act as a second to a distant acquaintance, Charles Willoughby. Willoughby confessed to him that he had invited a challenge the night before by behaving indecorously to a gentleman's sister. Bayley then refused to accompany him unless he agreed to make an apology.[15] Willoughby's account appears to have been entirely honest, but the point is that Bayley was entirely dependent upon that fact, and other seconds were similarly forced to depend upon the assertions of their principals. In reality it was only after accepting the role that seconds were left free to inquire properly into a dispute. Until then they were not at liberty to randomly interfere in matters between sovereign parties, no matter what the model conduct books might imply. Once appointed, they rarely felt obliged to quit their office. They could, though, offer their opinion. In 1815 a dispute arose between Admiral McNamara and Col. Beazley at the Bath theatre. McNamara's second:

> Felt that his principal had erred, and of course felt it his duty to make that representation ... Admiral M'Namara assured him he was most willing to take that course which seemed correct, and, as he had acted hastily, he was ready to express his consciousness of his error ... all differences were most amicably adjusted.[16]

However, the state of society was sometimes such as to make it difficult for an offending party to make restitution, even when conscious of his own error. The Duke of Wellington and Lord Winchilsea duelled in 1829, but Winchilsea had

---

14 Anon., *General Rules,* op. cit., pp. 19–20.

15 Bayley, *Diary,* op. cit., pp. 127–128.

16 *Hampshire Telegraph,* 25 Dec. 1815, p. 2, col. e.

already given a letter to his own second, Lord Falmouth, admitting that he had been in the wrong in the dispute. This letter was duly presented to Wellington's own second, Mr Hardinge, after the encounter. Falmouth:

> seemed greatly affected and stated he always thought and told Lord Winchilsea that he was completely in the wrong, on which Sir Henry remarked that if he did so and came with the writer of the letter to the ground, his Lordship had done that which he, (Sir Henry), would not have done for his dearest friend in the world.[17]

Hardinge, then, was rebuking Falmouth for putting friendship above the demands of justice. Yet the judgemental role to which some apologists expected the second to aspire did not marry easily with a mode of honour thinking that was not predicated upon the need to achieve justice. The infliction or acceptance of a symbolic reciprocal harm in order to equalise relations between parties might be required, but the goal of seconds was not to achieve recompense for broader moral fault. The duel was not a form of civic litigation. No one supposed that the purpose of the duel was to demonstrate the veracity of a claim. To deny a gentleman an opportunity to demonstrate his honourable courage merely because he was at fault would have been contrary to the purpose of an institution which was redemptive rather than judgemental. In truth, the second could function only as a very limited moral censor, and the emphasis the apologists placed upon ascertaining fault is highly questionable. I have found no instance wherein a second completely declined to continue to act for his principal once he had concluded that this principal was at fault. The claims of morality did not yet generally prevail over the demands of group loyalty, and it was to such loyalty that men appealed when seeking someone to act for them. Notwithstanding the fulminations of Bosquett or Hamilton, men who had had criminal conversations with other men's wives, who had seduced away daughters, who had committed unprovoked assaults, or who had libelled unjustly seem to have had little difficulty in finding their seconds.

Furthermore, not all seconds dispassionately sought reconciliation. Some were of a malignant disposition. Bosquett warned:

> There is great danger in adopting as your friend one who has been injured by, or bears enmity to the man you are to fight ... First, if not a man of honour, he will be adverse to an accommodation; and secondly, by carrying matters with too high a hand, under a pretended zeal for you, he may run the risk of sacrificing you to avenge himself: in other words, he might wish to fight your adversary through your ribs, which is no uncommon case.[18]

---

17 The British Library. Papers relating to Napoleon, Wellington and the Duke of York. Miscellaneous Papers of the 5th Countess of Jersey, LMA ACC/1128/220–223.

18 Bosquett, 'A treatise on duelling', op. cit., p. 86.

He recalled being asked to be second to a doctor. The doctor's challenger had appointed as his own second a man known to be hostile to the doctor. This second not only refused all offers of reconciliation from Bosquett but also actually challenged Bosquett's principal on the field, proposing that they should meet immediately after the first duel. All parties persuaded him to withdraw his challenge, and then the duel was arranged between the principals. Bosquett insisted upon setting the distance at the customary twelve yards, but his opposite number tried, unsuccessfully, to insist upon a mere seven. When, after the first fire, neither party was injured, Bosquett intervened to halt the proceedings, despite the vociferous objections of the other second. Both principals shook hands and eventually became firm friends, much to the consternation of Bosquett's opposite number.[19] The affair was not unique. The second to Professor Glashin challenged the opposing principal on the field. The challenge was accepted, but it was the challenger who was promptly despatched.[20]

Jonah Barrington, if indeed he can be trusted, gives us perhaps the most extreme example of a vindictive second in his *Personal Sketches*. The death of his brother, William Barrington, was allegedly occasioned by a second, Capt. Gillespie, following a duel between William and a Mr McKenzie. The principals had fired two shots at each other and had resolved to bury their differences when Gillespie interjected and tried to persuade his principal, Mr McKenzie, to continue with the duel. Both parties declined, and Gillespie became so agitated that he promptly fired and killed William Barrington. Indicted for murder, he was subsequently acquitted, with Jonah Barrington alleging that this was because the jury was packed with military men.[21] Seconds, then, were not necessarily innocent and objective assistants, and the danger of having as a friend a man who was overzealous in protecting one's reputation (but not necessarily his own) was parodied by *The Times* as late as 1843. Aside from borrowing money and turning up for dinner uninvited, such an intimate friend was said to be 'always ready to be my second in a duel' and 'so tenacious of my honour, that he will never hear of a compromise, though older and better men than himself have professed themselves satisfied'.[22]

However, if a principal might be unnecessarily endangered by his second, there were occasions upon which the second, too, might be placed into danger, in respect of both his honour and his life. Exertions on the part of one's principal might be rather dangerous if it came to be supposed that one was personally casting doubt upon the honour of any of the opposing parties. At the same time,

---

19 Ibid., p. 82.

20 *The Times*, 1 Jul. 1834, p. 4, col. e.

21 Barrington, *Personal Sketches*, op. cit., pp. 109–117.

22 *The Times*, 11 Sep. 1843, p. 6, col. c.

one had to be prepared to respond to any undue personal aspersions which another gentleman might be tempted to make during the course of the dispute. Seconds, then, might quarrel in consequence of the demands of their office. Kelly reports a duel between two seconds in Ireland in 1778 that was occasioned by their dissatisfaction at the outcome of the duel between the principals.[23] The fatal duel between Mr O'Callaghan and Lt Bailey in 1818 was occasioned by their quarrelling while acting for others.[24]

As already mentioned, during the course of an honour dispute the conduct of both disputants was frequently subject to intense public scrutiny. One tends to forget, however, that the conduct of the seconds was also under review and that seconds therefore also had to protect their interests and strive to place the appropriate interpretation upon their conduct. Little consideration has been given to the sensibilities of the second, but an interesting and rather unusual set of correspondence published in *The Times* in 1826 offers an insight into the potential difficulties of their situation. The correspondence was that which had passed between one second, a Mr Steele, who had been acting for a Mr Dickson, and another second, a Mr Murphy, who had been acting for a Mr John Taylor.[25] Of itself, the context was not unusual; such correspondence was often published at the end of an honour dispute. However, in this case, the dispute was never resolved and a duel was never fought, due, it appears, to the reluctance of Mr Taylor. Steele published the correspondence, seemingly to blacken Taylor's reputation and publicise his apparent cowardice. What is of most interest, however, is the passage of correspondence and the way that an additional contest of honour developed therein, this time between the seconds.

Dickson and John Taylor had quarrelled over an attack upon Dickson's character in *The Morning Herald*, and the seconds had agreed that there should be a duel at Norwood. However, on the way to the ground on 1 July 1826 Dickson had been arrested by a Bow Street officer and bound over to keep the peace. The seconds Murphy and Steele had apparently met thereafter at the intended duelling ground and they had agreed that a meeting would now have to be arranged at Calais. That same afternoon, however, Steele had discovered that it had been John Taylor's own brother, William, who had informed Bow Street of the intended duel and thus prevented the meeting. The correspondence published in *The Times* began with the letter that Steele had immediately despatched to Murphy. In the letter he implied that John Taylor had known of William's plan to prevent the duel and he demanded a firm date for the proposed meeting at Calais. In addition, though, he suggested that Murphy's own honour had been impugned by John Taylor, who had in Steele's view

---

23 Kelly, *That Damn'd Thing Called Honour*, op. cit., p. 176.

24 *The Times*, 13 Jan. 1818, p. 3, col. f.

25 *The Times*, 14 Jul. 1826, p. 3, col. f.

got Murphy to arrange a duel at Norwood that he had obviously had had no intention of fighting. He invited Murphy to consider his own position.

Murphy declined to do so. In the second published letter, dated 2 July, Murphy replied and expressed surprise at the conduct of William Taylor: 'He must answer for that himself.' He would not investigate whether John Taylor had known of his brother's intentions since: 'The high respect and admiration I have now long felt for his honour and integrity prevent the possibility of my asking him for a denial of conduct so mean and dastardly.' He had to report that his principal had now left London, but not before declaring that, in consequence of Dickson's arrest, 'it was impossible that he could ever again meet Mr Dickson under whatever circumstances.'

Steele replied immediately, pointing out that Murphy had pledged that John Taylor would meet with Mr Dickson at Calais but it appeared that Taylor was now refusing to honour the pledge of his second. Again he sought to engage Murphy's own honour in the matter. 'Sir, I do not know if you are aware of this – that Mr Taylor by violating your pledge after he had appointed you his friend has given you an insult as deep as a blow; and by leaving London after your promise, has branded himself for ever as a runaway and a coward.' A blow must be noticed, and he who did not do so had forfeited the status of gentleman. Steele explicitly suggested that Murphy, too, had to seek remedy.

Murphy did not reply until 4 July. He was in a difficult position and was prepared in some degree to acknowledge it, 'The strange and perplexing situation in which the conduct of Mr William Taylor has placed me, renders it extremely difficult to act with the promptitude which cases of this kind require.' However, he would not allow himself to be tainted by the increasingly plausible assertion that he had been ill-used by a principal who had thought nothing of violating his second's pledge. Murphy suggested that at Norwood he had merely promised to consider whether a meeting abroad was appropriate, and that no pledge had been given. But he was increasingly uncomfortable and expressed his own opinion that 'if the parties cannot accommodate their differences, they ought without delay, to quit the kingdom for the purpose of adjusting them'. Not mentioning William Taylor by name he declared that 'the information of a proposed duel must in all circumstances be communicated by persons who are more solicitous about the life than the honour of their friend'. Finally, he began to assert himself, for he could not allow himself to be bullied by Steele during a course of correspondence that was very likely to become public:

> In the meantime I think it necessary to request you will do me the favour to state whether I am warranted in collecting from the forms of your letter, any disposition upon your part that the relation in which you and I have stood hitherto in this unpleasant transaction should be changed – in short whether anything personally disrespectful to me was intended?

The response was spirited, but Steele was not to be distracted. On 5 July he sent Murphy a note and a statement from the surgeon (subsequently published) who had been engaged to attend the intended duel at Norwood. In the statement the surgeon affirmed that he too had been under the impression that Murphy had pledged that his principal would fight in Calais. Steele declared to Murphy that in conveying Taylor's refusal to fight, after the conduct of Taylor's own brother had become clear, 'You made yourself the vehicle of this determination of Mr Taylor.' The use of the word 'vehicle' was significant for it carried the connotations of being a mere means or a servant. Murphy had become, as Bosquett would put it, a mere automaton in the hands of his principal. Steele concluded his letter by declaring that although Taylor had 'utterly disqualified himself', Mr Dickson would still agree to the promised duel.

After receipt of this letter, Murphy apparently wrote to John Taylor asking him to return to London. By 9 July, however, Steele had received no offer of a meeting and upon that day repeated his offer. He no longer described Taylor as a gentleman, but as a 'person' who had 'retreated from London'. Murphy could only respond in sorrow that he was disappointed not to have received a letter from Taylor and that he was satisfied with the, 'fair and candid manner in which you have conducted this most unpleasant transaction'. This is the last letter published by Steele. He concluded his advertisement with a single sentence under Murphy's last communication: 'Up to this hour, ten o'clock a.m. Thursday, July 13, I have had no further communication on this subject of any kind whatever. Thomas Steele.'

One would very much like to have sight of the correspondence that passed between Murphy and his own principal and to know the story of the subsequent relations between them. The effect of his principal's conduct upon Murphy's own reputation is difficult to gauge. What does seem apparent from the defensive tone of his correspondence is that Murphy was aware that, at least to some degree, his reputation was in jeopardy. He upheld his principal's cause for as long as possible, but in the end had to abandon it and assert his own views and interests. In publishing the correspondence, Steele had indeed blackened the reputation of Taylor; however, he had also socially embarrassed Murphy, and his version of events had prevailed in the public arena.

If the correspondence serves to remind us of the all too often overlooked interests of the second, it also emphasises the careful attention paid at the time to the subtleties of language. Not least among the duties of the second was the careful crafting of the language of compromise, in such a way as to satisfy all possible sensibilities. Sometimes the second laboured in vain. In 1814 a Capt. Campbell and a Lt Russell quarrelled in Bombay. The cause of the dispute was that Campbell had chided Russell for failing to dispatch a report and that he had done so in the presence of another officer. Russell had allegedly made an insolent reply. The seconds laboured very carefully in order to diffuse the conflict, and eventually they were able to negotiate a compromise whereby Captain Campbell would state, 'It was not my intention to irritate or offend you when I addressed you the other evening in Lieutenant Robinson's quarters.' Lt Russell was to reply, 'It was not my intention to treat you with disrespect, or offend you on that occasion, and if I did so, I was sorry for it.' However, Russell then changed his mind, stating that instead of 'If I did so, I was sorry for it,' he would say 'I am sorry he should think I did.' Campbell observed that there was a glaring difference between expressing regret at one's conduct and expressing sorrow for another's conception of that conduct. Shots were exchanged and Russell was killed.[26]

The second in such negotiations acted as a species of honour critic. His purpose was to seek resolution, but not at any cost and not by being unduly judgemental in respect of the original cause of dissension. In teasing out a resolution, he had to be aware of the constraints that were laid upon the opposing principal; a second diligently seeking to effectively perform his task could not demand too much of the opposing side. Similarly, however, his duty was to prevent his own principal from conceding too much. Some principals might exhibit a greater enthusiasm for blood than was proper, and seconds might feel obliged to restrain them. Some, however, might, perhaps in the agony of the encounter itself, be unduly conciliatory and act in a way that might later be seen to have compromised themselves. By placing the conduct of the affair into the hands of seconds, gentlemen, to a degree, divested themselves of such a temptation.

The alternative term 'friend', often used instead of both second and principal, in many ways describes the relationship rather well. A gentleman could confer no greater honour upon a friend than to trust him to safeguard his reputation; a second could only reciprocate by striving to do the utmost in that gentleman's interest. Deciding what was in a friend's interest and what honour required, however, was a matter of some personal discretion. Some felt obliged to intervene to prevent the inappropriate resolution of disputes. When Mr Clayton and Mr Lambrecht quarrelled in 1830, both resolved to settle their differences without a meeting, but the friend of Clayton intervened to urge them as to the impropriety of such an act, and in the subsequent duel Clayton was killed.[27] In 1835 Mr Dickenson quarrelled with Mr Symons over a ball ticket. On the day of the duel, Dickenson's second approached his counterpart, Mr Brodhurst, and declared that his principal was sorry for his conduct and prepared to apologise. Dickenson, however, had actually jostled Symons, and Brodhurst accordingly declared that he could not consent to an apology until they had exchanged shots. Brodhurst was thereby endangering his own principal, but he did not, of course, consult him, for he must not hesitate in hazarding his life in order to protect his honour.[28]

Mention of the hazarding of life brings us to the management of the meeting, should, as in the aforementioned case, this be deemed indispensable. The duties of

---

26 *The Times*, 20 Dec. 1814, p. 4, col. a.

27 *The Times*, 13 Jan. 1830, p. 2, col. f.

28 *The Times*, 17 Nov. 1835, p. 3, col. e.

the seconds on the field were substantially determined by the weapons deployed. Until the 1760s pistols were not commonly used in British duels, although the first recorded use occurred during the duel between Sir Chomley Deering and Col. Richard Thornhill in 1711.[29] The preferred weapon until the 1760s was the sword, although it had ceased to be part of a gentleman's normal attire a generation or so previously. A period of transition followed in the 1770s, during which time swords were still deployed, but as secondary weapons; thus, when Richard Brinsley Sheridan fought Mr Matthews in 1772, swords were drawn after a single discharge of pistols and the parties fought desperately hand to hand.[30] The same occurred during the course of the duels between Capt. Stoney and Reverend Bate in January 1777 and between Count Rice and Viscount Du Barry in November 1778.[31] After 1780, however, swords were rarely deployed. Millingen in his *History of Duelling* records the weapons used in twenty-one duels between 1780 and 1789 fought either in Britain itself or by British subjects abroad, and in only one of these was the sword employed. It is significant that this single sword encounter in 1784 concerned a British naval officer embroiled with a German officer; for German gentlemen, as well as for Frenchmen, Italians and others, the sword remained the weapon of choice and was utilised up until the very end of duelling itself.

The rejection of the sword in Britain, then, marked a distinct departure from the continental norm. The adoption of the pistol may have contributed to the distinctly different historical trajectory taken by the duel in Britain from that elsewhere, for although the duel was essentially extinct in Britain by 1850 it endured in mainland Europe into the early twentieth century. At first sight, though, the adoption of the pistol in preference to the sword might be thought to have actually broadened the base of those able to duel in Britain. While the sword was an instrument of skill, which required an expensive and specialist education to master, the pistol could be mastered with relative ease by those without the advantages conferred by the tuition of a fencing instructor. That pistols were the more equable weapons was certainly argued at the end of the eighteenth century when the anonymous author of 1793 declared their adoption 'fortunate' since 'Every swordsman knows how rarely the parties are of equal skill.'[32] The point had already been made by Cockburn in 1720 when he declared that it was 'base, for one of the sword, to call out another, who was

---

29 *The life and noble character of Richard Thornhill, esq. who had the misfortune to kill Sir Cholmley Deering, Bart. ... in a duel in Tuttle-Fields, on Wednesday 9th of May, 1711 (London, 1711), A true account of what past at the Old Bailey, May the 18th, 1711, relating to the trial of Richard Thornhill, esq. indicted for the murder of Sir Cholmley Deering, Bart.*, 2nd edn, (London, 1711).

30 Millingen, *The History of Duelling*, op. cit., vol. ii, p. 97.

31 Ibid., vol. ii, pp. 101–102.

32 Anon. *Advice to seconds*, op. cit., p. 22.

never bred to it, but wears it only for fashions sake.'[33] Certainly, there were those who preferred the pistol in consequence of their unfamiliarity with swordsmanship. Shoemaker reports a duel in 1761 in which the participants opted for pistols and frankly admitted their incompetence with edged weapons, and in 1766 a challenger specified pistols, stating, 'I suppose neither you nor I know enough of sharps to risque anything upon them.'[34] The pistol made it possible for a gentleman, perhaps a parvenu, to challenge another without disadvantage.

However, Shoemaker has rather controversially suggested that the adoption of the pistol 'led to a huge reduction in the mortality rate',[35] an assertion standing in flat contradiction to Simpson's declaration that 'Reliance on the pistol transformed the nature of the duel. It made the encounter more deadly, and it democratised the institution.'[36] Shoemaker's deployment of statistics to support his argument is rather confused, but he bases it upon a statistical analysis of 206 accounts of duels from 1660 to 1800. He states that 'More than a fifth of the 105 participants in sampled sword duels were killed, and another quarter were wounded; only half (51 per cent) of the participants escaped without significant injury.'[37] The casualty rate seems extraordinarily high although he asserts that it declined in the later eighteenth century. Five out of eighteen participants in sword duels he sampled between 1700 and 1725 were killed (28 per cent), whereas in sword duels sampled after 1750 only four out of twenty-two participants were reported killed (18 per cent). This reduction in mortality rates may, he considers, be explained by the development of fencing as a predominantly defensive skill and an increasing willingness upon the part of combatants to disengage at the first sign of blood.

By way of contrast Shoemaker finds that 'only 6.5 per cent of the 214 participants in pistol duels were killed and 71 per cent escaped without any injury.'[38] Unfortunately, he does not analyse these figures to see if mortality rates changed over time. Certainly, firearms evolved enormously during the eighteenth century, but, Shoemaker suggests, the effectiveness of better weapons was negated since 'developing conventions

---

33 J. Cockburn, *The History and Examination of Duels, Shewing their Heinous Nature and the Necessity of Supressing them*, 2 vols (London, 1720), p. 137, cited in Shoemaker, 'The taming of the duel, op. cit., p. 529.

34 See the duel between Mr Brice and Capt. Jasper in 1761, LMA, Accession 1268, 17 May 1761 and the challenge of Mr Knill in 1766. PRO, KB 33/17/2, Trinity 6 Geo. III, both cited ibid. p. 529.

35 Shoemaker, 'The taming of the duel', op. cit., p. 528.

36 Simpson, 'Dandelions', op. cit., 119.

37 It is unclear why Shoemaker arrives at an odd number for the participants in these duels, nor, understandably, does he define what he considers to be a 'serious injury'.

38 Shoemaker, 'The taming of the duel', op. cit., p. 528. Assuming 214 pistol duellists equates to 107 duels and 105 (?) duellists equates to 52 duels, this leaves some 47 duels unaccounted for – duels, I presume, where the weapons employed are unknown.

prevented duellists from benefiting from the increasing accuracy of their pistols, and any skills they possessed ... what is impressive is how robust the rules for maintaining fair play and reducing bloodshed actually were.'[39] For example, duellists were not supposed to take aim, but to fire in a single movement.

Perhaps this was so but life and death were at stake, and we do know of duellists who practised at targets beforehand, who half rifled their duelling pistols to improve their accuracy, or who indeed fired with deliberate aim. Now, one may imagine that a determined sword duel, where parties slashed at each other, might well not end until both parties were wounded, fatally or not. It was said that if the swordsmen were of equal skill, 'a number of wounds may be received on both sides, before the conflict is ended. Every surgeon knows the ugly consequence of all such wounds, their extremities being so deep and small as to be hardly come at.'[40] By contrast, the wound sustained from a pistol ball was usually so conclusive that it terminated the affair at once, without harm to the other party. The total number of wounds in sword duels is then very likely to have been greater than in pistol duels, for both parties were very likely to receive some laceration from the encounter.

However, Shoemaker is on much more uncertain ground when he makes the asser-tion that 'The switch to pistols thus improved the chances of surviving a duel by a factor of approximately three.' The arguments against his hypothesis are compelling. First, it is notable that Shoemaker ignored the European dimension in considering the evolution of the duel. If, put crudely, it was observable to contemporaries that one was so very much more likely to survive a pistol duel than one fought with swords, one would have to come up with very powerful reasons why France, Germany, Italy and others did not adopt the pistol more readily! It cannot be that these nations wished to preserve the full danger of duelling through the nineteenth century for they clearly did so much to 'sanitise' sword duelling in the second half of the century. In fact in France and Germany a pistol duel was taken to be the more serious encounter, the choice of weapons indicating a particular determination for blood. European nations preserved the sword because they were able to finesse the encounters, to formalise the passes and to adapt both sword and clothing to such a degree that casualties in Euro-pean duels declined dramatically. I shall refer later to the very low fatality rates in later European sword duels – so low, in fact, that they became the subject of parody. Perhaps the second argument against Shoemaker's assertion that the pistol was seen as very much safer than the sword is that in the virile culture of the late eighteenth century I can find no evidence that anyone was ever taunted for having chosen this instrument of reparation. Shoemaker makes much out of a single reference to the diffi-culty of treating sword wounds, but I have found no occasion upon which the

---

39 Ibid., p. 533.

40 Anon., *Advice to seconds*, op. cit., p. 22.

choice of pistol over sword occasioned adverse comment. While honour theorists commented that the pistol was a fairer means of resolution, none of them affirmed that it was also safer. Third, and crucially, the smaller data set which Shoemaker employs somewhat unsystematically does little to rebut the evidence presented in Antony Simpson's much more systematic study of duels fought between 1785 and 1850.

In total Simpson has surveyed 840 duels involving 1680 duellists and noted some 229 fatalities, a death rate of some 14 per cent for the entire period, which is more than twice that suggested by Shoemaker.[41] For my own part I have revisited *The Times* reports via means of the digital archive and surveyed the accounts of 834 duels of British subjects at home and abroad between 1785 and 1844. These were overwhelmingly pistol duels and during their course some 277 duellists were reported killed, 16.6 per cent of the total number. A further 341 were reported injured, taking the death or injury rate to some 37 per cent overall. What both Simpson's survey and my own suggest is that casualty rates were not significantly lower in the early pistol duels of the later eighteenth century than they were in the sword duels of the second half of the eighteenth century. Perhaps they were a fraction less bloody, but then, as Shoemaker implies and others have argued, men, including gentlemen, were becoming less bloodthirsty as the eighteenth century wore on – whatever implement they employed. One cannot close, however, without admitting the difficulties with all these statistics. On the one hand, the sources rarely followed the progress of wounds and, with the uncertain medicine of the age, it is unclear how many wounds thought non-fatal actually turned out to be so. Upon the other, it seems logical to suppose that duels in which there were no serious injuries were far more likely to go unreported than ones in which death or injury had occurred. Our statistics may therefore make the duel appear a somewhat more dangerous enterprise than was actually the case. What is clear, however, is that there is no firm evidential foundation for the assertion that the rejection of the sword in favour of the pistol marked a fundamental diminution in the dangers of duelling.

This is not to say, of course, that all duels were equally hazardous. In so far as seconds were active during the final years of the sword duel, it was to observe the 'passes' between parties and to attempt to call a halt should one party be wounded. Not infrequently, however, they could but look on while the parties hacked each other. Aside from observing the absence of foul play, their role in determining the outcome of the actual combat was probably rather less important than it was later to become. When the pistol duel was adopted, however, the determination of the distance the parties were to stand at and the number of shots fired was most important in determining the likelihood of harm or fatality. Such crucial decisions were properly the province

---

41 Simpson, 'Dandelions', op. cit., Table 1, pp. 106–107.

of the seconds, and it seems that most gentlemen adhered to this unwritten rule. Following the duel between Wellington and Winchilsea, it was observed that upon the field itself:

> The principals are supposed to commit themselves entirely to the guidance of the seconds and they become in these hands almost passive agents ... The Duke conformed himself strictly to this rule and I could not help admiring how meekly and submissively he conducted himself through the whole of the affair.[42]

When Winchilsea, by contrast, had earlier begun to interest himself in the negotiations to end the matter bloodlessly, Wellington's second, Lord Hardinge, had promptly scolded him: 'Lord Winchilsea, this is an affair of the seconds!'

It became established that ten or twelve paces were the normal distances for an encounter.[43] The author of the *General Rules and Instructions for All Seconds*, however, protested in 1793 that:

> This being a matter entirely in the Breasts of the Seconds, where neither Heat nor Animosity can be supposed to exist, one cannot but wonder at the bloody distances which are sometimes given; Eight and Seven yards are not infrequent ... I certainly think that Ten Yards is the nearest Distance the Parties should be suffered to fight at ... in the settling of Trivial Disputes (which are far the greatest Number) Twelve or More Yards might well be given.[44]

The Times was scathing of an occasion where the distance was set at twenty paces but professed to be appalled at a duel in Gibraltar in 1831 where the seconds set a distance of only four paces. One pistol fortunately misfired and one party fired deliberately into the air. 'Had death ensued at this meeting, all living parties would most assuredly have been hanged.'[45] Much, it seems, depended upon the pugnacity of the opponents, the egregious nature of the offence, or sometimes the zealotry of the seconds. When a Lt W. and a Capt. I. met in 1803, the seconds of W. insisted that the encounter should be at no more than six paces. The seconds of I. objected, but

---

42 Papers relating to Napoleon, Wellington and the Duke of York, entry of 21 Mar. 1829. Miscellaneous Papers of the 5th Countess of Jersey, LMA ACC/1128/220–223, the British Library, London.

43 The distances set by the seconds were frequently omitted by the duelling reports. However, in a survey of seventy-nine reports where distances were named, I found two cases where duels were fought at the extreme distance of 20 paces (or yards), five cases in which a distance of 15 paces was set, one fought at 14 paces, one at 13, thirty-seven cases at 12, one at 11, and fifteen duels at 10. Close-quarter duels were not, however, that infrequent: there were two fought at 9 paces, six at 8, three at 7 paces, two at 6, one at 5, two at 4, and one at just 3 paces.

44 Anon., *General Rules*, op. cit., pp. 24–26.

45 *The Times*, 16 Aug. 1831, p. 2, col. f.

those of W. prevailed. The result was a rare instance when both parties were killed almost instantaneously.[46]

Although there were occasional and sometimes rather theatrical elaborations, by far the most common practice in pistol duels was for the seconds to pace out the distance and for the principals to stand sideways to their opponent at the appointed marks. First, though, they had to charge the pistols, itself a delicate operation. Abraham Bosquett reported that nervous seconds sometimes loaded badly or even wounded themselves or their principals by discharging a weapon accidentally. The seconds also had to decide upon the mode of firing, and three choices presented themselves. First, they might arrange that the parties fire at the same moment, upon a signal given by one of the seconds. Second, they might decide by the toss of a coin which of the parties was to fire first. Third, if there was a sense that one of the parties was in the wrong in the dispute, the wronged party might be given first fire.

The second and third alternatives allowed shots to be discharged un-hurriedly by the duellist without the anxiety that his opponent was about to fire. The *General Advice to Seconds* was scathing of these practices, asking, 'if this is not reducing the Business to *cool, alternative Firing*, provided it should even happen that the first shot miscarries. Now, if ever was a more *bloody* System introduced into the World, I leave the World to judge.'[47] Interestingly, the author denounced the notion that the aggrieved party should have first fire as 'absurd' and demanded to know 'from what authority they take upon themselves so great a Power ... can it operate to any good Purpose on the *Mind* of the injured person?'[48]

As I shall discuss later, in the final years of the duel there were an increasing number of formulaic encounters in which an aggrieved party would indeed fire first at his opponent (sometimes wilfully missing) and his opponent, if unscathed, would in turn fire into the air. This, though, both marked an important conceptual shift in honour culture and did much to discredit duelling. Much the most common practice for most of the history of the pistol duel was for both parties to fire together, upon either a word or a signal from one of the seconds. The *General Instructions for All Seconds* was clear that this was the most humane since the hurried aim of both parties resulted in fewer casualties. The parties readied themselves by standing sideways, thus reducing the area of the body presented as a target, while the pistol arm itself served as some protection to the vital organs. The pistol was held in the lowered arm, and upon the word or signal, the arm was raised and the pistol fired in a single movement. Although there were no formal sanctions available, pausing to take deliberate aim breached the etiquette prescribed in the duelling manuals. Thus, when Mr Trant took

---

46 Millingen, *The History of Duelling*, op. cit., vol. ii, pp. 165–166.

47 Anon., *General Advice to Seconds*, op. cit., p. 28, original italics.

48 Ibid., p. 29.

careful aim at Sir John Conway in 1787, Conway protested to his second, 'By the Lord! That damned Jesuit will shoot me!' A moment later he was dead.[49] Similarly, the use of more accurate, rifled barrels was deplored – hence the proposal to lay a criminal information against Castlereagh in 1814 for allegedly using them during his duel with Canning.[50]

If one of the parties was hit at first fire, it was the duty of his second to procure him medical attention. Not infrequently, surgeons were engaged to attend the duel. Although there were evidential difficulties in prosecuting attending surgeons as accomplices, some took the precaution of turning their backs at the moment of firing so as not to have witnessed the felonious act. Upon other occasions surgeons sometimes testified that they had 'chanced upon' wounded duellists, albeit at the most remote locations and in the early hours. The opposing principal and second were also obligated to assist the wounded man, remaining upon the ground until all possible assistance had been procured or, if necessary, conveying the corpse to a suitable location – before very likely evading the attentions of the law. If no injury had been occasioned, then the question arose as to whether the matter should proceed further. A goodly proportion of duels were settled in circumstances where the first fire had failed to cause a casualty. Offending parties were often afraid that should they apologise prior to a duel, that action would be interpreted by society as a sign of cowardice; similarly, those who had been offended feared that failure to go through with a meeting would be interpreted as a sign of a lack of resolve. Having exposed themselves to hazard, both could now be reconciled without stain upon their honour.

A considerable number of meetings, however, went to second, third or sometimes even more salvoes. Sometimes this was at the instigation of impassioned, determined principals who overbore the objections of moderating seconds, but occasionally it was at the insistence of seconds whose zealous sensitivity to honour seemed to far outrun that of their principals. Where principals displayed particular vindictiveness, seconds sometimes simply refused to participate further, leaving the parties the choice of proceeding without the witnesses. When Mr Barrow met Mr Hagan in Jersey in 1799, both exchanged three shots without success. Capt. Lee, the second to Barrow, proposed that both parties shake hands. Upon their refusal he quitted the ground in protest. Unfortunately, Hagan's second remained and the duel continued until Barrow was killed.[51] The meeting between Capt. T. and Mr H. in 1829 would have gone to a third fire but for the seconds, who declared their intention to withdraw despite the protests of both parties.[52] Few went so far as the second in 1818

---

49 Re-told in *The Times*, 14 Apr. 1829, p. 3, col. b.

50 *The Times*, 18 Aug. 1814, p. 3, col. c.

51 *The Times*, 8 Apr. 1799, p. 3, col. b.

52 *The Times*, 7 Oct. 1829, p. 3, col. d.

who, determined to prevent a duel at all, ran off with one of the pistols and was in return fired upon by one of the duellists.[53]

Sometimes, though, it might be the seconds who insisted that the demands of honour had not been met and that the matter required further salvoes. In 1821 a Mr Christie and Mr Scot duelled. However, at the first fire Mr Christie did not aim at his opponent. Christie's second, Mr Trail, had observed this, but not the other parties. Mr Trail then called out, rebuking his principal and instructing him to take proper aim next time, whereupon Scot, whose shot had simply missed, exclaimed, 'What! Did not Mr Christie fire at me?' Presumably, he intended to terminate the encounter there, but he was in turn rebuked by his own second, Mr Patmore, who declared, 'You must not speak, 'tis now of no use to talk, you have nothing now for it but firing.' Both men resumed their positions and Scot was mortally wounded.[54]

While honour may be internally felt, it was and is, seemingly inseparable from its public dimension. Honour exists in large measure insofar as it is acknowledged by others. Furthermore, it contains within it something of an uncompromising aspect, for so many of the compromises one makes for immediate self-interest have about them something of a dishonourable quality. In the honour-driven society of the late eighteenth and early nineteenth centuries, compromise was no easy thing. By appointing seconds, principals enunciated their desire for an honourable resolution. When they failed to do so, the absence of seconds was similarly indicative of a determination to go beyond what honour demanded and was therefore a manifestation of a malign disposition that might count against a defendant in court. In the nineteenth century no British subject is known to have been executed for having killed another in a duel save one: Maj. Campbell. While serving in a Scottish regiment in Ireland in 1808 he had quarrelled with a Capt. Boyd and they had met in a hurried duel behind closed doors and without seconds. Sabine put it succinctly: Campbell's offence was not that he had killed Boyd, but 'that he killed him contrary to established rules.' When Campbell was brought to trial, the presiding judge invited the jury to consider the words of the dying Capt. Boyd: 'You have hurried me; I wanted to wait and have friends. Campbell you are a bad man.' The judge directed that if these words were sufficiently proved, they 'did away with all extenuation ... the deceased will then have been hurried into the field; the contract of opposing life to life could not have been perfect.'[55]

The task of arranging such a contract fell properly to the seconds, and the reward for their efforts lay in the fact that a duel affirmed their own honour in the strongest of terms. When men, who guarded their honour more zealously than their lives,

---

53 *The Times*, 12 May 1818, p. 3, col. e.

54 Millingen, *History of Duelling*, op. cit., pp. 244–252.

55 Sabine, *Notes on Duels and Duelling*, op. cit., p. 72.

entrusted that honour to the care of others, they conferred the highest of compliments. The seconds, however, required strong nerves, for the social capital that they had accrued could be dissipated in an instant by some unworthy conduct. The seconds who fled the field in 1838 after the duel between Mr Eliot and Mr Mirfin were widely despised. We cannot know, but we may suppose that there were those who accepted their appointment as a second in the belief that a dispute could be readily settled. When that proved not to be the case, there must have been some seconds who regretted their choice and who regarded the looming prospect of an actual encounter with dread. Such men were the counterparts of those duellists who hastily gave or accepted a challenge and then lived, or did not live, to regret it.

Ultimately, the particular form of honour culture that characterised late eighteenth and early nineteenth-century England depended upon the final willingness of some men to risk a possible physical extinction rather than a certain social one. This, though, was very much the final resort. It was the seconds who provided the mechanism by which most honour disputes eventually resulted in a peaceful resolution. It was they who enabled reconciliation, by warranting to the rest of society that though an accord had been reached, it had been concluded upon terms that did not compromise the interests of the broader society of gentlemen. On those rare occasions when an accommodation could not be reached, it was the duty of those selfsame men to assist upon the field and to restrain the arbitrary and indiscriminate violence that would supposedly have otherwise resulted. As we shall see, however, it remains a moot point whether the seconds were, by the nineteenth century, indeed necessary to prevent the return to the violent affrays of the early modern period or whether their encouragement and occasional instigation of duels merely served to prolong the life of an institution doomed to collapse in the face of the advance of modernity.

7

The Contest in the
Courtroom: Duelling and the
Criminal Justice System

Chapter 6 alluded to the very public nature of honour disputes, disputes that were often played out through the medium of the press. It gives one some pause for thought to reflect that by turns seconds or principals were advertising their intent to commit a criminal offence or recording in print that an offence had already been committed. Here, then, I intend to explore the relationship between honour culture and the law, but the very fact that unlawful acts were openly advertised of itself says much about the general effectiveness of the legal system in punishing duellists. Nevertheless, some have attributed the demise of duelling, at least in part, to the allegedly increasingly severe attitude taken by the courts to those who had killed during the course of a duel. For reasons that will become apparent, I shall doubt that that was indeed the case.

The common law position that to encompass the death of another in a duel was murder has already been considered in Chapter 1. There were in addition a number of statutes available to the courts which might theoretically have been deployed in this context. However, neither the Stabbing Act 1604,[1] which dealt with fatal stabbings committed in heat, nor the Black Act 1723,[2] which among many other things dealt with shootings, was ever intended to be and was ever applied to the penalisation of duellists. Yet in 1803 Parliament passed a further act which seemed ideally suited to application in the suppression of duelling. The so-called 'Ellenborough Act' made it a capital offence to 'shoot at, stab or cut' another, regardless of whether any injury was inflicted.[3] In a sense, the very severity of the act might be supposed to have made some reluctant to apply it in the context of duelling, although to an extent this objection was nullified by a later reform of the act in 1837 which made the offence capital only if an injury had occurred.

---

1   2 Jac. I, c. 8.

2   9 Geo. I, c. 22

3   43 Geo. III, c. 58.

In practice, however, the Ellenborough Act was not to be deployed against duellists – although lawyers and parliamentarians were aware of the possibility that it might be. Following the duel between the Duke of Wellington and Lord Winchilsea (over the foundation of King's College) in 1829 the peers briefly considered whether or not to try Wellington under the Ellenborough Act, but the political implications were such that they quickly abandoned the idea.[4] In truth, right up until the end of duelling the state acknowledged no active duty to intervene and prosecute offenders in cases where duels had not in fact led to a fatality. This might be partly explained by the fact that it was not until 1834 that the first public prosecutors were introduced into the Old Bailey by Lord Brougham. Magistrates could bind over for trial, but they rarely chose to do so unless there had been a homicide. Thus when Gen. Moore wounded Mr Stapleton in 1832, he was indeed bound over, but once it became clear Stapleton would survive, the prosecution was dropped. In 1843 *The Times* could still lament the absence of a public prosecutor to lead in duelling cases and declare, 'We must claim for the future that our criminal procedure be no longer trusted to the hesitating hands of individuals.'[5] One difficulty in appointing a public prosecutor in such matters lay in the fact that political contentions lay behind some of the animosities that resulted in duels. Public prosecutions in such circumstances would inevitably be tainted by the suspicion of political partisanship. One can scarce imagine the consequences had the, in the event harmless, duel of 1829 led to the trial and conviction of Wellington.

However, where a death had occurred in a duel, the duellist might find himself indicted either by a coroner's jury or else prosecuted on behalf of the estate of the deceased. Yet in 1738 Samuel Madden had written that it was safer to kill a man in a duel than steal a sheep or cow.[6] This was still entirely true in 1814. In an oft-cited passage, *The Edinburgh Review* declared:

> This law is a mere dead letter; for what with the unwillingness of prosecutors, the connivance first of police-officers, then of judges – the feelings of juries, and the corresponding feeling in the place of last resort, no instance is known of the law being executed against any person for being engaged in a duel, fought in what is called a fair manner.[7]

This despite the fact that in 1803 and the case of *R. v Rice* Mr Justice Grose J. had declared that to kill a man in a duel was murder and 'to every lawyer this is a

---

4   University College London, the Brougham Papers, HB/34247. Letter of George Eden, Earl of Auckland, to Henry Brougham, 25 Mar. 1829.

5   *The Times*, 20 Jul. 1843, p. 4, col. b.

6   Samuel Madden, *Reflections and Resolutions Proper for the Gentlemen of Ireland* (Dublin, 1738), cited in Kelly, *That Damn'd Thing Called Honour*, op. cit., p. 65.

7   *Edinburgh Review*, 1814, p. 74.

proposition perfectly clear'.[8] Even as late as 1841 the *Morning Chronicle* was printing a letter which, it claimed, captured the flavour of the duelling trial:

> The counsel for the Crown details the case, lays down the law ... then concludes by telling the jury, that, if the facts are as he has stated them, he cannot see how they can avoid pronouncing the verdict of guilty; but he feverently hopes that something may arise to relieve them of that duty. In the examination of the evidence, everybody is aware that the Judge, the counsel on both sides and the witnesses, are straining all their ingenuity to prevent a verdict against the prisoners; and everybody sympathises with their endeavours. His Lordship, in his charge to the jury, explains to them again that every man killed in a duel is murdered; but he at the same time shows that there are some technical defects in the evidence, which he places before them in a strong light. The jury turn around for a few minutes and find a verdict of not guilty. Upon this there is a considerable applause manifested among the auditory, which meets with the reprehension of his Lordship, who threatens to commit the offenders. The court is now cleared, all the world is pleased to find that poor Smith is acquitted, agrees that duels are horrid things, and hopes that, as they become common, the Judge will direct the next man who fights one to be hanged.[9]

Among many other things, the letter suggests that the declarations of the court upon such matters could not be taken at face value: there was much happening in the duelling trial that could not be openly acknowledged. Of course, very few duellists were actually brought to trial in the first place. I have found evidence of only thirty-six proceedings initiated against duellists and/or their seconds for homicide between 1785 and 1845. No doubt there are more, but of these, in two cases the indicted parties absconded and were never tried, and in six cases the final verdicts are not known. Of the rest, there were eighteen trials that concluded in verdicts of acquittal, seven that resulted in verdicts of manslaughter and three that resulted in murder verdicts. In the case of the murder convictions the capital sentences were later commuted to terms of imprisonment.[10] When one considers that there were at the very least two hundred deaths in England and Wales occasioned by duelling during this period, one observes that the probability of any particular duellist being indicted and then convicted was small indeed.

The Crown's officers may have been at times lethargic, but one of the reasons that so few duellists were indicted was that many gentlemen refused to cooperate in

---

8 *R.* v *Rice* 1803, 3 East 581.

9 *Morning Chronicle*, 22 Feb. 1841, reproducing an article from *Knight's Quarterly Magazine c.*1820.

10 Note that these statistics refer to the number of court cases rather than the number of parties concerned. For example, both Mr Young and Mr Webber were indicted together in 1838 for their role as seconds in the duel that led to the death of Mr Mirfin, and I have counted their joint conviction for murder as one instance of a trial that ended with that verdict.

prosecuting them. In 1843 *The Times* found it remarkable that during the inquest upon the duellist Col. Fawcett no one volunteered to identify the body, despite the fact that many of his friends and family were in the room at the time. Social pressure or conscience operated powerfully, even so as to prevent the dying from naming their adversary. Mr Stewart, who was found mortally wounded in Liverpool in 1800, would not do so.[11] In 1804 Lord Camelford positively forbade a gardener to detain the man who had shot him and subsequently instructed his family not to prosecute.[12] In 1809 Assistant Surgeon O'Hagan urged his opponent to flee before the arrival of constables.[13] In 1830 Mr Clayton begged as he lay dying that there be no prosecution as all had been conducted fairly.[14] Non-cooperation was the order of the day at the trial of Col. Wood at Aylesbury Assizes for killing the Honourable Mr Cooper: none of the subpoenaed witnesses attended, and the judge had to order the jury to acquit.[15]

In respect of the trial process itself, however, examination of the aforementioned thirty-six proceedings shows that once duellists were indicted grand juries rarely quashed those indictments against then, presumably because they did wish the conduct of the parties to be assayed at trial. This is interesting because the grand juries were recruited from precisely those classes of men within the penumbra of the duel. The grand jury at Norfolk Assizes in 1772, for example, consisted of the Honourable Henry Hobart, Sir Armine Wodehouse Baronet, Sir Edward Astley Baronet, Sir Harbord Harbord Baronet and eighteen others listed as esq.[16] By contrast, Beattie characterises trial jurors at Kingston as 'tradesmen and craftsmen of the town and small property owners'.[17] The petty jurors for Essex in 1783 were farmers, shopkeepers, tradesmen, oyster dredgers, bricklayers and weavers.[18] In other words, although men within the penumbra of the duel were sending duellists on to trial, it was men below the status of gentlemen who were required to judge them.

The charge under consideration being a felony, duellists brought to court laboured until 1836 under the 'felony counsel restriction' whereby defence advocacy was limited to putting forward points of law, cross-examining prosecution witnesses and calling witnesses for the defence. Furthermore, until the Criminal

---

11 *Hampshire Telegraph,* 4 Aug. 1800, p. 4, col. c.

12 *The Times*, 13 Mar. 1804, p. 3, col. d.

13 *The Times*, 21 Jun. 1809, p. 3, col. d.

14 *The Times*, 3 Apr. 1830, p. 5, col. d.

15 *Manchester Mercury*, 15 Mar. 1825, p. 4, col. c.

16 Norfolk County Records Office WLS/XLVI/8-12/425.

17 J. M. Beattie, *Crime and the Courts in England 1660–1800* (Oxford: Clarendon Press, 1986), p. 388.

18 Essex Record Office Q/J 1/11.

Evidence Act 1898[19] the defendant was not competent to give evidence on oath and be examined, but was confined to a statement to the jury. The consequence was that the duelling trial was constructed rather less as a matter of evidence and argument and rather more as a contest of honour. The defendant strove to represent himself as a gentleman who should not be captured by the processes applicable to the chastisement of the common felon, as a man upon whom the criminal process had no claim. Not all judges were prepared to challenge this assertion. Some demonstrated their sympathies by displaying an exceptional solicitude for the well-being of the defendant, which signalled from the first that this was no ordinary defendant brought before the courts. When the wounded Capt. Watson appeared at Kingston Assizes in 1796 charged with the murder of Maj. Sweetman, Baron Hotham:

> With his accustomed humanity and politeness, paid every attention to the prisoner. This excellent judge, the mild ornament and pride of British justice, ordered the windows to be let down to admit the fresh air, and the avenues and approaches of the Court to be cleared of the mob, that the unfortunate young Gentleman, who was brought on men's shoulders to the bar of the court to be tried, might be every way accommodated.[20]

When Henry Hunt was tried in 1818 for issuing a challenge, the judge allowed him to sit among the barristers and turned down the request of the prosecution that he be brought to the bar like any other defendant.[21]

In terms of procedure, duelling trials, like most others of the period, were extremely short. The prosecution commenced with an opening address and then summoned his witnesses. The depositions lodged in respect of these were not available to the defence, but at this stage the judge might question the witnesses upon them. This normally concluded the prosecution's case. Having opened, the prosecuting counsel was not permitted to close or to rebut the defence that followed. He could therefore neither challenge the character of the defendant as given by witnesses nor assault the veracity of the statement made by the defendant himself. Whilst the prosecutor was restricted in his ability to make reference to character, the defence, via statement and witness, was not. The duty of the prosecution, then, would appear to have been limited to the proof of fact. However, the fact of the killing itself, and the identity of the perpetrator, was not contested during any of the trials detailed below. When opening the case against Mr England in 1796 Sgt Adair noted, 'The fact that death was occasioned by the prisoner at the bar, will, I am afraid, not be a matter of much

---

19 61 & 62 Vict. c. 36.

20 *The Times*, 25 Mar. 1796, p. 2, col. d.

21 *The Times*, 27 Oct. 1818, p. 3, col. c.

doubt or enquiry.'[22] Mr Knopp was correct (and correctly critiqued the verdict) when he opened against Capt. MacNamara in 1803 with the contention that there was 'very little law in the case'.[23] By the time of the trial itself, a coroner's jury and usually a grand jury had already considered the evidence. The factual inquiry had to be complete before the trial proper began; the prosecution could not hope to bolster its case upon the errors or omissions of the defence.

The limitations of the process were exemplified by the prosecution of Lt Fisher in 1806 for the killing of Lt Torrence. The grand jury had, unusually, thrown out the bill of indictment, so Fisher was arraigned upon the coroner's inquest. The prosecution summoned as a witness the regimental surgeon who had attended the duel. However, he declined to give evidence. A fellow officer reported that on the evening before the duel Torrence had come to his room and admitted that he had struck Fisher on the parade ground (an event presumably witnessed by many) and that he intended to duel with him. The officer reported that Torrence had then called for his pistols and left. Torrence's servant reported that he had found his master dying the following morning but that he had not named his killer. At this point the Lord Chief Baron intervened: the circumstantial evidence against Fisher might be thought overwhelming, but the fact that there was no witness to the duel itself led the Baron to conclude that there was no evidence at all against the defendant. He immediately directed the jury to acquit. The defence, therefore, never presented, and Fisher was never called upon to deny that he had shot Torrence.[24]

The ability of the prosecution to find witnesses to duels was greatly impaired by the criminal culpability of the seconds and, indeed, anyone else aiding and abetting. Notwithstanding this, seconds were upon occasion prepared to incriminate themselves in order to testify that a duel had been properly conducted. In 1784 Mr Delaney gave evidence for his principal, Mr Allen. In 1794 Gen. Stanwix, the second of the deceased Mr Roper, gave evidence in favour of the man who had shot Roper, Mr Purefoy.[25] In *R. v England* 1796[26] the court considered whether the court could offer Mr Donnisthorpe, one of the seconds, immunity from prosecution in order to elicit testimony. Mr Justice Rooke and Sgt Adair, for the prosecution, opined that the attorney general could grant a 'nolle prosequi' upon the application of the court. For the defence Mr Erskine and Mr Garrow objected that this would be 'making a promise that the Court cannot legally do' and pointed out the novelty of such an

---

22 *R. v England* 1796, 2 Leach 767, 168 ER 483. *Old Bailey Proceedings Online* (www.oldbaileyonline.org, 1 Oct. 2009), 17 Feb. 1796, trial of Richard England (ref. t17960217-27).

23 *The Times*, 23 Apr. 1803, p. 2, cols d–f.

24 *R. v Fisher* 1806. *The Times*, 28 Jul. 1806, p. 3, col. b.

25 *R. v Purefoy* 1794. *The Times*, 16 Aug 1794, p. 3, col. b.

26 R. v *England,* 2 Leach 767, at 769.

immunity. Rooke eventually agreed that the court had no power to promise immunity from prosecution. He then instructed Donnisthorpe as follows:

> [The court] cannot compel you to be examined, but if you chuse to be examined, you must fulfil the terms of your oath, which is, to tell every thing you know, the truth the whole truth and nothing but the truth ... if you are examined, you will be liable to the whole cross-examination of the counsel for the prisoner; and you must tell everything you know respecting this business.

Faced with the possibility of prosecution Donnisthorpe declined to give evidence at all.

As well as the seconds, it was also possible to construe a surgeon engaged to attend the field as an aider and abettor of the offence. This circumstance led a number of surgeons to claim that they had chanced upon wounded men in the early hours at some very remote locations. At the very least, surgeons were disposed to turn their backs at the moment of firing, so as to be able to say in truth that they had not witnessed the fatal act. The surgeons could, of course, not be compelled to give evidence. For example, in 1841 the physician Sir James Eglinton Anderson was summoned by the prosecution in the case of Capt. Douglas to give testimony as to his presence at the duel between the Earl of Cardigan and Harvey Tuckett. He declined to answer any questions from Mr Justice Williams, who conceded that he might not be questioned to his own incrimination.[27]

There were, then, many evidential difficulties which the prosecution had to surmount in order to establish the actual occurrence of a duel and the participation of the defendant. Furthermore, prosecutors were aware of the instinctive sympathies of juries and that, if they wished to secure a conviction, then they would have to convince the jury that the death complained of had occurred in circumstances that took the matter outside of the honour paradigm. Juries were rarely prepared to convict where both parties had conducted themselves honourably and both had been at equal hazard. It was for this reason that the unusually vigorous prosecutors engaged by the relatives of the deceased in the prosecutions of both Mr Allen in 1782 and Mr England in 1796 concerned themselves much with the prior conduct of the defendants and rather less with the details of the homicidal acts themselves.

Mr Allen had become embroiled in the law in consequence of an advertisement he had placed anonymously in a newspaper in 1779. This had cast aspersions upon the character of an American landowner. The English brother of the landowner, a Mr Dulany, had responded by placing his own advertisement calling upon the man who had slighted his brother to declare himself. No reply had been received, and Dulany himself had had to leave England on business for two years. Upon his return

---

27 *R. v Douglas* 1841, Carrington and Moody 193, 174 ER 468.

to London he had received a note from Allen via his second, Mr Morris, who was also later indicted. This note had admitted Allen's authorship of the original piece and had dared Dulany to challenge him. They had met that same afternoon, 18 June 1781, and Dulany had been killed.

The duel had been witnessed by a number of passers by and Mr Silvester who was prosecuting summoned these witnesses first. Interestingly though, he left until last three witnesses who had no knowledge of the duel at all. They were called to testify to having witnessed Allen doing target practice immediately before the duel. Such would have constituted a breach of the honour code, and since he had not seen depositions, Mr Mansfield, for the defence, was momentarily discomforted. He then remarked to no one in particular that 'no such evidence was given before any Justice of the Peace ... This story of firing was perfectly new to every person acquainted with the case.' Allen's second addressed the jury to the effect that the accusation was untrue and the defence had, by chance, witnesses on hand prepared to swear to having been with Allen at the time of the alleged target shooting. In short, the defence did not dispute the encounter at all, but took pains to refute the allegation of dishonourable conduct.

In *R. v England*[28] the prosecutorix was the mother of the deceased, a Mr Rowls. The duel had arisen in consequence of a debt allegedly owed by Rowls to Mr England, which had caused the latter to publicly declare at a racecourse that no one should bet with Rowls since he did not pay his debts. Sgt Adair opened for the prosecution by distinguishing the encounter from that of the paradigmatic duel. He stressed that England had fled abroad for several years and had therefore failed to submit himself honourably and courageously to judgement. He alluded to the number of shots fired as evidence of malice and suggested that the defendant was motivated by an attempt to enforce a monetary payment, which took the affair outside the ambit of honour:

> The parties did not appear to be satisfied with that sort of vindication of their honour, which has prevailed in this unfortunate, fashionable mode of deciding differences; they did not satisfy themselves with exchanging each a shot, shewing they had kept their appointment, but shot after shot was fired ... the object of the duel was not so much the satisfaction of his [the prisoner's] honour, as either the fulfilling of his revenge for the injury he had sustained, in not being paid the full amount of the debt he had demanded, or enforcing that payment ... the subject of duelling when it is applied not to the restoration of injured honour, but to enforce the payment of debts, is equally repugnant to the principle of honour as of law.[29]

---

28 *Old Bailey Proceedings Online* (www.oldbaileyonline.org, 1 Oct. 2009), 17 Feb. 1796, trial of Richard England, (ref. t17960217-27).

29 Ibid.

The fact that the defendants were convicted in both the above cases, albeit of manslaughter, is perhaps testimony to the success of the prosecution in distinguishing the conduct of the accused from that expected of the idealised duellist.

Other prosecutions, though, commenced with something like an apology. *The Times* reported that the attorney general prosecuting Lt Rea at the Old Bailey in 1802 opened by stating that:

> Although an act of this kind was declared by law to be a murder, he must say, that in point of the moral guilt attached to it, it differed materially from other cases of murder. They all knew that what was called the law of honour, still sanctioned this crime, and the severity of public opinion sometimes unavoidably led to its commission.[30]

Mr Gurney who prosecuted Mr Lambrecht in 1830 conceded generously to the defendant that:

> He did not learn from the parties on the ground any thing that could suggest the idea of any unfair advantage being taken of Mr Clayton by Mr Lambrecht. When Mr Clayton fell, Mr Lambrecht approached him with feelings of great concern, and Mr Clayton returned his kindness by offering him his hand and expressing his full forgiveness.[31]

Mr Gurney concluded his address by informing the jury that the prosecution had been instituted in obedience to the findings of the coroner's jury, and the parish officers had been bound over to prosecute – in other words, that they had had no choice but to do so. Mr Broderick, also for the prosecution, then called the first witness, a surgeon, who promptly declared that he had found the wounded man, who had affirmed that all had been conducted fairly and had begged that there should be no prosecution. After such an opening, it is unsurprising that Lambrecht was acquitted, although the final direction of Mr Justice Bayley was robust, and seemingly directed as much at countering some of the barely concealed advocacy for leniency presented by the prosecution as well as the defence.

The very act of prosecution, it seemed, required justification, to be found in a disinterested duty to lay the matter before law's tribunal. In *England* it was said that the mother of the deceased was 'directed by the principles of public justice only ... if you should find yourselves warranted ... to release the prisoner at the bar, I trust the animosities will be buried in the grave of her son, and that she will be perfectly satisfied with your verdict.'[32] In *MacNamara* Mr Knopp informed the

---

30 *The Times*, 22 Sept. 1802, p. 3, col. a.

31 *R. v Lambrecht, Bigley and Cox. The Times*, 3 Apr. 1830, cols d–f, at col. d.

32 *Old Bailey Proceedings Online* (www.oldbaileyonline.org, 1 Oct. 2009), 17 Feb. 1796, trial of Richard England (ref. t17960217-27).

jury that the prosecutor had 'instructed him to lay the case, simply as it stood, before the jury; wishing only that it might undergo a fair investigation without desiring to gratify any thing like resentment.'[33] Similarly, in *Christie* Mr Walford declared the prosecution had been instituted by the relatives of the deceased, who 'disclaimed all vindictive feelings and were only anxious that the facts should be examined before the proper authorities and such conclusions be drawn from them as the law authorised.'[34]

For their part, defence counsels rarely cross-examined witnesses on the evidence; rather, they sought to elicit a statement that the duel had been fairly conducted. The trial, then, was constructed as a duality, with the prosecution speaking as to evidence and the defence as to character. A denial of ill will from the defendant was crucial to uphold that character. Addressing the jury, Mr Allen declared that he 'bore no malice, and had no intention to fight.'[35] Mr Purefoy asserted that he 'entertained no malice against the deceased and that he, felt not the asperity of revenge.'[36] Mr England claimed, 'my own conscience acquits me of malice.'[37] Capt. MacNamara declared that he had had no desire to take the life of his opponent. Finally, the counsel of Mr Lambrecht, Mr Adolphus, read out an address from Mr Lambrecht to the jury in his defence which dwelt extensively on the theme. He claimed that he was actuated by no feelings of malice:

> I am charged with the crime of wilful murder, of this high offence you cannot pronounce me guilty unless you are satisfied that in committing the act which unfortunately produced Mr Clayton's death, I was actuated by preconceived malice against him – unless in the language of the law, the act was committed with malice aforethought. I shall call before you witnesses who have been acquainted with my past life, and who know that so far from being capable of forming a malignant design against the life of man, that I am wholly incapable of entertaining malicious feelings of any kind.[38]

What is remarkable about these words is that the counsel must have known that they completely misrepresented the law by conflating the legal term 'malice aforethought' with the common language of maliciousness or evil intent.

---

33 *The Times*, 23 Apr. 1803, p. 2, col. d.

34 Millingen, *The History of Duelling*, op. cit., vol. ii., pp. 244–252

35 *Old Bailey Proceedings Online* (www.oldbaileyonline.org, 1 Oct. 2009), 5 Jun. 1782, trial of Bennet Allen (ref. t 17820605-1).

36 *The Times*, 16 Aug. 1794, p. 3, col. b.

37 *Old Bailey Proceedings Online* (www.oldbaileyonline.org, 1 Oct. 2009), 17 Feb. 1796, trial of Richard England (ref. t17960217-27).

38 *The Times*, 3 Apr. 1830, p. 5, cols d–f, at col. f.

The true legal definition of this term of art was given by Mr Justice Patteson in the trial of the seconds of Sir John Jeffcot in 1833. He directed the jury impeccably:

> It was charged that Sir John Jeffcot had done this with malice aforethought. Unless it was done with malice aforethought, the crime of murder was not committed. Malice afore-thought was not to be supposed to lead to the conclusion that any of those gentlemen had any private malice or ill will against Dr Hennis, or that they had the least wish he should fall ... Malice aforethought was not that of private ill will towards the party but it was the malice the law presumed when persons went out intending to commit an act which was in itself unlawful. If they found themselves obliged to find these gentlemen guilty, it would not proceed upon the supposition that they had ill blood but that they had done an act which the law said was murder.[39]

Legally, the term 'malice aforethought' was simply synonymous with an intent to commit an unlawful act; it was in no sense negated by the absence of the emotion of malice. However, judges who were sympathetic to duellists were not above misdi-recting juries in their summing up as to the law. Sometimes judges themselves adopted the definition of malice as propounded in *Lambrecht*. That is to say that they correctly distinguished between, upon the one hand, 'malice aforethought' – or as it was also referred to, 'implied malice' – and, upon the other hand, demonstrations of ill will that amounted to 'express malice.' They then went on to claim that, in contradic-tion to well-established principle, in duelling express malice had to be found before a verdict of murder could be returned. Of course, in the paradigmatic duel the rituals of act and expression were formulated precisely to suppress personal resentments, and where the duel had been properly conducted some judges were therefore erroneously suggesting that the offence could be only mere manslaughter.

Some judges were also keen to point out that the killing was similarly manslaughter if a partial defence of provocation could be accepted. However, the defence was actually rather clear: a killing done after provoking conduct from the deceased and committed while the perpetrator was still in hot blood might be deemed to be but manslaughter, if, that is, the provocation had been of sufficient seriousness. If, however, the blood had cooled by the time of the homicide and the act had therefore been deliberate, the offence was that of murder. Since, again, most duels were carefully arranged affairs occasioned by causes that were objectively slight, the provocation defence would not seem to have been one that should have been available to many duellists, but judges could be creative in suggesting that it might.

If one begins, though, with the exemplary direction of a judge who was known to be unsympathetic to duellists, one can see how a judge might be correctly dismissive

---

39 *R. v Halstead, Holland and Melford* 1833. *The Times,* 29 Jul. 1833, p. 6, col. b. Millingen, *History of Duelling,* op. cit., vol. ii, pp. 327–334.

of claims that non-legal issues should be allowed to interfere with verdicts. Mr Justice Buller directed in *Allen*[40] that 'Good character is no answer to the charge; and as far as the verdict goes we must adhere to the laws of the land.' When a witness claimed that nothing unfair had occurred in the duel, he observed, 'Taking that for a fact it makes no difference as to the law. If they went there for the purpose of fighting this duel deliberately, as death did ensue, it was murder in all concerned.' When it came to considering whether the partial defence of provocation might apply, he pointed out that three years had passed since the publication of the contentious article and the duel. Allen had been immediately challenged upon his return to England, before he had met his putative opponent and before anything else had passed between them. In other words there had been no sudden provoking act.

> Where then is the ground upon which you can say that there was any sudden quarrel or provocation? When they get to Hyde Park; Mr Delancey says, he remembers not a word was said by Mr Allen, except complaining that he had got a cold and thought it was damp ... Is this the conduct of a man in passion? Upon this evidence did they, or did they not, meet with a design to fight this duel; not upon any immediate provocation, or sudden quarrel, but from some motive which rankled in their minds for the space of three years together? If you are of opinion that they did, it is my duty to say to you, in direct words what the law is. And the law upon that case is that it is murder in the person that kills the other.

Contrast this, though, with Mr Justice Rooke's direction to the jury in *England*. He noted that after one exchange of shots between the parties, Lord Cremorne, who had 'chanced' to observe the encounter, had interfered and attempted to terminate the affair. At that point England had told Cremorne that he had been injured in his honour and cruelly treated. Rooke asked the jury the following:

> Consider whether these were the words of an angry injured man, who had received that morning any particular insult; or of a man who did what he did in consequence of what had passed the day before at Ascot races – If you think they are the words of a deliberate man, they make against him. If you think they are the words of an angry man, as relating to something that passed immediately before the duel, they are in his favour.

The objections to this direction are twofold. First, the evidential burden, the duty, that is, of producing some evidence that the defendant had been provoked, lay upon the defence, but the defence in *England* made no such claim. England and Rowls did not meet on the morning of the duel, other than at the moment of taking to the field, and there was no evidence of any communication passing between them. Second, it

---

40 *Old Bailey Proceedings Online* (www.oldbaileyonline.org, 1 Oct. 2009), 5 Jun. 1782, trial of Bennet Allen (ref. t 17820605-1).

mattered and still matters very much at what point the intent to commit the unlawful act is formulated. To give a modern analogy, suppose a man designs to shoot another; he acquires a pistol and goes off to where the man may be found. The victim may foully curse his would-be assassin such that at the moment of actually pulling the trigger the perpetrator is angry. This, however, would not suffice to ground the partial defence of provocation and reduce the offence to manslaughter, for the intent to commit the act will have been formulated before any infuriating conduct on the part of the deceased. The malice prepensed of murder would be evident both in the use of a weapon and in the pre-existing design. In *England* the challenge had been issued (itself an indictable misdemeanour) and accepted. Both had then come to the field armed, after the blood had cooled (from the day before), in contemplation of the commission of a felony. Rooke, though, speculated upon the basis of no evidence that something might have passed between the parties before the discharge of pistols and, furthermore, directed that if the defendant had been angry at the moment of the homicide then this would in law negate his calm and pre-existing determination to perform the unlawful act. Finally, the earlier authorities were adamant that it was not enough that the perpetrator was provoked at the time of the killing; he had to be able to show that the provocation offered by the deceased had been substantial.

The judge's direction then was unsound for three reasons. First, there was no evidence of provocative conduct immediately before the duel. Second, even if there had been, provocative conduct at the time of the homicide should not have been allowed in law to negate the already formulated intent to commit the unlawful act. Third, even if it had been allowed (wrongly) to do so, the court should still have had to consider the nature of the provocation. Neither in law nor in evidence was there room for a defence of provocation, but the jury nonetheless accepted the proffered invitation and returned a verdict of manslaughter.

Other judges were similarly indifferent to the requirements of evidence. In the 1818 case of *O'Callaghan*[41] very little was known to the court about the duel other than the fact that the defendant and the deceased had quarrelled a full day before the fatal affair. The defence chose to make no defence to the charge at all. O'Callaghan himself presented a brief written statement as to his regret at the death and his willingness to accept the verdict of the court. The two seconds indicted with him said nothing, and neither did counsel upon their behalf. Mr Justice Parke, though, noted to the jury that he had 'already said that malice might be expressed or implied. In duelling it must be expressed. It was for the Jury to say whether malice was expressed in this case'.[42] In other words, the charge could not be established unless the prosecution proved through express declaration the malignant intent to kill.

---

41 *The Times*, 17 Jan. 1818, p. 3, cols c–d.

42 Ibid.

Shortly afterwards Parke went even further when he not only placed upon the prosecution the onus of rebutting a partial defence of provocation that the defence had not pleaded but also entirely fancifully envisaged circumstances under which the jury might feel that the homicide could have been carried out in hot blood. His difficulty was that the only known quarrel had occurred twenty-four hours before the duel:

> If the prisoners went deliberately to the field, where the deceased was shot, it was murder, but, if they went thither suddenly and in the heat of blood, *and no appearance to the contrary was proved,* they might, for ought that appeared, have passed the preceding night in a tavern, and gone forth before their blood had cooled in a kind of furore, if this was the case it was manslaughter ... Here it did not appear when the quarrel took place. The circumstance that had caused the quarrel had happened on the preceding morning; *they might have afterwards met in a tavern or playhouse and proceeded to fight in the heat of blood.*[43]

The men may have repaired to taverns after their quarrel, he suggested, and with a bout of prolonged drinking, their hot tempers may not have cooled during the long hours up until the duel. Lest this be too ambitious, Parke also fell back upon the approach adopted in *England*. Perhaps the men had not formed the intent to commit the unlawful act after their initial quarrel, perhaps there had been a further quarrelsome meeting immediately before the actual duel and they had then fought in an immediate passion. Needless to say, there was evidence for none of this.

There was, perhaps, some virtue in the fact that Parke attempted to fit the facts to the law; he was not as overt as Baron Hotham, who was prepared to simply subvert it. Hotham presided over the trials of Mr Purefoy in 1794 and of Lt Rea in 1802. In *Purefoy*, *The Times* reports, Hotham ended his direction to the jury with the following remarks:

> Homicide, after a due interval left for consideration, amounts to murder. The laws of England in their utmost lenity and allowance for human frailty extend their compassion only to sudden and momentary frays, and then, if the blood has not had time to cool or reason to return, the result is termed manslaughter. Such is the law of the land ... His [Purefoy's] whole demeanour in the duel, according to the witness you are most to believe, General Stanwix, was that of perfect honour and perfect humanity. Such is the law and such are the facts, if you cannot reconcile the latter to your consciences, you must return a verdict of guilty, but if, the contrary, though the verdict may trench upon rules of rigid law, yet the verdict will be lovely in the sight of God and man.[44]

---

43 My italics.
44 *The Times*, 16 Aug. 1794, p. 3, col. b.

The appeal to the perfect honour and perfect humanity of the defendant is obviously an appeal to qualities which should only be considered in mitigation of sentence. More remarkably, Hotham states the law (correctly), but he does not invite the jury to act according to the law but rather to consider whether they can reconcile the law to their consciences. Indeed, he goes further: he subordinates the law by suggesting that a verdict in contradiction to its 'rigid rules' (rigid being a term suggestive of inappropriate inflexibility) might accord with the values of society and even merit divine approval. Furthermore, the omissions are quite as interesting as the content. He directs that if they cannot reconcile the facts to their consciences, then they must bring in a verdict of guilty. However, he does not say what the jury should find the defendant guilty of. The challenge and the duel had taken place on 21 December 1788 in consequence of Purefoy's dismissal from the army for insubordination in 1787. The resentment had long been nurtured, and the initial challenge had come from Purefoy. Where there was evidence of such preconceived design, judges less sympathetic to duellists were directing that juries must return a verdict of guilty of murder. Hotham, however, was silent upon this.

Can we really divine such sympathy for the duellist from a brief trial report? I believe we can. In *Rea*, eight years later, the defendants (the principal and two seconds) made no statements to the jury; counsel merely called evidence as to character. According to the law report of *The Times*, Hotham closed his summing up of the evidence in the following terms:

> There were many facts not disclosed at all, which would have been very material in this case. There was no evidence as to the original cause of the quarrel, how the provocation took place, or where circumstances had occurred, which if disclosed this day would have altered the case entirely. It was possible that the Prisoner Rea might have endeavoured to prevent the duel, and that the fatal catastrophe was occasioned by the wrong headed conduct of the deceased, which might have been such as the other could not endure ... the lives of three persons were at stake and it was for them to say whether they could, thus in the dark find the Prisoner's guilty, when there might be circumstances which, had they known, they would sooner have cut off their hands than down those persons to the fate that must follow their verdict of guilty. His Lordship then dwelt upon their excellent characters ... and observed that if any doubt remained on the minds of the Jury, evidence as to character must preponderate.[45]

First, one observes that whereas Mr Justice Buller in *Allen* had been explicit that character was no defence to the charge, it seems that for Hotham it sufficed to oust the presumption of malice of the law. Second, earlier in the trial Hotham had conceded to the attorney general who was prosecuting that the jury must return a verdict of

45   *The Times*, 22 Sept. 1802, p. 3, cols a–c.

murder or acquit, that the circumstances were not such as to admit the reduction of the offence to manslaughter due to provocation. Nevertheless, in his summing up for the jury, Hotham deliberately raised the issue of provocation in the jurors' minds by using the word. He dwelt upon what was not known, which was 'the original cause of the quarrel.' He suggested that the duel might have been occasioned by the 'wrong headed conduct of the deceased', which the other could not bear. Finally, he concluded with a simple emotive appeal. The jury are 'in the dark'. Might they not regret their verdict? Could they 'down those persons to the fate that must follow'? Since no duellist had been executed in England during Hotham's lifetime, this was a remarkable observation.

In 1816 in a somewhat pompous editorial *The Times* declared, 'The law of the land does not recognize any fellowship with the law of honour ... No English judge would suffer a Counsel to build a defence on so unsteady a basis as the customs and manners of fashionable life.'[46] Yet Lord Erskine, in his early career, acting in defence of Lt Bourne upon a criminal information for a challenge, addressed the bench as follows:

> I build my principal hope of a mild sentence upon much more that will be secretly felt by the court, than may be decently expressed from the bar ... Your lordships must speak to him the words of reproach and reprobation for doing that, which if he had not done, your lordships would scorn to speak to him at all as private men.[47]

However, we need not believe that such sentiments were necessarily avowed by all of the judiciary. In contrast to Erskine, Lord Kenyon had declared of duels, 'Beyond all contradiction all the parties are murderers, and a judge who would fritter away the law in such a case, would but ill deserve to continue on the seat of justice.'[48] In the trial of Mr Lambrecht in 1830, Mr Justice Bayley was at pains to carefully restate the doctrine of implied malice after the erroneous statement of the defence:

> If a party wilfully and intentionally did an act likely in its result to produce death and death actually ensued, the act so done by him was done with what the law called malice aforethought and the party was guilty of the crime of murder. This being the law, there could be no doubt, that if parties went out with deadly instruments one against the other and by those instruments produced death they were guilty of malice aforethought.[49]

---

46 *The Times*, 20 Aug. 1816, p. 3, col. a.

47 Anon., 'The life of Lord Erskine', *Law Mag. Quart. Rev. Juris.*, 22 (1839), pp. 121–147, at pp. 129–131.

48 Anon., 'The life of Lord Kenyon', *Law Mag. Quart. Rev. Juris.*, 17 (1837), pp. 252–297, at p. 281.

49 *R. v Lambrecht, Cox and Bigley* 1830. *The Times*, 3 Apr. 1830, p. 5, cols d–f.

In *Helsham* Bayley again rebutted any presumption that fair conduct sufficed to exculpate the prisoner or alleviate the charge:

> Intentionally using means calculated to produce death, if that death result, did most undoubtedly constitute the crime of murder. With regard to the present case, it appeared, beyond all doubt, that it had arisen out of a duel; now he was bound as a lawyer to tell the jury, that if parties went out to fight a duel and that death was the result of that meeting, the surviving parties to the transaction were equally guilty of the crime of murder, whether fair or foul means had been used.[50]

Mr Justice Patteson, concluding the trial of the seconds involved in the duel between Dr Hennis and Sir John Jeffcot in 1833, was entirely unwilling to countenance fictions to do with provocation. The defence had suggested the defendant had been provoked, but to the jury Patteson 'confessed he had extreme difficulty in seeing how they could arrive at such a conclusion; how it could be said this duel took place in the heat of passion and anger'.[51]

There existed, then, a genuine difference of conviction within the judiciary, but the number of duelling trials is too small to allow more than the very tentative conclusion that judges seemed to become less favourably disposed to duellists as the nineteenth century progressed. This may be explained in part by the fact that the legal profession was generally, if incompletely, turning its back upon the duel and by the fact that the social composition of the bench was changing.

A gradual change in the disposition of judges, however, could be of limited effect so long as the jury were prepared to resist the implications of a judge's direction. Considering the directions given, some acquittals do not surprise. However, Capt. MacNamara admitted at his trial for manslaughter to having fired the fatal shot, and yet he was acquitted against express judicial direction in only twenty minutes. At the trial of Mr Christie in 1818 he too admitted he fired the fatal shot. The judge strongly directed towards manslaughter in preference to murder, yet the jury acquitted of both. It took ten minutes for Lieutenant Rea to be acquitted in 1802 and fifteen for Mr O'Callaghan in 1812. Perhaps the most remarkable verdict of all was actually given at a coroner's jury upon a French officer killed by another in a duel: 'Death by the visitation of God.'[52]

The reluctance of juries to convict in capital cases is well known, and Martin Wiener's work has highlighted the independent attitude of juries throughout the nineteenth century. From his study of ninety-three spousal murder trials during

---

50 *The Times*, 9 Oct. 1830, p. 3, col. f.

51 *The Times*, 27 Jul. 1833, p. 3 ,col. g.

52 *The Times*, 6 Nov. 1812, p.3., col. e.

the 1860s, he concludes that of the thirty-five manslaughter verdicts, twelve were in opposition to the instructions or clearly expressed views of the judges, and that upon conviction the jury made twenty-four recommendations for mercy, of which only ten were supported by the judges.[53] Hence the complaint of the barrister, Sir George Stephen, in the 1850s: 'Nowadays a man cannot get hanged, let him try for it ever so anxiously.'[54] Wiener cites a particularly bad-tempered exchange between a judge and the jurors intent upon returning a manslaughter verdict:

> You can give what verdict you please. It is the evidence you are sworn to act upon. It is entirely a question for you. You have the power of disbelieving every witness who has been called. You may think the whole is fiction, but you do so on your own responsibility – that of your oaths ... Of course you may constitute yourselves judges or the law; if you do so you violate the oaths you have given.[55]

Juries in duelling cases were aware of the sympathy of society and were unwilling to return murder verdicts unless some serious defect on the part of the defendant had rendered the encounter flawed. In some cases they can have been in little doubt where the sympathy of the presiding judge lay. Where judges were prepared to apply the law without partiality, juries were not above defeating their attempts. In *Lambrecht* the foreman of the jury asked if they could return a manslaughter verdict instead of that of murder. As aforementioned, Bayley told them that there were no circumstances which could be put to them in mitigation of the homicide. The jury deliberated for some two hours before asking Bayley to reiterate the testimony. They wished to know whether the loud talking a witness had referred to upon Clayton's part suggested that he was angry. They further wished to recollect the distance at which they had stood. Clearly they were seeking evidence which would enable them to conclude that the affair had been gone through in heat. There was none. After a further hour the jury could not bring themselves to convict and acquitted.

With respect to such acquittals, it is difficult to determine whether juries acquitted because they simply refused to regard duelling as a criminal offence, or whether they accepted that duelling was a criminal act but were unwilling to sanction the penalties that might follow upon conviction. In 1842 a barrister suggested that juries would convict duellists yet were dissuaded by the 'impolitic severity of the law which was utterly at variance with the opinions and feelings of the present age'.[56] Adopting the

---

53 Martin. J. Wiener, 'Judges v jurors: courtroom tensions in murder trials and the law of criminal responsibility in nineteenth century England', *Law and History Review*, 17 (1999), pp. 467–506, at p. 480.

54 *The Juryman's Guide* (London, 1867), cited in Wiener 'Judges v Jurors', op. cit., fn 17.

55 *R. v Hynes* 1860. *The Times*, 17 Jul. 1870, p. 12, col. f.

56 Anon., 'Defects of the criminal law', *Law Mag. Quart. Rev. Juris.* (1842), p. 28.

CHARLES MOHUN

LORD MOHUN.

Plate 1 Charles Lord Mohun 1672–1712 © The Mary Evans Picture
Library.

Plate 2 Duel with Pistols c. 1820 Artist unknown © The Mary Evans Picture Library.

Plate 3 *The Field of Battersea*, William Heath (1795–1840) here depicts Lord Wellington duelling with Lord Winchilsea in 1829. He is shown as a lobster, a disparaging term for a soldier and his support, albeit tardy, for Catholic Emancipation is mocked by his wearing of robes and a rosary. Hume watches from the grass whilst a sign invites onlookers to view the 'Battersea Shooting Grounds Grand Pigeon Match'. Reproduced by courtesy of the University Librarian and Director, The John Rylands University Library, The University of Manchester.

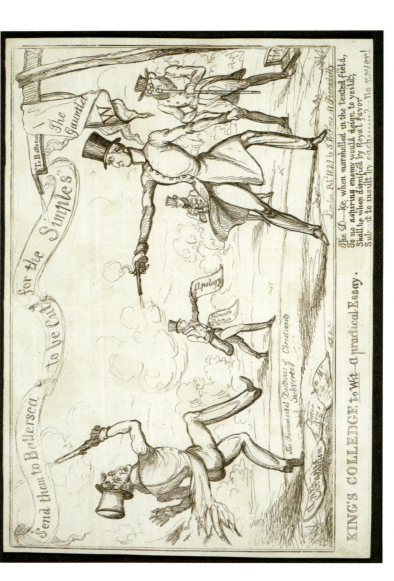

Plate 4 Kings Colledge to wit a practical essay, Thomas Howell Jones's depiction of the Wellington duel. In the background Lord Falmouth has an apology ready to be given to Lord Hardinge and in the foreground at Winchilsea's feet lies an anti-Catholic petition. Reproduced by courtesy of the University Librarian and Director, The John Rylands University Library, The University of Manchester.

same arguments that had been applied against many capital statutes, he argued that lesser penalties would be more vigorously enforced. Killing in a pre-meditated duel remained however, murder and juries remained reluctant to convict.

Sometimes the fiction of mere manslaughter was embraced, a felony within benefit of clergy. Until 1822 a duellist so convicted could only be sentenced to a maximum of twelve months imprisonment.[57] Benefit of clergy was pleaded by Ben Jonson when he was branded for the murder of Gabriel Spencer in 1598 and Lord Byron escaped execution by such means in 1765.[58] After 1822, however, the penalty for manslaughter was substantially increased. It was enacted that persons so convicted could be transported and imprisoned for three years or fined.[59] Yet there was a dearth of manslaughter convictions after 1822 for duelling. One can only hypothesise as to the reasons for this. Perhaps, the reluctance of some judges to allow speculative provocation defences to reduce the offence of murder to manslaughter merely resulted, as in *Lambrecht*, in acquittals. Perhaps, jurors were aware that the penalties for manslaughter had grown more severe and no longer regarded a manslaughter conviction as a moderate and acceptable middle course. Ironically, tougher judicial direction and heavier penalties may merely have increased the chances of acquittal.

What is clear is that it was not that the law was wanting in provisions for the punishment of duellists, but rather that legal processes were invaded by, and easily subverted by, the values of honour culture. The absence of public prosecutors, the climate of non-cooperation and the pressures of society were such as to inhibit the onset of the legal process. Where cases did indeed come to court at the instigation of the state, prosecutions were sometimes half-hearted. Even private prosecutors acting upon behalf of the deceased felt, upon one hand, the need to defend themselves against the accusation of vindictiveness and, upon another, unease at the logical consequences of a conviction. The judiciary themselves seemed divided upon the matter. While some were scrupulous, others were not, and it was they who were prepared to direct in ways that seemed to confirm the trial as a contest of reputation rather than of evidence and of law. The juries listening to the contest either struggled to understand or else refused to accept principles that seemed to contradict their own rough and ready perceptions of fair play.

This, however, was not the whole picture: duellists whose behaviour had taken them outside the paradigm of the honourable duel could not necessarily count upon the indulgence of the court. Some judges were not prepared to tolerate duellists, and the number of such judges, the balance of the evidence suggests, was probably growing. Juries, however, preserved a strong sense of independence and were not

---

57 18 Eliz. I., c. 7, s. 2.

58 A. L. Cross, 'The English criminal law and benefit of clergy during the eighteenth and early nineteenth century', *American Historical Review*, 22:3 (1917), pp. 544–565.

59 3 Geo. IV, c. 38 s. 1.

as yet prepared to surrender that independence and be governed merely by strict principles of law. The legal climate was growing somewhat more difficult for duellists, the legal process less advantageous. However, it is apparent that those who killed others in duels in the 1830s were no more likely to face the full force of the law than those who had done the same a hundred years before.

Faced with this fact, it is tempting to conclude that the law was entirely impotent in the face of honour culture and could do nothing to deter duelling. This however, would only be true in respect of the ability of the courts to penalise parties who had agreed to a meeting. The courts were more successful in offering a remedy to gentlemen who did not want to duel and who asked for legal protection to help them avoid it. Such gentlemen could prosecute a challenger by laying an information before the court of King's Bench. To challenge another, to invite that is, a breach of the King's Peace was a misdemeanour. Unfortunately, the prosecution of would be challengers has attracted little attention from those interested in the history of the duel. Where legal processes have been considered, it has nearly always been in the context of the homicide trial with the predictable conclusion that the law was rather ineffectual. The glamour of the fatal act and of the murder trial has turned attention away from apparently minor and pedestrian legal actions. Yet there were actually a goodly number of such prosecutions relative that is, to the number of duels actually being fought. Furthermore, the punishments consequent upon conviction were such as might give gentlemen pause.

If we take for example the period between 1800 and 1805 there were at least eight convictions for this misdemeanour in King's Bench and in each terms of imprisonment were awarded. In 1800 a Cambridge undergraduate (possibly a student of law, since he was said to be accompanied by two attorney's clerks) was convicted of assault upon a cavalry captain, conducted in an attempt to provoke a duel. He was imprisoned for six months and fined 400 guineas.[60] In 1801 the Reverend Augustus Beavor received only three weeks imprisonment for writing scurrilous letters with similar purpose.[61] However, that same year a major received twelve months imprisonment and a fine for having challenged his commanding officer Maj.-Gen. Eyre Coote.[62] In 1802 a Lt Stodthard was convicted of having provoked the master of ceremonies of the Ipswich Assembly Rooms by pulling his nose. He was imprisoned for four months and fined.[63] In 1803 a Mr Heydon was imprisoned for two months for having challenged Mr Hunter of the navy office[64] and a lieutenant of the navy was

---

60 *The Times*, 19 Nov. 1800, p. 3, col. c.

61 *The Times*, 8 May 1801, p. 3, col. b.

62 *The Times*, 11 Jun. 1801, p. 3, col. c.

63 *The Times*, 26 Jan. 1802, p. 3, col. a.

64 *The Times*, 23 May 1803, p. 3, col. b.

imprisoned for a month for having challenged his captain.[65] That same year a rule was granted against Mr Philips, an election candidate for Carmarthen, in consequence of a challenge issued to a rival, Mr Thomas.[66] In 1805 a Capt. Thornhill was committed to Marshalsea for three months for having challenged the master of a gamekeeper who had ordered him off his land.[67] Finally, that same year Mr Pierrepoint Dormer also served three months in Marshalsea for having challenged his brother-in-law in consequence of the treatment of his sister.[68]

To put the terms of imprisonment awarded for issuing challenges into context, of seven duellists convicted of manslaughter in the course of a duel in English courts between 1785 and 1845, two served twelve months, two only six months, two three months and one but a month. The terms of imprisonment seem almost inconsequential today, but then all sentences were short, for conditions were harsh. Furthermore, the particular rigours of imprisonment for gentlemen should not be underestimated. Upon a material level, if a gentleman's wealth might ameliorate prison conditions somewhat, as the prison system became more systematised and rule based it became more difficult to soften the impact of incarceration.[69] Imprisonment and more particularly submission to prison discipline were, I think, particularly damaging to the reputation of men of honour. The man of honour was, after all, a man who would sooner die than fail to requite a blow, a man who tried to maintain an absolute bodily autonomy. His very claim to be a gentleman was based upon prioritising honour ahead of consequence and maintaining the distinctness of his being. Confinement might be tolerable, under certain circumstances, but to be absorbed into the amorphous body of common prisoners, denied the basic conditions of gentility and obliged to obey the common jailor these were matters for horror. Matters too not easily forgotten upon release, for honour society cannot easily have accepted back into it those who had been obliged to passively endure all those affronts which gentlemen found so abhorrent.

The penalties then that King's Bench might impose upon a would be duellist were very far from nugatory and perhaps it was in consequence of an awareness of the seriousness of the offence that judges sometimes refused to accept informations from parties who did not come to court with clean hands. In *R. v Cook* 1803, the complainant, a Mr Bruin, alleged that Mr Cook had described him as a coward and

---

65 *R. v Rice* 3 East 581, 102 ER 719.

66 *The Times*, 9 Nov. 1803, p. 3, col. b.

67 *The Times*, 26 Nov. 1805, p. 2, col. d.

68 *The Times*, 29 Nov. 1805, p. 3, col. b.

69 Note for example the onerous discipline applied to Messrs Young and Webber after their conviction for their part in the duel between Mr Eliot and Mr Mirfin, *The Times*, 12 Apr. 1839, p. 7, col. a. *R. v Young and Webber* 1838, 8 Carrington and Payne 644.

a blackguard while dining at his, Bruin's house. He further claimed that Cook had thereafter pursued a campaign of vilification against him, designed to inveigle him into combat. The court however, refused to commit Cook for trial when the origins of the affair were revealed. Cook's conduct had been occasioned by the dishonesty of Mr Bruin and a business partner in refusing to repay money that Cook had lent to them.[70] In *R. v Flint* 1806 the King's Bench refused to accept an information from a complainant who had been horsewhipped by another for refusing to fight a duel, once that is, they found out that the original challenge had been inspired by the refusal of the complainant to honour a legitimate wager.[71] In addition, the King's Bench declined applications from plaintiffs whose social status inclined the court to think them in no need of protection from the demands of the society of honour. In 1825 a rule granted against an attorney in Lincoln upon behalf of a Mr Gresham was overturned once the court were informed that Gresham had once been a waiter in a tavern.[72]

Where informations were accepted, the prosecution might still be beset by evidential difficulties. Many honour disputes erupted in private without witnesses and where there were witnesses they were not always willing to give evidence. Sometimes this difficulty could be obviated by the code of honour itself. Being unabashed about one's conduct, even if consequences ensued, was itself a mark of honourable conduct and sometimes gentlemen testified to their own detriment in contexts where their guilt could otherwise not have been proved. When Lord Ranelagh used provoking language in John Adolphus's office in 1819, Adolphus declared his intention to prosecute and asked if Ranelagh would disavow in court the words he had used. Ranelagh responded that he would 'certainly not' and he was subsequently convicted.[73] Words though had to be accurately recalled. Where no assault had been committed or challenge committed to paper, cases frequently turned upon memory and upon the interpretation of angry words. It was not necessarily easy to determine which party had actually challenged the other first. Furthermore, judges, in their capacity as prisoner's friend, were inclined, even doctrinally obliged, to construe words according to their most benevolent construction.

One question for the courts to consider was whether trying to provoke another person into issuing a challenge was as much of a misdemeanour as actually issuing a challenge oneself. In *R. v Phillips* 1805 the court concluded that it was:

> An endeavour to provoke another to commit the misdemeanour of sending a challenge to fight is itself a misdemeanour indictable; particularly where such provocation was

---

70 *The Times*, 17 Nov. 1803, p. 3, col. b.

71 *Annual Register*, 48 (1806), p. 367.

72 *The Times*, 25 Jan. 1825, p. 3, col. e.

73 *The Times*, 9 Dec. 1818, p. 3, col. f.

given by writing, containing libellous matter, and alleged in the prefatory part of the indictment to have been done with intent to do the party bodily harm and to break the King's peace; the sending of such writing being an act done towards procuring the commission of the misdemeanour meant to be accomplished.[74]

The court had also to decide what would constitute evidence of the intention to provoke another to issue a challenge. They concluded that where a person had performed an illegal act, such as a criminal libel or an actual assault, the intent to provoke another could be presumed by the court. However, where no unlawful act had been performed, as for example where a gentleman had merely insulted another, the court could only conclude that the offending party had tried to provoke another into a challenge if the complainant could show some additional evidence that had indeed been the intent. Since, as aforementioned, the court was obliged to give words the construction that was most favourable to the defendant it was difficult to succeed in a prosecution if the defendant had confined himself to provoking remarks to which other meanings might be attributed.

Yet another consideration for the court was whether the court should accept an information from a complainant and convict where it was apparent that the complainant himself was as much to blame for the dispute as the defendant. With some reluctance they concluded that they would. In *R. v Rice* 1803 Mr Justice Grose spoke of being, 'Astonished to hear and read the numerous and severeties passing from the Prosecutor to the defendant, not by words only, but by orders carried into execution.'[75] Nevertheless, he accepted that the defendant had indeed challenged the prosecutor and sent him to prison for a month. It was a sentence which reflected not only the strong mitigation but also the fact that Rice had been confined pending the hearing. In *R. v William and Charles Davies* 1818 a ship's captain was censored, by Lord Ellenborough, for having unjustly and disproportionately punished his midshipman, Charles Davies, and for having pursued him with a false charge of embezzlement. Mr Justice Bayley concurred with Ellenborough that Davies had been greatly exasperated by what he thought tyranny and cruelty. Nevertheless, Bayley went on to declare that the court must prevent individuals becoming the avengers of their own wrongs and Charles Davies was sentenced to two months imprisonment.[76]

The court was then, something of a blunt instrument neither able to take into account the provocation that may have been offered by a complainant nor indeed to deal with some of the intricacies of honour culture. In 1810 King's Bench dealt with the complaint of William Bates who had become involved in a shooting

---

74 *R. v Phillips* 6 East 464, 102 ER 1365.

75 3 East 581, 102 ER 719.

76 *The Times*, 30 Apr. 1818, p. 3, col. f.

dispute with Gen. William Carr. During the dispute the general had challenged him to a duel. Supposing that this was mere hot headedness Bates had not turned up at the rendezvous. He had then received a letter declaring him a coward who could no longer be looked upon as a gentleman. It was this letter which had provoked Bates to lay an information against Carr. However, Ellenborough would not grant a rule against the general. His reasoning was that although Carr had issued a challenge, his subsequent assertion that Bates was no longer a gentleman was in effect a declaration that he could and would under no circumstances meet him. In short, Carr was no longer inciting a breach of the King's Peace. The court looked to the present circumstance rather than the lapsed invitation.[77] Such however, was scarcely a satisfactory conclusion for Bates. It seemed that although Carr had behaved unlawfully by issuing a challenge, he had returned his conduct to lawfulness by declaring that Bates was now incapable of giving satisfaction. Such a declaration was as socially damaging to Bates as any could be. If however, Bates chose to rehabilitate his reputation by trying to provoke Carr into agreeing to a meeting then it would be he who was now liable to prosecution. Of course, if all those who espoused the cause of the duel had at the same time repudiated the legal process, then one would not have had to fear that someone such as Carr might then turn to the courts. However, it is clear that there were men who used the courts opportunistically, who appealed to the demands of honour or to the power of the law as it suited them. This became very apparent during the prosecution of William Yates Peel in November 1818.[78]

In early 1818 William Yates Peel, son of Sir Robert, had put himself forward as parliamentary candidate for Tamworth against Sir Charles Townshend. The complainant in the later case, a Mr Floyer, had been an agent for the Townshend family. He had responded to Peel's candidature by publishing handbills which asserted that by standing against the Townshend's William was violating a promise given by his father. In one handbill, on 17 June 1818, Floyer had declared that, 'I will meet the Hon. Baronet upon the hustings, and if he denies a single syllable of what I have uttered, let him call upon me.' This then could scarcely be interpreted as anything other than an invitation to issue to challenge and William Peel had indeed visited Floyer thereafter and, 'desired an interview in a field'.[79] But Floyer's response had not been as expected, he had declined and expressed his intention to apply to King's Bench.

No further challenges had been forthcoming from William Peel but a vigorous pamphlet war had commenced. In October 1818 Floyer had sought advice from the barrister Scarlett as to whether he could bring an information against William Peel for his challenge. Scarlett had advised that he could not, as two quarter sessions

---

77 *The Times*, 28 Nov. 1810, p. 3, col. d.

78 *The Times*, 16 Nov. 1818, p. 3, col. b.

79 Ibid.

had passed during which he might have indicted him, and therefore his application would be deemed stale. Floyer had decided therefore to provoke Peel into issuing a fresh challenge so that he could be prosecuted. On the 6 November 1818 Floyer had published another pamphlet reporting a purported conversation with William Peel, during which Floyer claimed he had said to Peel, 'If you mean to call me out, give me a sufficient provocation and you will find me ready.' The implication was that Peel had been afraid to challenge him, and to reinforce this Floyer had posted notices in coffee houses around Tamworth describing both the elder and younger Peel as cowards.

It seems clear that at this point the Peels could have prosecuted Floyer at King's Bench but perhaps they were too incensed or too honourable to have done so. Instead, William Peel had promptly travelled down to Floyer's seaside home in Worthing, shook a horsewhip over his head and told him that he should consider himself horse-whipped.[80] Floyer however, had not responded with the bravura that his pamphlets had implied, instead he had promptly laid an information at King's Bench. The question now before the court was then whether a man who had behaved as Floyer had was entitled to lay an information? Mr Justice Best in the minority would not accept one 'upon the application of a complainant who had so conducted himself as Mr Floyer'.[81] For the majority, the Lord Chief Justice disapproved the conduct of Floyer but was prepared to grant a rule because if the court declined to accept it, they would be holding out 'an inducement to others to take the law into their own hands'. Not only was the information accepted but upon conviction both Peel and a second who had accompanied him to Worthing were each sentenced to one month in Marshalsea prison and fined £500 and bound over for five years in the enormous sum of £8000.[82]

The case of William Peel demonstrates that not all those who filed informations were necessarily repudiating the duel per se. For some it was but one strategy of action in a social or political contest. Peel's counsel pointed out that Floyer had already engaged in a duel as a principal and had twice acted as second. He was 'perfectly acquainted with the mode of provoking and accepting a challenge'. What it also shows however, is that King's Bench were prepared to penalise those who issued challenges, however egregious the provocation. They were prepared to offer a remedy – if, that is, gentlemen were prepared to resort to them in a timely fashion. However, it is noteworthy that it never occurred to William Peel to do so, although Floyer gave him several opportunities. It seems that there was some social cost in turning to the law. Not perhaps for someone such as Lord Sidmouth who prosecuted so dubious a

---

80 Ibid., col. c.

81 Ibid., col. c.

82 *The Times*, 4 Feb. 1820, p. 2, col. e.

gentleman as Arthur Thistlewood in that same year.[83] It seems however, that a certain suspicion lingered in the minds of gentlemen in respect of the motives and courage of fellow gentlemen who sought to prosecute challengers. Amongst some sections of gentlemanly society there was a general attitude of derision towards those who responded to affronts by recourse to the legal process.

In *R.* v *Rice* Mr Justice Grose admitted that men were either not aware of the consequences of, or had become insensible to the mischief of, sending challenges to fight duels. Two years later in *R.* v *Dormer* 1805 he lamented of the defendant's challenge:

> Although this may be consistent with the false laws of honour, it is totally inconsistent with the law of the land. It is much to be lamented that after the unwearied pains taken by this Court to publish the law upon this subject, you, as a gentleman of education, should have been ignorant of it.[84]

The warm praise spoken in favour of those who pursued the legal process against challengers is in itself suggestive of the contradictory sentiment in society. *R.* v *Woolcombe* 1833 arose from another election quarrel in which the conduct of the complainant Sir Edward Codrington was criticised by the court. Nevertheless, the court declared itself to be 'entertaining feelings of gratitude to Sir Edward Codrington who had displayed high moral courage in preferring an appeal to the laws of his country to that appeal that you wished to provoke'.[85]

While a copious quantity of abolitionist pamphlets and printed sermons were circulating through society by the beginning of the nineteenth century depreciating the duel, nevertheless apologists were still arguing that recourse to law instead of recourse to the field was indicative of character weakness. Bosquett declared succinctly that he had never, 'seen a man whose heart was in the right place bring an action for damages against another for seducing a beloved wife, daughter, etc. For these and such offences the law can make no adequate retribution.'[86] Romantic literature did much to continue to propagate this view. For example, at one point in Mary Shelley's novel *Falkner*, a companion informs Falkner that Mrs Neville has eloped with a lover and that they are being pursued by her husband. This initiates the following exchange:

> 'Then there will be a duel to the death?' Asked Falkner in the same icy accents.
> 'No', replied the other, 'Mrs Neville has no brother to fight for her and her husband breathes law only. Whatever vengeance the law will afford, he will use it to the utmost — he is too angry to fight.'

---

83 Philip Ziegler, *Addington; A Life of Henry Addington, First Viscount Sidmouth* (New York, 1965), pp. 356–357.

84 *The Times*, 29 Nov. 1805, p. 3, col. b.

85 *The Times*, 18 Nov. 1833, p. 3, col. e., per Mr Justice Parke.

86 Bosquett, *A Treatise on Duelling*, op. cit., p. 87.

'The poltroon!' Exclaimed Falkner, 'and thus he loses his sole chance of revenge.'

'I know not that', replied his companion, 'he has formed a thousand schemes of chastisement for both offenders, more dread than the field of honour — there is, to be sure, a mean as well as an indignant spirit in him, that revels rather in the thought of inflicting infamy than death ... he will wreak all that a savage and yet a sordid desire of vengeance can suggest. Poor Mrs Neville! After all, she must have lived a sad life with such a fellow.'[87]

Recourse to law is clearly portrayed as an indication of a defect of character, of a lack of courageous spirit and a surfeit of malice. Yet, although the romantic novelists played their part in shaping the attitudes of the age, they are an unreliable guide to the day to day conduct of gentlemen. The fact is that the evidence suggests that there was a constituency of such gentlemen whose reaction to a challenge was to immediately lay an information. How then in return did gentlemen react to the prospect of such a prosecution? A peculiar incident in the life of Thomas Pitt 2nd Baron Camelford suggests that while publicly they purported to be indifferent to the operation of the law their private feelings were quite the reverse.

Nikolai Tolstoy has ably chronicled the extraordinary adventures of Thomas Pitt the 2nd Lord Camelford, the 'Half-Mad Lord' indeed.[88] His short life saw a period of naval service in which he shot and killed a fellow officer in a dispute over seniority and discharged a broadside from his ship into one of her Majesty's shore batteries. The battery officer had had the temerity to challenge his ship when it approached harbour at night unlit and unannounced. After the navy had, with some difficulty, got rid of him he pursued in civilian life the violence that was henceforth denied him in service of his country. There were numerous outrageous acts, including a vicious assault at the theatre, innumerable and deliberate brawls with radicals, and most famously an attack on his former ship's Captain immortalised by Cruickshank in his 'Caneing in Conduit Street.' Seemingly anxious to do his country some service, he paid a number of clandestine visits to France which Tolstoy has plausibly interpreted as solo attempts to get close to and assassinate both Citizen Barras and thereafter Napoleon. Camelford, in brief was something of a legend in his own lifetime, feared and, by some, admired. Hester Stanhope later recalled, 'His taking me one evening to a party, and it was quite a scene to notice how the men shuffled away, and the women stared at him.'[89]

In February 1800 however, Camelford quarrelled with an erstwhile friend Peter Abbott and attempted to provoke him into a duel. Abbott however, responded by laying a criminal information against him at Bow Street on 1 March 1800. That

---

87 Mary Shelley, *Falkner* (London, 1838), Literature Online (http://chadwyck.co.uk, 2 Jul. 2009) at p. 84.

88 Tolstoy, *The Half-Mad Lord*, op. cit.

89 Cited in ibid., p. 91.

information, along with subsequent correspondence concerning the affair has survived in a bundle within the Dropmore papers[90] originally from Dropmore House, Buckinghamshire the home of Camelford's sister and of Lord Grenville and now in the British library. Perhaps because of the faded quality of the documents concerned, they do not appear to have been investigated by Tolstoy, nor, so far as I am aware, by any other historian but they reveal much about the private affairs of gentlemen. First among the papers is the copy of the criminal information itself.[91] The rest of the documents are of four types. First, there are the legal papers which passed between Camelford and those he appointed to defend him against Abbott's charge. Second, papers which passed during the case between Camelford's solicitors and Abbott's. Third, the bundled folios contain private intimate correspondence belonging not to Lord Camelford but to Peter Abbott. Finally there is a postscript, a memorandum added by the secretary to the succeeding Lord Camelford, the 3rd Baron, explaining how Peter Abbott's letters came to be in the bundle and dealing with a subsequent demand for money.

According to Abbott's information the quarrel between them had begun congenially enough. On 25 February 1800 Abbott had dined at Camelford's house, and 'Every mark of goodwill appeared.' At the end of dinner Abbott had acceded to a request from Camelford to accompany him upon a drive into town. During the journey however, he had become aware that Camelford had directed the coach driver to turn aside from the normal route onto a remote road and that a case of pistols had been placed in the coach. Camelford had then informed him that he, Abbott, had in conversation after dinner, implied that he, Camelford, was addicted to an unnatural sexual vice. Consequently, one of them must die at the other's hand. Abbott had immediately 'disavowed having made any such insinuation'. However, Camelford,' was sure I had charged him with it and was therefore resolved to have my blood.' Terrified had Abbott leapt out of the moving carriage and had run down the road and into a nearby cottage. Camelford had pursued him into the house, struck him twice and had then ordered his valet to offer him a sword, 'I was impelled by resentment to take it-but I saw that the Moment I should touch the sword and before I could take a posture of defence, Lord Camelford would run me through.' Abbott had declined and Camelford had left abusing him as he went. It is perhaps important that at no point during what was to follow did Camelford suggest that Abbott's description of the basic events was untrue.

Upon learning that an information had been laid against him Camelford had immediately appointed solicitors, who made the relevant inquiries upon his behalf and then wrote back to him informing him that a grand jury would sit upon the bill against him on the 24 or 26 May 1800. Camelford had responded with a diatribe

---

90 The British Library, The Dropmore Papers, (series II) vol. cxxxxvii.

91 Folio 1.

lambasting Abbott for, 'Turning a challenge to fight into an attempt of assassination ... this affront is so blended with buggery and assassination that to pacify this man of conscience we must let him have it all his own way and admit either one or the other or both.'[92] This however, was smoothly transliterated by his solicitors into a conciliatory statement:

> Lord Camelford ... declares that he then was and still is deeply concerned that such events should have taken place between himself and a person with whom he had lived upon terms of intimacy and equality ... Lord Camelford has much satisfaction in making the above statement which he perceives must answer all honourable purposes.[93]

The solicitors also engaged the services of the barrister Erskine who, in an opinion of 25 May, strongly advised an out of court settlement, 'If he [Camelford] can a forehand avoid the judgement by an honourable arrangement he may do it without disgrace.'[94] Erskine pointed out the social embarrassment that Abbott's prosecution might bring upon Camelford's family and although, 'in Lord Camelford's situation the countenance of his powerful kindred will be most important,' he urged that he did not involve himself in politics, 'whilst his nearest relations are so deeply implicated in the government of the state.'

The following day the grand jury sat and found a true bill and the trial date itself was set for July, although it was later put back to the end of November. In the interim Camelford's solicitors tried to negotiate, but they were hampered by Camelford's insistence that he would not come to a pecuniary settlement with Abbott. On 5 July Erskine delivered a second opinion anticipating that at trial the court would take an approach similar to that which was in fact later taken in both *Charles Davies* and *Peel*. That is to say that however much Camelford might feel himself aggrieved that could not negate the offence of having issued a challenge. The insinuations made by Abbott, 'though most important for the consideration of the court cannot procure any acquittal, a challenge being under any possible provocation a misdemeanour. We are of the opinion that the plea of not guilty should be withdrawn and the facts fully disclosed to the Court.'[95]

Camelford would not change his plea nor pay money to Abbott, for he had his own scheme afoot. He was never tried upon Abbott's information. Instead, on 22 November shortly before the onset of the trial opposing counsels for both sides met:

---

92 Folio 22.

93 Folio 17.

94 Folio 23.

95 Folio 59.

as a sort of Court of Honour – to direct upon what terms (not being pecuniary terms) the proceedings should be abandoned ... Lord C. was indebted for this change in his situation to the possession of Abbott's letters (which were kept secret from A) ... and A.'s consequent dread of exposure to the world.[96]

This description of events is set down in the memorandum written by a secretary to the 3rd Lord Camelford after the demise of the 2nd and explaining the circumstances under which the prosecution of his father came to be withdrawn. The nature of Abbott's letters was not specified but bundled in with the memorandum is another document headed, 'Copy of Letters written to Mrs Turner, dated From June 19th to July 7th 1800.' Seven letters, lettered A–G are copied in this one document, each is signed P. A. [Peter Abbott].[97] A note in the margin at the end of letter E explains:

> All the above five letters were received from Mrs Turner by Mr Whayley on Saturday 5th July-delivered by him to Lord Camelford on the 6th July (Sunday) and produced by Lord C at the Consultation at Mr Erskine's house that morning. The remaining two letters were received by Mrs T after Mr W had interviewed her at Slough on the aforementioned Saturday 5th July at which she gave him the five letters aforementioned.

All seven are intimate letters to a 'Sophia' making reference to a money-making scheme. It appears that at the time the letters were written Sophia was on friendly terms with Lord Camelford's and she and Abbott appear to have agreed that she was to feign concern for the Baron and to offer to effect the withdrawal of the action against him for an undisclosed sum of money. The letters begin on 19 June when Sophia was already in contact with Camelford's solicitors – with Abbott's knowledge and approval. To give a flavour of the letters, letter B from Abbott dated 30th June 1800 informed Sophia that:

> If he [Camelford] proposes to you to come to Town he ought to pay handsomely, you ought to have a very handsome sum, more than you expected before as the Business is very serious to Lord C-may you prosper my Angel. But take care to do nothing without first receiving proper Security.

At this stage it was anticipated that Lord Camelford's trial would commence in July and on 1 July, in letter C, Abbott wrote to Sophia that:

> I wish to God something was settled the Time presses, either it must be settled one Way or the other by Friday as I shall not have it in my Power afterwards to do anything but

---

96 Folio 74.
97 Folio 74.

what the Law requires. Bless you my Darling a thousand Times let me hear from you immediately, I would do anything in my Power to make you happy.

Further letters followed in this vein. Alas however, for his money making scheme and alas it seems for the course of true love – for by 5 July five of his private letters were in the hands of Camelford delivered by Mrs Turner and two more were to follow.

It is of course not necessary to conclude that Sophia and Mrs Turner were one and the same, but, put briefly, the details in the memorandum to the 3rd Lord describing the acquisition of the letters makes it very likely. Shortly after the death of Thomas Pitt in 1804 a Lady Cox approached his successor asking for money. It was this demand that seemingly prompted the secretary to draw up a précis of the whole affair. Lady Cox had, according to the secretary, been paid £150 to pass Abbott's letters to her over to Camelford. However, she was now claiming that she had also received a promise that she would receive a further £500. That promise that had not been kept by the date of the death of the second lord and she now expected his successor to stump up. The secretary summed up her role thus:

> At the time of Lady Cox's interference she was Abbott's friend and not Lord C's ... her object in the first instance was, in concert with Abbott to obtain money from Lord C for being the means of accommodating the dispute and suppressing the dispute at law. The answer given by Lord Camelford that it was his own decision not to come to any accommodation upon pecuniary terms, lest it be construed by malignants into a device to hush up the insinuations made by Abbot, she must have become immediately sensible of the impossibility of effecting the above purposes ... she then changed her means with a view to effecting the same End, that of obtaining money from Lord C and determined to sacrifice Abbott to him for her own benefit.

The identification of Lady Cox with both the Mrs Turner who had delivered the letters and with Sophia who had, from the correspondence between them, clearly connived with Abbott to get money from Camelford seems irresistible, the more so because all three are at points in the correspondence described as living in Slough. Abbott in other words had been double-crossed. When he was confronted with the letters by Camelford's solicitors immediately prior to the trial, he must have realised that his motives would be discredited and he withdrew the prosecution. We do not know whether Lady Cox got her money, but from the comments of the third lord's secretary we may doubt it, 'No sense or feeling of honour (as far as could be collected from the Documents and from the circumstances which occurred, so many of which seem to speak trumpet-tongued to the contrary) appears to have entered into Lady C's share of the transactions.'

Aside from providing a further insight into the life of a colourful historical personage and a somewhat melodramatic tale of betrayal, the dispute between the two men provides us with some interesting insights into the misdemeanour in question. We learn that to be tried for such a misdemeanour was a serious matter, even for someone as powerful as Camelford. To suppress such a prosecution a complainant might hope to receive a significant sum. In the case of Camelford that sum was not to materialise, but the lord was prepared to spend time and money in order to suppress the dispute – by applying a little 'blackmail' of his own. His legal advisors were sanguine about his prospects in court urging private reconciliation and pointing out the damage to his familial and political connections once matters became public. In the absence of a settlement, Erskine did not believe that any evidence of provocation would avail Camelford in court and urged a guilty plea. There is then, no sense in any of this of a court in which judges and counsel, with the complicity of a sympathetic jury, could be expected to strain to acquit the defendant. Nor any sense that the sanctions available to the court were nugatory.

In summary then, in focusing upon homicide trials, where indeed the legal system appeared ineffectual in penalising duellists, studies of English duelling have tended to ignore the potential remedies offered by the courts to those who did not wish to duel. There is very little evidence to support a contention that in respect of homicides the courts were treating duellists with much greater severity at the end of our period than at the beginning. However, while a more systematic study of the prosecutions for the misdemeanour of issuing a challenge would clearly be desirable, the evidence thus far does suggest that by the beginning of the nineteenth century criminal informations were being regularly laid by gentlemen against those who had challenged them, or who had sought to provoke them to issue a challenge. They were doing so in the knowledge that there was a good chance of success before King's Bench and that upon conviction the court would apply meaningful sanctions against the malefactor. Obviously, we cannot know how many gentlemen were dissuaded from issuing a challenge by the prospect of being hauled before the courts. William Peel had, it appears, first been so dissuaded, but then he had given way in the face of quite intolerable provocation. It seems though very likely that the courts were operating with some meaningful deterrent effect. Whatever public persona gentlemen might project, whatever romantic memoirs or honour theorists may suggest, by the beginning of the nineteenth century would be duellists certainly did not regard the prospect of being prosecuted before the King's Bench with insouciance.

8

The Years of Decline, the European Middle and the Domestic Duellists

Notwithstanding the operation of the courts, to observers at the beginning of the nineteenth century the duel probably appeared to be in as rude a health as it had ever been. There were perhaps more honour disputes during the first decade of the nineteenth century than in either of the two previous decades. Many of those disputes were undoubtedly engendered by the stresses and strains of war, but the cessation of hostilities probably did not lead to an immediate decline in duelling. We know that after the war there were a number of duels between officers of the army of occupation in France and their French counterparts, who were eager to requite national humiliation through personal combat. Similarly, at home there were meetings to settle old grudges that had had to be postponed due to the inconveniences of conflict. Few, I suppose, can have anticipated that by the middle of the century the English duel would be defunct, this notwithstanding the fillip given to the institution when the Duke of Wellington met Lord Winchilsea in 1829. Even in Ireland, long held by Englishmen to be the breeding ground of quarrelsome and habitual duellists, the duel had entered a terminal decline by the second decade of the nineteenth century. By 1838 it was being declared, rather curiously, at the Royal Dublin Society that 'There is not one hostile meeting for twenty-three there used to be in this country.'[1] The very last duel on English soil was a remarkable and fatal affair fought in 1852 between two Frenchmen who had decamped from Calais for the purpose.

A discussion of the reasons for the decline and demise of English duelling after the Napoleonic Wars will occupy most of the rest of this book, and some very particular explanations will be required in order to explain the disappearance of honour culture from these islands. Why did the English gentlemen give up the duel, when it remained an important part of the broader European cultural milieu for at least another half century? The search for some answers can be profitably be begun by a

---

1   John Rigby, speech at the Royal Dublin Society, 1838, cited in Michael Barry, *An Affair of Honour: Irish Duels and Duellists* (Fermoy: Eigse Books, 1981), p. 8.

brief consideration of the history of the duel upon the Continent, in particular in three countries, France, Italy and Germany.

'The first tool of civilization, the only means man has found to reconcile his brutal instincts and his ideal of justice.' Anatole France's remark upon the sword was one that might have been readily uttered in eighteenth-century England, when regular protestations were made that it was the sword alone that guaranteed polite society. The place, however, was Paris, and the year 1886.[2] The Comte de Tilly had declared at the end of the eighteenth century that France was 'the birthplace of duelling'. In point of fact this was not correct, but it was perhaps in France that duelling was most prolific in the seventeenth and eighteenth centuries.[3]

Briefly, the duel had arrived in France at the end of the fifteenth and beginning of the sixteenth centuries in consequence of the campaigns of Charles VIII and Louis XII in Italy. As it spread from the army into the court, the French kings had at first done little to suppress the activity, and indeed François I had himself issued a challenge to the Holy Roman Emperor Charles V in 1527. Thereafter a series of sporadic attempts had been made to restrain duelling, and in 1602 and 1609 Henry IV had issued edicts making duelling, acting as a second or even merely issuing a challenge a capital offence. Indeed, two members of his guard were executed in 1610. This did not, however, prevent the duel reaching its zenith during his reign, and it has been estimated that between 1588 and 1608 some 7,000–8,000 noblemen perished in duels.[4]

Perhaps it was this surfeit of fatalities that provoked a serious attempt at suppressing honour culture in the succeeding reign. Louis XIII was only eight when he came to the throne in 1610. The inspiration behind the subsequent 'campaign' against duelling was not him but Richelieu, who became Louis's chief minister in 1624. In 1617 and 1624, Louis XIII reissued Henry IV's edicts, but in 1626, under Richelieu's direction, a new approach was adopted. An edict of 24 March 1626 relaxed the penalties to be imposed upon those who had fought but had not killed their opponents in duels. Henceforth they were to be banished for three years, deprived of a portion of their property and of any royal pensions that might accrue to them, and dismissed from any official office. Death remained the sanction for those who had killed, but for the rest it was hoped that the real prospect of humiliation would prove a sharper deterrent than the unlikely fate of extinction.

---

2   Anatole France, 'La Vie à Paris', *Le Temps*, 18 July 1886.

3   Robert Nye records the last formal challenge to a duel made by a Gaullist party deputy in 1967. See Robert Nye, 'The end of the modern French duel', in P. Spierenburg, ed., *Men and Violence: Gender, Honor and Rituals in Modern Europe and America* (Ohio: Ohio State Press, 1998), pp. 82–101.

4   P. de L'Estoile, *Memoires-Journaux* IX, 277 (Paris 1875–96), cited in Richard Herr, 'Honour versus absolutism: Richelieu's fight against duelling', *Journal of Modern History* 27:3 (1955), pp. 281–285, at p. 282.

On 12 May 1627, however, François de Montmorency, Comte de Bouteville, fought a duel with the Marquis de Beuvron in the Place Royale in Paris. The seconds engaged as well, and one of them, the Marquis de Bussy d'Amboise, was killed. Beuvron escaped but Bouteville was captured and subsequently executed together with his second, the Comte de Chapelles. Richelieu was subsequently to claim of both the 1626 measure and the subsequent executions that 'the relaxation of the penalty and, on the other hand, the inflexible steadfastness in not exempting anyone have been profitable, considering that since that time this rage which has been so ardent, has been calmed and duels are now hardly mentioned'.[5] The truth, however, was that Bouteville had aroused the king's particular ire because prior to the fatal encounter he had already fought a duel and absconded to Brussels. The King had let it be known that he could return to France and that he would not be arrested so long as he did not come to Paris or the Royal Court. In returning to Paris Bouteville had, by combating in the most public place possible, flouted the king's command and scorned his mercy. This marked Bouteville for condign punishment, but the king was far more lenient in the cases of other duellists who had not so explicitly contravened his royal commands; by 1640 he was readily pardoning them. Not surprisingly, then, when another edict was issued in 1643, again drafted by Richelieu, it lamented that the 1626 edict had not achieved its purpose.

Louis XIV was neither more consistent nor more successful than his predecessor. He issued ten further edicts including the *Édits des Duels* in 1679, which prescribed the death penalty for all principals and seconds, as well as confiscation of property and even deprivation of a Christian burial. Even this extreme measure did not prevail, not least because the king often turned a blind eye to duels in his court, leading some commentators to suppose that he in fact regarded them with secret approbation. Louis had set up a court of honour in 1679 to which disputes were to be referred, but it was rarely consulted, and no more so in the succeeding reigns. Among the most notorious of the subsequent duels occurred in 1734 when the Duc de Richelieu killed the Prince de Lixen following a dispute about dress and deportment at the siege of Philippsbourg.

As the eighteenth century wore on, the duel appeared as firmly entrenched as ever and, importantly, it remained so while preserving its attachment to the sword. There were actually a fair number of French pistol duels fought in the nineteenth century; however, French duellists did not in general adopt the pistol in the way that English gentlemen did. By 1790 sword duels had become extremely rare in England, but they still formed the majority of French encounters. The fact that the French remained devoted to the sword was later to allow them to finesse and sanitise the duel in a way that was denied to their English counterparts. The outbreak of revolution, however, challenged the very existence of the duel, redolent as it was with the values of the

---

5   Richelieu, *Memoires* v. 274, cited in ibid., p. 285.

ancien régime. This was all the more so because, once ousted from power, members of that regime frequently sought to gain their revenge upon deputies of the new National Assembly by challenging them to duels. Thomas Carlyle reported that when Charles de Lameth, a constitutional monarchist and deputy of the National Assembly, was wounded after having been provoked into a duel by the Duke de Castries, a mob promptly descended upon the Hôtel de Castries and sacked it.[6] A Monsieur Boyer thereafter raised a corps of swordsmen sworn to defend the deputies against challenges from reactionary royalists, but matters had already turned even more ugly and the royalists were obliged to leave Paris and seek redress elsewhere.

The revolutionary government thereafter made a number of attempts to prohibit duelling entirely, with the mayor of Paris petitioning the National Assembly for a law banning an activity 'incompatible with the character of a free benevolent people'.[7] It seems, though, that the militarisation of society consequent upon the almost continual warfare up until 1815 had the effect, much as it did in England, of stimulating duelling activity. Duels were not uncommon in Napoleon's armies, and although he expressed a consistent disapproval of them two of his generals, Destaing and Regnier, duelled in 1802 and two more, Ornano and Bonnet, in 1815. Robert Nye, writing of late nineteenth-century duelling, remarks that 'Honour did not have to be reinvented in this era, for it survived the Revolution of 1789 and the triumph of bourgeois society more or less intact.'[8] Of course, the restoration of the Bourbons marked a return to the pretensions of a returning and resentful aristocracy, but it is clear that concepts of personal honour had also become deeply rooted among the Bonapartists. As discussed previously, a good number of duels were fought in 1815 and 1816 by Bonapartist officers smarting at their defeat and seeking revenge upon the officers of the occupying forces.

It would, however, be a mistake to suppose that because duelling persisted in France it must have proved immune to the social and economic developments of the first half of the nineteenth century which, as we shall see, did so much to undermine honour culture in England. There is evidence to suggest that after 1815 duelling went into decline in France in much the same way as in England and that during the 1840s when the duel became extinct in England it very nearly became so in France. French society in the 1820s and 1830s turned its back upon militarism and military prowess, and after 1837 the Court of Cassation made a significant and seemingly successful attempt to penalise duellists and curtail duelling. In 1845 a report of the Association for the Discouragement of Duelling in London cited a set of statistics from the French minister of justice which showed that from 1827 until 1834 the

---

6   Thomas Carlyle, *The French Revolution: A History*, 2 vols (London, 1837), vol. ii, chap. 2. 3. 3.

7   See Baldick, *A History of Duelling*, op. cit., p. 90.

8   Robert A. Nye, 'Fencing, the duel and Republican manhood in the Third Republic', *Journal of Contemporary History*, 25 (1990), pp. 365–377, at p. 366.

Court of Cassation had recorded 189 fatalities in duels, a little less than 24 per year. However, after the drive against duelling had commenced in 1837 the number of fatalities had dropped dramatically. In the five years from 1839 to 1843 the court however, recorded only twenty-eight fatalities.[9] English abolitionists were much encouraged by the seeming success of the court and the association's report that year concluded that without doubt the French duel was in terminal decline. The survival of the very skill of swordsmanship was in question, for by 1840 there remained only ten fencing halls in the whole of France.[10]

Ultimately, though, the duel endured because it was reinvented as a tool of a democracy, 'aristocratic in its manners and sentiments'.[11] It should be observed that, judging by the number of fatalities, even at its lowest ebb duelling in France was still occurring with a frequency that it had rarely attained in England. Honour and honour culture were already being appropriated in France as the attributes of the idealised Republican male. In the developing and increasingly bourgeois society of England the duel came to be regarded as both ludicrous and irrelevant, a manifestation of the offensive claims of a small clique to be above both the law and the rules of normal social intercourse. In France, by contrast, the duel was thrown open by Republicans who claimed for all free Frenchmen the privileges hitherto confined to the few. Honour and its attributes were henceforth to be the inheritance of any worthy citizen.

Nye remarks that 'It may seem paradoxical to consider that a cultural discourse born in a sixteenth century world of unlettered, warring nobles could play a functional role in a democratic industrial society.'[12] Perhaps so, but in a sense the duel had always had a certain democratising function; it had served to protect the interests of the well-born from the tyranny of the even-better-born and more powerful. To extend the penumbra of the duel to the broader population was to make an important statement about the value of the individual citizen, his personhood and his role in the state. The duel, then, was revived after 1840, and 'by the mid-nineteenth century both fencing and the duel had been adopted by middle class men and integrated into bourgeois society.'[13] After 1848 France fell increasingly under the somewhat stifling autocracy and bureaucracy of Louis Napoleon. However, in their resistance the political opposition to the Second Empire took to the duel since it:

> served to dramatize and symbolically represent the basic elements in Republican ideology – individual liberty and equality – and helped to set the foundations for the

---

9   Anon., *2nd Report of the Association for the Discouragement of Duelling* (London: Alvey, 1845), p. 19.

10   Nye, 'Fencing', op. cit., p. 370.

11   Ernest LeGouve, *Un tournoi au XIXe siecle* (Paris, 1872), p. 10, cited in Nye, 'Fencing', op. cit., p. 368.

12   Ibid., p. 366.

13   Ibid., p. 370.

civic value system of the Third Republic. In principle, any man, no matter what his origins, could cultivate the art of fencing and engage in duels, because the Republican man was a free agent responsible for his actions.[14]

Defeat in the Franco-Prussian War brought national reflection and a prolonged period of political indecisiveness, but in numerical terms the duel was nothing diminished, rather the reverse. Personal honour rather than national prowess became the focus of malehood; fencing became a popular pastime with clubs in most towns.[15] France's middling orders not only adopted the duel, they also made it their own. According to Hughes, after 1870 the duel became 'a rallying point of bourgeois Republicanism'.[16] Nye concurs and believes that by 1875 the duel 'was aligned firmly with generally progressive political forces in the new Republic'.[17] While in England, then, the increasing influence of the middle classes, as signified perhaps by the Reform Act 1832, is sometimes said to have inevitably challenged the culture of honour, in France, on the contrary, the onset of a more broadly based, progressive politics served to reinvigorate it.

Something not too dissimilar was occurring in Italy. Hughes points out that the adoption of duelling by the middle classes was not the mere aping by some of its members of aristocratic values (as Simpson alleges in the English context); rather, duelling became genuinely inculcated as part of the values and identity espoused by that middle because 'it performed a variety of political and social functions that were inherent in the arrival of a liberal, constitutional regime on the peninsula'.[18]

In France, Nye asserts, the duel retained a distinctively civilian form, whereas in Italy, according to Iacopo Gelli's statistics (as employed by Hughes), the military remained the single largest group of duellists. About one-third of known Italian duellists between 1888 and 1895 were from the military. In both cases, however, it was the hurly-burly of democratic politics and the general vibrancy of public debate which engendered encounters. Gelli recorded journalism as the greatest cause of duelling in Italy between 1879 and 1895, and after disputes of no known cause, politics comprised the third category. As for duellists themselves, although the military comprised the largest single group, journalists, lawyers, capitalists and politicians were well represented.

---

14   Nye, 'Modern French duel', op. cit., p. 86.

15   *L'Escrime Française*, 5 Mar. 1889.

16   Steven Hughes, 'Men of steel: dueling, honor and politics in liberal Italy', in P. Spierenburg, ed., *Men and Violence: Gender, Honor and Rituals in Modern Europe and America* (Ohio: Ohio State Press, 1998), pp. 64–81, at p. 75.

17   Nye, 'Modern French duel', op. cit., pp. 82–101.

18   Hughes, 'Men of steel', op. cit., p. 65.

Note, though, that most of these duels were sword duels, and there comes a point at which one must question whether the term duel proper continued to be appropriate for encounters that were fought with epées with the assistance of protective clothing and under formal fencing conventions. For example, Iacopo Gelli's study from Italy suggests that fatality rates were as low as half of 1 per cent.[19] Nye has estimated that there were between 200 and 300 'duels' per year in France between 1875 and 1900, but he also estimates that of the 10,000 to 15,000 protagonists, only perhaps two dozen were killed.[20] If we compare then the single fatality or so occurring each year in French duels at the end of the century with the twenty-four per year being recorded by the Court of Cassation prior to 1834, then we can see how little French duelling at the end of the nineteenth century seems to have resembled French duelling towards the beginning of the same century. In the English pistol duels of the early nineteenth century, 15–17 per cent of all participants were killed; French casualty rates in the duels of the Third Republic were perhaps one one-hundreth of this. In 1880 Mark Twain parodied the later French duel thus: 'Much as the modern French duel is ridiculed by certain smart people, it is in reality one of the most dangerous institutions of our day. Since it is always fought in the open air, the combatants are nearly sure to catch cold.'[21] This was perhaps a little unkind but surely no more so than would have been the observations of those who could remember the duel of some forty years before.

For much of its history, then, the French duel described a trajectory not dissimilar to that found in England and elsewhere. That is to say that it arrived from Italy and spread through the court, notwithstanding the apparent disapprobation of the kings. Soon strongly lodged within the military and aristocracy, it resisted with vigour all attempts to curtail it and was clearly in rude health in the middle of the eighteenth century. When the English switched over to the pistol duel towards the end of the eighteenth century, the French continued with a general adherence to the sword, and thus the forms of duelling began to diverge. However, there are reasons to suppose that in both countries the duel was under pressure in the early nineteenth century. The difference was that while the English duel succumbed, the French duel evolved into a new form, both practically and ideologically. Having spread into Republican armies, the duel was associated with the ideals of *liberté*, *egalité* and *fraternité*. In practice this did not mean that the duel was available to all, but rather that with the decline of the military estate and prestige the duel was able to transfer itself into civilian life and take on a distinctly bourgeois form; in short, it evolved from a badge of aristocratic

---

19 Iacop Gelli asserted that there were 3, 918 duels in Italy between 1879 and 1899 and that these resulted in a mere twenty deaths. Cited by Hughes in 'Men of steel', op. cit., p. 73.

20 Nye, 'Fencing', op. cit., p. 88.

21 Mark Twain, *A Tramp Abroad*, 2 vols (London, 1880), vol. i, p. 5.

difference to an emblem of liberal and Republican opposition. Visceral duels still occurred, but for the most part the process of adapting to the bourgeois life saw the duel shorn of its most deadly attributes. It became much more of a contest and much less of an earnest hazard of life and death.

However, while the English duel was disappearing and the French and Italian duels descending into mere neutered swordplay, the German duel was by contrast in full flourish. Indeed, there may have been more fatal duels in Germany in the second half of the nineteenth century than in the first. Men still fought with swords, students especially in the *Mensur* but it was the lethal tradition of the pistol duel that accounted for the bulk of the casualties. The contrasting vigour of duelling in Germany led Germans such as Adolph Kohut to be not a little disparaging of their continental cousins: 'The duel in France has deteriorated into a trivial game. Neither high mindedness, nor noble sentiment, nor preservation of true manly honour are the mainsprings of the affairs of honour, but in most cases enormous vanity.'[22] For Kevin McAleer both the state of the French duel and the disappearance of the British duel 'symbolised for Germans corrupt western *Zivilisation* opposing the German duel's expression of superior *Kultur*'.[23]

In origin, of course, the German duel was also an import from Italy, though as in other nations this was wilfully forgotten later. The transmission came partly through German scholars bringing honour culture back from Italian universities such as Salerno and Bologna and substantially through the occupation of foreign armies during the course of the Thirty Years War (1618–1648). Duels were being recorded by the second half of the sixteenth century, and fencing had become part of the university curriculum by this time. In 1617 Matthias the Holy Roman Emperor issued an edict against duelling, and McAleer records that by the mid seventeenth century almost all German territories had anti-duelling laws. This included Prussia, where initially, as in England, an attempt was made to take a vigorous stance against the duel. Friedrich Wilhelm of Brandenburg issued Prussia's first anti-duelling law in 1652; Friedrich III followed in 1688, and a number of duellists were actually hung at the end of the seventeenth century. A Prussian decree of 1713 specified the death penalty for all who presumed to duel.

However, as was so often the case, such law failed in the enforcement. Friedrich Wilhelm I of Prussia (1713–1740) occasionally penalised duelling but openly tolerated the practice within the army as did his successor, Friedrich the Great. While law codes did not relax their vigour as the eighteenth century wore on, society seems to have become habituated to the existence of the duel and resigned as to the possibility of eradicating it. In civilian life, duelling had by now become so entrenched in the

---

22 Dr Adolph Kohut, *Das Buch berühmter Duelle* (Berlin, 1888), p. 171.

23 Kevin McAleer, *Dueling: The Cult of Honor in Fin-de-Siècle Germany* (Princeton, NJ: Princeton University Press, 1994), p. 81.

student body and eligible gentlemen had become so accustomed to carrying the necessary accoutrements that when Karl Philipp Moritz travelled to England in 1782 he noted with surprise that no one carried a sword in the public street, the English having given up the habit a generation previously.

Formally, the position of Prussian law remained firmly opposed to duelling, and in 1794 Friedrich Wilhelm II's Prussian Law Code imposed a penalty of three to six years detention for issuing a challenge and a penalty of ten years to life imprisonment for actually fighting a duel. This was far more severe than the penalties for such activities in England or France. Yet the appreciation of honour had developed so far by then as to make it understood that such penalties were only to be applied in cases of the most egregious offence and cases of the most presumptuous behaviour by those who could not properly claim to be within the penumbra of the duel. That such penalties be imposed upon officers and gentlemen rightly reacting to affront was never seriously contemplated. As McAleer puts it, the code:

> Imposed an elitist bias by attributing a more fully developed sense of honour to this upper crust. A double standard also existed in cases when an insult crossed formal social divisions: an insult from high to low usually incurred a fine, where insults directed from low to high were almost always punished with imprisonment. Similarly armed clashes between members of the bourgeoisie were denied treatment under the duelling statues and prosecuted under those of murder and assault ... this distinction began to evaporate from German jurisprudence only in the 1820s and 1830s.[24]

In effect, then, German law codes implicitly recognised the special honour situation of the elites and of those in the military in particular. The crushing defeat of Jena in the Napoleonic War further enhanced honour sensibilities, and at the conclusion of the conflict German officers in the army of occupation in France found themselves, like the British officers, regularly challenged by Bonapartist sympathisers.[25]

The arguments advanced in favour of the duel were in some respects much the same as those observable in England, yet duelling in England was rarely so explicitly linked to claims of national superiority or quite so firmly expounded as a group obligation:

> The duel is for the sake of the individual only insofar as he is a member of an entire caste, his honour being identified with caste honor, with that of the caste ... For this reason it testifies to egoism if someone, despite acknowledgment of the aforementioned says 'What do I gain if I am insulted and on top of everything, if I am killed for it,' because he places the 'ego' in his case higher than the totality, for whose welfare he is pledged to work.[26]

---

24 McAleer, ibid., p. 22.

25 Alfred Vagts, *A History of Militarism* (New York, 1959), p. 177.

26 *Von einem Praktiker, Unser Ehren-und Waffen* (Thorn, 1893), p.11, cited by McAleer, *The Cult of Honor*, op. cit., p. 35.

Caste honour was particularly developed in Germany, and so too the capacity of society and the state to apply sanctions against those who did not uphold their social position.

However, the fact that the German duel was still vigorous towards the end of the nineteenth century does not mean that it was not challenged and there were those powerfully placed who doubted its utility. In fact, after 1815 the German duel seems to have experienced something of the decline that afflicted its French and English counterparts. This seems to have been consequent upon an attempt to restrain combat among the officer corps by Friedrich Wilhelm. In 1821 he established honour courts within the army to mediate disputes and investigate cases of misconduct. He issued declarations against duelling in 1823 and 1828 and in a fourth declaration in 1829 promised to prosecute duellists within the army. Between 1817 and 1829 officers were punished for taking part in thirty-nine serious duels; during the period between 1832 and 1843 that number dropped to twenty-nine.[27] By 1840 Millingen was asserting that duels 'are rare among German officers',[28] and McAleer has accepted that duels did indeed decline in the face of a serious attempt to suppress them.[29]

Yet duelling rebounded in the officer corps in the 1840s, and it may never have declined in the universities. The question, of course, is why this happened when the duel was routed or neutered elsewhere. For Ute Frevert, the resilience of the German duel must be ascribed, first, to the entrenchment of duelling within the universities in a way that had simply not happened in France or Britain and, second, to the embourgeoisement of both the universities and the duel that occurred from the mid eighteenth century onwards. There emerged in Germany a *Bildungsbürgertum*, an educated professional middle class, with aspirations to a culture of nobility and manliness. Within the universities, the sons of such men were socialised in values whose origins lay, originally, in the views of their social betters. Duelling and the values of honour were no small part of that socialisation process, and when he left school, regional student associations (*Landsmannschaften*) and student fraternities (*Burschenschaften*) ensured that the graduate remained inculcated with the values of the student fraternity. Success in the higher professions or in the state service in particular was thereafter to no small degree predicated upon previous success in student life and required constant reference back to the values of *Bildung*. In a sense, then, in Germany the student was educated in the schools of honour and never allowed or given incentive to leave; honour became an enshrouding life experience for the professional or for the successful civil servant in a way that was clearly not the case elsewhere.

---

27 Karl Demeter, *Das Deutsche Offizeerkorps in Gesellschaft und Staat, 1650–1945* (Frankfurt am Main: Bernard Graefe, 1962), p. 123.

28 Millingen, *The History of Duelling*, op. cit., vol. i, p. 347.

29 McAleer, *The Cult of Honor*, op. cit., p. 91.

One consequence of this was that although the professionals developed independently they remained intimately connected to an honour system of pre-modern origins. Even more importantly, the state, though modern in its appearance and to a degree its outlook, remained composed of middling administrators, functionaries and bureaucrats who arrogated themselves a place within honour culture and who barred advancement to those who did not share their values. Those outside of the state or the professions who were merely economically prosperous were denied entry to the system of honour thinking. More importantly, the truly economically active bourgeoisie did not set the tone of society. Rather, it was the educated elite, either professional men or state servants, who played the dominant role in determining the mores of the middling classes – in contrast to the situation in England, where, it is suggested, the independent and commercially minded shop keeping classes were beginning to assert themselves.

> What distinguished Germany from England in this respect was above all the dominant role of the formally educated within the middle class formation, and the special place that the *Bildung* had in the *Bürgertum's* self-awareness and lifestyle ... In England there was neither an omnipotent state that ennobled its servants and set them apart from other social groups, nor was there an independent and socially influential *Bildungs-bürgertum*. [30]

Frevert stresses that the middle in Germany did not merely ape the duel but rather developed their own distinctive duelling milieu, which was capable of existing independently of the highest classes and which, in an increasingly bourgeois society, was capable of maintaining the duel in the face of social change.

> Unlike in England, there were two 'ideal' types of duelling culture in Germany – the estatist and the bourgeois. The genuinely bourgeois emphasis on individual Bildung together with the already existing feudal (standisch) traditions in the army and the universities combined to create a potentially explosive mixture. It ensured the survival of the duel, even when the feudal element in German society declined as a result of social and political change. [31]

Of course, it was in the army that the fiercest duels were fought, but even in 1860 35 per cent of Prussian officers had middle-class backgrounds. By 1917 this number had risen to 70 per cent. [32]

---

30 Frevert, 'Honour and middle class culture', op. cit., pp. 234–235.

31 Ibid., p. 236

32 Frevert, 'The taming of the noble ruffian: male violence and dueling in early modern and modern Germany', in P. Spierenburg, ed., *Men and Violence: Gender, Honor, and Rituals in Modern Europe and America,* (Ohio: Ohio State University Press, 1998), pp. 37–64, at p. 52.

Others, though, have not agreed with the emphasis that Frevert has placed upon duelling in the middle orders. McAleer accepts, of course, that middling-order Germans constituted many of the nineteenth-century duellists but argues, 'The one undeniably non-liberal, non-bourgeois institution in Germany – the army – was the duel's chief procurator. It was under the moral and political sway of the German empire that the bourgeois sector of the German empire experienced social militarization.'[33] By the end of the century, the enormous reserve meant that many lived both the life of the bourgeois civilian and that of the officer corps. In effect, then, the military socialised the civil, and leadership of the military, McAleer stresses, was distinctively in the hands of the aristocracy, who still adhered to ideas that were feudal. The paradox of Frevert's arguments, McAleer asserts, is that 'While endeavouring to show the extent to which the German bourgeoisie willingly dueled and were masters of and not mastered by the practice, Frevert has thoroughly demonstrated the extent to which the bourgeoisie was in fact dominated by preindustrial forms.'[34] For McAleer, then, duelling was not an articulation of middle-class *Bildung* and individuality but rather a manifestation of the success of ideas antithetical to liberalism and glorifying war and authoritarianism.

V. G. Kiernan, writing from a Marxist perspective, is even more emphatic upon this point, 'Europe's old nobilities were stragglers from an epoch whose three score years and ten were long over, and could only be spun out by more or less black arts.'[35] Honour culture was one such black art, with the bourgeoisie 'succumbing to atavistic neo-feudalism and strident militarism'.[36] For Kiernan the very purpose of the duel was to serve as a measure distinguishing the poor but proud squirearchy from the new industrialists, against whom honour culture was a 'necessary bulwark'. Duelling, then, was a state-sponsored and above all aristocratic institution necessary to maintain the aristocratic (and militaristic) elements at the head of society. Attached to the aristocracy proper were those who might economically be but of the middling rank, but who, through manners, education and honour attached themselves firmly to the fortunes of the classes above. They were greatly assisted in this by the ubiquitous presence of a large, confident and well-organised administration: 'Prussian bureaucratic minuteness was applied to the task of propping up the phantom virtue of a bygone age.'[37]

If both Kiernan and McAleer stress the aristocratic leadership of the duel, for Kiernan duelling appears rather more as a conscious and artfully adopted strategy, a fabrication designed for the achievement of class ends. McAleer's analysis seems to

---

33 McAleer, *The Cult of Honor*, op. cit., p. 200.

34 Ibid., p. 199–200.

35 Kiernan, *The Duel in European History*, op. cit., p. 276.

36 Ibid., p. 271.

37 Ibid., p. 274.

me to be more firmly grounded in historicity, considering the evolution of an honour culture within which the participants were quite as much imprisoned as they were acting freely with true design and volition. The duel was not a privilege; it was rather the price of one's social position, sufficiently deadly that those outside its penumbra were rarely eager to force their way in. It was 'a form of tribute paid in lives for the privileges naturally obtaining to the exalted sectors of German society',[38] an institution 'whose menacing countenance seems to have generated greater public dismay than envy ... never was remorse expressed over the duel's exclusionary clause'.[39]

Kiernan, by contrast, will persist in characterising duelling as childish, although clearly it was not a matter of children. He writes of dying for honour as the product of an 'infantile inability to peer beyond the momentary burst of applause into the long silence of nothingness'. Yet honour culture represented a successful strategy of living (and occasionally dying) for many cultures over many centuries; his characterisation of it as infantile tells us more about him than about them. The systems of thought through which we interpret our place in the world, the ways in which we judge success or failure in life or deal with the fact of our ephemeral existence, cannot be based upon objectively verifiable realities – there is in a sense no true way of living – except that the man of faith may think he has found it. Honour culture was but one strategy of making sense of a world, and one no less rational than many others. Kiernan, in his desire to make the aristocracy the villains of a teleological history, is ever eager to find class conspiracy. Clearly, the effect of duelling was to maintain social separation and stratification, but this was not the redundant exercise that Kiernan seems to suppose, nor were its only victims those who were excluded from honour.

Kiernan has scarcely tackled the subject of student duelling, and so has not had to consider the role of the universities in sustaining duelling generally. It is important that many of the students were of a genuinely bourgeois origin as opposed to *Junkers* of middling economic power. McAleer for his part has acknowledged that 'students and former students together seem to have constituted not only the vanguard but moreover the body of the empire's duelling elite', but questions whether student duelling in the nineteenth century really should be regarded as true duelling at all since by the middle of the century it had moved so far from its earlier deadlier form.[40] Until the early nineteenth century student duels had predominantly been fought with the rapier (*Stossdegen*), and McAleer notes that the penetrative power of the weapon had resulted in many fatal internal injuries. However, after Breslau banned the weapon in 1819, many universities followed suit, and the very last fatality occasioned by the rapier was in 1847.[41]

---

38 McAleer, *The Cult of Honor*, op. cit., p. 38.

39 Ibid., p. 39.

40 Ibid., p. 131.

41 Ibid., p. 121.

Replacing the rapier was the *Schläger*, a curved weapon without a point. The consequence was that it became difficult to inflict penetrating injuries. Furthermore, padding was introduced to protect the limbs, and after 1857 the use of goggles shielded the eyes. Student 'duels' had by this time ceased to be a matter of affront and had become prearranged matches to test courage: 'Occasionally serious affairs were played out with curved sabers and no upholstery, and sometimes with standardized duelling pistols, but the vast percentage of so called *Ehrenhändel* among German students after 1871 were confined to the formal *Mensur*.'[42] Deaths from freak accidents still occurred, but these were rare since the *Mensur* was not truly a duel with deadly weapons. The student sword duel, then, in some respects, followed the pattern of the duel in France, being finessed into the formal fencing match. The gold standard of German duelling was the pistol duel as practised by the military.

However, as already mentioned, duelling within the military seems to have declined significantly during the period between 1815 and 1840. McAleer traces its revival to a two-part cabinet order issued on 20 July 1843 and drafted by War Minister Hermann von Boyen. The order firstly not only refurbished but also expanded the remit of military honour courts, making everyone who had ever been in uniform subject to their rulings, including militia officers, gendarmes and military pensioners. Each regiment was to establish a three-man council of honour which would refer qualifying disputes to a full military court. Most significant, however, was the second part of the order. It declared that 'In order to prevent as far as possible duels among my officers ... the court of honour should function as umpire in all disputes and insults among officers insofar as they are not directly connected with an act of service.'[43] The very wording of the article envisaged that it would not always be either possible or indeed appropriate to prevent duels. If the honour council were to learn of an impending duel, then it was to appear at the combat to ensure fair play in the proceedings! What was to follow thereafter was not a little farcical. The combatants, having formally broken the law, were to be taken into arrest, but so many excusatory grounds for duelling were envisaged that a brief incarceration was all that was likely to ensue. McAleer remarks that:

> to assert that in 1843 the officer duel was more or less legalised is scarcely an exaggeration ... In the thirteen year period after 1843 the number of duels reported in the army rose at least 25 percent over those documented in the decade previous to Fredrich Wilhelm IV's toothless measure.[44]

Duelling among civilians received its own fillip when in 1851 the Prussian Code revised the penalties for civilian duellists downwards. The actual fighting of a duel now

42 Ibid., p. 125.
43 Ibid., pp. 88–89.
44 Ibid., pp. 90–91.

attracted a penalty of only six months imprisonment, in contrast to the maximum of life imprisonment that could, theoretically, have been imposed previously. Even in the event of a death, the surviving duellist might serve as little as two years in prison. Furthermore, unlike in England, duellists were distinguished from normal felons and accorded the privileges of gentlemen whose parole, for instance, could be trusted to ensure their return to formal incarceration after a day of ease outside the prison.

After 1851, then, the number of civilians duelling increased. McAleer lists the participants as 'doctors, judges, engineers, architects, lawyers, civil servants, academics – men who had been to university, the so-called Bildungsbürgertum – and wealthy businessmen, industrialists, bankers, entrepreneurs, the so-called Besitzbügertum'.[45] In examining the list, one sees, of course, that men of some of these professions also duelled in England, but not for prolonged periods, and that there were men in many professions who duelled in Germany but not, it seems, in England. According to August Bebel, by the end of the nineteenth century about 5 per cent of German males were *satisfaktionsfähig*, capable of giving satisfaction.

The tolerance extended to duelling in the army was further formalised by Kaiser Wilhelm I, who declared that he would not tolerate in his army 'an officer capable of offending the honour of one of his comrades in a frivolous manner' nor 'an officer unwilling to defend his honour' in his army. By a decree of 2 May 1874 the Kaiser recognised that honour courts were not always obliged to seek a peaceful resolution to honour disputes and might in appropriate circumstances insist upon a meeting. In effect the power of honour courts to force officers to duel upon pain of dismissal was formalised. Officers who did duel and were injured in the encounter were to be allowed recuperative leave and, if necessary, granted pensions in consequence of their injuries.

The effect of the decree was to further emphasise the special legal status of not only professional officers but also officers of the reserve as compared to that of those wholly in civilian life. Indeed, this was further recognised in the right of officers to act instinctively to protect their honour (*Ehrennotwehr*) and the honour of their caste against outrages upon the part of bumptious civilians. What function, however, did the particular adulation of the cult of honour that seemed to be a characteristic of Wilhelmine Germany serve? Kiernan's answer is that the duel:

> Helped to keep the German army keyed up for action, in the years between 1871 and 1914 when German officers saw scarcely any active service and had to fall back on other ways of manifesting courage. A soldier who never fights comes to border on the ridiculous, or must feel that he does. Meanwhile, French, Russian, and above all British officers had continual opportunities to distinguish themselves in colonial wars, and pile up ribbons.[46]

---

45 McAleer, *The Cult of Honor*, op. cit., p. 36.

46 Kiernan, *The Duel in European History*, op. cit., p. 274.

The desire to test oneself and one's courage harkens back to the observations about masculinity and Thomas Hobbes that I made in Chapter 2 – that only by testing oneself and prevailing over others can some men banish doubts about their masculinity. Bereft of an arena in which to test its mettle, the army that did not fight stood upon its dignity and turned in upon itself. The very decline or disappearance of the duel in other countries may have helped to prolong it within Germany, since self-evidently the debased state of the French duel and the corresponding vigour of the German but reflected the differences in national character apparent in the war of 1870.

Summarising the later history of duelling in the three countries, then, one notes points of both similarity and difference. In none of the three did the sword duel retain its vigour into the second half of the nineteenth century; in each case the deadly encounter became finessed into something quite different. In great part, though, in France and post-unification Italy sword duels were the only duels upon offer, and casualty rates in meetings thereby declined until they were the merest fraction of what they had been at the beginning of the century.[47] In Germany, however, the pistol duel retained its vitality – yet not without challenge. If McAleer is right, pistol duelling within the military came under sustained pressure from about 1820 to 1843. This pressure, furthermore, was from the very top and resulted in a measurable reduction in the number of encounters. After 1843, however, the sovereigns were complicit in the development of a fetishised cult of honour that if not at all Germanic in its origins was particularly Germanic in its final form.

In each country the middle played a particular role. The reinvention of duelling as a liberal anti-authoritarian and even democratic institution in both France and Italy gives the lie to Kiernan's portrayal of duelling as but the dusty vestige of feudalism and chivalry. Duelling in those two countries became quite decisively a bourgeois enterprise. In Germany the picture is rather more complex, or at least two distinctively different interpretations have emerged, with Frevert emphasising the development of an independent bourgeois duelling culture and McAleer stressing the dependence of bourgeois duellists upon the mores and, crucially, the protection of the aristocracy and the state. Of course McAleer, viewing from the German perspective, scarcely accepts that later French duelling should be characterised as duelling at all. For McAleer duelling was a spent bullet in France by 1850:

> In democratic France, innocuous duelling was a normalized solution to private discord entirely compatible with the bourgeois state of society, thus not really, 'duelling' at all, as

---

47 McAleer, *The Cult of Honor*, op. cit., p. 189, reports upon the ways in which the dangers of French pistol duels were commonly mitigated by subterfuge on the part of the seconds. By contrast, he assures us that the German duel was 'not a cynical affair where men went through the motions of combat, firing over each others heads or ending sword bouts with token first blood'.

such is by historical definition an illegal activity. But in Germany, where duelling was both criminal and deadly, a code of honor permitted an elite to place itself above the law.[48]

Whether one accepts Frevert's or McAleer's view of duelling in Germany, it does not invalidate the observation that in that country, as in France and Italy, middling duellists played a crucial role in sustaining the duel into the second half of the nineteenth century and in accommodating it to the advance to modernity. Given then the prominence of the middling orders in the duels in these three nations, it comes as no surprise that almost all the reasons advanced for the decline of the duel in Britain have been predicated upon discussions of the attitude of the middling orders. But if the middling orders sustained the duel in France, Italy and Germany, what are we to make of Antony Simpson's argument that in England it was precisely the fact that the middling orders had adopted duelling that occasioned its demise?

Before dealing with that hypothesis, though, it is useful to consider who the English middle were. Hobsbawm reminds us that the middle classes did not form a coherent natural order. Rather, he divides them into three broad groups. First, there were the mercantile and financial interests whose wealth remained greater than that of the manufacturers for most of the nineteenth century. Second, there were the professional classes, who shared with the aristocracy the profits of the Old Corruption up until at least 1832. Among these we can number military officers, barristers, judges, administrators and holders of political posts and sinecures. Third, there were the industrialists, but these were far from being the most influential group, not least because it was not until after 1880 that profits from manufacturing exceeded those from the landed interest. If the first and the third groups were at least financially independent, the second group was not: 'The professional classes of "Old Corruption" on the other hand, could have no collective presence as a middle class, being parasitic on the state and estates of the landed interest ... they were part of what rational bourgeois reform wished to abolish.'[49] Notably absent from the list are those receiving salaries from private employment; salaries, other than from public offices, were not recognised as sufficiently important to comprise a separate category of income for tax purposes until 1898. Hobsbawm thus cautions us not to overestimate the importance of salaried employees or small businessmen within the nineteenth-century middle relative to the long-established influence of the financiers and those benefiting from public office.

Now according to Simpson's hypothesis, to which I alluded in Chapter 4, these were people who began to duel in the first half of the nineteenth century. The paradoxical effect, Simpson suggests, was that whereas embourgeoisement seemed to

---

48 Ibid., p. 208.

49 E. Hobsbawm, 'The example of the English middle class', in J. Kocka and A. Mitchell, eds, *Bourgeois Society in Nineteenth Century Europe* (Oxford: Berg, 1993), pp. 127–150, at p. 130.

strengthen the duel in France, Germany and Italy, in England it served to undermine it. The English elite, according to Simpson, turned their back upon the duel because it was becoming too popular with the wrong sort of people and without the support of the elite the middle were unable to sustain the institution, which consequently collapsed. However, neither Shoemaker's study of the social status of duellists prior to 1800, nor my own study, nor James Kelly's research in the Irish context, suggest that the social status of duellists declined significantly in the later eighteenth and into the nineteenth century. To be fair my data does suggest that the duel went into something of a decline after 1815–1816, but that there was, in simple numerical terms, a modest increase in duelling between 1821 and 1830. This might, somewhat speculatively, be linked to an increased participation in duelling by middling groups. However, the evidence suggests only a very small increase in the number of encounters, and the aforementioned studies aside, there are a number of further objections to Simpson's contention that middle-order duelling induced the elite to repudiate the practice.

Hobsbawm's argument that the professional classes of the Old Corruption could have no independent collective existence outside of their betters seems to me to be compelling; the extent to which they were perceived as a separate and threatening group seems doubtful. Ute Frevert concurs in pointing out that unlike, she believes, in Germany, no distinctly bourgeois form of duelling can be identified. In England, according to Frevert, there was no 'independent and socially influential *Bildungsbürgertum*'.[50] The very openness of the elite prevented the development of a distinct bourgeois culture which might have been viewed as a threat to better society. True, some of the middling orders did duel for a time, but duelling never became entrenched as part of their habitus, their view of the world. The lawyers, for example, flirted with duelling around 1800 but by 1820 had substantially renounced the practice; the surgeons came to it tardily and experienced the fashion right at the end of the institution itself. Aspiring military officers had of course always duelled, but no self-respecting officer of the 1830s or 1840s would have considered himself as being in any way 'bourgeois'. The Napoleonic Wars opened the way for rather more men of middling position to enter the officer corps. Some subsequently duelled. However, it would be wrong to assume that such was a necessary condition of advancement, for I have shown, in Chapter 4, that even within the military there was an influential constituency opposed to duelling. What is largely absent from Simpson's argument is evidence that middling officers who did duel were perceived as a particular threat to the established society of honour.

In respect of Hobsbawm's third group, the new industrial interests, it is really rather clear that there were very very few duels among the new commercial classes slowly emerging in the rapidly expanding towns of manufacture. This did not change

---

50   Frevert, 'Honour and middle class culture', op. cit., p. 235.

as the duel proceeded towards its final extinction. My, admittedly rather limited, survey of the local press supports that impression that the regions of England, Scotland and Wales are unlikely to have been hiding reservoirs of duellists invisible to the national press. Furthermore, had there been a contemporary perception that the middling orders were newly addicted to duelling, might we not expect to find this denounced in the reports from 1844 to 1847 of the Association for the Discouragement of Duelling? Yet those reports concentrate almost entirely upon the need to suppress the institution in the armed services. Incidentally, the reports of the society do much to confirm that the duel at the end of its life was indeed the very rarified event suggested by the national press. The 360 members of the above society, which included clergymen, judges, magistrates, city gentlemen, soldiers, sailors and rural landowners, were well placed to know what was happening in the nation. We can be pretty confident that when the society reported but a single duel for 1845 and declared at the end of 1846 that 'not a single instance of duelling is believed to have occurred within British dominions' the assertion was correct, or very nearly so.[51]

There were then, very few duels in the late 1830s and into the 1840s and these were not noticeably embarked upon by parvenus. It was comparatively late in the history of that duel that Wellington and Winchilsea met. If we consider the final years between 1840 and 1845, we find among the duellists not only the usual host of military officers, junior and senior, but also peers – Lord William Paget, Lord Sussex Lennox, Sir Richard Cardington and, most sensationally, the Earl of Cardigan – in company with well-heeled beaus such as Mr Craven Berkeley and Mr William Wellesley. Of course, there were lesser individuals, but so there were in the eighteenth century; this explanation for the demise of the duel begins to look like no explanation at all.

Furthermore, one might legitimately ask whether the portrait of the English aristocracy that the Simpson thesis suggests is one that we can accept. Do we believe that the English aristocracy were so incensed by the trespass by some of the middle onto their preserve that they quickly and decisively rejected their own two-hundred-year-old ritual system? One of the strengths of the English elite was precisely that it did not consist of a rigidly bounded group. Mosse notes that:

> Being commercially minded, members of the ruling aristocracy were ready to ally themselves with – indeed absorb – wealthy and talented representatives of commerce ... the political history of England could almost be written in terms of the history of the upwardly mobile descendants of trade and industry.[52]

---

51 Anon., *Third Report of the Association for the Discouragement of Duelling* (London: Alvey, 1846), p. 7.

52 W. Mosse, 'Nobility and bourgeoisie in nineteenth century Europe: a comparative view', in J. Kocka and A. Mitchell, eds, *Bourgeois Society in Nineteenth Century Europe* (Oxford: Berg, 1993), pp. 70–102, at p. 85.

Between 1760 and 1832 the peerage doubled, intermarriage between the aristocracy and financial and mercantile interests was not frowned upon, and 'The English nobility and gentry therefore contained titled and untitled members whose activities were impossible to distinguish from those of non-aristocrats.'[53] There were always parvenu duellists and always rather sniffy complaints about them, but what seems to be missing from the discourse of duelling in the nineteenth century is any consistent discourse upon the part of the aristocracy that articulated a fear of middle-class duellists. The anecdotal complaints about vulgarian shootists are little more than mere repetitions of the same anxieties about protecting the territory of honour that were being espoused two generations before. In fact, even earlier than that Daniel Defoe was complaining in the *Complete English Tradesman* of shopkeepers who wore swords and acted the gentleman. There had always been newcomers rising to the level where they were capable of giving satisfaction. To my mind it is quite implausible to suppose that an energetic consensus repudiating former practices and constructed around a resistance to vulgarity could emerge so rapidly among the metropolitan elite without being articulated in the literature of the period.

There are, then, sound reasons to doubt that the established duelling fraternity was so discommoded by the activities of parvenu duellists as to renounce the practice altogether. Neither the general disposition of the elite nor the evidence of the number of the middling orders who actually duelled would support this assertion. Simpson has, however, rested much of his argument upon comments made by the press in the aftermath of a single duel that took place between Mr Eliot and Mr Mirfin in 1838. The dispute had been inspired by a minor traffic accident, and in the resulting duel Mr Mirfin was killed. Simpson's contention, in brief, is that initially the press commented favourably upon the behaviour of the parties, but once the social status of the duellists became apparent, press and public became relentlessly hostile. Although Eliot was never tried, two seconds, Mr Young and Mr Webber were; both were, most unusually, convicted of murder. In Simpson's eyes this rare condemnation of the seconds of duellists is then evidence of the elite's reaction to middle-class duelling. These were the sorts of dandelions that filled the elite with revulsion. As Simpson puts it:

> It is not quite clear which was the most heinous aspect of this case: the capital crime charged, or the social rank of the defendants ... Much was made of the fact that 'the parties concerned in this affair, though aping the barbarous code of refined honour, could apparently claim only very doubtful gentility'. Of the six young men involved in the affair, one was the nephew of a Taunton innkeeper, and two were, or had been, linen-drapers in Tottenham Court Road. The provenance of the other three is not recorded.

---

53 Hobsbawm, 'The example of the english middle class', op. cit., p. 132.

One can understand why the gentry were less than pleased by such presumption and the attitude of an aristocratic judge in 1838 is understandable in view of his own class position. The reaction of the middle-class press to this 'raffish exhibition of squabbling shopmen' was extreme. Initial reports of the encounter, which variously described the antagonists as, 'a young man of independent fortune' and the 'son of a major-general' were neutral – even approving. Once their true social status was revealed, the focus of the press changed and the social attributes of the participants became the major object of attention.[54]

There are, however, a number of difficulties with this interpretation, which in part depends upon an assessment of the social status of the parties that was made by Millingen in 1841. Robert Baldick in 1965 had followed Millingen in describing the two as 'mere hempen homespuns', and V. G. Kiernan subsequently adopted this terminology.[55] However, there is another story to be told. Millingen describes Mirfin as the son of a mercer and the keeper of a linen-draper's shop and Eliot as a former officer in the British Auxiliary Legion and the nephew of an innkeeper. He adds for good measure that one of the seconds was the son of a brickmaker. Perhaps, but Mirfin's father was described by *The Times* as an alderman of the corporation of Doncaster and a businessman of very considerable property. The sons owned drapers businesses in Doncaster and Manchester, chemists businesses and other property. One was in the legal profession and sufficiently prosperous as to be able to maintain his own hunting establishment near Uxbridge.[56] The Mirfin family, then, was indeed in trade, but as I have observed before with epithets such as 'brewer', such terms in fact described men of very much more substance than might be supposed by the description of shopkeeper.

Charles Mirfin was described by newspapers as 'a gentleman of independent fortune' and this was no mere fancy but the words of his servant at the coroner's inquest.[57] In addition to wealth he was, crucially, educated as a gentleman, finishing in Paris and thereafter passing his time in gentlemanly sporting pursuits. His opponent Eliot only held the rank of second lieutenant in the British Legion, but on the other hand he was also the son of a retired major. One of the seconds was indeed the son of a builder, although we are unsure exactly what that designation really meant. Millingen fails to mention that the other second, Broughton, was trained to the Bar and was the nephew of Baronet Sir John Broughton. These then were no earls or dukes, but they were men of substantial property who were educated as gentlemen and connected through family to the law, to the military, and to gentry. Men such as

---

54 Simpson, 'Dandelions', op. cit., p. 105.

55 Baldick, *A History of Duelling*, op. cit., pp. 109–111.

56 *The Times*, 10 Sep. 1838, p. 6, col. f.

57 *The Times*, 27 Aug. 1838, p. 6, col. c.

these had been duelling for over a hundred years – and most of society had treated them as gentlemen. Why then were the men in this case treated with such distain?

Not, I would suggest, because these men were 'middle class' but because of the shocking details of the background to the duel and of its actual conduct which began to emerge some time after the initial reports of the encounter. First, the survivor, Eliot, was an experienced duellist. He had, according to one report, already fought five duels in Spain and killed two opponents.[58] An officer who had served with him in Spain, however, replied to *The Times* that to his knowledge he had fought only three duels and wounded two officers (who had clearly believed him at the time to be a gentleman).[59] Although a party might be lauded for a duel, it was always the case that habitual duellists were liable to be regarded as social monsters dangerous to their fellows. The deceased, Mirfin, by contrast became the object of public sympathy once it became clear that he was a young man with no experience of firearms. Furthermore, it was Eliot who provoked the encounter after a coach accident by striking the injured Mirfin. In addition, Eliot behaved so atrociously on the field as to take the affair entirely outside the ambit of honour. He approached the field casually whistling and declared that he was used to duelling and little bothered by it. More importantly, *The Times* reported that at the inquest a witness swore that he had heard Eliot say, immediately after shooting Mirfin, 'I have done for the *****.' According to the newspaper, 'a thrill of horror here ran through the persons present at the unfeeling conduct of the individual'.[60]

A declaration of the absence of malice, a rebuttal of the murderous intent that the law would otherwise presume, was crucial in the defence of a defendant duellist. Solicitude for the fallen was to be expected and to be cited in mitigation. Eliot's remarks, his murderous triumphalism, were dishonourable. His conduct and that of all the seconds immediately afterwards was even more so, for they simply ran away, leaving the body in the custody of the surgeon and assaulting a cabman in the process. Furthermore, all parties then refused to submit themselves to justice and decamped to France. It had counted strongly against Maj. Campbell at his trial in 1808 that he had assumed a false name and hidden in London in disguise before eventually surrendering himself. The successful duellist was expected to demonstrate that same courage and dignity in submitting himself to the judgment of the law as he had displayed in submitting himself to the dangers of the field. In terms of its own code, then, the conduct of this duel was deplorable. This amply explains the strong revulsion expressed by the jury at the trial of the seconds and the public hostility expressed after the details of the unequal encounter came to light at the inquest.

---

58 *The Times*, 10 Sep. 1838, p. 6, col. f.

59 *The Times*, 13 Sep. 1838, p. 7, col. c.

60 *The Times*, 27 Aug. 1838, p. 6, col. c.

When the two seconds, Mr Young and Mr Webber, surrendered themselves for trial, Simpson suggests, the judge Mr Justice Vaughan displayed a prejudice against them. Yet from the report of the latter's direction I can find no evidence of this. Vaughan began by reminding the jury that they were bound to dismiss from their minds all the impressions which they had received out of court that were injurious to the prisoners at the bar. He went on to correctly cite the law to the effect that all persons who had assisted in a duel in which death took place were guilty of murder as principals in the second degree. However, considering the conduct of the parties, he was rather generous:

> Now with regard to the manner in which the duel was conducted, it did not appear that any unfair advantage had been taken by either party. Indeed, on the contrary, so far as he (Mr Justice Vaughan) knew anything of such matter, the affair appeared to have been managed with a strict regard to the practice usually followed upon similar occasions.[61]

The summing up did not in fact indicate any particular hostility. Indeed, once the verdict was given, Justice Vaughan hastened to assure the defendants that although the penalty of death would be recorded against their names, it would not be carried out but would be commuted. In the event the sentence was indeed commuted to twelve months' imprisonment.

The Eliot and Mirfin duel would perhaps have served as a rather better test of Simpson's 'middle-class' hypothesis had it indeed been conducted according to the normal practices of honour. As it stands, however, the pejorative view taken of the backgrounds of the parties does not seem to have arisen independently of the circumstances of the duel. That is to say that once a picture of the events emerged, it became necessary to uphold the integrity of a duelling system whose values had been parodied. It became necessary to explain the occurrence in such a manner as would leave the values of the duel itself intact. Hence the parties were to be banished to the very margins of the duelling fraternity. 'What can one expect of mere linen drapers?' Millingen seems to have said in his history, echoing the sentiments expressed in the comic morality tales that *The Times* had run and was running. Yet he derived his material substantially from that paper and was surely aware that the parties had a rather better claim to gentility than he allowed in his history. All this, of course, does presume a certain prejudice against linen-drapers. This is by no means the same as saying that the parties were necessarily derided as middle-class duellists. It was rather that the disapprobation generally expressed of their conduct manifested itself in an accentuation of those facets that cast doubt upon their claims to gentility and a suppression of those facets which would have served to uphold their claims. Nor

---

61   Millingen, *History of Duelling*, op. cit., vol. ii, p. 354.

must the degree of contemporary pejorative comment be overestimated. Following the conviction of the seconds *The Times* ran a number of articles protesting that twelve months imprisonment was too severe a penalty to have been imposed.

In summary the evidence that gentlemen were repudiating duelling because the bourgeois were adopting it, is really very thin and the trial and conviction of Mr Young and Webber does not in fact strengthen that argument. Indeed, the Hon. Grantley Berkeley, in declining an invitation to join the Association for the Discouragement of Duelling in 1845, regretted that the duelling franchise was not further extended, 'a man having an undoubted source of income from trade being considered as having no claim except by statute law upon the protection of society'.[62] Some among the middling orders at best merely copied, without ever genuinely incorporating, the duel; thus, when the elites ceased to resort to it – when they, as Frevert puts it, 'agreed on a different concept of honour' – the rest of society acquiesced.

---

62 *The Times*, 24 Jun. 1845, p. 5, col. c.

9

The Reformation of Space,
Place and Mind

If Simpson's 'dandelion' hypothesis is to be discarded, as I am afraid it must be, then a contrary hypothesis suggests itself: that duelling disappeared not because the middle were adopting it to the alarm of the elite, but because the middle were resolutely opposed to it and imposed their will upon their betters. The belief that the demise of duelling can be ascribed to the rise of a new commercial middle class, whose values were (allegedly) necessarily antithetical to the culture of honour, has gained broad acceptance.[1] Donna Andrew has suggested that:

> The most important effect of the growth of commerce was that by encouraging personal freedom and political liberty, a new and energetic class arose, a class that could both oppose itself to the classes above it, while claiming to represent the real interests of all of society ... It could and did reject the established norms of gentlemanliness, which the code of honour represented and substitute its own redefinition of the term ... Duelling was identified as a failing of the upper classes and, as such, roundly condemned.[2]

According to Andrew, it was the onset of Christian commerce in place of the code of honour that served to displace the duel and the middle classes that struggled the hardest to suppress duelling, 'thus the debate about duelling was an important element in the formation of the middle class, and the gestation of middle class culture'.[3] Kiernan seemed to accept Andrew's argument when he declared that the abandonment of the duel was an important symptom of the decline of aristocratic hegemony.[4] James Kelly again reiterated the

---

1 Cautious commentators have, though, seen no contradiction in holding this to be the case, while also espousing Simpson's Dandelion hypothesis.

2 Andrew, 'The code of honour and its critics', op. cit., pp. 428–429.

3 Ibid., p. 434.

4 Kiernan, *The Duel in European History*, op. cit., p. 220.

argument in his work on the duel in Ireland. According to him the demise of the duel was:

> A triumph for the rule of law over that of traditional privilege and for the emerging middle class over traditional aristocratic mores. These contrary tendencies had been engaged in a visible struggle for pre-eminence since at least the 1780s when there was a perceptible increase in public commitment to law and morality ... From one perspective this was the inevitable result of the emergence in industrialising Britain of a propertied middle class increasingly determined to enforce its social priorities and ideological concerns.[5]

Certainly, what we do see emerging by the end of the eighteenth century is a new type of masculine persona possessed of 'an entrepreneurial, individualistic masculinity, organised around a punishing work ethic, a compensating validation of the home and a restraint upon physical aggression.'[6] Wiener has no doubts about from whence this new persona comes:

> In the rapidly growing and increasingly influential religious middle class, male self-hood came to depend less upon physical virility and more on occupation, on 'rational' public activity and on one's role as husband and father – a shift which was to spread both to the aristocracy and to the working classes during Victoria's reign.[7]

I have though, some reservations about all this, most notably about the implicit assumption of some commentators that the demise of duelling is indeed to be regarded as, 'the inevitable result of the emergence in Britain of a propertied middle class'. This seems a somewhat inadequate explanation when in continental countries, the middle adopted the duel, and even to an extent made it their own and when Robert Nye can confidently assert that 'virtually everywhere in the West, the duel was an engine for the integration of bourgeois and aristocrat.'[8] The middle orders in Europe were not, in short, implacably opposed to duelling. True, in Britain during the later eighteenth and early nineteenth centuries, there was a clear shift in mentalities, and the dominant social values became more hostile to duelling. However, I am uncertain whether it can be correct to ascribe these changes merely to the activities of a new

---

5   Kelly, *That Damn'd Thing Called Honour,* op. cit., p. 277.

6   John Tosh, 'Masculinities in an industrializing society: Britain, 1800–1914', *Journal of British Studies,* 44 (2005), pp. 330–342, at p. 331.

7   Martin J. Wiener, 'The Victorian criminalization of men', in P. Spierenburg, ed., *Men and Violence: Gender, Honor and Rituals in Modern Europe and America* (Columbus: Ohio State University Press, 1998), pp 197–212, at p. 201.

8   Nye, 'The end of the modern French duel', op. cit. , p. 84.

species of middle class-whose influence it is all too easy to exaggerate. Identifying the middle classes is, to a degree, a modern enterprise and one in a sense doomed to failure since notions of class exist in part independently of objectively verifiable considerations of income, education and so on. To my mind Wahrman is entirely right to point out the dangerous circularity of an argument which identifies certain values as distinctly middle class and then searches for the proponents of those values in society as evidence that a middle class has indeed come into being. For Wahrman the notion of the middle class is a 'charged and contingent historical invention' and conceptualising society around a middle class was 'a particular construction chosen for it, for which there were a number of alternatives'.[9]

Classes in society exist because they are thought to exist, sometimes in the absence of any objectively verifiable substance. They are spoken and in an act of performative magic they come into being by being thought into being. In the early stages of formation, the articulator of such a class is 'an impostor endowed with the skeptron' who acts on behalf of a group that in reality comes to exist only through his own act of representation.[10] The values that were to come to be characterised as middle class were present in all classes of society in the first half of the nineteenth century and indeed before. They did not come into being as a by-product of the evolution of a wholly new social group whose coincident interests and attitudes inevitably coalesced into the creation of a new and self-aware class. Rather, the social environment at this time was populated by many speakers of many different persuasions seeking to speak the society of their own preference. Through processes which will probably always be obscure to us, ideas became associated. A particular construction was chosen, perhaps indeed because it had an observable attraction to particular groups. Particular values, having been declared as middle class, slowly became, through repetitive labelling, sufficiently discrete to be cognitively recognised and socially employed, even though the middle neither had sole ownership of such practices and attitudes nor necessarily always employed them.

Certainly, we must be very wary of assuming that because society increasingly espoused what we have come to call middling values, transformation can be credited to leadership from the middle. If we consider society in simple economic terms, we must, to repeat, observe that the duel was in terminal decline long before manufacturing capital had become more important in society than the power of the landed interest. In political terms it was in decline before the Reform Act 1832, and in practical terms we will see that the campaigns against duelling were led by those who would have been horrified to be viewed as expounding 'bourgeois values'.

---

9 Dror Wahrman, 'Middle class domesticity goes public: gender, class and politics from Queen Caroline to Queen Victoria', *Journal of British Studies*, 32:4 (1993), pp. 396–432, at p. 432.

10 Bourdieu, *Language and Symbolic Power*, op. cit., p. 109.

Ute Frevert has pointed out, to my mind rightly, that the arguments used to explain the death of the duel in England, 'stand on rather weak foundations'.[11] In particular, she rejects the contention that its demise can be attributed either to immediate instrumentalist steps taken to suppress the institution in the 1840s, most notably the amendment of the Articles of War in 1844, or to the advance of the bourgeoisie. In respect of instrumental steps against the duel she notes that punishment had no observable effect upon the popularity of the German duel, just as Herr had already demonstrated that in France even the autocracy of Louis XIV could not suppress honour culture. Furthermore, the significance of the amendment of the Articles of War in 1844 has in itself been exaggerated since those articles had long since contained fulsome provisions against duelling. Courts martial had, on occasion, deployed those provisions, and the 1844 amendment marked but a renewed determination to apply what was already present rather than a significant innovation in military law.

In respect of the role of the English bourgeoisie, Frevert notes that the elite had always been open to them and had long succeeded in coopting the most successful into their ranks. However:

> Acceptance into this social elite was conditional on the newcomer's adopting its culture and standards of behaviour. As long as the hegemony of the landed classes continued, which it did, on the evidence of historical research until the 1880s, criticism by outsiders of their lifestyle and socio-cultural norms would not have been given a hearing or gained acceptance within the elite itself.[12]

Frevert, of course, has still to explain why, if it was not due to pressure from below, the elite did actually repudiate the duel. For her it was the reform of education as delivered by the English public schools that held the key:

> In the private schools newly established or reformed after the 1820s, individuality or independence of mind was not highly valued. A complex system of self-management, in which the younger boys were subordinate and obedient to the older boys, for whom they acted as servants, combined with a merciless ritual of punishment and initiation, encouraged a sense of community and social conformity ... The duel was based upon highly ritualised forms of communication, yet what was given expression in these forms was not collectivity, but absolute individuality. The priority of the group or of the collective taught in the English public school system of the nineteenth century was diametrically opposed to this principle of individuality and was probably of decisive importance in bringing about the observed change in the behaviour of the English social elite.[13]

---

11 Frevert, 'Honour and middle class culture, op. cit., p. 223.

12 Ibid., p. 225.

13 Ibid., p. 226.

This, though, merely invites a further question, which Frevert does not answer: What was it that caused such an apparently profound transformation in the educational ethos of English schools? Might this not merely take us back to the assertion that educational reform was the product of the inexorable rise of middle class values? Furthermore, the regime of bullying and brutality to which Frevert alludes could be interpreted entirely differently. It might be supposed to create just the sort of gentleman, physically tough and pugnacious, eager to assert the adult bodily autonomy that was to feature so strongly in the duelling reports. In addition, the timetable for this volte-face in educational attitudes and their effects seems somewhat tight. Was not Eton, for example, particularly influential in determining the mores of young gentlemen? Yet the reign of the headmaster Keate, from 1809 to 1834, was profoundly conservative. In 1825, for example, he defended precisely the type of individualistic behaviour that Frevert asserts the schools had turned against, which is to say bare-knuckle boxing. It was only with the arrival of Edward Hawtrey and, in particular, the retirement of Provost Goddall in 1840 that the culture of Eton began to change. The duel had already died out long before any of the pupils of the new Eton had ascended to the head of society.[14]

Yet the behaviour of the social elite clearly did change during the first half of the nineteenth century. However, so did the behaviour of many other sections of society. What one observes during the later eighteenth and early nineteenth centuries is the spread of a set of dispositions, propositions and perceptions which, to repeat, in time came to be labelled as and therefore attributed to the middling orders, even though the middling orders neither solely invented, solely owned nor solely employed them. Together the slow accumulation of ideas, attributes and perceptions seems to have led to the development of mentalities that were rather more functionalist in their outlook. By this I mean that men became better equipped to postpone gratification and suppress immediate emotional impulses in favour of planning to achieve long-term and seemingly rational objectives.[15] Methodical rational planning and the prioritisation of distant goals equipped those who possessed such mentalities with a calculating futurology antithetical to the culture of honour. I do not suggest that the facets of such mentalities described were wholly novel (what project could be more ambitious, meticulous and further projected into the future than the completion of a cathedral?) any more than E. P. Thompson would suggest that the desire to keep to

---

14 Christopher Hollis, *Eton: A History* (London: Hollis and Carter, 1960), for the tenure of Keate see pp. 185–221.

15 I say seemingly because the accumulation of ever increasing amounts of property – often through overwork and neglect of other interests – may of itself be regarded as a form of honour culture no more rational than the systems of thinking it has replaced.

time was a wholly novel impulse in the eighteenth century.[16] However, it was during this period that such mentalities became rather more important and so eventually reconfigured the social environment, creating a society orientated around future expectation, rational planning, profit and progress.

Reconfiguring a social environment was of course a matter of immense complexity, and the disappearance of duelling was but one facet of the process. In the face of so many changes in society in the first half of the nineteenth century, it is probably futile to assign the demise of any customary behaviour to a single operator or cause. Certainly, I shall not do so in respect of duelling. Thinking broadly, I would prefer rather to identify species of direct and indirect causes; direct causes relating to steps taken to discourage duelling by those consciously willing and aiming for its demise. Indirect causes reflecting the fact that acts and changes within society that were undertaken for quite different objectives nevertheless had the effect of hindering the operation, transmission and ultimately the viability of honour culture. It bears repeating that although the disappearance of the duel by the mid nineteenth century was perhaps not inevitable, duelling was a rather more marginalised activity and rather more vulnerable than the publicity given to it would sometimes suggest. The idea of duelling as a mark of social distinction was, I believe, very important, but the lead was given by but a very small number in society.

Important things were signified by the final demise of duelling, but that demise becomes somewhat easier to explain when one appreciates that duelling was not a practice that had to be uprooted, root and branch, from every small town and parish in England. Rather it required a reformation in the attitudes of a comparatively small number of gentlemen who were at the centre of metropolitan society or who held positions within the government bureaucracy and military. Honour culture, though, as the whole history of the duel suggests, could be remarkably difficult to eradicate, and notwithstanding the small number of duellists, socially they were very well placed. It is doubtful that direct attempts to suppress the duel in the nineteenth century would have succeeded had not duelling been exposed as an increasingly anomalous act in a society that was reconsidering appropriate behaviour and appropriate use of public space.

Shoemaker was probably correct to argue that by the onset of the nineteenth century duelling in civilian life was but 'a pale reflection' of its former self, although the war with France invigorated the military duel. In proportionate terms the peaks in English duelling were most probably during the reign of James I and in the period immediately following the Restoration. In a sense, then, duelling had been declining

---

16 For a discussion on the relationship between the perception of time and capitalism, see Edward P. Thompson, 'Time, work-discipline and industrial capitalism', *Past and Present*, 38 (1967), pp. 56–97.

for a very long time, although there were numerical spikes in, for example, times of war. This decline does not seem to have been in consequence of any particular initiatives against it, and the decline has, at least to some degree, to be located within that broader Elian civilising process wherein violence in society is said to have become ever more circumscribed. This is a process where we are often 'forced ... to explain the decline in terms of heavy generalisations about the civilising effects of religion, education and environmental reform'.[17]

Nevertheless, the general decline in violence seems to have been real enough. Beattie, for example, commenting upon the decline of homicide rates in Surrey between 1660 and 1800, remarks that men and women became 'more controlled, less likely to strike out when annoyed or challenged, less likely to settle an argument or assert their will by recourse to a knife or their fists, a pistol or a sword'.[18] Stone has shown that homicide rates in medieval England were about ten times those of today and were still about five times the modern level in the early seventeenth century, but that they declined between 1660 and 1800 to rates commensurate with those of today. Controversial, however, is his following assertion:

> The decline in the level of recorded violence – notably homicide – I still believe can plausibly be attributed to a cultural softening of manners, a greater sensitivity to cruelty and violence, and to the social rise of a middle class culture and a more market orientated society.[19]

It is the attribution of this increased civility to an alleged middle class and commercial culture that is difficult. Beattie points out that the decline in homicide rates was such as can only be explained by a change in sentiments throughout society, by a reformation in attitudes to violence among those well below the status of a commercial middle class. One could, of course, argue that a burgeoning middle class were proselytising among the lower orders and inculcating them with their values of commercial civility, but to argue that they were doing so as early as the seventeenth century would seem problematic. Cockburn warns of the irregular and piecemeal nature of social change and notes:

> The distorting potential of a monocausal approach is well illustrated by Stone's strained attempt to demonstrate that 'the commercialisation of values' during the eighteenth century was accompanied by a 'slow revulsion of public opinion against physical cruelty'.[20]

---

17 Gatrell, 'The decline of theft and violence', op. cit., p. 300.

18 Beattie, *Crime and the Courts in England*, op. cit., p. 112.

19 Lawrence Stone, 'The history of violence in England: some observations: a rejoinder', *Past and Present*, 108 (1985), pp. 216–224, at p. 219.

20 Cockburn, 'Patterns of violence in English society', op. cit., p. 103.

I am not concerned here with tackling the broader issue of the general decline in violence in society, except to note that, for whatever reason it occurred, scholars almost unanimously accept that it did. With this drop came a concomitant decline in homicides perpetrated by gentlemen. Shoemaker notes that there was a dramatic decrease in homicides in London in the eighteenth century, 'caused by the formulation of new understandings of masculinity in the context of the changing social-cultural significance of honour in urban society'.[21] Gentlemen were changing the way they behaved in urban space. For a start they were no longer duelling within it: of thirty-four duels sampled by Shoemaker between 1660 and 1724, one-third took place within the built up area of London, whereas only seven out of a hundred duels studied in the last quarter of the eighteenth century did so.[22] It was not only that duels were no longer fought on the streets, but also that they were no longer occasioned there: 'Killings provoked by insulting words, jostling on the street and insults to gentlemanly honour declined substantially after 1750.'[23]

To what, then, do we owe the decline in violence between gentlemen? I argued earlier that the ability of a gentleman to display pugnacious physicality was a necessary concomitant to the maintenance of bodily integrity and proxemic distance in the context of disordered public space. It was a matter of utility quite as much as outlook. It is no coincidence, I believe, that the slow improvement in the way that gentlemen seem to have conducted themselves towards each other in the eighteenth and early nineteenth centuries, and hence the decline in those trivial social disputes which so often engendered duels, went hand in hand with a largely successful attempt to prioritise the interests of the better classes, to subdue public space, to tame the unruly elements within it, and to make passage through it more commodious for gentlemen. None of this was, of course, undertaken with a view to dissipating quarrels among gentlemen. Rather, the changing nature of public space owed much to new technical possibilities and new initiatives in planning and architecture. In addition, however, there developed in the eighteenth century a particular desire to subdue and suppress activities within public space that either were repugnant to the morals of the evangelical revival or aroused fears about the gathering of unruly groups in the context of a society increasingly infused with radical ideas. As public space became less combative, less difficult, so too, I suggest, did the necessity of gentlemanly pugnacity begin to disappear and the harshness of social interaction begin to abate. The very behaviour of gentlemen began to change.

In respect of London, the process began at the end of the seventeenth century with the construction of the new residential squares. At first these were inhabited

---

21 Shoemaker, 'Male honour', op. cit., p. 190.

22 Shoemaker, 'The taming of the duel', op. cit., p. 537.

23 Shoemaker, 'Male honour', op. cit., p. 203.

by all manner of people, but towards the end of the eighteenth century the move to extend private rights gradually ousted other elements to create comparatively secure environments for the well-to-do. At the same time, London gentlemen seem to have adopted new modes of behaviour within public space. What one observes is an increasing emphasis on privacy and a turning away from display, part of the process of turning one's back upon Georgian ostentation. Lawrence notices the changes through the medium of gardening. The purpose of early London squares had been fulfilled by visual openness; one promenaded publicly to see one's acquaintances and to be seen. By the end of the eighteenth century the design of the gardens therein began to reflect a new desire for privacy from both the few and the many. Thus, for example, when Grosvenor Square was enclosed in 1774, the trees therein, hitherto pruned short, were allowed to grow up to obscure the view across it; St James's Square came, by 1817, to be concealed by a deep plantation along its old iron fence.

On the streets themselves passage became easier and more secure due to the gradual implementation of lighting and paving, changes which, although presented as having indisputable benefits, again prioritised a particular constituency of interest. Schivelbusch's study of light, politics and policing in Paris notes the early identification of light not with the ability to move and interact but with the ability to survey and control. The role of commercial torchbearers as police informants and the iconic grandeur of the lamp standards as declarations of royal power, protected by the fiercest prohibitions, necessarily connected the rather ineffectual illumination of the city with a particular type of repressive social ordering. Hence when Foulon, Berthier and others were 'lanternised' in 1789, the convenience of these points of suspension was matched by the delight at a very symbolic mode of revenge.[24]

Physical improvement in London was closely associated with the closer supervision and suppression of the undesirable; what was changing was not merely the appearance of public space but the sense of what public spaces were for. Slowly, streets came to be theorised as an environment through which objects moved, rather than an environment in which objects were placed. The movement of bodies not only suited the purposes of the private gentlemen seeking to pass as quickly as possible to nodes of private interest but also, and even more importantly, helped to constitute a new social trope. As Sennett puts it:

> Individual bodies moving through urban space gradually became detached from the space in which they moved, and from the people the space contained. As space became devalued through motion, individuals gradually lost a sense of sharing a fate with others.[25]

---

24 Wolfgang Schivelbusch, 'The policing of street lighting', *Yale French Studies*, 73 (1987), pp. 61–74.

25 Richard Sennett, *Flesh and Stone: The Body and the City in Western Civilisation* (London: Faber and Faber, 1994), p. 323.

The street, in short, was no longer the place in which one displayed oneself and competed against one's rivals, but rather the space through which one moved as quickly as possible. As an example of the new prioritisation of interests Sennett cites the construction of Regent Street and the Park. Uncontested passage was achieved by the use of traffic designed to thin out space; the pressure of linear pedestrian movement made it difficult to remain stationary, to form crowds or to be addressed.[26]

As public space was reconceptualised, opinion formers began to see some of the long established usages of the streets as no longer appropriate. Moral reformers were particularly suspicious of public space as the traditional locus of unlicensed recreations which aroused disreputable passions among the lower classes. Language was among the many weapons that these reformers deployed to justify the seizure of public areas and their arrogation to their own interests. To illustrate, in 1784 Robert Raikes came across a group of children playing in the street in Gloucester. It was Sunday, naturally; otherwise most of these children would have been at labour. Raikes, however, fumed to a newspaper that the street was 'filled with multitudes of these wretches, who, released on that day from their employment, spend their day in noise and riot, playing at chuck and cursing and swearing'.[27] No great harm seems to have been afoot, but Raikes spoke of observing their 'misery and idleness'. The association of play with idleness seems contradictory unless one shares Raikes's sense of appropriateness; similarly, it was a very particular construct of the social good which described the playing children, released for a time from their labours, as 'miserable'. In Raikes's perception the occupation of the streets seemed to have been synonymous with a kind of moral stagnation. So long as they were out of place, these children were not children but 'wretches' and they could only be designated again by useful productive terms once relocated and reclassified as workers, or as pupils and worshippers in new Sunday schools.

If children playing in the street were an irritation, violent acts in the public thoroughfare were to be more strongly deplored. The state played its part in removing many of its own violent acts from the public eye, with the abolition of the Tyburn procession in 1783, the end of the burning of women in 1790, the relocation of whipping to the prison, and the demise of the gibbet and the pillory. In addition, in the midst of all this there also emerged a strange concern for the welfare of animals. Robert Darnton has characterised the violent acts perpetrated against animals by apprentice printers in eighteenth-century Paris as resistive acts playing out upon a symbolic level the necessarily suppressed desires of urban workers for revenge upon their exploitative masters.[28]

---

26 Ibid., pp. 324–325.

27 *Manchester Mercury*, 6 Jan. 1784.

28 Robert Darnton, *The Great Cat Massacre* (Harmondsworth: Penguin, 1991), pp. 79–104.

It is interesting, then, that between 1800 and 1835, while children were being lashed in London's prisons or confined for days in total darkness and complete solitude, there were eleven bills promoted by the patrons of the Society for the Prevention of Cruelty to Animals.[29] An 1835 act[30] formalised what had been a largely successful campaign against bear baiting, cock fighting, dog fighting, badger baiting and bull running.

A measure of the change in the flavour of life in the streets at the end of all this can be gained from the recollections of Francis Place. Within his lifetime the bawdy street entertainers had been displaced from the streets and public opinion would not sanction their return.[31] The instruments to ensure that this was so were on hand with the passing of the Metropolitan Police Act 1829 and the Municipal Corporations Act 1835. Notwithstanding doubts about the effectiveness of the new police, Critchley notes the contrast apparent between Bristol and London after the Lords rejected the Reform Bill in October 1831. In Bristol, where the mayor had no police and had to rely upon the *posse comitatus*, the disturbances spread out of control and twelve were killed. In London, by contrast, the police were able to contain the disturbances and no deaths occurred. Shoemaker has argued that:

> Other features of modernisation and the 'civilising process' commonly identified by historians such as the increasing role of the state and the growth of middle class and industrialisation, appear to have had had little direct role in taming the duel in London ... London's evolving police force played a very limited role.[32]

In the direct sense I would agree with him, but the reconstruction of public space, the containment and the displacement of violent acts had, I believe, a progressive and salutary effect upon the general behaviour of the elites which could not but in turn affect their views on the commission of violent acts against each other. Put simply, by 1840 the experience of life as publicly lived had changed for gentlemen. Less was drunk, less was gambled; violence in all its classes was less often publicly observed. A broad social consensus as to acceptable behaviour, assignable to no single cause and no single period of time, was palpable.

---

29 'The common people may ask with justice, why abolish bull baiting, and protect hunting and shooting? What appearance must we make, if we, who have every source of amusement open to us, and yet follow these cruel sports become censors of the sports of the poor?' William Wyndham as reported in Cobbett's *Parliamentary History*, 18 April XXXV, (1800), p. 207.

30 Cruelty to Animals Act 1835.

31 'The old blackguard songs were in a few years unknown to the youths of the rising generation ... if the ballad singers were now to be left at liberty to sing these songs ... the public in the street would not permit the singing of them'. Francis Place Papers, BL Add. MS 27826 fo.144.

32 Shoemaker, 'The taming of the duel', op. cit., p. 544.

None of this necessarily need have resulted in the suppression of those duels that were fought between stiff-mannered gentlemen over considered points of honour; Wellington and Winchilsea were not driven to confrontation by the hubbub of the common street. However, a considerable number of the duels in the metropolitan environment had been engendered by the behaviour of a young, ill-disciplined but privileged elite culturally orientated towards drunkenness, gambling and violent pastimes. Such behaviour had been predicated upon the indulgence of their superiors and the resigned toleration of the surrounding society. Toleration of disorder in all its forms was, however, very much on the decline in the period after the Napoleonic Wars, and slowly these younger disruptive elements began to rein in their behaviour. For example, the patronage of violent sports began to decline, not least because of the increasing reprobation of gambling. For example, the publication of the final volume of Egan's *Boxiania* in 1829 marked the beginning of the decline of pugilism. Patronage of boxing, of cock and dog fights and of bull baiting was to be replaced by patronage of the races. Gentlemen continued to kill things, but this increasingly took place not in public but upon their own lands in the face of equals or their servants. Significantly, they no longer boxed publicly. They ceased to attend the fives court to strip and spar with their inferiors. Society was displaying an increasing antipathy towards the expression of overt violence by gentlemen as a method of communicating with either their equals or inferiors. As already mentioned, this was in part but a reflection of the broader trend of declining interpersonal violence traceable back to the fourteenth century.[33]

The shift away from ostentation and public competition, which, to repeat, had engendered many disputes, was accompanied by a new ideology of a private life which was closely connected to the religious revival. Men were increasingly encouraged to define themselves through their connections to family, faith and productive activity. They were urged to contented passivity to accept the arguments of William Howitt that 'happiness is a fireside thing ... and the deeper and truer it is, the more it is removed from the riot of mere merriment'.[34] Privacy became extended into the public, and after the report of the 1833 Parliamentary Select Committee and the opening up or creation of new parks, leisure began to become highly scripted and the importance of parks as the loci of social contest further declined. Rather, control of performance culture was to enable the well-to-do to achieve a new kind of privacy within public leisure space. The terror of being submerged and the consequent need to impose oneself upon social space was replaced by the freedom of anonymity, by a kind of retreat into the public. Public spaces became, as Mitchell describes them,

33 Lawrence Stone, 'Interpersonal violence in English society 1300–1980', *Past and Present*, 101 (1983), pp. 22–33.

34 William Howitt, *Rural Life* (London: Longman, 1840), p. 420.

places of 'controlled and orderly retreat where a properly behaved public might experience the spectacle of the city'.[35]

So brief an overview can do but inadequate justice to the many changes in the use and construction of public space that occurred in London over the course of the eighteenth and early nineteenth centuries. Of course, there were large areas of the city that remained as dangerous and as squalid as ever; it was the better areas that were paved, lit and policed. However, these were the areas that predominantly concerned gentlemen, and in them the interests of the respectable classes had come to prevail. Whereas Hazlitt's truculent bore had conducted himself as though expecting at any moment to be obstructed or assailed, the gentleman of the 1840s was generally able to proceed without such expectation. He did not anticipate receiving offence and therefore he did not have to stand ready to give it.

One not inconsiderable consequence of the successful prioritisation of their interests was that the physicality of gentlemen waned. In broad terms, gentlemen were becoming less habituated to displays of individual physicality. As Tosh puts it:

> Military manliness was still at a premium during the Napoleonic Wars, but it rapidly lost ground after 1815. With the abandonment of the duel, the growing professionalism of the armed forces, the exercise of violence became specialised.[36]

The decline of physicality should not be overstated, and, indeed, the cult of violent physicality has a long way still to run. However, increasingly, as Ute Frevert argues, such physicality was to be expressed not through boxing, fencing, wrestling or athletic feats such as pedestrianism – activities which had hitherto reflected an overweening concern for personal reputation – but rather through collaborative physical activity in which individual prowess was seen to be harnessed for the accomplishment of group goals.[37] Gentlemen were less competitive in respect of themselves and were in addition becoming equipped with a new sense of the interior life, a new sense of what we might call dignity which seemed to be lacking in their forebears. Such gentlemen were increasingly able to remain passive in the face of offence or criticism, to resist being terrified into action by fear of the loss of public face.

By the 1830s the compulsion to duel, which had sustained the institution as much as the actual desire to duel, was abating and duelling was on the decline. Furthermore,

---

35 Don Mitchell, 'The end of public space? People's park, definitions of the public and democracy', *Annals of the American Association of American Geographers*, 85:1 (1985), pp. 108–133, at p. 115.

36 John Tosh, 'The old Adam and the new man: emerging themes in the history of English masculinities 1750–1850', in T. Hitchcock and M. Cohen, eds, *English Masculinities 1660–1800* (London: Addison Wesley Longman, 1999), pp. 217–238, p. 222.

37 See Peter Radford, *The Celebrated Captain Barclay: Sport, Money and Fame in Regency Britain* (London: Headline, 2001).

the duel, while it lasted, was not immune to the changes that were happening in the society around it, although this fact has been much neglected by previous commentators. The tendency has been to speak of 'the duel' as though it were rigid and unchanging, whereas the term 'duel' has in fact been used for differing but related sets of behaviours covering chance medleys where all parties, including retainers, rushed in with drawn swords or else highly mannered exchanges of fire by singleton combatants. There has been little consideration of duelling as a system with its own internal rules and logical in its own terms. Not a few studies have reported the history of duels without ever remarking upon the point of it except in the most general of terms. Yet one can observe that as the pugnacity of the elites declined, not only were there increasing numbers who foreswore the duel but also what it meant to duel began to change. Among some gentlemen the duel came to mean something quite different to what it had meant a generation previously, whereas to traditionalists new modes of so-called duelling appeared entirely deplorable. Fractures began to appear within the culture of honour which were liable to make the whole edifice unsustainable.

Given the number of manuals and histories of duelling, it seems somewhat surprising that the internal dynamics of duelling have been little studied. What the protagonists were doing and why has rarely been questioned. Perhaps this has been because the answers have been thought blindingly obvious – the participants were going to the field to avenge outraged honour in accordance with the prescriptions set out in the duelling manuals. Thus, all that has remained is to chart the circumstances that led to duels and record the incidences thereof. In fact, though, there is very much more to be said, for many of the nuances of honour culture have been missed. In particular, the fact that there were differing duelling forms, each in a sense competing for predominance, has been overlooked. By differing forms I do not mean that they were fought with different instruments at different distances and so forth; rather, I mean that superficially similar modes of performance were sometimes predicated upon quite different and sometimes contradictory understandings about the purpose of the duel and the social logic that underpinned it. What the duel was, in short, was an object of controversy upon the field of ideas – hence, indeed, the fact that so many duellists felt the need to write manuals upon the subject of proper duelling. For example, the move to the establishment of dispassionate seconds, complete before 1780, was an important shift in not just the conduct of the duel but in the conceptualisation of its social purpose. So far as we know, this shift was unopposed. At least, there is no later literature that argues that the second should be thought of as the partisan of the principle protagonist and should engage in the combat – as had been customary fifty years or more before.

However, in the nineteenth century there appeared a very damaging dissension as to what the purpose of the duel should be. At the end of the eighteenth century the orthodoxy was clear: a duel was a way by which a man whose reputation had been stained by receiving offence could rehabilitate himself in the eyes of the peers.

The focus was very much upon the obligation of the offended to atone for having received an offence which had called his place among the order of gentlemen into question; it was his opportunity to reaffirm his right to belong among them. What was missing from this construction was a moral content which judged the behaviour of the offender. Indeed, the rights or wrongs of the affair were, morally speaking, hardly to be engaged in the issue at all. By 1790 some, such as Lieutenant Stanton in his *Principles of Duelling*, were attempting, with no seeming success, to add moral content by insisting that seconds should not act for principals whose causes were manifestly unjust.

By the nineteenth century, however, some gentlemen were intent upon adding further moral content, both by placing increasing emphasis on honourable reconciliation and by refocusing the duel itself, directing attention not towards the acts of the offended party and his need to remove the stain on his honour but towards the obligations of the offending party. Such men insisted that the duel was to be viewed as a mode of apology, of atonement for fault, in which the offender expiated his offence by offering himself up to the fire of his adversary. The offended party was to be satisfied by the admission of responsibility made by the transgressor, either when he apologised or when he agreed to receive fire. Society, in return, was to respond as if the expression or demonstration of regret on the part of the offender nullified the stain on the honour of the offended, as though the mere apologetic will of the transgressor could re-establish the equilibrium between the dishonoured gentleman and society.

To critics of such new values this might well appear like an exercise in balancing the books, a system, indeed, of duelling for shopkeepers. For adherents to the Clonmel Code the bilateral relationship between parties was but incidental. When offences were construed as serious, the erasure of their stain could not be accomplished by mere apology. It was the display of fortitude in the face of hazard that enabled the offended gentleman to restore his honour, not the acknowledgment of error upon the part of his opponent. By the 1820s, then, there were two different strands of thinking in operation: one in which it was deemed absolutely essential for both parties to be engaged in full and earnest combat in order for the honour of both, but in particular the honour of the aggrieved party, to be reaffirmed and another in which what mattered was that an offender offered recompense, made a public declaration of his error by apology or by facing the fire of the party he had outraged. These two contrasting ideas interacted uneasily, and the new construction of appropriate behaviour led both to a decline in the number of duels being fought and to a decline in casualty rates and a failure of what I would call 'necessary ambiguity'.

To begin with, though, to substantiate the general impression gleaned from the sources that duelling was becoming objectively less dangerous, I have returned again to the reports in *The Times* and quantified the number of duellists reported killed or wounded as set out in the graph below. I accept the limitations of such an exercise, insofar as it is very likely that not all wounds occasioned by duels were recorded and it is perhaps even more likely that duels in which no harm whatever was occasioned often went completely unrecorded. Furthermore, there are occasions in which the subsequent fortunes of wounded duellists are unknown; thus it is difficult to know how many wounds thought to be minor in fact led to the death of the patient.

With these caveats, the graph below records those reported as killed or wounded between 1785 and 1844. The 277 reported killed comprise some 16.6 per cent of total duellists, close to Simpson's own estimate of a 15 per cent fatality rate in the nineteenth century. A further 341 were reported wounded, making an average death or injury rate of 37 per cent. However, while between 1785 and 1804 some 41 per cent of participants were killed or wounded and between 1805 and 1824 the figure is 43 per cent, during the period between 1825 and 1844 the rate had declined to just 23 per cent. There do not seem to have been any sudden structural changes in the manner in which the duel was fought that may explain the significant decline in casualty rates after 1824. For instance, I have found no evidence that duels were being fought at a greater distance. Of course, as firearms developed one might have expected casualty rates to actually rise, but this at least was restrained by the conventions that pistol barrels were not to be rifled[38] and that parties were to raise weapons and fire in one movement without pausing for steady aim.[39] How, though, does one explain the decline in fatality rates? There is a great deal of evidence, admittedly anecdotal, to support the contention as suggested above that the very notion of what constituted a duel had changed. More specifically, the actual interchange of shots was in many quarters no longer viewed as de rigueur.

In 1777 the Clonmel Code[40] had done all in its power to avoid any suggestion of an inappropriate compromise upon the part of aggrieved gentlemen. In effect it had given them little chance, once matters had proceeded to the field, of avoiding bloodshed. For instance, it had expressly prohibited firing into the air or gentlemen avoiding receiving fire by deciding to apologise on the field. The influence of the code is open to dispute, but as mentioned by Barrington, some duellists thought it binding. There were certainly social costs in adopting practices that were later to be thought entirely normal and even praiseworthy. For example, a letter in 1789 to the

---

38 An attempt was made to lay criminal information against Castlereagh in 1814 for allegedly using rifled barrels during his duel with Canning (*The Times*, 18 Aug. 1814, p. 3, col. c).

39 When Mr Trant took careful aim at Sir John Conway in 1787, Conway protested to his second, 'By the Lord! That damned Jesuit will shoot me!' A moment later he was dead (*The Times*, 14 Apr. 1829, p. 3, col. b).

40 Sabine, *Notes on Duels and Duelling*, op. cit., pp. 31–34. For a discussion of the code and its application to his own duel with Mr Daly see Barrington, *Personal Sketches*, op. cit., pp. 292–300.

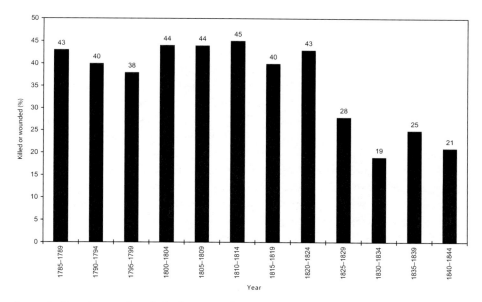

Figure 6 Casualties in British duels reported in *The Times*, 1785–1844

Coldstream Regiment publicly castigated an officer who had declined to fire on a signal after agreeing to a duel:

> In such a case as this, is not a breach of Promise a breach of Honour? And does not a man's public assent to terms which he is Privately determined not to abide by, become an act of DUPLICITY incompatible with the character of an Officer and a Gentleman ... Can he, according to the laws of honour, come into the field under a solemn engagement to fire his pistol on a certain signal, and yet when that signal was given, reserve his fire, and refuse openly to fulfil what he had PUBLICALLY engaged to perform?[41]

The obligation to fire insisted on above becomes understandable once one appreciates that only by receiving fire could a gentleman demonstrate his courage and relieve any doubts about his honour. Thus in 1790 Mr Curran was not grateful but rather complained bitterly when his opponent Maj. Hobart refused to fire upon him: 'I am sorry sir, you have taken this advantage; but you have made it impossible for me not to be satisfied.'[42]

Towards the end of the duel a great many 'duellists' were in fact refusing to fire upon their opponent, knowing that this refusal would bring the duel to a conclusion. In 1839 the Marquis of Londonderry received the fire of Mr Gratton

41 *The Times*, 6 Jun. 1789, p. 3, col. a.

42 Millingen, *The History of Duelling*, op. cit., vol. ii, p. 136.

on Wimbledon Common and terminated the dispute by firing into the air.[43] In the same year Mr Roebuck received the fire of Lord Powerscourt and similarly discharged into the air,[44] as did Mr Fiske in his meeting with Lord Paget.[45] It is hard to believe that marksmanship among the aristocracy had reached such a low ebb that Lord Loftus and Lord Harley had genuinely intended to hit each other when, also in 1839, they exchanged numerous salvoes to no effect at Boulogne.[46]

Now, some men had always been unwilling to fire in earnest; perhaps they acknowledged their culpability or appeared on the field despite their personal convictions. However, firing into the air was adopted not only as an act of humanity but also, at times, as an act of calculation. If one's opponent had missed, then one might decide to return fire to try to hit the opposite number. However, if one also missed then the duel might continue to another round and one's life would again be in hazard. Over time it came to be understood in some quarters that parties should no longer fire together, or even toss for first fire, but that the offended party should discharge first – with the offender then having the opportunity to respond. It seems that, increasingly, the transgressor, if unharmed, would respond by firing into the air to terminate the affair. The Germans entirely understood that such gestures were not motivated by simple generosity, for in Germany:

> Prominent misses were perceived as a craven show of clemency in the hope that the gesture would be returned ... Should the bad aim persist, seconds were to again foreshorten the battle and declare the transgressor unsatisfaktionsfähig and ineligible for further combat.[47]

However, in England and among some duellists firing into the air came to be regarded as an entirely acceptable form of behaviour. Indeed in some quarters offending parties were perhaps even expected to do so. This mode of proceeding, of course, seemed better to accord with principles of morality in an increasingly moral age and was, in addition, a great deal safer.

However, it took some time before the strategy of firing into the air could be said to be a canny and foolproof stratagem to terminate an affair. Mindful of earlier imprecations about the honourable necessity of engaging in earnest, some duellists at first merely ignored these pacific gestures from their opponents. In October 1803 a Mr B. and a Mr H. met on Hampstead Heath. Mr H. apologised for an offence given,

43 *The Times*, 30 Aug. 1839, p. 5, col. c.

44 *The Times*, 22 May 1839, p. 5, col. f.

45 *The Times*, 24 Dec. 1839, p. 8, col. b.

46 *The Times*, 11 Dec. 1839, p. 4, col. e.

47 McAleer, *The Cult of Honor*, op. cit., p. 69.

but his opponent would not accept his apology. Mr B. fired, and Mr H responded by discharging in the air. However, Mr B. insisted on firing again. His ball passed through Mr H.'s hat, and Mr H. again replied by firing into the air. Mr B. merely declared that he still was not satisfied and shot again! Mr H., who must have had the patience of a saint, fired skywards for the third time, and the parties left the ground without being reconciled.[48] The attitude of the pugnacious Mr B. is not as significant as the fact that, at this point in time, neither of the seconds felt that the action of Mr H. obliged them to intervene. Similarly, when the offending party at an exchange of shots in October 1805 was observed to shoot into the air, the seconds merely asked his opponent if he were now satisfied. He, however, declared he was not, and each fired again in earnest, this time wounding the other.[49]

It seems that by the 1820s, though, the seconds were regularly intervening and declaring categorically that the affair must be concluded once one party had intentionally missed his opponent.[50] Sometimes it remained the custom to ask the party who had observed his opponent's harmless act if he was now satisfied. Theoretically, that party could insist that the duel continue, but it was becoming difficult to display such obstinacy. For one thing, should the opponent be killed, the duellist might come to trial, and an important and necessary element in his defence would be a rebuttal of the presumption of malice, the presentation of a frank and honourable conduct that would impress the jury. The act of refusing to be reconciled after the first fire might of itself be taken to indicate malice, but how much more indicative of malice and less expressive of manly virtue was the act of continuing to discharge shots at a party who did not fire in return? By the 1820s, then, there was a constituency among gentlemen who felt that the requirement of honour had been entirely satisfied where parties had appeared at the field, where an offended party had fired at the other (perhaps not with the intent to strike the target) and where the offending party had obliged in return by discharging his pistol in the air.

The most famous 'duel' of the 1820s was precisely such an affair. According to his second Lord Hardinge, Lord Wellington had in 1829 not aimed at the body of Lord Winchilsea but at his legs. The shot had missed, and Winchilsea in return had discharged into the air. However, let us consider how such formulaic duels were to be viewed by the lights of traditional honour theory. Traditional duellists could not but believe that firing wide was an additional hostile act. If one was obliged to expunge the stain on one's honour by a display of compensatory courage – not by the firing of shots but by hazarding the danger of receiving them – then to be denied that

---

48 *The Times*, 11 Oct. 1803, p. 3, col. a.

49 *The Times*, 10 Oct 1805, p. 4, col. a.

50 As, for example, did Mr Castlereagh's second during his meeting with Gerard de Melcy in 1838 (*The Times*, 18 Jun. 1838, p. 4, col. e.)

opportunity was to be denied the opportunity of rehabilitation in the eyes of society and in the eyes of oneself. The traditional duelling system relied upon the assumption that both sides would enter the combat with equal determination. However, should offending parties consistently refuse to fire in earnest, then the duel would lose its restorative capacity. The party whose honour had been violated would be seen to have set little or nothing at hazard by challenging his offender. Rather, it would become the offender whose courage the duel would affirm. True, the offender had transgressed upon the honour of another, but in a virile society, who did not in part secretly admire him for doing so? Furthermore, by setting himself at hazard in reparation, the offender would have shown not merely courage but also generosity. By contrast, the offended gentleman would be cast into a very difficult position. He had somehow conducted himself in such a way as to suggest to others that his honour might be trespassed upon with impunity. The very act of having been insulted had cast his gentility into doubt. Now, however, the road to rehabilitation was closed to him, his offender refusing to engage him in combat.

It was in consequence of adherence to traditional honour theory that, paradoxically to the modern mind, gentlemen who had been sorely offended sought to insist that their opponents promise to fire upon them in earnest. For instance, when Sir Jacob Astley met Capt. Garth in 1828 in consequence of Garth's alleged relationship with Astley's wife, he was incensed when Garth refused to fire back at him after his first fire. The seconds convened a meeting, with those for Astley urging 'The necessity of Captain Garth's giving his pledge to return the Honourable Baronet's next fire.'[51] The intervention of the police prevented the resolution of a problem that had been apparent since the days of the Clonmel Code: how to restore honour when the challenged refused to put the life of the challenger into hazard.

There were plenty of later duels in which both parties were determined to do the utmost harm to each other. Duelling in England never descended to the absurdities of the French duel of the 1880s parodied by Twain. Duels occasioned by deep-seated feelings of animosity were still being fought with ferocity. In the 1820s and 1830s, however, one increasingly observes single-shot duels in which the transgressor consented to receive a shot without ever intending to return it in earnest. Under the older system of thinking these duels could retain some restorative power only so long as there remained an ambiguity as to the transgressor's intentions. There had to be a very real possibility that he would fire back at his challenger. So long as this ambiguity was present, then such duels conferred the maximum of possible advantages upon the challenger, the offended party. When he challenged, he gained the right of first shot to satisfy his animosity. At the same time, should he miss, there was a considerable likelihood that this opponent would not attempt to kill him in return.

---

51 *The Times*, 16 Jun. 1828, p. 6, col. f.

His honour was still to be restored, since he had risked retaliatory fire, yet the danger of being harmed by such was much diminished. Sometimes, of course, benefits were also conferred upon the offending party, for, believing it unlikely that the offender would seek to return fire in earnest, the offended might himself either fire aside or aim, like Wellington, to find a non-lethal target.

The difficulty with all this, of course, was that the offended party was, like those of generations before trying to redeem his reputation but trying to do so by what was now an inferior display of courage. The language and coinage of honour were becoming debased. The debasement of precious metal coinage perhaps serves as a useful analogy. Where a base metal is introduced to adulterate the coin it may, for a time go unobserved, or be deemed so inconsequential as to not damage the circulation of that coin. Adulteration then, can prove advantageous in the short term, but the temptation to repeat the process is rarely resisted. Eventually, the baseness of the metal becomes apparent and a crisis of confidence ensues which can drive out good coin as well as bad. So too with duelling, there had always been a certain number of stage managed encounters, but as the number of duels increased in which the challenger had never in fact been at hazard, so too cynicism about the authenticity of encounters increased. This is turn meant that the power of the duel to rehabilitate or to enhance a reputation began to wane.

Although later duellists were demanding the same powers of social purchase that taking the field had conferred upon their predecessors they were engaging in a system which was slowly being remodelled. Expiation of shame was being replaced by restitution for fault. However, conducting the duel as a mere mode of restitution for fault disturbed the rough equality of hazard that had hitherto been deemed necessary for a meeting of honour. Duels were not true duels where one party, and possibly two, were not in danger. Some, and I stress some, duellists were engaging in a kind of brinkmanship which threatened the whole system itself. Cynicism about bloodless duels became, I think, widespread and was manifested both in the caricatures and in the increasingly sardonic reporting of *The Times* of duels, 'of no interest except to the parties concerned'.[52] Not only did such cynicism infect those duels which did indeed appear to have been stage managed, but it also undermined the resolution of those who desired a full-blooded encounter. Men such as Sir Jacob Astley never desired to be killed or maimed, but they risked such a consequence in anticipation that, should they emerge unscathed, they would regain social capital. But what if one emerged from a contest of deadly earnestness only to find one's expectations of repute to be confounded, either by the increasing indifference of one's peers or by the assumption, spoken or unspoken, that one had not really been at hazard in the first place?

---

52 *The Times*, 31 Dec. 1831, p. 3, col. f.

As cynicism about the motives of duellists spread through society, so it seems that anti-duelling campaigners took heart and pressed home their attacks. By and large attacks upon duelling in the eighteenth century had come from pious Christians arguing from the stance of high moral principle. Since they were often by implication criticising the activities of social superiors, such criticism was often general and circumspect rather than focused upon individual persons and acts. As previously mentioned, it was very noticeable how little the established Church, as a body, had to say in respect of duelling. Individual and general homilies were the order of the day. However, by the 1830s this had begun to change as anti-duelling campaigners became more confident, aware that they were at the head of a constituency of opinion that had real social power and could apply significant social sanctions against duellists.

That duelling was no longer socially advantageous can be illustrated by the private correspondence which passed between two election agents, William Bulwer and William Rous, in 1834.[53] Both had candidates for the forthcoming Yarmouth election. Rous was horrified to discover that his candidate, Mr Wodehouse, had challenged his opponent, Mr Windham, and that Windham had considered accepting. Rous wrote immediately to Bulwer to declare that Wodehouse had acted 'without the knowledge, (as it must be without the approbation) of any man whatsoever'.[54] He proposed that the two act immediately to publish a joint statement that both men had been reconciled before the intervention of any other party and had had no intention of proceeding with the affair. He and Bulwer were agreed upon the 'ruinous consequences to the credit of the parties concerned in case the business had not been amicably settled'.[55] After the initial challenge, both candidates had been bound over, and Bulwer declared that it was important that the public knew that the two men had reconciled themselves before the law had intervened.[56] Bulwer and Rous wrote a humble apology to be published upon the candidates' behalf in the local newspapers and instructed their men to say nothing on the affair. The matter was smoothed over with alacrity. Although a challenge was still a social possibility in Yarmouth in 1834, it was by this time not to be boasted of and publicised for political capital.

In April 1839 the archdeacon and clergy of Bath placed an advertisement in the *Bath Chronicle* referring to the conduct of a Bath MP, Lord Powerscourt, in having duelled with Mr Roebuck. The clergy expressed 'deep regret that, by a recent duel, your Lordship's sanction should have been given to a practice so injurious to the best interests of society, at variance with the laws of the land, and in direct violation of

---

53 Bulwer of Heydon Family Papers, 5 BUL 16/28/3-7, Norfolk County Records Office.

54 Ibid. 5 BUL 16/28/18/3.

55 Ibid. 5 BUL 16/28/18/6.

56 Ibid. 5 BUL 16/28/18/5.

the precepts of the Gospel'.[57] The churchmen called upon him to publicly express his remorse. This was both an organised collective act and an expression of confident opinion. This was not a generalised speech from the pulpit to a congregation but rather a direct admonition of the conduct of a named prominent individual circulated by churchmen who were influential within his constituency. At the same time Powerscourt received deputations from his constituents threatening to withdraw their political support unless he publicly disavowed his actions. The press, so often the tool of the duellist, was now being employed to counter the public face of the culture of honour. What was advanced against the duellist, though, was not merely the claim that he was immoral or unchristian, but rather that he was cowardly. He was in effect now being challenged upon his own terms. Powerscourt was declared to have 'lacked moral courage'.

The opponents of duelling had long sought to break the connection between duelling and appropriate virility, to characterise the duel as impelled by fear rather than urged by manly virtue. By the 1830s such a strategy was at last bearing fruit. What was significant about Powerscourt's response was not that he acknowledged that his conduct had been unethical, but that he was prepared to publicly declare that his conduct had been governed by fear rather than by courage or conviction.

> My own opinion upon the subject of duelling coincides with that expressed in your address ... I confess that I have been deficient in that exalted moral courage which could alone have enabled me to despise the scoffs of the world ... I do not however, urge this either to justify the practice or vindicate myself from an act ... which my judgment and conscience must condemn.[58]

Many who had not supported the duel had nevertheless admired the duellist as a man whose conduct was governed by internal principles which were held higher than life itself. Now they were becoming persuaded that the duellist was in fact but a lightweight social dupe, in the thrall of social practices that were increasingly archaic or peculiar. The duellist was becoming a man of timid and even servile mentality. The anti-duelling campaigners had correctly identified that ethical principles alone were unlikely to prevail against duelling. Courage was to remain a pre-eminent virtue, and there was no lack of courage in Victorian society. Their success was to lie in relocating true courage elsewhere. They were able to do so because they understood the weaknesses of honour culture; they understood that its dynamics were maintained as much by fear as by courage and that this could be exploited. Again, though, mere argument might not suffice against those species of men able to resist material or political loss, ignore moral censure, and bear the prospect of pain or punishment.

---

57 *The Times*, 22 May 1839, p. 5, col. f. Headed 'Bath 24th April 1839'.
58 Ibid.

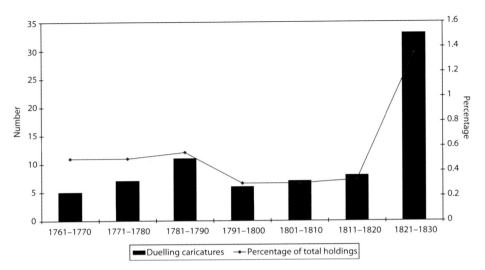

Figure 7 Caricatures in the British Museum collection, 1761–1830

However, campaigners did not depend upon mere rational argument, for they also understood that the very way in which honourable men defined themselves made them peculiarly vulnerable to a further and very particular form of social criticism. Duellists might bear being loathed or lectured, resist being reasoned with or rebuked, but few of them could tolerate being laughed at.

When the duel underwent something of a modest revival in the 1820s, this occasioned in response not merely an increase in anti-duelling sentiments, sermons, and literature, but also a comical and withering counterblast from the popular caricaturists. There are some 14,000 descriptions of English caricatures and prints in the British Museum paper catalogues covering the period from 1750 and 1830.[59] Figure 7 illustrates both the number of duels or duellists, factual or fictional, depicted in popular illustrations of that time and the proportion of images of duelling as a percentage of the total collection holdings for each ten-year period in question.

As may be observed, both the number of duelling caricatures and the proportion of the total collection that they represent increased markedly during the period between 1821 and 1830. The caricatures themselves were uniformly hostile to duelling. Some merely represented the political affiliations of the cartoonist, reflecting nothing more than a partisan desire to attack character. However, others were rather

---

59 M. D. George, *Catalogue of Political and Personal Satires Preserved in the Department of Prints and Drawings in the British Museum*, vols II–XI, F. G. Stephenson and D. George, eds (London: British Museum, 1877–1952).

more sophisticated and conveyed general sentiments about the duel itself. A distant gibbet, for example, was a popular augmentation made to the background, reminding the observer of both the illegality of the act and perhaps also causing him or her to reflect sardonically upon the inactivity of the law. By the 1820s caricatures had become savagely critical of the institution of duelling itself. When Thomas Landseer, for example, portrayed two typical duellists in 1827, he depicted them as monkeys gathering under a sign which said, 'Rubbish may be shot here!'[60]

While then the anti-duelling campaigners were endeavouring through speech (typically via the sermon) and through print in essays, pamphlets, and advertisements to break any supposed connection between admirable masculinity, courage, and duelling, the caricaturists were advancing the attack pictorially. The duellists in caricature are not primarily unethical monstrous beings (although they are that as well), for that would not have suited the caricaturists' purpose. They were rather vain, silly and ludicrous creatures, often cowardly, often fraudulent. When Mr Osea had come to the field to fight in 1791, he had declared, 'die nobly, die like demi-gods!'[61] Such a man might be reproached or even hated, but reproach can contain within it a certain grudging admiration and vehement hatred often serves to increase the stature of those upon whom it is bestowed. Ridicule, however, deflates and never dignifies; it disenchants absolutely. Ridicule was precisely the right sort of instrument with which to bring such demi-gods down to earth.

If we leap forward to 1847 and 1848, we find even so cautious a newspaper as *The Times* mocking the duellist when it dissected the attributes of what it described as the typical 'old style' and a 'new style' gentleman in two pieces. In respect of the 'old style' gentleman:

> He may be seen in a stall inside a theatre, but not at a stall outside one ... He may kill a man in a duel, but must not eat peas with his knife. He may thrash a coal heaver but mustn't ask twice for soup. He may pay his debts of honour but he need not trouble himself about his tradesman's bill.[62]

By contrast, the 'new style' gentleman:

> Has never been known to dress up as a jockey, or try practical jokes on watermen, or empty flour bags upon chimney sweeps ... He allows a performer to talk louder than himself at the theatre, and does not spring on the stage if there is a row at the

---

60 *The Crisis Or The Point Of Honour*. Designed & etched by Thomas Landseer. Published By F. G. Moon, 20 Threadneedle St, London, 6 Aug. 1827.

61 *The Times*, 17 Jun. 1791, p. 3, col. c.

62 *The Times*, 23 Dec. 1847, p. 3, col. f.

Opera ... He has never proved his cowardice by fighting a duel ... He does not bully his servants or joke with them ... He does not think it essential to his reputation to keep late hours, to pull down signboards, bait policemen and besiege toll keepers.[63]

These were, of course, stereotypical portrayals, but they were nevertheless ones which reflected a genuine shift, measured in degree rather than in absolute terms, away from display and pugnacious physicality towards privacy and civil discourse.

In August 1839 the dean and vicar of Ripon Cathedral and 29 clergy of the town, inspired perhaps by the mobilisation of opinion against Lord Powerscourt, placed an advertisement in the *Durham Advertiser*. In it they declared their regret that the Marquis of Londonderry, in compliance with the unchristian usage of the upper classes of society, had duelled with Henry Grattan. They were:

Compelled to view this transaction in connexion with that church for who's excellencies and privileges your Lordship is a strenuous advocate and to exhibit it as detrimental to the spread of spiritual influence, without which religion is but an empty name.[64]

Londonderry, however, was made of sterner stuff than Powerscourt. He replied, in a tone of mock humility and sarcasm, declaring that it was flattering that so many clergymen were interested in his actions. He noted that they had not so chided Wellington when he had duelled in 1829 and declared that in remonstrating the clergy 'seem to wish for publicity'. Finally, he pointed out that the duty of the soldier and that of the preacher were quite distinct. He was a soldier bound to fight to uphold church and altar: 'for this high duty our garments must be unsullied as yours ... you must leave to the British soldier, the unfettered right of being the best judge and arbiter of his own honour.'[65] The time, however, when a serving officer could make a special claim upon the field of honour was passing rapidly.

---

63 *The Times*, 24 May 1848, p. 5, col. a.

64 *The Times*, 30 Aug. 1839, p. 5, col. c.

65 *The Times*, 10 Sep. 1839, p. 4, col. d.

10

Dishonourable Duellists and the Rationalisation of Punishment and Warfare

The duellist, as we have seen, was a peculiarly public creature, particularly, even obsessively, concerned with self-image. Certainly, he was disposed to look outward rather than inward and to find his estimation of himself not through contemplation but through envisaging how he appeared to others. Henri Rochefort put it succinctly: the duel would die 'if there weren't always four gentlemen available to draw up a duel report, and fifty newspapers to print it. In ninety-one out of ninety-two cases, one duels for the gallery. Suppress the gallery and you exterminate the duel.'[1] Changes in the way that duels were reported and the increasing danger of being mocked were then particularly liable to affect the duellist. However, to expect the press to take a principled and consistent stand against duelling would perhaps have been too much. In general, attitudes in the press were changing, albeit somewhat tardily, but still they were opportunistic, never inclined to let principle obstruct the path to good copy. They were prepared to both glorify and vilify duellists depending upon the circumstance. It was significant, then, that within the space of five years four duels took place that were both sensational and entirely disreputable and which ensured that the duel was the subject of negative copy at a time when it was clearly already in serious decline.

The first of these was the duel between Mr Eliot and Mr Mirfin in August 1838, the disgraceful conduct of which I have already alluded to. The second was that between Lord Cardigan and Col. Harvey Phipps Tuckett in September 1840. Of the four duels, that between Cardigan and Tuckett was the exception insofar as there was no fatality and insofar as the parties did not flee but surrendered to justice. Much of the hostility to this duel, therefore, was engendered not by the duel itself nor by its aftermath but by the circumstances that had preceded it. Cardigan was at the time the subject of vehement public antipathy. His mismanagement of his 11th Light Dragoons after his appointment in 1837 is too convoluted to relate, save that in consequence of his

---

1   Henri Rochefort, duellist and journalist, in Dr Adolph Kohut, *Das Buch berühmter Duelle* (Berlin, 1888), p. 173.

conduct, nineteen officers voluntarily left his regiment. He came to the hostile attention of the *Morning Herald* in August 1838,[2] and in 1839 he challenged its editor.[3] The following year the 'Black Bottle' affair so alienated the public that Cardigan was harangued by large crowds wherever he went, and yet it was during this same period that he chose to challenge and meet a former officer, Harvey Tuckett.

Perhaps the most remarkable aspect of the whole affair was, given that Tuckett was merely wounded, that Cardigan was ever tried at all. Although brief threats to prosecute under the Ellenborough Act had been made against Wellington, the act had never been seriously applied to duelling. Wandsworth magistrates, however, charged Cardigan under 1 Vic. c. 85 s. 2, wherein wounding with intent to commit murder was a capital felony. The prosecution before Cardigan's peers famously failed because Sir John Campbell neglected to call Tuckett into court and to ask witnesses to identify him as the man seen upon the field. Instead he relied upon the wounded man's card, which he had surrendered after the duel. Unfortunately, the indictment against Cardigan specified his opponent as Harvey Garnet Phipps Tuckett, whereas the card merely identified the bearer as Capt. Harvey Tuckett. Failure to prove that these were one and the same led the judge, Lord Denman, to declare that in an ordinary court such a defect would have led to an acquittal. The peers duly followed, with only the Duke of Cleveland declaring, 'not guilty, legally, upon my honour'.[4]

Sections of the public were entirely cynical about the verdict, though it must be pointed out that indictments in ordinary courts did indeed sometimes fail in consequence of such flaws. Cardigan himself was not so confident of the verdict that he neglected to transfer his estate to a nephew (at considerable cost) to avoid the danger of confiscation upon conviction.[5] The whole affair, which was followed closely by the press, animated public opinion. The radical newspapers, the *Globe,* the *Morning Chronicle* and the *Herald*, were resolutely against Cardigan. Even *The Times* could seriously propose that a peer should be treated like a common felon, its editorial, incidentally, entirely contradicting Simpson's claim that the newspaper adopted a prejudicial view of the Mirfin duel merely because of the origins of the parties:

> Let his head be cropped, let him be put on an oatmeal diet ... Let not the occasion be given for anyone to say that the same which was visited as a felony on the associates of the linen-draper Mirfin is excused as an act worthy of a man of honour in the Earl of Cardigan.[6]

---

2   *Morning Herald*, 14 Aug. 1838.

3   *Morning Chronicle*, 16 Aug. 1839.

4   Millingen, *The History of Duelling*, op. cit., vol. ii., p. 402.

5   Saul David, *The Homicidal Earl: The Life of Lord Cardigan* (London: Abacus, 1997), p. 208.

6   *The Times*, 29 Sep. 1840.

Despite the acquittal, the trial sparked debate in the Lords. For the prosecution, the attorney general had opened with a declaration of satisfaction that the charge against Cardigan was 'not one that suggested, moral delinquency'. Lord Eldon and the Bishop of London disassociated themselves from such a conclusion. Lord Mountcashel asked the government to take new measures against duelling; when they declined, he tried to stimulate them into action by threatening to move for the repeal of 1 Vic. c. 85.[7] The government did, however, abolish benefit of clergy in respect of peers, which Cardigan had intended to claim if convicted.[8] The trial of course alerted the society to the possibility of a felony prosecution for the mere act of fighting a duel. In addition, the claims of Cardigan as a man of honour were somewhat discredited by the discovery, after an examination by gunsmiths, that he had gained an unfair advantage over his opponent by using a rifled barrelled weapon with a hair trigger in the duel.

Two further disreputable encounters followed. In July 1843 Lt Munro killed his brother-in-law Col. Fawcett following a quarrel between Munro and his sister, Fawcett's wife, at a social function. The connection between the parties led to much hostile comment, so too the fact that all the surviving parties fled, with the exception of one of the seconds, Mr Gulliver. Gulliver was subsequently tried and acquitted, but Lt Munro did not surrender himself to justice until 1847. He was tried at the Central Criminal Court on 18 August 1847 and found guilty of murder, but the judge 'felt justified in merely ordering judgement of death to be recorded and in assuring him that the sentence would not be carried into effect'.[9] In the event, he was to serve twelve months imprisonment. In the meantime, however, Mr Hawkey had in 1845 shot down Mr Seton in response to Seton's alleged advances to his wife. Hawkey had shown no solicitude to the fallen Seton, merely remarking immediately to his second, 'I am off to France.' As with the case of Munro, it was this refusal to submit to justice that most offended. Hawkey, too, was ultimately persuaded to surrender himself and stood trial in July 1846 at Winchester Assizes. He was acquitted, and *The Times* fulminated that 'There was evidence to convict twenty murderers, and not an attempt was made to disprove a tittle of it.'[10]

These four duels, then, did much to bring the already enfeebled practice of duelling into disrepute. Yet none of these were sham duels of the sort referred to in the previous chapter. What was shaming to adherents of honour culture was how far the participants had fallen short of the ideals of their predecessors. What was also

---

7 Debate of Friday, 12 March 1841, *The Times*, 13 Mar. 1841, p. 3, col. b.

8 Townshend, *Modern State Trials*, vol. i, p. 212.

9 *The Times*, 19 Aug. 1847, p. 6, col. f.

10 *The Times*, 20 Jul. 1846, p. 4, col. d.

alarming to the thoughtful members of society was how vividly the encounters had demonstrated that all were not equal before the law and that the operation of the law was deeply imperfect. Others were not slow to point this out. It was no coincidence that the bitterest critics of the Cardigan trial were newspapers of radical persuasion. Others were determined that if for the moment it was not possible to make the duellist the equal of the common felon in the courtroom, at least they would try to make sure that he was shown to be so if he was sent down from it.

By the 1830s duelling was beginning to appear an increasingly anomalous act in the context of a gentlemanly society that was, in relative terms, softer and more conciliatory than the one of a generation before. Violent acts were, in general, increasingly disapproved of and penalised – even violent acts committed by gentlemen. Of eighteenth-century justice, Beattie has observed that all men were not equal before the law and that this was not sought as an ideal. In the early nineteenth century courts in duelling cases continued to conduct themselves in such a fashion as to support Beattie's observation. Yet as *The Times*'s commentary on the preferred fate for Lord Cardigan illustrates, the idea that all should be equally punished by the law was gaining ground. If this was not yet apparent in the courtroom, it was becoming so in the prison yard.

In the eighteenth century the state, such as it was, still believed in the sufficiency of pain and was engaged in an articulate discourse with the populace, carried out through a theatre of punishment that was immediate, visible and barely systematised. The duellist was largely immune from this discourse of punishment. Branding had become a private and token punishment long before the duel's abolition, and duellists were neither whipped nor hung. A gentleman might be, for a time, incarcerated, but the privilege of his station guarded him from the worst of its inconveniences. He might lodge with his jailor, purchase his food, receive visitors and, of course, desist from all labour.[11] By the third decade of the nineteenth century, however, punishment had been reconceptualised. The criminal justice system had become intellectualised and systematised; it had a greater understanding of the possibilities of power and was grasping the complexities of creating institutions to give that power effect. Slowly reform gathered pace, led in particular by the Prison Discipline Society.[12] After 1818 the treadmill was generally adopted, with guidelines as to the daily revolutions. In 1823 the Gaol Act laid down standards of diet, hours of labour, visiting restrictions and so forth. Uniforms were specified, silent regimes introduced and solitary confinement extended. In 1835 Elizabeth Fry could declare, 'In some respects I think there is more cruelty in our Gaols than

---

11 When Gilbert Wakefield was confined in Dorchester Penitentiary in 1799, he purchased rooms with his jailor and dined with him for £100 per annum.

12 Philip Priestly, *Victorian Prison Lives* (London: Pimlico Press, 1999), p. 127.

I have ever seen.'[13] That year the Prisons Act was passed to effect uniformity in the regulation of prisons in England and Wales.

As we have seen, court practice and social sympathy had often served to negate the contention that the defendant duellist was but an ordinary felon. Indicted by the court, in the court of society his credit remained, if he had behaved honourably, substantially intact and even, in some quarters, enhanced. Upon conviction however, this was a circumstance that was to change. In the systematisation and bureaucratisation of imprisonment, however, the justice system had found its own mode of representation that might challenge and indeed negate that given by the gentleman and the duellist. The erasure of physical distinction, through the uniform and the prison haircut, served as an assault upon the very claim of gentility. The monotonous tramp in the prison yard, the treadmill and the forced repudiation of the right to an extended proxemic sense diminished the control and poise the gentleman exhibited when moving through space. Prison not only exhibited the ability to cast one into the pit of equality, it also inverted the hierarchy by substantiating the warder as state agent, as governor of his social unequal.

It might be objected that the pains of the prison could be as nothing compared to risk of death or injury which duellists courted on the field. Objectively, perhaps, but the duellist was sustained by what one might call a necessary failure of imagination. He was inculcated with those stories of duelling in which, like the stories of the martyrs, pain never disfigured or broke down courage. The duel could endure through the pain that was not imagined and the tale that was not told. It could not so easily endure the sight of the duellist shaven, shambling and bereft of dignity. This was not lost on the more thoughtful of contemporaries. The barrister Henry Joy noted that it was in vain to hope that the penalty of death would deter the duellist since it was by his very showing of a disregard for life that he hoped to gain the esteem of society. However, Joy did note the following:

> If instead of being a felony, punishable with death or transportation, fair duelling were now in all cases to become a misdemeanour punishable by a few months imprisonment *with hard labour*, the young men of ultra-fashion, who quarrel over champagne and hazard, though they might form a correct estimate of the value of their lives, would not choose to soil their boots and gloves with the dust of the tread-mill.[14]

However, the pains of the penitentiary were not imposed upon gentlemen of honour without a struggle within the penal system itself, as the fate of Mr Young

---

13 Cited in M. Ignatieff, *A Just Measure of Pain: The Penitentiary in the Industrial Revolution 1750–1850* (London: Peregrine, 1989), p. 179.

14 Henry Joy, Letter of 1842 in *Law Magazine Quarterly Review of Jurisprudence*, 28 (1842), p. 32, original italics.

and Mr Webber, the two seconds sentenced to twelve months for their part in the Eliot–Mirfin duel, illustrates. They were lodged in Guildford Penitentiary, but in January 1839 a Mr Hawes MP laid a complaint at the Surrey Quarter Sessions about their treatment. Its substance was that the two had been allocated a cell to themselves to distinguish them from other felons and, furthermore, they had been allowed a special diet.[15] It was contended that they had been sick, but Hawes thereafter interrogated the jail surgeon, who admitted that only one of them had been suffering from a serious ailment and that the favourable regime had been imposed in respect of both and after the invalid had returned to full health. The Prison governor was summoned and interrogated and admitted that Lord Russell had sanctioned the relaxation in these men's confinements, although upon what principle he could not clearly say. A supporter of Hawes proposed a motion censuring the conduct of the magistrates and the prison in allowing this special treatment, and it was but narrowly defeated.

On one level the matter was trivial, yet I think it serves to illustrate how upon many levels and in many ways, great and small, the duellist was being increasingly discomforted. The zeal, energy and passion of Hawes to see that gentlemen convicts were treated the same as the other inmates would not have been understood a generation or so before. Furthermore, he prevailed: Young and Webber were thereafter both placed under normal prison discipline, about which they complained bitterly at the following Quarter Sessions.[16] They found the water gruel allowed them for breakfast by the regulations of the prison 'particularly distasteful', saying that it caused 'violent retching and sickness'. They requested permission to purchase milk instead, to correspond with friends, to read newspapers. All these requests were denied. If duellists or seconds in the 1830s were no more likely to find themselves facing the full force of the law than their predecessors in the eighteenth century, still I believe the pains of the lesser penalty had, for gentlemen, increased. The culture of honour was now withering at the gates of the prison. Small wonder, then, that when in 1830 Capt. Smith of the 32nd Regiment was sent to prison for twelve months for killing Standish O'Grady he burst into tears, declaring, 'My God! Take my life! Is it come to this! ... Oh I wish they would take my life! Shame and disgrace and everything else have come upon me'.[17]

By 1845 shame and disgrace had come upon duellists generally. Not least among the effects of these four duels was that they helped to break down the connection between duelling and personal courage or personal honour in the minds of the public and the press. The leading protagonists in these four duels had proven themselves deficient in those virtues, which duellists claimed were particularly their own. Denounced in the press, derided in public opinion, and displaced from public space,

---

15   *The Times*, 2 Jan. 1839, p. 6, col. d.

16   *The Times*, 12 Apr. 1839, p. 7, col. a.

17   Millingen, *History of Duelling*, op. cit., vol. ii, p. 318.

the duel had become but a vestige of its former self. And yet it might possibly just have survived, had it not been for a slow but steady sea change of opinion that had been occurring in the places where the duel had found its most natural home: among the messes of the army and the navy.

In 1835 a conman, Mr Thomas Hasker, pondered how he might plunder the pockets of the nobility. The scheme he hit upon was to present himself as an army officer dismissed for assisting in a duel. Having presented fake testimonials to this effect, he managed to elicit money from Lord Fitzroy Somerset and the Earl of Sandwich. Unfortunately, he then he fell foul of a Col. Stanhope, who was acquainted with the handwriting of the supposed authors of those testimonials and had him arrested.[18] What interests about the story is that it reveals something of the state of attitudes to duelling within the army. For the ruse to succeed, the tale had to be such as would invite sympathy from the aristocracy and yet at the same time be entirely plausible. By 1835 one could contend without arousing suspicion that one had been dismissed for duelling, while at the same time one could reasonably expect that this would arouse such sympathy as to induce gentlemen to dip into their pockets.

That one might be dismissed for duelling in 1835 was not such a novel circumstance as might be suggested by the evidence advanced in Chapter 4 that a significant proportion of duellists were military officers. One should point out that the fact that many duellists were military officers does not logically lead one to the conclusion that most officers duelled. To argue from silence is always difficult, especially when one argues against the confident assertions of honour theorists that the entire officer corps was deeply inculcated with the values of the duel. However, the *Biographa Navalis*, the six-volume biography of naval officers from 1660 to 1798, mentions only a very few duels, notably the duel between Capts Innes and Clarke on 12 March 1750.[19] Of course, this might simply reflect the fact that this was not the sort of material in which the author was interested. However, I supplemented this with a reading of eight biographies or memoirs of naval officers and found references to only two honour disputes – one at Gibraltar in 1752 and one in Penang in 1809 – neither of which proceeded to a meeting.[20]

---

18 *The Times*, 30 Apr. 1835, p. 6, cols c–d.

19 Charnock, *Biographa Navalis,* op. cit.

20 The resolution of an honour dispute at Gibraltar is reported in Erskine and Kimber, op. cit., p. 129. The dispute at Penang is recorded by Napier in *Henry at Sea*, op. cit., vol. i, p. 101. The other memoirs consulted were: J. Barrow, *A Private Memoir of the Life and Services of the late William Barrow* (London: privately printed, 1850); A. Crawford, *Reminiscences of a Naval Officer, 1788–1869*, 2 vols (London: H. Colburn, 1851); D. Dawkins, *The Life and Times of Capt. John Pilford RN* (Horsham: Horsham Museum Society, 1988); D. Ford, *Admiral Vernon and the Navy* (London: Fisher Unwin, 1907); D. Gask, *Cm. John Mundell R.N. 1776–1833* (Cawsand: privately printed, 2001); J. E. Talbott, *The Pen and Ink Sailor, Charles Middleton and the King's Navy 1778–1813* (London: Frank Cass, 1998).

Furthermore, inveterate duellists were always the subject of reproach and suspicion. Col. Bayley reported in his diary the outcome of a quarrel between a Capt. K. in the 33rd Regiment and a young lieutenant in the 12th Regiment in Cape Town in 1796. The captain was an experienced duellist and 'a notorious marksman', and his own second, Lt Buckeridge, took pity upon his inexperienced opponent. The second therefore charged the captain's pistol with only a fraction of the usual charge, so that when the lieutenant was indeed shot down, his wound was not severe. The captain challenged his second in response, but the officers of the regiment intervened. They forbade Buckeridge to accept the challenge and sent the captain to Coventry until he was forced to quit the corps.[21]

It should similarly not be supposed that the existence of a culture of honour within the officer ranks was not perceived as problematic for military institutions. Indeed, the survival of the duel was symptomatic of a social order that had imperfectly adapted itself to the military function. At his trial in 1803 for the killing of Col. Montgomery, Capt. MacNamara declared:

> I am a Captain of the British navy ... to maintain my character in that situation I must be respected. When called upon to lead others into honourable danger, I must not be supposed to be a man who sought safety by submitting to what custom has taught others to consider as a disgrace.[22]

MacNamara's statement suggests the difficulty of leading in the absence of good name. No doubt this is a matter contemporary officers must still consider. However, the problem was particularly acute in the early nineteenth century when hierarchies of authority had not yet solidified and become institutionally enforced. At that time the degree to which a commander could depend upon military discipline to uphold his authority was rather limited. His freedom of action was severely circumscribed by the values of individuality and equality propagated in the culture of honour. The instinctive, reflexive modes of subordination which military discipline today strives so hard to inculcate in the junior ranks were the very antithesis of the values honour culture espoused. Values which their exponents asserted entitled, even obliged, them to challenge any exercise of authority that they deemed to trespass upon their personal dignity. This leads on to a general question: How well can any complex organisation function or how efficiently can any complex task be accomplished, when those serving the directing mind espouse values which entitle them to question, weigh and, if necessary, reject the instructions emanating from their superiors? How

---

21 Bayley, *Diary*, op. cit., pp. 39–40.

22 Millingen, *The History of Duelling*, op. cit., vol. ii, p. 160.

secure in their command can officers be if their junior officers regard themselves as personally entitled to place their superiors' lives at hazard?

In contemporary military service it is anticipated that in the context of accomplishing, in its broadest sense, the military purpose, the subordination of the junior will be unquestioning and complete. A certain core of private dignity is allowed the soldier, but there exists a comparatively sophisticated and mutually accepted understanding of the distinction between the private and the professional. When one observes, however, the contexts in which military duels occurred in the eighteenth and nineteenth centuries, it becomes clear that such distinctions were but imperfectly formed. The contest between contradictory imperatives had not yet been resolved. Men inclined to regard subordination in order to accomplish the military purpose as both legitimate and honourable were less inclined to find offence at the hands of their superiors. However, such men were pitted against others more immediately self-regarding. Such self-regarding men prioritised their own image and their right to be uninhibited in their conduct above the achievement of military objectives.

In an atmosphere in which the very principle of subordination was regarded with suspicion, command required a delicate array of skills. An officer had to obey his superiors, yet in such a way as did not suggest to even the most punctilious of his officers that he had ever displayed undue subservience. He had to interact with his equals in a competitive military environment, and yet never suggest that he regarded them with other than approbation. He had to obtain the obedience of his subordinate officers, possibly under the most stressful conditions, and yet never trespass upon their sensitivities. Small wonder that when one observes the causes of disputes between officers they often seem to have arisen in consequence of the exercise of what we today might regard as perfectly legitimate authority.

I have for example already referred to the dispute between Ensign Purefoy and Col. Roper in 1788. When the junior officers of the regiment misbehaved Col. Roper revoked their leave and one might think this a common enough exercise of military authority. Yet Purefoy, a mere ensign, responded by so berating Roper that the colonel had him court-martialled and dismissed. Purefoy however, applied to the code of honour. Roper stood upon his military authority, but when Purefoy posted him as a coward, Roper had no choice other than to meet him. He was killed in the encounter.[23] Again, the death of Lt Col. Aston in India in 1799 resulted from both the legitimate exercise of his authority as commanding officer and from a minor indiscretion which led to the most deleterious consequences.[24]

The fatal duel between Maj. Campbell and Capt. Boyd in 1807 originated in consequence of Campbell being corrected by Gen. Kerr over the precise words to be used

---

23 *The Times*, 24 Dec. 1788, p. 3, col. b.
24 Bayley, *Diary*, op. cit., pp. 61–66.

in a command given on the parade ground. Boyd subsequently took the view that Campbell had indeed been in the wrong, and this induced the quarrel. Finally, the death of Lt Russell in Bombay in 1814 was occasioned by a Lt Campbell, while on duty as guard captain, chiding Russell for failing to send him a report from his station. Russell is alleged to have responded, 'In noticing the omission Sir, you have done your worst, I defy you.' Yet this was precisely the type of omission that any conscientious officer should have noticed. Campbell was nevertheless challenged, though he prevailed on the field.[25] The failure in these instances to subordinate personal inclinations in favour of the accomplishment of military purposes is striking.

That honour culture was capable of subverting the military enterprise had long been appreciated. Gustavus Adolphus was said to have eliminated duelling from his reformed Swedish army simply by requiring that a duel was to be fought to the death in front of the army and stipulating that the survivor was to be immediately executed. Absent, of course, from the duelling chronicles are records of disputes which from their nature might have led to duels but which did not; missing are reports of officers who regarded duelling as unprofessional or desisted from it for personal reasons.

W. Hough's *Casebook of Courts Martial*[26] demonstrates that by 1821 not only was there in existence within the Articles of War a comprehensive list of provisions against duelling, but also that they were upon occasion enforced. Hough's reports of courts martial for duelling make it clear that is that those duellists convicted by court martial were quite likely to be sentenced to be cashiered or reduced to the list of half-pay officers. However, at review lesser penalties were generally substituted. Seconds, though, who were perceived to have aggravated disputes, were less likely to have their sentences overturned.

To illustrate, in 1813 Ensign E. McG. was capitally convicted at Winchester Assizes of the murder of Lt B. of the 101st Foot.[27] Convicted with him were three seconds: Lt D., Ensign G. and Ensign O'B. However, on 8 September 1813 the king published a letter in General Orders. He declared his intention of granting a royal pardon to all the parties. From the report of the court martial he observed:

> It appears that the original disagreement between Lieutenant B. and Ensign McG. arose from a trivial cause; that no attempt was made to reconcile the parties, but, on the contrary, that instead of those efforts, which, if properly and seasonally exerted

25 *The Times*, 20 Dec. 1814, p. 4, col. a.

26 William Hough, *A Casebook of European And Native General Courts Martial Held From the Years 1801–1821, On Officers, Non Commissioned Officers And Privates in His Majesty's And The Honorable East India Company's Armies. To Which is Annexed The Forms And Precedents Observed At Courts Martial* (Calcutta, 1821), pp. 182–210.

27 Ibid., pp. 189–190.

might have had the happy effect of preventing the meeting ... great pains were most unwarrantably taken to instigate and promote it.[28]

The pardon having been granted, the commander-in-chief was left at liberty to deal with the recommendations of the military court martial and he noted in the General Order that he was:

induced to think, of all the parties concerned, the unfortunate officer who lost his life, and the yet more unfortunate one, by whose hand his Comrade fell, were the least culpable; they appear not to have been actuated by any personal animosity, but to have been instigated and governed by the advice of others.[29]

He accused the seconds of magnifying the dispute but declared that he particularly intended to single out Lt D., who, from his rank and standing in the army, ought to have set a different example. All three seconds were cashiered, but only Lt D. was declared incapable of ever holding military rank again. The surviving duellist retained his appointment.

This apparent policy of adopting greater severity towards seconds than duellists themselves makes complete sense in the context of a military aware that their officers were gentlemen and expected to be regarded as such, but also aware of the damage duelling might do to the functioning of the regiment or ship. Most subversive of military disciple were those who sought to more safely requite personal quarrels by inducing others to place themselves at hazard. The ease with which this might be accomplished is illustrated by the case of Capt. C. C. of the 89th Foot who was convicted of:

Maliciously endeavouring to excite a personal quarrel between Lt. Philan 89th Foot and Ass. Surgeon Train, on the night of the 4th instant by saying on the return of the latter Gentleman (Ass. Surgeon Train) who had previously quitted the room, I have been fighting your battles in your absence, Doctor, I would not allow any one to speak of me in that way, and if you want a friend on a certain occasion.[30]

There was, then, and I suggest there always had been, a sense within the military that duellists or those who slyly instigated duels had the potential to subvert military discipline and even endanger the military enterprise. However, reconciling the exigencies of subordination and the demands of command with the claims of honour was no easy task, and this was not lost upon fellow officers. In 1789 HRH the

---

28 Ibid., p. 190.
29 Ibid., p. 190
30 Ibid., p. 183.

Duke of York was obliged to give satisfaction to Lt Col. Lennox, and the officers of the Coldstream Regiment were in turn obliged to consider Lennox's conduct. After a meeting of the mess, they concluded with the utmost delicacy 'that, Lieutenant Colonel Lennox has behaved with courage; but, from the peculiar difficulty of his position, not with judgment'.[31]

When, however, Duke of York learned of the encounter between the Marquis of Londonderry and Ensign Battier in 1824, he issued a General Order declaring he had been obliged:

> To submit to the King a transaction at variance with the principles of subordination, and therefore of a tendency injurious to the discipline of the army. The King has consequently conveyed to his Royal Highness his Majesty's concern and displeasure, that an officer of Lord Londonderry's high rank and military reputation should have committed himself in personal collision with an inferior officer, by accepting a challenge for any supposed aggression proceeding from the exercise of his authority as Colonel of the Regiment.[32]

At times one is perhaps tempted to characterise expressions of disapprobation of the duel as examples of mere hypocrisy. In 1816, Prince George had vowed to dismiss any officer who had duelled,[33] but he later greeted the news of the Wellington–Winchilsea affair with delight.[34] It seems, though, that men found it genuinely difficult to reconcile, on the one hand, rational considerations of necessity and function with, on the other, the emotive appeals of the culture of honour. Hence, they might vacillate between the two according to context. The officers of Lennox's regiment could not but approve Lennox's courage, but at the same time the implications of his challenge were disturbing for military and political life. Similarly, when Londonderry was publicly rebuked, the language used reflected such a tension. Londonderry was not rebuked for duelling. Rather, he was rebuked for having accepted a challenge from an inferior officer and for accepting one that arose in consequence of his exercise of his functions as a military commander. Honour itself was not rejected, but the idea that it was appropriate to test it in opposition to the requirements of military discipline was. Inclinations of honour should not lead to transactions 'injurious to the discipline of the army'.

---

31 Millingen, *History of Duelling*, op. cit., vol. ii, p. 133.

32 Ibid., pp. 282–283.

33 Philo Pacificus, *Two Extracts from a Pamphlet Entitled, 'The Friend of Peace: Containing A Special Interview Between The President of the United States and Omar, An Officer Dismissed For Duelling; With Six Letters From Omar to the President; And Omar's Solitary Reflections, The Whole Reported by Philo Pacificus* (Stockport: J. Lomax, 1816), p. 5.

34 Maxwell, *The Creevey Papers*, op. cit.. Letter of the Earl of Sefton to Mr Creevey, 25 Mar. 1829.

In consequence of his challenge, Ensign Battier was removed altogether from the Army List. Londonderry was merely rebuked, but the effect of such should not be underestimated. Although many of the penalties imposed upon duellists do not seem severe, their efficacy has to be judged in the context of the men and the society to which they were addressed. That is to say that precisely because the culprits were men of honour, court martial, symbolic humiliation and public rebuke were measures most likely to influence their conduct.

As Hough's *Casebook* makes clear, there had long been a constituency within the army that was hostile to duelling in principle – or, less certainly, hostile to certain forms of duelling and certain modes of instigating it. It appears that this constituency grew more confident over time, though it was not until 1845 that they could clearly be observed to prevail against the defenders of duelling such as the Marquis of Londonderry. The reasons they were ultimately to do so, however, were perhaps first explained by John Taylor Allen during a reading of his essay in the theatre at Brasenose College, Oxford in 1807. In his essay, Allen dealt with precisely the contention, which the Marquis of Londonderry was still advancing in 1839 that an officer's honour and his willingness to defend it were necessary attributes for one charged with the defence of the realm. Allen, however, noted that:

> The important changes which have, of late years, taken place in military tactics and the ancient mode of warfare, have rendered the plea of necessity no longer tenable. The fortune of the field does not now depend upon the exertions of individual prowess; it is from the concentrated efforts of a well-disciplined army; from the bravery and firmness of united battalions, that the fate of battles and empires must now be decided. [35]

Gen. Sir Rupert Smith has recently argued that it was the Napoleonic Wars that marked the beginning of the era of 'industrial war', during which society's aspirations, accomplishments and endeavours were to be subsumed into the collective national patriotic struggle.[36] Not only was society mobilised for war in a way not previously comprehended, but the mechanics of war also moved on apace, with both technical innovations, such as the Congreve Rocket and military semaphore, and the consequent establishment of specialist repositories of military knowledge such as the Royal Engineer Establishment, founded in 1812.

It was becoming increasingly plain that success depended less on personal courage than on military science and subordination within a disciplined command structure and the conduct of quarrelsome, sensitive and to a degree amateur officers was being to look like dangerous self-indulgence. However, one consequence of the sheer scale

---

35 John Taylor Allen, *Duelling An Essay Read In The Theatre, At Oxford, 10 June 1807* (Oxford: Brasenose College, 1908), pp. 19–20.

36 Sir Rupert Smith, *The Utility of Force: The Art of War in the Modern World* (London: Allen Lane, 2005).

of warfare during the contest with France was that the officer corps was becoming increasingly professionalised, as men joined from rather humbler walks of life. Such men were entirely dependent upon the military for their livelihoods, they anticipated they would serve until almost the end of their days and accordingly applied themselves methodically to learn military science. One such was Lt Nixon, who served with Capt. Aston in India in 1798 but who refused to act as a second in the fatal duel because he had no other income other than his military pay and he would accordingly not jeopardise his military career.

Examining for a moment the mores and mentality of but one of these new careerist officers who wrote a detailed account of his service, Maj. George Simmons, it becomes apparent just how much the behaviour of such a man might differ from that of the well-born gentleman officer. Maj. George Simmons served in the regular forces from 1809 to 1845, but he began as a militia officer and gained a regular commission by persuading one hundred militiamen to volunteer for a regular regiment. When he first served in Spain, he had to walk with his men since he was initially too poor to buy a horse or a mule. It is difficult to convey the flavour of his journal and correspondence other than to say that in tone it appears the very antithesis of the dashing, insouciant and condescending memoirs of Col. Bayley.

A recurring theme throughout Simmons's correspondence was his appreciation of his position as the main provider for his parents and siblings: 'If I live you shall always command my last shilling. I live for my family, and hope to see them all happy; it shall ever be my greatest pleasure to assist them.'[37] He recorded the money he had saved, the remittances home, gave instructions as to where to buy second hand uniforms for brothers about to enter service. Above all, both his personal conduct and his advice given to younger brothers suggest that he regarded the army as a vocation in which, for such as he, advancement was to be achieved through a thorough professional military education. He did not gamble, drank very little and he did not duel. In addition he was scornful of the well-connected officers who served as adjutants and when his brother Joseph joined the regiment, Simmons warned him away from such men. There was to be no roistering rakish lifestyle for Joseph, his brother proposed to instruct him in the technicalities of warfare and the obligations of military service and to do this he intended to 'keep him five hours a day at his studies'.[38]

Robert Connell has described the changing nature of the military enterprise thus:

> Real warfare became increasingly organised. The armies of the revolutionary and Napoleonic Wars became standing conscript armies with permanent officer corps ... Violence

---

37 Lt Col. Willoughby Vernier, *A British Rifleman: The Journals and Correspondence of Maj. George Simmons, Rifle Brigade, During the Peninsula War and the Campaign of Waterloo* (London: A&C Black, 1899), p. 107, letter of 30 Sep. 1810.

38 Ibid., p. 265, letter of 12 Dec. 1812.

was now combined with rationality, with bureaucratic techniques of organisation and constant technological advance in weaponry and transport ... It was the social technique of bureaucratically rationalised violence, as much as sheer superiority of weapons, that made European states and settlers almost invincible in the colonial wars of the nineteenth century.[39]

It is significant that when the Association for the Discouragement of Duelling was founded in February 1842 it counted among its very first members senior military figures such as Lt Gen. Orde and Lt Gen Maitland as well as a number of admirals, lords, two earls and the Duke of Manchester. However, it started quietly at first declaring its intention to proceed with caution: it would espouse its opposition to duelling 'in a quiet and unostentatious way' and would not 'take steps of a more public character' without the approval of its committee members.[40]

The position of the Association changed however in 1843 following the duel between Lt Munro and Col. Fawcett. The association held a special meeting at which it came to the conclusion that 'the matter might fairly be submitted to the public'. It recorded this determination in the pages of *The Times*, but significantly, it did not hope that duelling might be extirpated by a campaign in the newspapers, 'as the opinions of the newspapers were addressed chiefly to the middle class of society.'[41] There was no acknowledgment of the existence, as some have supposed, of a significant constituency of middle-class duellists; rather, 'the committee felt it their duty to invite the attention of the higher class to the subject', and to reach them it proposed to appeal to the sovereign.

The Munro–Fawcett duel was debated in the Commons and the debate highlighted the divisions within the military on the subject of duelling. Capt. Bernal pointed out that Munro had consulted many officers and five generals before deciding whether to challenge Fawcett and that, allegedly, all had advised him to do so. Sir Henry Hardinge responded that for the previous twenty-four years, the sixty or seventy officers of the Royal Artillery had messed at Woolwich without a single duel occurring, and that the Advocate General had recently intervened to order a court martial to look again at a charge laid against an officer who had failed to notice an assault.[42] Hardinge's comments can, of course, be read both ways; it seems that an officer who did not notice an assault might still fall foul of the 'Devil's Article'. Hardinge, however, had already struck a significant blow against military duelling by, in February 1844, taking the unprecedented step of refusing a pension to the widow of Col. Fawcett and undertaking that the government would do the same in future in respect of all

---

39 Robert W. Connell, *Masculinities* (Cambridge: Polity, 1995), p. 192.

40 Anon., *Ist Report of the Association for the Discouragement of Duelling* (London: Alvey, 1844).

41 *The Times*, 5 Aug. 1843, p. 6, col. f

42 *The Times*, 9 Mar 1844, p. 3, col. f.

men killed in duels.[43] Whether this was a decisive step is not entirely clear; insurance companies were offering policies which promised to pay out to dependents should an insured officer be killed in a duel – provided of course that they had paid a number of years premiums. Certainly, however, it gave uninsured officers a good reason not to duel, and it provided an important weapon for those in the army who wished to avoid the field. Furthermore, on 30 March 1844 the judge advocate general issued a letter reiterating that an officer 'cannot be subjected to a trial and punishment for leaving undone that which the law expressly forbids'.[44] The following month the War Office promulgated amended Articles of War.

In the main, the revisions merely reiterated or rephrased previous prohibitions. The amended articles, though, acquitted 'of disgrace or opinion of disadvantage, all officers, who ... refuse to accept challenges'. Officers were ordered not to 'evince dissatisfaction with or to upbraid another officer for refusing or not sending a challenge'.[45] The article 107 declared that it was not merely those who participated in a duel who were liable to be cashiered, but any who knew of one and who did not try to prevent it. However, it was the determination to enforce such articles, subsequently expressed after 1844, rather than their new content per se that mattered. The court martial of naval lieutenant Bridge in December 1844 was an important test of that determination, for it questioned how the authorities might act when faced with the anomalous situation created by the articles. Bridge had been provoked into issuing a challenge by the insults heaped upon him by a civilian. In his defence he pointed out that since the articles bound only serving officers he now stood to be punished while the aggressor would remain scot-free. This seemed to make officer vulnerable to insult, not just from civilians but also from the officers of foreign countries where duelling was not penalised. Nevertheless, Bridge was cashiered.

With public sentiment negatively influenced by the circumstances of recent encounters, and given the hostile disposition of the press, the constituencies within the churches and within the military were greatly emboldened. It remained only to add the influence of the sovereign to weigh the balance against the men of honour. Victoria had, however, displayed no strong disapprobation of the duel. When two lieutenants of the Royal Marines were cashiered in 1841 for attempting to provoke a duel, she restored their commissions. Cardigan was a personal favourite of hers, and prior to his trial she had hoped that he would 'get off easily'.[46] Public pressure mounted, however, after the death of Col. Fawcett. On 15 March 1844, during a

43 *The Times*, 29 Feb. 1844, p. 4, cols a–b.

44 Anon., *2nd Report of the Association for the Discouragement of Duelling*, pp. 15–16.

45 Ibid., pp. 10–11.

46 Royal Archives, *Queen Victoria's Journal*, 25 Apr. 1841, cited in David, *The Homicidal Earl*, op. cit., p. 208.

Commons motion urging the house to condemn duelling, it was suggested that no party to a duel should henceforth hold public office and that if the sovereign did not receive them at court, 'this usage which existed only among the higher classes would soon be at an end'. Victoria acquiesced.[47]

The manifest demonstration of a willingness to apply the Articles of War, the withdrawal of the sovereign's clemency, the genuine possibility of criminal sanctions – reiterated following the conviction of Seton in 1847 – and pressure both from within and without the military served to finally extinguish the duel within the services. For a time the association in the public mind between the military and the duel continued. There were in fact duels within the army in India well into the 1850's. However, at home to find an officer prepared to countenance a duel, let alone to participate in it became extremely difficult. In 1851 two civilians a Mr James Cherry and a Mr George Palmer quarrelled during a council meeting at Great Yarmouth. Mr Cherry challenged Mr Palmer to a duel but he was unable to find anyone willing to be his second. He applied, first, to a friend who was a captain in the army and then to another who was a captain in the navy. Both declined the position each citing the severe consequences for their military careers.[48] After 1850 the duel was spent in the officer corps and the culture of honour was subordinated to the needs of the functionalist and technical military enterprise.

---

47 Debate of Thursday 14 Mar. 1844 as reported in *The Times*, 15 Mar., p. 4, cols a–b. It is again interesting to note that the Commons had no cognisance of 'dandelion duellists'.

48 Ferrier of Great Yarmouth Family Papers, MC 268/117.694, Norfolk County Records Office.

Conclusion

Reviewing all that has gone before, it is clear that notwithstanding its emblematic importance, duelling as mode of settling differences between gentlemen was not a particularly common phenomenon. At best it was located within very specific sections of gentlemanly society. Certainly, this was so by the later eighteenth century. In London duelling found a place among the troublesome, and to a degree anti-patriarchal, young metropolitan elite and for a short time was adopted by a rather limited number of aspiring men of the legal and then medical professionals. The duel followed such men out to the places of their rural recreation, to the sporting venues and the hunting grounds. There they quarrelled with each other or occasionally with the small numbers of like-minded gentlemen at the very top of rural society; men with intimate connections to London and to the militia.

However, the duel did not succeed in recommending itself to those who were prosperous and yet below the level of these county leaders and it did not succeed in establishing itself in the older market towns or in the expanding centres of manufacture. The natural home of the duel lay in the military. Outside of London then, it was the dispersal of military officers which in great measure determined both the frequency and the geographic distribution of duelling. However, as the Chapter 10 suggests, even within the military there was always an important constituency opposed to duelling. Although the sensibilities of the mess sometimes cajoled men into combat habitual duellists were deeply unpopular. There were many officers who were never challenged and who never duelled, and others who when challenged resorted to military tribunal. There were others who did duel, despite their personal judgement, because they felt impelled to do so.

Yet despite both the danger and the manifest illegality of duelling, it endured; in doing so, it served, for a time, to legitimate social difference. The possibility of being called to the field, the privileges and hazards of honour, justified claims to a bodily autonomy that was denied to other members of society. In that sense all gentlemen, even those who did not duel and who were not likely to do so, inherited a certain social capital from those who did. Duelling must have played a role in constructing the masculinity and secret fantasy of many men who lived their outward lives in apparent tranquillity. That some men were bold enough to translate fantasy into reality was a consequence of their general familiarity with violence and of their education within a culture that prized assertiveness, physicality and pugnacity.

Since the duel was a form of boundary behaviour, it is not surprising that much energy was expended discussing who should and who should not be within its penumbra; there were always anxieties about interlopers. However, honour culture did not stand entirely apart and alone; rather, it not only distinguished the gentleman but also connected him to a broader cultural system based upon 'honest British violence'. The notion of honest, fair violence contributed much to the appreciation of and formation of the general national character. Hence the sympathy of jurors of lesser social status when judging duellists and the institution from which they themselves were excluded. More broadly, rough, violent popular performance culture legitimated the notion that disputes must be personally resolved and negated the obligation or impulse to deliver their resolution up to authority. The strength of the duel, then, lay not merely in its espousal by subgroups within the social elite, but also in its relation to popular values to which, superficially, it might appear the very antithesis. The codes of honour were sustained not by the values of gentlemanly society alone but by their relation to popular culture. The duel existed within a broader framework of notions of legitimate violence and, perhaps paradoxically, was but one manifestation of a series of connections that linked the most privileged to the most humble.

By the end of the period in question those connections had been substantially broken. In terms of the sports they patronised, the language they spoke, the very geography they inhabited, the elite and the poor had moved further and further apart. In no small part this was a consequence of the broad attack upon street culture and upon popular sports, well documented by Malcolmson and others. The very conception and nature of public space was changing at the end of the eighteenth century, and by the mid nineteenth century the interests of the better classes were being protected by policemen who were not only enforcing the law but also acting as domestic missionaries, bringing 'the arm of municipal and state authority directly to bear upon the key institutions of daily life'.[1]

Of course none of this was undertaken with the explicit objective of weaning gentlemen away from duelling. However, the securing of the streets – the paving, the lighting, the policing and prioritising of interests – coupled with a broad general decline in interpersonal violence reduced the need for young gentlemen to exercise courage and pugnacity within urban space. A species of gentleman developed that was rather less familiar with pain and with the exercise of personal courage. Such gentlemen were less resolute at the prospect of being shot on the field and more inclined to turn to the police or the magistrate when challenged. The very notion that gentlemen should resolve their disputes personally was increasingly being questioned in a society that was now emphasising submission before the law. Spirited gentlemen could, in time, no longer be confident of the unqualified approbation of ordinary men and women.

---

1 Storch, 'The policeman as domestic missionary', op. cit.

Both the subjugation of public space and the reconstruction of popular culture were long-term phenomena that took place steadily throughout the eighteenth and early nineteenth centuries. In the meantime, the eighteenth century was also, according to Tosh, 'Pivotal in entrenching an entrepreneurial, individualistic masculinity organised around a punishing work ethic, a compensating validation of the home and a restraint upon physical aggression.'[2] Although, for reasons I have already explained, I have doubts about attributing the rise of the 'new man' to middle-class values, what one does observe by the end of the eighteenth century is the increasing prominence of the rational functionalist mentality.

Men equipped with such mentalities looked towards the future: They saved. They insured. They were capable not merely of envisaging distant goals but also of methodically devising the means to achieve them. Such men were not feckless; they could restrain their immediate impulses, delay or deny the gratification of appetites, and maintain sustained expressions of will. They were self-critical and reflected upon their own conduct and at least tried to amend the defects in their character. In examining themselves, they also had the disposition to examine people and institutions around them and to ponder modes of improvement in both. Of course, many men of the nineteenth century were only imperfectly endowed with these attributes, and the consequences of such attributes were not always benign. Some of the sour Gradgrindian moralisers of the Victorian Age seem less desirable than the rakes of the Regency. Nevertheless, when we consider the great Victorians it is no accident that compared to them men such as the brilliant but lazy and dissolute Fox, the irresponsible Col. Aston or the entirely impulsive Lord Camelford – can appear as but spoiled and wilful children.

If the dispositions apparent in these new men were not in truth entirely new, their spread still seems to owe much to the evangelical revival, with its message as to the efficacy of guiding present conduct by future expectations. Clearly, they were also intimately related to the development of commerce and science and the increasingly obvious benefits of detailed rational planning. Perhaps, too, they emerged in response to the demands of a larger state, necessarily bent towards maintaining its sovereignty in the face of more sophisticated threats from within and without. What was most certainly the case was that the calculating mentalities of such new men were antithetical to the values of the men of honour, for whom the methodical calculation of ends contradicted a central tenet of honour: that life was to be mastered by rising above considerations of cost, benefit, or utility and being prepared to lay it down for trifles.

One consequence of the increasing technical change and commercial and industrial development in the early nineteenth century was of course an appetite for more.

---

2   Tosh, 'Masculinities', op. cit., p. 331.

The changes were not merely technical and scientific, however; perhaps more than anything they were managerial. As the power of management techniques, the utility of statistics and the value of rule-based systems of governance became apparent, so too there emerged new aspirations and expectations. The organising classes of society were, in short, equipped with new ideas about the appropriate way to live and were setting themselves increasingly ambitious objectives. Unfortunately for the men of honour, as I have shown, not least among the deleterious effects of the duel was its capacity to subvert, even overthrow, those hierarchies of authority necessary to the operation of any sophisticated organisation or the accomplishment of any complex task.

If one takes warfare, for example, the desire to progress, to cultivate the ability to wage it more effectively was not merely driven by imperial ambition but also by imperial anxiety. War as a new 'social technique of bureaucratically rational-ised violence' required a new spirit of discipline. It required that individuals, even gentlemen, suppress their personal inclinations in order to accomplish the collec-tive purpose. The professionalisation of the military endeavour was, of course, hardly a matter of choice when others were doing the same. Necessity, too, was the driving force in reforming the haphazard administration of an empire acquired, in Sir John Seeley's memorable phrase, 'in a fit of absence of mind'. Where areas of authority were left indeterminate, where different arms of government were allowed to compete, damaging disputes proved to be the consequence. However, over time those indeterminate areas slowly began to shrink or disappear. Honour disputes themselves played a role in accomplishing this. By highlighting areas of contention, they obliged governments to establish administrative norms and delineate spheres of authority. Colonial officers who urged that central authorities must protect them against personal challenges to their authority rarely repudiated honour culture per se. Rather, they referred to their position and to their particular circumstances and pointed out the dangers of challenges to their authority in an empire that was but sparsely held. Only by bureaucratising colonial administration could the overseas possessions be secured and exploited.

The same was true at home too. As society grew more complex, its management became less a matter of bravura and personality and more a matter of hierarchical authority and rule-based norms. A civil service emerged, and the professions became truly professional as we understand them. The legal profession, subverted for a time by the codes of honour, is a case in point. The lawyers themselves duelled and aped their betters. Indeed, one wonders if this was a necessary stage through which the profession had to pass on the way to respectability. That phase ended, however, as the profession developed its own nexus of mores and practices and its own free-standing cultural forms. The formalising of qualifications, the development of education and the establishment of professional bodies and systems of regulation were all part of the process that liberated the law from servility. Judges, for example, as Duman has shown, ceased to regard themselves as mere aspiring landed proprietors and came to view themselves as men accomplished in their own right, participating in an alternative and, at the very least, equally valid system of social placing. The pursuit of the law became not a mode of entry into the mores of the landed gentility but an entirely plausible alternative to it. The doctors were rather tardier, passing through the duelling phase right at the end of duelling itself. The other professions, such as architects, engineers and accountants, naturally multiplied with the advance of manufacture and the expansion of commerce, but they were either never attracted to the duel or arrived late enough to be spared the experience of it.

As mentalities became increasingly calculating, the conduct of those who gave way to their violent passions and who displayed a defiance of, indeed, a contempt for, the virtues of consequentialism became increasingly anomalous. Those who continued to adhere to the older forms of interaction and retain the older sensibilities found that society was reconfiguring in such a way as to limit the opportunity for offence and honourable resolution. New men were more likely to resort to law in matters of dispute. They were less likely to give public insult and less likely to respond to insult with violence. The effect of this was cumulative; that is to say that as the tyranny of society was relaxed, fewer and fewer gentlemen felt compelled to challenge or to duel.

Abolitionists were quick to characterise the duellist as an arcane creature of yesteryear, and ridicule was a powerful weapon deployed against men of honour. These abolitionists no doubt hastened the day when duelling was no more. However, they did not themselves accomplish the demise of duelling, other than in the most immediate and trivial sense. For two centuries they had been railing and writing pamphlets against duelling, complaining about the inadequacy of the courts, demanding that duellists be socially ostracised and so forth. Yet, for example, they never succeeded in creating a climate of opinion such that juries would convict honourable duellists of murder and such that judges would allow the full majesty of the law to take its course. The truth is that the duel was something of a rattling corpse ere the abolitionists finally stifled it. Duelling did not succumb to any single onslaught; there was no single reason for its disappearance. Rather, from the eighteenth century onwards the spaces in which honour culture had existed, in spite of a powerful Christian counter ideology, began to slowly disappear. Honour culture was steadily squeezed out of society like water from a dishcloth, and as often as not this was as much an incidental consequence of broader cultural change as it was a result of anti-duelling endeavour. For example, the securing of public space and the expectation of an increasing decorum within it were not envisaged primarily as ways of improving the behaviour of gentlemen; nevertheless, they had this effect. The penal reforms designed to regularise and systematise punishment were not intended to increase the pains of detention for duellists, but they did so.

An objection, though, might be raised to my assertion that it was the advance of modern functionalist mentalities that occasioned the demise of the English duel. That is to say that if such mentalities occasioned the demise, how then did the duel endure in European societies that were also modernising and industrialising? Part of the answer lies in the observation that in France and Italy the duel did not in fact continue into the second half of the nineteenth century with the same vigour as before. The same was true of a number of other countries, whose history space has not permitted me to explore – the Scandinavian countries, Belgium, Holland and Switzerland, for example. The actual number of encounters may not have diminished – indeed, it may well have increased – but deployment of the sword allowed them to be finessed into an activity that was very much safer and less threatening to the proper functioning of society. Among the industrialising powers, the great exception to this was, of course, Germany, although again there is evidence of a sustained and, if McAleer is right, at least partially successful assault upon duelling during the very period that the institution was declining dramatically in France and England.

Nevertheless, the duel did survive, in a somewhat attenuated form, in both France and Italy. In part, the difference can be explained by the fact that the duel had in both countries reached further down the social scale in these countries. It had indeed become, to a degree, democratic and symbolic of national virility. In France and in Italy the move to modernity was to reform the duel but not yet to eliminate it. In Great Britain the duel was not so entrenched. It never gained a sufficiently broad constituency in England such that its preservation could plausibly be identified with the preservation of national masculinity. Duelling failed to join those patriotic attributes of Englishness that were to be included within the national pantheon and celebrated in the course of the new imperialism.

However, there was a further factor that hastened the demise of the English duel. That is to say that when one observes the changes in the nature of governance during this period, one observes that those changes were driven as much by a desire to preserve as to reform. Fear as well as optimism lay behind the desire to quell the disorder in society. Continental revolution, domestic radicalism, frame breaking, the activities of Captain Swing and the campaigns of Chartism – the period under question was one of profound turbulence in British society. Furthermore, after about 1810 the English crowd often possessed 'an unmistakeable consciousness ... that what they [were] in rebellion against [was] the established order of society, laid down by Parliament, upheld by the courts and enforced by a standing army'.[3]

What we observe after the French Revolution and then with the growth of radicalism is a crisis of confidence within the British governing classes. It was the reaction of the British elites, rather than the experience itself, which was to distinguish the

---

3   Webb and Webb, *English Local Government,* op. cit., vol. iv, pp. 412–413.

British experience. Their reaction, by and large, was not to retreat back to autocracy and simple authoritarianism. They were quite simply more creative and intelligent than that. In the context of felony, for example, the views of those such as Paley that hanging was not punishment enough did not prevail. Rather, the better orders re-evaluated; they demonstrated a capacity for self-appraisal and criticism. In short, they indeed demonstrated the flexibility of an open elite. The conclusion drawn from their introspections was that old modes of governance and traditional modes of communication with the rest of society would no longer suffice to contain the exuberance of a restive and growing populace. It was no longer safe to allow crowds to congregate at an execution, to allow violent sports to course through the streets, to rely upon the watch and the magistrate to manage the mob.

One consequence of this was the impulse to subdue public space, the pursuit of which, as I previously argued, did so much to diffuse the pugnacity of gentlemen. Another was that notions of civility were reinforced. It had become necessary in such times to make aristocracy acceptable to the middle, and one way of doing so was to practise discretion in the exercise of social power. Men, even of the highest social standing, were to become less loud, less contemptuous and less overt in the exercise of privileges that might offend the new social norms. To generalise, as one must, even young London gentlemen began to pay their tailors, conceal their mistresses, curtail their gambling and conduct themselves with some decorum. Whether, though, they indeed became less aggressive per se is hard to ascertain. As Peter Tosh puts it:

> It is at least worth reconsidering the suggestion that a masculine culture not yet reconciled to the outlawing of interpersonal violence was drawn to the empire as a career posting and as an imaginative space where physical exertion could be given free rein.[4]

At home, though, men of privilege began to consider how society might best be reformed in order to secure it for their interests. Between the elites and the middle there developed a coalition of interests forged to no small degree out of fear of those below. There was no doubt that it remained the elite themselves who were to be the senior partner in the construction of a new kind of national society. For the elites, the abandonment of immunity from the law, class-bound violence, and honour culture was a price that had, somewhat reluctantly, to be paid. However, by paying it, gentlemen were able to secure their leadership of this new society, a society with, allegedly, collective interests and equal liberties – and, of course, increasingly patriotic and imperialistic ambitions. The physical constraints henceforth laid upon gentlemen were amply compensated for by the increased safety and dignity they experienced as they moved through society. Gentlemen no longer needed fisticuffs.

---

4   Tosh, 'Masculinities', op. cit., pp. 340–341.

A gentleman's interests were rather to be secured by the expanding institutions of a state that had grown adept at suppressing popular culture and radicalism. They were also to continue to be secured by the judges of the law, who were to remain 'sat atop a pyramid of violence, dealing'.[5]

The problem of legitimacy, however, became more and more acute with the spread of radical ideas. One response was to rejuvenate the image of, and proselytise the virtues of, a society formally equal under the Sovereign and the Rule of Law. When *The Times* argued that an earl who had committed a felony should be treated like a common criminal, it was expounding a form of legal equality that had, by and large, been absent from the practice of eighteenth-century criminal justice. Yet that all should be equal before the law was not a new assertion. Those who called for formal equality were able to present themselves as both progressive and traditional. They sought to improve society, but their propagandists, such as Hannah More, couched such improvements in terms of the return to (allegedly) old English virtues of just governance and liberty based upon formal equality.

In this context, however, the duel stood exposed. The duel could only undermine the necessary forgetfulness implicit in this construction of the new national image. Each unpunished duellist demonstrated that all men were not equal before the law. Each duel undertaken revealed that there were men at the very pinnacle of society who preferred to indulge their personal inclinations rather than do their duty to the sovereign, to her laws and to the nation. This was indeed a scandal. By the 1840s, I argue, the time when the duel could be claimed to be necessary to sustain society had long since passed. It had become unpatriotic, antisocial and uncomfortable in its allusion to the realities of social power. The duellist would not comply with the stage directions given in the new national drama; he remained questioning, awkward and contradictory, subverting the plot and revealing its contrivances. Each duel was a declaration of the power of privilege to subvert those rules governing the rest of society. Increasingly, the anomalous treatment of gentlemen duellists disturbed a respectable public conscience that was itself required to believe in formal equality in order to speak with conviction to those below. *The Times* captured this when it linked the Cardigan duel to the issue of public order and social stability: 'An opinion, most dangerous to the aristocracy prevails, that in England there is one law for the rich and another for the poor.'[6]

Objectively this was an obvious social truth, but one that had to be wilfully forgotten in order to habituate restive groups to the existing social order. Such wilful forgetfulness was not, however, easily accomplished when the inequality of society was so loudly and proudly proclaimed by those adhering to the old codes of honour.

---

5   Cover, 'Violence and the word', op. cit., p. 1609.

6   *The Times*, 18 Feb. 1841, p. 4, col. a.

Much had to be given up in order to construct the new representations of nation and of self, to create the illusions upon which the new society would be built. The duel had lost its utility in the construction of the social vision. The last words here then, are appropriately those of a writer for *The Times* who was well aware of the potential of the duel to dispel the façade of equality that was essential to the new social mirage:

> No more pernicious or anarchical principle than that of the defenders of duelling was ever broached by Chartism or even Socialism itself.[7]

---

7   *The Times*, 20 Feb. 1841, p. 4, col. d.

Appendix
Selected Duels in England, Scotland and Wales, 1750–1852

Unfortunately, considerations of space prohibit me from presenting a list of all the duels that I have discovered in England, Scotland and Wales. Such a list, however, would not necessarily be very informative. There are many duels about which we actually know very little. Brief newspaper reports may record the fact of a duel's occurrence, but the 'when', the 'where' and the 'why' often elude us, and so too the fate and even the identity of the parties. It must also be said that some reports were quite unreliable; not infrequently newspapers found themselves retracting reports of duels that had turned out to be based upon nothing more than unsubstantiated rumour. It has thus been necessary to choose which encounters to select for inclusion below. Some duels have been included because at the time they were felt to be politically important or socially significant, even though the encounters themselves may have proved harmless. The duel between the Duke of Wellington and Lord Winchilsea is a case in point. Others have been selected because they occasioned notorious fatalities, or were carried out in a fashion that resulted in particular public approval or disapprobation. Many have been chosen because they gave rise to legal proceedings and thus serve to illustrate the effectiveness, or the lack thereof, of the criminal courts in suppressing duelling. To that end I have also included one duel from Ireland, that which resulted in the execution of Col. Campbell in 1808, since this was both a unique legal consequence and was widely discussed at the time. Above all, though, I have tried to select accounts that illustrate the circumstances in which gentlemen might come into conflict and the nuances of honour culture which led men to take to the field. In sum, then, I hope that this appendix will provide a useful snapshot of the later history of duelling.

May 1751 (?): Mr Dalton and Mr Paul at a Private London House

The date of this duel is uncertain since a year is not given in the Walpole Papers; it has been variously dated to 1751 and 1765. Mr Dalton was engaged to a Miss Mary Green, who had previously had the unfortunate habit of taking too much snuff.

He had therefore confiscated her snuffbox. One day he chanced to visit her house at the same time as an old friend, Mr Paul. Mary asked Dalton for some snuff, which he refused; however, when she asked Mr Paul for some of his, he gave it to her, and 'at this trifling circumstance the then present Company perceived Mr Dalton to be somewhat Affected'.[1] Mary asked Mr Paul to try some of the snuff in her snuffbox, then in the possession of Mr Dalton. However, when Dalton gave Mr Paul the snuffbox, Miss Green immediately asked him to give it back to her instead of to Mr Dalton, 'The whole Company thereby understanding her meaning to be that she might recover Possession of her Box so as not to be debarred the liberty of taking Snuff when she pleased.' An argument arose over who was entitled to get the box back, with Mr Paul choosing to return it to Miss Green. At that point Dalton promptly assaulted him. Mr Paul left, acquired a sword and some time later went to Dalton's house. According to Paul, they met in a locked room without any seconds, first embracing before drawing swords. Dalton was killed, and Paul fled to France. He subsequently published a letter exonerating Miss Green from all blame and declaring that before the incident he and Dalton had been the firmest of friends. According to Millingen, he never returned to England and was outlawed.

1752: Capt. Grey and Lord Lempster in London

They quarrelled over a gambling debt and fought with swords. Grey was killed, and Lempster was tried at the Old Bailey and found guilty of manslaughter.[2]

1760: Maj. Glover and Mr Jackson in Manchester

Maj. Glover served in the Lincolnshire militia. He was passing down a street one day when an apothecary, Mr Jackson, touched him playfully on the back. When Glover encountered Jackson later that day, Glover poked him with a switch in return. Jackson challenged at once. The major offered his apologies, but Jackson would not accept them. They fought immediately in a nearby coffee house, and Jackson was run through.[3]

1761: Maj. Egerton and Col. Grey on Putney Heath

Egerton was returning from the theatre with a lady when Grey ran into him. Egerton called Grey a 'stupid booby', and Grey tried to draw his sword in response.

---

1 British Library Add. 74087, the Walpole Papers vol. cccxviii, f.17. Millingen, *The History of Duelling*, op. cit., vol. ii, pp. 49–50.

2 Sabine, *Notes on Duels and Duelling*, op. cit., p. 189.

3 Truman, *The Field of Honor*, op. cit., p. 208–209.

Egerton knocked him down, and Grey challenged the following day. They met at ten paces, and after the first unsuccessful exchange of shots, the seconds attempted to intervene. Grey insisted on another exchange; he was killed whilst Egerton was wounded.[4]

October 1762: Lord Talbot and Mr John Wilkes at Bagshot

The duel was caused by remarks about Talbot made anonymously by Wilkes, a politician and demagogue, in issue twelve of the *North Briton* on 21 August 1762. Wilkes would neither admit to nor deny authorship of the piece. The pair dined together before the duel at the Red Lion Inn, and Wilkes claimed later that he 'knew his Lordship fought me with the King's Pardon in his pocket, and I fought him with a halter about my neck'. Accompanied by seconds, the two then strolled into the garden and exchanged a single shot each – to no effect.[5]

November 1763: Mr Samuel Martin and Mr John Wilkes in Hyde Park

Martin was a secretary to the Treasury who had been lampooned in the *North Briton* some eight months previously. In November he attacked Wilkes in Parliament and in a private letter challenged him, describing him as 'a cowardly as well as a malignant scoundrel'. They exchanged one shot apiece in the park, and Wilkes was wounded, not seriously, in the abdomen.[6]

January 1765: William, Fifth Lord Byron and Mr Chaworth in Pall Mall

The duel arose out of a dispute at a public dinner over the best method of preserving wild game. Each of the two men boastfully claimed to have more game on his estate than the other. The dispute seemed trivial to the other members of the company, but Byron invited Chaworth into an adjacent room and invited him to draw. There were no witnesses or seconds. The men fought by candlelight, and Chaworth was killed. Byron was tried by his peers at Westminster hall; he was acquitted of murder but convicted of manslaughter. He pleaded benefit of clergy and was symbolically branded with a cold iron and fined.[7]

---

4   Ibid., pp. 189–190.
5   Millingen, *History of Duelling*, op. cit., vol. ii, pp. 66–76.
6   Ibid., pp. 76–81.
7   Ibid., pp. 60–66.

May 1765: Lord Kilmaurs and a French officer

The duel was caused by Kilmaurs being told off for talking loudly in the theatre. The complainant thereafter accused Kilmaurs of staring at him and dragged the lord into the street, where he then struck him with the flat of his sword. Kilmaurs drew but was wounded in the stomach.[8]

1769: Mr Andrew Stewart and Mr Edward Thurlow in Kensington Gardens

Thurlow later became the Lord Chancellor, but in 1767 he was counsel at the Bar for Mr Douglas in *Douglas* v *Duke of Hamilton*. He was challenged after making some critical remarks about Stewart, who was working for the Duke's legal advisors. Thurlow accepted the challenge upon condition that the meeting take place after the case had closed. They subsequently exchanged shots in Kensington Gardens without effect.[9]

1772: Capt. Matthews and Mr Richard Brinsley Sheridan at Kingsdown, Kent

Two somewhat different accounts of the duel are offered by Sabine and Millingen. It seems Sheridan pursued a singer, Miss Linley, with little success, until a jealous admirer, Captain Matthews, published an attack upon her character in the press. Sheridan challenged, and two duels followed: the first in Henrietta Street, Covent Garden, in which Matthews was disarmed, and the second at Kingsdown in Kent. In the second, the combatants fired pistols and then fought with swords, with both parties being seriously wounded. Each recovered, but it was Sheridan who married the lady.[10]

January 1777: Rev. Bate and Capt. Stoney in London

The Rev. Bate was the editor of the *Morning Post* and had published some paragraphs reflecting upon the honour of Lady Strathmore. The captain challenged Bate, and they fought first with swords and then pistols. Both were wounded but neither fatally. The captain subsequently married Lady Strathmore.

---

8 Ibid., pp. 92–94.

9 Sabine, *Notes on Duels and Duelling*, op. cit., p. 295.

10 Ibid., pp. 276–278; Millingen, *History of Duelling*, op. cit., vol. ii, pp. 96–98.

November 1779: Mr Adam and Mr Charles James Fox in Hyde Park

The quarrel between the two men arose over a parliamentary debate. Mr Adam, who supported the government, alleged that if they came to power the Whigs would make abject concessions to the rebellious American colonists. Fox in reply, mocked Adam's speech as a sign of desperation from a failing government. Adam thought that Fox had attacked him personally and he subsequently asked Fox to insert a paragraph in a newspaper denying any personal malice. Fox refused, saying that he was happy to declare personally that he had no malice, but how others interpreted his speech was for them. Two shots each were fired at the subsequent meeting in Hyde Park, and Fox was lightly wounded.[11]

March 1780: Col. Fullarton and the Earl of Shelburne in Hyde Park

Fullarton, who was the MP for Plympton, challenged the earl because Shelburne had suggested that Fullarton's regiment was as ready to act against England's liberties as it was to defend it against England's enemies. They met at twelve paces with Lord Cavendish acting for Shelburne and Lord Balcarras for Fullarton. After one exchange neither party was hit, but at the second fire, Shelburne was hit in the groin. Shelburne himself had still to fire, though, so Fullarton returned to his position to receive Shelburne's shot. Shelburne, however, fired into the air, and the men were reconciled.[12]

April 1780: Mr Donovan and Capt. James Hanson in Surrey

Donovan had intervened to prevent the captain fighting with another person. Hanson had then abused him, and they had fought with pistols. Hanson was wounded and died twenty-four hours later. Donovan was tried at Kingston Assizes in Surrey, where Mr Justice Gould spoke of the humanity Donovan had shown towards the wounded man and declared that the circumstances 'were as favourable to the prisoner as in such a case could be'. He was found guilty of manslaughter and fined ten pounds.[13]

---

11 Sabine, *Notes on Duels and Duelling*, op. cit., pp. 176–178; Millingen, *History of Duelling*, op. cit., vol. ii, pp. 104–107.

12 Sabine, *Notes on Duels and Duelling*, op. cit., pp. 275–6; Truman, *The Field of Honor*, op. cit., pp. 193–194; Millingen, *History of Duelling*, op. cit., pp. 108–110.

13 Ibid., pp. 111–12.

June 1782: Rev. Allen and Lt Lloyd Dulany in Hyde Park

Allen published an anonymous paragraph in the *Morning Post* on 29 June 1779 attacking the character of the principal men involved in the American Revolution. One of these was the brother of Lt Dulany, who tried unsuccessfully to find out the identity of the author before having to leave England for two years. On his return he received a note from Allen declaring authorship. They met on 18 June 1781 with seconds, and Dulany was killed. Allen was tried at the Old Bailey together with his second. The second was acquitted, but Allen was convicted of manslaughter, fined a shilling and sentenced to six months' imprisonment.[14]

April 1783: Mr Cunningham and Mr Riddell

Riddell was an officer of the Horse Grenadiers and Cunningham of the Scots Greys. Following a quarrel over cards, Riddell challenged Cunningham, who declined. However, Cunningham's fellow officers pressured him until, after some considerable time, he indicated he was prepared to fight. Riddell, however, consulted his own officers, who declared that Cunningham had forfeited his right to give satisfaction. Cunningham, desperate to rehabilitate himself, then spat in Riddell's face to provoke a fresh challenge. They met the same day at only eight paces. The seconds tossed for the right of first fire, which Riddell won. Riddell shot Cunningham through the chest, but Cunningham returned fire and Riddell was fatally wounded in the groin. Riddell died the following day, and a coroner's jury brought a verdict of manslaughter against Cunningham, though there is no record of him ever being brought to trial. He may himself have died sometime afterwards since both Millingen and Douglas report his own estimate of having been 'mortally wounded', but there is no record of his death.[15]

September 1783: Col. Cosmo Gordon and Lt Col. Thomas in Hyde Park

Both had been officers in the American war, and Gordon had been court-martialled at Thomas's instigation for neglect of his duty. He was acquitted, and once back in England, he challenged. The two met in Hyde Park at only eight yards. At the first fire Gordon was hit in the thigh and Thomas killed. According to Sabine, Thomas left a will in which he asked for 'mercy and pardon for the irreligious step I now

---

14 *Old Bailey Proceedings Online* (www.oldbaileyonline.org, 1 Oct. 2009), 5 Jun. 1782, trial of Bennet Allen (ref. t17820605-1).

15 Douglas, *Duelling Days in the Army*, op. cit., pp. 69–71; Millingen, *History of Duelling*, op. cit., vol. ii, pp. 116–118.

(in compliance with the unwarranted customs of this wicked world) put myself under the necessity of taking.'[16]

June 1784: Mr England and Mr Rowls at Cranford Bridge

Rowls had lost a bet to England in 1780 and had owed him £500, which at the time he had been unable to repay. Eventually, a compromise had been agreed whereby the debt was settled for £250. However, in 1784 they met again at Ascot Races, where Rowls was taking bets. England urged those present not to bet with Rowls as he would not pay up if he lost. Rowls responded by threatening to strike him, at which point England invited a challenge. They met on 18 June, and both sides fired four or five shots each. At some point during the interchange Rowls offered to pay a sum of money to England, which the latter declined. Lord Cremorne chanced upon the duel and attempted to interfere but was instructed to withdraw lest he himself be declared 'impertinent' by Rowls. Rowls himself was then killed in the exchange, and England fled abroad, not returning until four witnesses to the encounter had died. He was indicted at the Old Bailey on 19 February 1796. The prosecution attempted to characterise the affair as one outside of the ambit of honour, since the heart of it was a pecuniary dispute between the parties and since England had failed to submit to justice for twelve years. The jury, however, brought in a verdict of manslaughter after forty-five minutes, and England was fined a shilling and imprisoned for twelve months. However, reports from *The Times* show that in July he was pardoned by the king.[17]

September 1784: Lord Macartney and Mr Sadleir in Kensington

In a conflict over the politics of the East India Company, Macartney and Sadler had quarrelled in Madras and then at the Council Board in Bombay on 16 March 1784. On their return to England they met at twelve paces, and at the second fire Macartney was seriously wounded.[18]

---

16 Sabine, *Notes on Duels and Duelling*, op. cit., pp. 293–294; Millingen, *History of Duelling*, op. cit, vol. ii, pp. 119–120.

17 See *Old Bailey Proceedings Online* (www.oldbaileyonline.org, 1 Oct. 2009), 17 Feb. 1796, trial of Richard England (ref. t17960217-27); *The Times*, 20 Feb. 1796, p. 3, col. b; *The Times*, 9 Jul. 1796, p. 3, col. b.

18 *The Times*, 19 Apr. 1785, p. 2, col. d; Truman, *The Field of Honour*, op. cit., pp. 207–208.

February 1785: Capt. Brisco and Mr Bulkley, both of the Guards, at Paddington

For reasons unknown Capt. Brisco sent a critical letter to Capt. Bulkley. Bulkley however, far from dealing with the matter personally, made a complaint to a court of enquiry about Brisco's conduct. The effect was the reverse of that which he had anticipated since the court and all his fellow officers voted to send him to Coventry rather than to act against Brisco. Once Bulkley had however, duelled with Brisco the officers met and decided to speak to him again.[19]

January 1786: Lt Gamble and Lt Mollison at Chatham

The duel was caused after Gamble lost a bet with Mollison at Brompton in London. The following day both men returned to their billet at Chatham lines and appointed seconds. Each fired a single shot, with Gamble being wounded in the thigh and Mollison in the arm, which was subsequently amputated.[20]

June 1786: Lord Macartney and Maj. Gen. Stuart at Kensington

The duel was fought over a dispute concerning the politics of the East India Company; Macartney had already been wounded in a duel with Mr Sadleir in 1784 over a dispute in Bombay. In this duel, fought at twelve 'short paces', Macartney was again wounded.[21]

August 1786: Lt M. and Lt S. at Newington

'A duel took place at Newington between Lt M and another commissioned officer of the navy, occasioned by a dispute that arose on Monday evening at a tavern in Holborn. The ground being measured, the latter officer fired, and wounded Lt M in his sword arm; notwithstanding Lt M fired, and wounded his antagonist in a manner it is thought he cannot survive.'[22]

September 1787: Maj. Browne and Sir John MacPherson

In 1785 Sir John had been the Governor General of Bengal, and Browne had been the East India Company resident to the King of Delhi. Browne had received orders

---

19 *The Times*, 3 Feb. 1783, p. 3, col. a.

20 *The Times*, 23 Jan. 1786, p. 3, col. b; Millingen, *History of Duelling*, op. cit., vol. ii, pp. 125–126.

21 Ibid., vol. ii, pp. 126–128; Truman, *Field of Honor*, op. cit., pp. 207–208.

22 *The Times*, 29 Aug. 1786, p. 3, col. b.

of recall back to London, but he refused to return until Sir John had ordered him to leave India. Browne was at this point suspected of some unspecified intrigue in Delhi. Browne was forced to return home, but when Sir John himself came back to England, Browne challenged him. Six shots were exchanged to no effect.[23]

March 1788: Mr S. and Capt. H. on Shooters Hill

This was but one of a whole series of duels that were caused by a dispute at cards and in the subsequent duel Capt. H. was wounded. According to *The Times*, 'The gentlemen were playing at hazard ... when Mr S went several times against the whole table, excepting Captain H-g individually and by name. Capt H-g desired to know if any thing of a personal nature was intended by the exception. Mr S-r refused to give any answer.'[24] The two men then exchanged angry words and then blows.

December 1788: Col. Roper and Ensign Purefoy at Maidstone

Purefoy had been an ensign in Roper's regiment on station at St Vincent. Owing to the misconduct of some junior officers, Roper had cancelled all their leave, including that of Purefoy. The ensign had then berated Roper, and this had resulted in his court martial and the loss of his commission. Both had returned to England, and the duel took place on 21 December 1788. The seconds of the parties agreed that on the field each would turn on their heels and fire quickly, but Purefoy broke his ground, laid his pistol on his arm and took deliberate aim and fired, killing Roper with the first shot. A coroner's jury brought in a verdict of wilful murder,[25] but Purefoy had already fled abroad. However, he was arrested at Nieuport in 1793[26] and brought back to face trial at Maidstone Assizes on 14 August 1794. Remarkably, Gen. Stanwix, Roper's second in the duel, gave evidence for Purefoy at the trial, saying that Purefoy 'had entertained no malice against the deceased; he had been laid by a call of honour, or, more properly speaking, driven by the tyranny of custom, to an act which in early life had embittered his existence; but without which, he was taught to believe that he should lose all consideration which society could afford.' The jury without hesitation brought in a verdict of not guilty.[27]

---

23 *The Times*, 14 Sep. 1787, p. 2, col. c; Millingen, *History of Duelling*, op. cit., vol. ii, pp. 129–130.

24 *The Times*, 29 Mar. 1788, p. 3, col. a.

25 *The Times* 24 Dec. 1788 p. 3, col. b.

26 *The Times*, 12 Nov. 1793 p. 2, col. c

27 For an account of the trial see *The Times*, 16 Aug. 1794, p. 3, col. b. See also Millingen, *History of Duelling*, op. cit., vol. ii, pp. 146–147.

February 1789: Mr C. H. and Mr J. W. in King's Park, Edinburgh

Both men were advocates, and the quarrel originated while Mr H. was acting for a Mr Fennel in a case against Mr Wilde and several others. During the trial he used expressions that the defendants found personally objectionable. Accordingly, they drew lots and it fell to Mr W. (presumably Mr Wilde) to challenge Mr H. No one was wounded in the encounter.[28]

May 1789: Col. Lennox and HRH the Duke of York on Wimbledon Common

Frederick Augustus, the Duke of York, was the second son of George III. While colonel of the Coldstream Regiment, he was alleged to have remarked that 'Colonel Lennox had heard words spoken to him at Daubigny's [a gentleman's club] to which no gentleman ought to have submitted.' When Lennox heard this, he demanded on the parade ground an explanation of the remark. The duke subsequently offered, as a private gentleman, to give the colonel satisfaction. Lennox then sent a letter to all the members of Daubigny's asking if any had ever heard words spoken to him which he should have resented and had not. None suggested that such was true, and Lennox demanded a meeting. Lord Rawdon seconded the Duke of York, and Lord Winchilsea seconded Col. Lennox. On Wimbledon Common the duke received Lennox's fire, which was said to have grazed his cheek; the duke in return declined to fire at Lennox. There was much adverse comment about a member of the Royal family being hazarded in a duel and on 1 June 1789 Lennox convened a meeting of the officers of the Coldstream Regiment to judge his conduct. [29] The meeting prepared a written statement declaring that Lennox had 'behaved with courage but from the peculiar difficulty of his position, not with judgment'. Lennox soon after exchanged his commission for another regiment. [30]

June 1789: Capt. Tongue and Capt. Patterson

The duel originated in a drunken quarrel in the street, and 'though Mr T, who gave the insult, offered to make any apology, yet such was the idea of modern honour that no mediation but that which hazarded life was deemed sufficient. The principals and the seconds therefore met, and to avoid as much as possible

---

28   *The Times*, 5 Feb. 1789, p. 2, col. c.

29   *The Times* reported the duel on 27 May (p. 3, col. a.) and again on 28 May (p. 2, col. b), but it also carried a letter on 6 June criticising the duke for refusing to fire on his adversary (p. 3, col. a).

30   Millingen, *History of Duelling*, op. cit., vol. ii, pp. 131–133.

any lucky escape from the ball, the distance was set at seven yards, so that with the length of the arm, the muzzles were not above four yards asunder. In this position the word fire was given, which did not however happen for a full minute afterwards, when Mr Tongue received his adversaries ball under the bone of the right hip ... Mr Tongue's second desired him to fire, but he declined it, saying that he gave the insult, was sorry for it, and of course had no animosity against Mr Paterson.'[31]

October 1789: Mr R. C. and Lt J. N. L. at Hammersmith

The duel was caused by Lt J. N. L. speaking disparagingly of the character of a friend of Mr R. C. The gentleman in question was away in Dorsetshire and hence unable to defend his reputation, so Mr C. challenged in his stead. The duellists met at ten paces, and at the first exchange of fire Mr C. was slightly wounded. However, he refused to end the meeting, and at the second exchange Lt L. was wounded in the hip.[32]

1790: Mr McLeod and Mr MacDonnell in Edinburgh

The duel was caused by a quarrel at a ball. Mr MacDonnell felt that Mr McLeod had given him an impertinent look and thus struck him with a cane. Mr McLeod challenged at once, and the two met the following day. On the duelling ground Mr MacDonnell indicated his willingness to make a full apology, but McLeod's second interposed and said that MacDonnell must agree to the same punishment that he had inflicted on McLeod. MacDonnell refused and at first fire killed his opponent. He was subsequently tried for murder but was acquitted.[33]

March 1790: Lt H. T. H. of the Royal Navy and Lt L. at Blackheath

'Friday morning a duel was fought on Blackheath, between Lieutenant H.T.H. of the Royal Navy and Lieutenant L. of the Marines, the parties met by agreement at half past five o'clock and took the ground at fifteen paces and on Mr H. – having the advantage by getting the first fire, Mr L. received a wound in the right shoulder and immediately declined the contest.'[34]

---

31 Millingen, *History of Duelling*, op. cit., vol. ii, p. 134.

32 *The Times*, 26 Oct. 1789, p. 3, col. c.

33 Sabine, *Notes on Duels and Duelling*, op. cit., p. 231.

34 *The Times*, 29 Mar. 1790, p. 2, col. c.

March 1790: Parson W., a chaplain to a regiment, and Mr A-D. in Hyde Park

'On Friday morning a duel was fought in Hyde Park between a Parson W. a chaplain to a regiment, and a young man who calls himself the son of General A-D. Mr A-D was wounded in the thigh, and taken to his lodgings in the Strand, where the ball was extracted.'[35]

April 1790: Sir George Ramsay and Capt. Macrae at Musselburgh

Sir George had a sedan chair waiting for him at the door to an Edinburgh theatre, but Capt. Macrae ordered Sir George's servant to remove it. The servant, James Murray, refused to do so, whereupon Macrae assaulted and severely injured him. Murray then laid a criminal complaint against Macrae, who responded by writing to Sir George and insisting that he dismiss Murray from his employ. Ramsay refused, whereupon Macrae declared him to be a scoundrel and no gentleman. They met at Musselborough near Edinburgh, and Ramsay was killed. Macrae fled, and in July the High Court of Justiciary pronounced the sentence of outlawry upon him.[36]

May 1790: Lt Reid and William Ross

The duel was caused when Mr Ross called for an apology from Lt Reid and his brother, seemingly for an attempt to seduce his sister. Ross, as the challenger, fired the first shot, and then Reid. After this exchange the seconds attempted to resolve the dispute, but Reid refused to offer the required apology, and in the second exchange of fire Ross was killed.[37] The case served to illustrate the degree to which duelling and its consequences were becoming a cause for public debate. On 19 May 1790 there appeared this announcement in the classified advertising section of *The Times*:

> Westminster Forum, Panton Street Haymarket
>   Held every Wednesday. Evening admittance 6 d, Gallery 1 shilling. 'Appeal to the Heart.' This Evening (at the request of several Ladies who patronise this society) will be debated, 'Is that Brother justifiable, who punishes with death the seducer of his Sister's honour?' A most important debate will doubtless arise on this question; not a father, a brother, nor member of civil society, but is interested in this discussion. The beauteous circle of Ladies who attend this society, must animate the speaker on such a theme.

---

35 *The Times*, 15 Mar. 1790, p. 2, col. f.

36 Details of the correspondence which passed between the two men were published in *The Times*, 4 May 1790 p. 3, col. a. See also Millingen, *History of Duelling*, op. cit., vol. ii, p. 136–137.

37 *The Times*, 12 May 1790, p. 3, col. a; 14 May 1790, p. 3, col. a.

Gentlemen are requested to be as tender as possible in their allusions to the late fatal duel between Messes Ross and Reid. Who we acknowledge, gave rise to the above question, which simply asks how far the feelings of a brother might excuse him for taking vengeance upon the author of that family dishonour, the effects of which are indeed irreparable.[38]

June 1790: Mr MacDuff and Midshipman Prince at Bridlington

Mr Macduff was a captain's clerk on the sloop of war *Racehorse*, and Mr Prince a midshipman. The reasons for the duel are unknown, but according to *The Times*, the only witness was a boy. Macduff was killed, but the fate of Prince is unknown.[39]

July 1790: Mr Alcock and Mr Sewell at Guildford

Little is known about this duel except that it serves to illustrate the hazards of the field. The duel was caused by a dispute at the Guildford elections, and at the second fire Sewell accidentally shot himself through the foot.[40]

September 1790: Mr Anderson and Mr Stephens, Secretary to the Admiralty, near Margate

The duel was caused by a dispute over the shutting of a window in a public room. At the second fire Stephens was killed. Stephens had particularly objected to the words spoken by Anderson to other gentlemen present at the time: 'Don't mind that upstart puppy.' Anderson gave evidence at the inquest that the deceased began the affair by assaulting him and that he had tried to resolve the dispute after the first exchange of fire. The coroner's jury returned a verdict of manslaughter, but Anderson was nevertheless subsequently indicted for murder. However, the indictment was thrown out by the grand jury as defective 'in point of form'.[41]

January 1791: Mr Osie and an officer at Blackheath

The officer in question had been wooing a lady for two years, but after three weeks acquaintance with Mr Osie she decided to elope with him. The officer challenged,

---

38 *The Times*, 19 May 1790, p. 1, col. a.

39 *The Times*, 15 Jul. 1790, p. 3, col. f.

40 *The Times*, 6 Jul. 1790, p. 2, col. c.

41 Millingen, *History of Duelling*, op. cit., vol. i, p. 138; *The Times*, 25 Sep. 1790, p. 2, col. c; 23 Dec. 1790, p. 3, col. f.

and at second fire Osie was wounded in the leg. According to *The Times*, Mr Osie 'entered the field with all the naïveté possible, pronouncing, with emphasis, "Die all, die nobly, die like Demi-Gods!"' The final outcome is uncertain since it seems the lady had been corresponding with her former suitor during the elopement and may have encouraged the challenge.[42]

January 1791: Mr Campbell and Mr Taylor, both of the Royal Navy, at Southsea

This duel was caused by an unknown dispute that led to the wounding of Mr Campbell. The interest in the duel is that it was reported as having taken place at the exceptionally short distance of seven paces.[43]

March 1791: Mr T. Hassel and Capt. Picton at Haverford West in Wales

The duel was caused by a difference of opinion at a public meeting. This was an unusual duel in respect of the status of one of the participants. Mr Hassel was said to have formerly kept a public house in Wolverhampton. In addition, 'No seconds were present at this affair, but they [the protagonists] were discovered measuring the ground and seen to fire at the same time by some countrymen.' Picton was wounded in the encounter.[44]

July 1791: Mr Graham and Mr Julius at Blackheath

Graham was a lawyer and Julius was a pupil in another firm of attorneys. They quarrelled over religion while at dinner. Graham was killed in the duel, and a coroner's inquest brought in a verdict of manslaughter against Julius, but it seems that he was never brought to trial.[45]

August 1791: Mr C-h. and Mr S-n. at Nantwich

Little is known about this duel save that it followed a dispute at cards during the Nantwich races. *The Times* claims that the two parties rushed forward from their allotted positions and shot each other at the same time – seemingly mortally.[46]

---

42 *The Times*, 17 Jan. 1791, p. 3, col. c.

43 *The Times*, 26 Jul. 1791, p. 2, col. 2.

44 *The Times*, 26 Mar. 1791, p. 3, col. b.

45 Millingen, *History of Duelling*, op. cit., vol. i, pp. 139–140; *The Times*, 18 Jul. 1791, p. 3, col. c.

46 *The Times*, 1 Aug. 1791, p. 2, col. d.

October 1791: Mr Julian and Mr Ross in Liverpool

This duel was caused by a political quarrel at a private dinner, one man being a supporter of the current ministry and the other of the opposition. Mr Julian was seriously wounded in the neck.[47]

November 1791: Mr Applewaite and Mr Rycroft at Newmarket

Caused by a quarrel, which erupted while Rycroft and others were dining in Applethwaite's rooms. A Mr Pampin had lent money to a friend of Mr Applewaite, a Mr Corby, and, when Corby had been unable to repay the money, had had him imprisoned for debt. During the dinner Rycroft justified Pampin's actions and made some derogatory remarks about Corby. Applewaite begged him to drop the conversation and then, when he refused to do so, told Rycroft that he had not behaved like a gentleman. Rycroft, who had been drinking heavily, left immediately but left behind a written challenge. At first Applewaite ignored the challenge, but Rycroft renewed it two days later, demanding that either Applewaite must give a written apology or ask pardon on his knees. The former seemingly declined all attempts to resolve the dispute, and was ultimately killed at first fire on Newmarket Heath.[48] Applewaite surrendered himself for trial at Bury St Edmunds Assizes, but the grand jury did not find a true bill against him.[49]

May 1792: Mr Bond and Mr Warden in Shropshire

Warden owned an estate in Shropshire over which Bond had hunted his dogs without permission. Warden ordered him off his land, and in consequence of the subsequent quarrel they agreed to a meeting. According to *The Times*, no seconds were appointed but Warden was killed in the encounter.[50]

June 1792: Mr Frizell and Mr Clark in Hyde Park

Both men were law students who had gone out to drink at a coffee house with two others. At about one in the morning Frizell decided he wanted to go to bed, but Clark objected to him terminating the evening's drinking. Clark declared that Frizell was using his friends ill in doing so, to which Frizell replied that he did not mean to give offence but if he had done so he was prepared to give satisfaction. He then went to bed

---

47 *The Times*, 4 Oct. 1791, p. 3, col. d.

48 *The Times*, 28 Nov. 1791, p. 2, col. a; 8 Dec. 1791, p. 4, col. a.

49 *The Times*, 27 Mar. 1792, p. 3, col. a.

50 *The Times*, 2 May 1792, p. 3, col. a.

in a room at the coffee house, but Clark roused him at three o'clock that same morning and insisted on a meeting. Pistols were procured, and the two met in Hyde Park at ten yards. Frizell was fatally wounded at the first fire, and Clark and his second, Mr Evans, were arrested by soldiers. However, they were freed on the instruction of an officer and promptly fled – it seems they were never brought before a court.[51]

June 1792: Capt. Cuthbert of the Guards and the Earl of Lonsdale in London

Cuthbert had ordered that Mount Street should be closed to traffic after a disturbance in the road. Lonsdale's coach was prevented from travelling down the street, and he said to Cuthbert, 'You rascal do you know I am a peer of the realm?' Cuthbert is said to have replied, 'I don't know that you are a peer, but I know that you are a scoundrel, for applying such a term to an officer on duty; and I will make you answer for it.' Each fired two shots at the subsequent meeting, one of which deflected off Cuthbert's coat button.[52]

July 1792: Gen. Benedict Arnold and Lord Lauderdale at Kilburn Wells

This was an unremarkable duel, except that it serves to demonstrate the difficulties occasioned when one party refused to fire upon the other. Lord Lauderdale had said in the Lords that the Duke of Richmond was 'the greatest political apostate his Majesty had in his service, since General Arnold had left it.' This occasioned bloodless encounters with both Arnold and the duke. On the field Lauderdale received the general's fire without injury, but he refused to fire in return. The seconds retired for ten minutes and then collectively called upon Lauderdale to fire back at the general. He refused to do so. He declared that he would not retract his remarks and if the general was not satisfied with having fired at him he must continue firing until he was. The duel was then concluded. Sabine made the following observation: 'that such a gentleman as his lordship's antagonist was so far recognised as a gentleman as to be permitted to fight a duel is wonderful.'[53]

February 1793: Capt. D. and Dr D., a surgeon, near Uxbridge

This was one of many disputes that were caused by an argument at the theatre. At least five duels were engendered by such between 1793 and 1795.[54]

---

51 Millingen, *History of Duelling*, op. cit., vol. ii, pp. 141–143.

52 Ibid, pp. 143–4; *The Times*, 11 Jun. 1792, p. 2, col. d.

53 Sabine, *Notes on Duels and Duelling*, op. cit., p. 227; Millingen, *History of Duelling*, op. cit., vol. ii, p. 145.

54 *The Times*, 18 Feb. 1793, p. 3, col. b.

November 1793: Mr H. and Capt. Y. at Falmouth

The duel was caused by Capt. Y. breaking off his engagement to Mr H.'s sister. Mr H. was shot through the thigh, and Capt. Y. set off abroad pending news of the progress of the wound.[55]

December 1793: Lt Brown and Ensign David near Bristol

This was the result of yet another unspecified dispute at the theatre. Brown was hit in the knee and died from the wound sometime afterwards.[56]

February 1794: Lt A. and Lt B. at Portsmouth

The dispute was caused by Lt B. failing to remove his hat at the theatre when the rest of the audience were singing 'God Save the King'. Lieutenant A. removed B.'s hat, and this occasioned the challenge.[57]

April 1794: Two gentlemen in Edinburgh

This duel was the consequence of a scuffle at the theatre. Neither party was seriously wounded.[58]

June 1795: The Hon. Mr Butler and a gentleman in Hyde Park

This was another dispute originating at the theatre. Four shots were fired, but neither party was wounded.[59]

July 1795: Mr H. and Mr W., both officers of the North Lincoln Militia, at Mulford Bridge

Neither officer was injured in a dispute over how to carve a leg of mutton.[60]

---

55 *The Times*, 9 Nov. 1793, p. 3, col. c.

56 *The Times*, 17 Dec. 1793, p. 3, col. c.

57 *The Times*, 18 Feb. 1794, p. 3, col. d.

58 *The Times*, 18 Apr. 1794, p. 3, col. c.

59 *The Times*, 8 Jun. 1795, p. 3, col. d.

60 *The Times*, 10 Jul. 1795, p. 3, col. a.

August 1795: Lt Hall, 39th Foot, and Lt Hibbs at Blackheath

This duel was caused by a dispute between the two parties on the passage back from the West Indies. They waited until arriving home before deciding to settle their differences. Four shots were fired, but neither was hit.[61]

November 1795: Mr Dalton and Capt. Eyre at Gainsborough

This was a dispute over shooting rights. Neither party was wounded.[62]

January 1796: Maj. Sweetman and Capt. Watson at Cobham

The two men had formerly served in the same regiment, but for an unknown reason a coolness had developed between them. Sometime thereafter, they met at the opera and one of them chanced to step on the other's toe, at which point a challenge was instantly issued and accepted. The day before the duel they dined together and made their wills. On the field itself they were placed by the seconds at only four paces – because Sweetman was short-sighted. In its first report *The Times* claimed that both parties had been killed,[63] but in March it reported that Watson was tried at Kingston Assizes and 'there being no evidence against him he was immediately acquitted.' The sympathies of the judge were apparent:

> Baron Hotham with his accustomed humanity and politeness, paid every attention to the prisoner. This excellent judge, the mild ornament and pride of British justice, ordered the windows to be let down to admit the fresh air, and the avenues and approaches of the Court to be cleared of the mob, that the unfortunate young Gentleman, who was brought on men's shoulders to the bar of the court to be tried, might be every way accommodated.[64]

May 1796: Mr C.-K. and Maj. L. at Bath

The duel was caused by a dispute that arose while the two parties were playing the game of hazard. Mr C.-K. was wounded in the thigh at the first fire.[65]

September 1796: A young gentleman and a naval officer at Highgate

The unknown gentleman was alleged to have made advances to a lady at the Haymarket Theatre while she was under the officer's protection. The officer immediately inflicted

---

61 *The Times*, 3 Aug. 1795, p. 3, col. d.
62 *The Times*, 3 Nov. 1795, p. 2, col. d.
63 *The Times*, 9 Jan. 1796, p. 2, col. d.
64 *The Times*, 25 Mar. 1796, p. 2, col. d.
65 *The Times*, 2 May 1796, p. 3, col. a.

upon him 'severe personal chastisement', whereupon his victim challenged. During the duel the gentleman was wounded twice.[66]

May 1797: Mr W. Cowen and Lt John Elliot, 22nd Foot, on Lexden Heath

Little is known about this duel except that Elliot was killed and the coroner's inquest returned a verdict of wilful murder against Cowen, his second, and the deceased's second. Cowen appears to have been a regimental surgeon.[67]

June 1797: Lt Col. Bell and Dr Crigan at York

The duel was caused by a quarrel in the West Indies. Crigan was killed, and a coroner's inquest subsequently brought in a verdict of manslaughter. Bell was then tried at York Assizes, where he was found guilty of manslaughter, fined 6s 8d, and sentenced to one month's imprisonment in Ousebridge Gaol. His second was acquitted.[68]

August 1797: Mr Anderson and Mr Barker at Leith

Mr Barker, a brewer by occupation, had made some sarcastic remarks about the rules for the running of the Leith assembly rooms – which Anderson had drafted. Anderson challenged and succeeded in wounding Barker in the leg, while his own nose was shot off.[69]

August 1797: Lt Luckley and Capt. Smith in Jersey

Both men were officers of the Loyal British Fencibles; their unknown quarrel resulted in Luckley striking Smith. After several exchanges of shots, Luckley was killed.[70]

April 1798: Mr Fenwick and Lt Prother on Kennington Common

Fenwick was wounded in this duel, which was caused by some insulting remarks he had made about Prother's character.[71]

---

66 *The Times*, 13 Sep. 1796, p. 2, col. d.

67 *The Times*, 29 May 1797, p. 2, col. c.

68 *The Times*, 11 Aug. 1797, p. 3, col. b.

69 *The Times*, 28 Aug. 1797, p. 2, col. b.

70 Millingen, *History of Duelling*, op. cit., vol. ii, p. 153; *The Times*, 12 Aug. 1797, p. 2, col. c.

71 *The Times*, 12 Apr. 1798, p. 2, col. c.

May 1798: Lt Fitzgerald and Capt. Brown in Hyde Park

Both men were of the Irish Brigade and met in Hyde Park to resolve a dispute between them that had arisen while they were serving in the West Indies. The duel was fought at only five paces, and both parties were wounded.[72]

May 1798: Mr William Pitt and Mr George Tierney on Putney Heath

Pitt, the younger of the two men, was prime minister at the time, while Tierney was a member of the Whig opposition. Tierney opposed Pitt's proposals for the revitalisation of the navy, and this caused Pitt to accuse Tierney in Parliament of a 'desire to obstruct the defence of the country'. When Tierney demanded a retraction, Pitt merely reiterated his remarks. This provoked Tierney to challenge. They met at twelve paces, and at the second exchange of fire Pitt fired into the air and terminated the duel.[73] No one was injured, and ironically, Tierney was to go on to be appointed treasurer of the navy in 1803. The duel was caricatured by James Gillray in *The Explanation*.

January 1799: Lt Andrews and an unknown gentleman at Poole

The duel was caused by Andrews ordering a gentleman, who was due to take up a commission in Andrews's regiment, out of a church pew because he did not have his regimental uniform on. Andrews was subsequently injured in the thigh.[74]

July 1800: Lt Smith and Ensign Obree, both of the 9th Regiment Foot, at Botteley

The reasons for the duel are unknown, but the two parties met at ten paces and Smith was killed at the first fire. Obree was subsequently convicted of manslaughter at Winchester Assizes, sentenced to six months imprisonment and fined 6s 8d.[75]

November 1800: Mr Granger and Lt Stapleton at Portsmouth

Granger was killed during this duel, the cause of which is unknown. Stapleton was subsequently convicted of manslaughter at Winchester Assizes and sentenced to twelve months' imprisonment, although his sentence was later cut short.[76]

---

72 *The Times*, 18 May 1798, p. 3, col. c.

73 *The Times*, 28 May 1798, p. 2, col. a.

74 *The Times*, 26 Jan. 1799, p. 3, col. a.

75 *The Times*, 15 Jul. 1800, p. 3, col. c; 25 Jul. 1800, p. 3, col. c; 30 Jul. 1800 p. 3, col. c.

76 *The Times,* 10 Nov. 1800, p. 3, col. a; 1 Jul. 1801, p. 3, col. b.

February 1801: Lt Minster, Marines, and Lt Laschen, Royal Navy, near Queenborough

The two men had quarrelled during a game of cards aboard the ship *Latona*. The ship's captain had made both swear to keep the peace on pain of court martial. However, Minster arranged his transfer to another ship, the *Monarch*, and upon appointment there, immediately challenged the Lt Laschen. In the duel, Minster was killed at once and the other was 'shot through the body with very little hope of recovery'.[77] Both of the seconds absconded.

March 1802: Lt John Breamer and Lt Henry Rea at the Cape of Good Hope

Although the duel took place abroad, I have included it because Rea was tried at the Old Bailey on 21 September 1802 under a statute of Henry VIII. Rea was a marine and Breamer a naval lieutenant. They quarrelled aboard ship and had themselves rowed ashore to settle their differences. There were no witnesses prepared to testify as to the conduct of the duel itself, but a servant gave evidence as to the immediate aftermath and the statements of the dying Breamer, who was shot in the groin at the third fire. The trial is notable for the extremely favourable direction given by Baron Hotham, who first doubted that the seconds of the deceased might be convicted, directed that the accused could only be convicted of murder or be acquitted, and then strongly intimated that circumstances unknown might make a murder conviction inappropriate. In the event, the jury acquitted Rea and the seconds after ten minutes' deliberation.[78]

October 1802: Cap. P. and a gentleman from the East India Company in Hyde Park

The duel was caused by a quarrel at the theatre over a young lady. The two men met between five and six in the morning at only seven paces, but Capt. P. fired his pistol into the water at the first exchange and the duel concluded harmlessly.[79]

January 1803: Mr S. of the City and Lt P., Royal Navy, in Hyde Park

The reasons for the dispute are unknown, but having missed in the first salvo, the two parties closed to just six paces and Mr S. was wounded in the thigh.[80]

---

77 *The Times*, 17 Feb. 1801, p. 3, col. a.

78 *The Times*, 22 Sep. 1802, p. 3, col. a.

79 *The Times*, 14 Oct. 1802, p. 3, col. b.

80 *The Times*, 22 Jan. 1803, p. 2, col. d.

January 1803: Lt B. and a surgeon, Mr A., in Hyde Park

The duel was allegedly caused by a dispute over a game of billiards at St Domingo in December 1797. One of the protagonists was severely wounded. [81]

March 1803: Lt W., Royal Navy, and Capt. I., Army, in Hyde Park

Notwithstanding the studied courtesy with which most duels appear to have been fought and the frequent denials of personal malice, feelings of animosity were not always restrained. This duel was fought at only six paces at the insistence of the friends of Lt W. At the first fire the lieutenant lost two fingers but insisted that the duel go to a further round. At the second fire the captain was killed instantly, while the lieutenant was mortally wounded in the chest. Millingen reports that the lieutenant, having inquired whether the captain had been killed and being told that he had, thanked God that he had lived long enough to learn of his enemy's demise. He left a ring for his sister and before dying instructed his seconds to inform her that this had been the happiest day of his life.[82]

April 1803: Lt Col. Montgomery and Capt. MacNamara at Primrose Hill, London

The dogs of the two protagonists fought while their respective owners were riding in Hyde Park. Montgomery separated the dogs and allegedly remarked, 'Whose dog is that? I will knock him [the dog] down.' To which MacNamara replied, 'You must knock me down first.' A meeting was immediately arranged on Primrose Hill at seven o'clock that evening. Montgomery was hit in the chest and died soon after; MacNamara was wounded. Millingen says of MacNamara that he was an accomplished duellist who had fought two or three times previously. Indicted by the coroner's jury for mere manslaughter, the captain made an oft-quoted statement at his trial at the Old Bailey on 22 April 1803:

> I am a captain of the British Navy. My Character you can only hear from others. But to maintain my character in that situation I must be respected. When called upon to lead others into honourable danger I must not be supposed to be a man who sought safety by submitting to what custom has taught others to regard as a disgrace ... It is impossible to define in terms the proper feelings of a gentleman but their existence has supported this country for many ages, and she might perish if they were lost.[83]

---

81   *The Times*, 29 Jan. 1803, p. 3, col. a.

82   Millingen, *History of Duelling*, op. cit., vol. ii, pp. 165–166.

83   Millingen, *History of Duelling*, op. cit., voil. ii, p. 169.

Mr Justice Heath directed straightforwardly, noting that 'fortunately for the prisoner' the court could not investigate whether MacNamara might not have been better charged with murder. The only question the jury had to decide was whether, upon the evidence, the prisoner had indeed slain the deceased, in which case they must return the verdict of manslaughter. The jury, though, went against his direction and after twenty minutes returned a verdict of not guilty.[84]

Truman's report is rather fuller than that of Millingen and notes that MacNamara declared that it was his particular fear for his reputation, being a stranger to the town, that induced him to react as he had:

> The origin of the difference as you see it in the evidence was insignificant ... It was not the deceased's defending his dog, nor his threatening to destroy mine that led me to the fatal catastrophe; it was the defiance which most unhappily accompanied what was said ... The offence was forced upon me by the declaration that he invited me to be offended and challenged me to vindicate the offence by calling upon him for satisfaction ... If under these circumstances, the words which the deceased intended to be offensive and which he repeatedly invited to be resented, had been passed by, and submitted to, they would have passed from mouth to mouth, have been ever exaggerated at every repetition and my honour must have been lost.[85]

May 1803: Mr Hobart and Mr O'Reilly at Chalk Farm

The duel was occasioned by insults exchanged at a ball in Fitzroy Square. According to witnesses the men met at about sixteen paces, but O'Reilly was wounded in the thigh at the first fire. He died of the wound, and a warrant was issued against Hobart and the seconds for murder. Hobart fled but in 1804 surrendered himself to the magistrate at Bow Street. He was tried at the Old Bailey on 18 May 1804, but the jury returned a verdict of not guilty.[86]

September 1803: Mr Moodie and Mr Spark of *HMS Leydon*, at anchor off the Essex Coast

Both men were midshipmen of about nineteen-years-old, and the quarrel occurred after Moodie had been reprimanded by the captain for some misconduct. Moodie accused Spark of having told tales upon him to the captain and challenged him in the mess. They met upon deck with the ship's surgeon and a fellow midshipman as seconds. According to a witness who later gave evidence, they stood so close to each

---

84 *The Times*, 23 Apr. 1803, p. 2, col. d.

85 Truman, *Field of Honor*, op. cit., pp. 204–206.

86 *The Times*, 19 May 1804, p. 2, col. f.

other in the encounter that their pistols overlapped. Spark was killed at the first fire, and Moodie and his second, Mr Booth, were confined. Both men were tried at the Old Bailey on 2 July 1804. Sir James Mansfield directed that if they, the jury, were satisfied that the men had fired at each other with the intention of killing, then both the principal and the second were guilty of murder. However, the jury returned a verdict of manslaughter, and both men were fined 10s and imprisoned for six months.[87]

October 1803: Mr B. and Mr H. on Hampstead Heath

The cause of the duel is unknown, but the conduct of the affair is interesting insofar as this was one of those instances at the beginning of the nineteenth century where the conduct of one party in firing into the air was not felt to require that the meeting be terminated. Mr H. came to the ground unattended and apologised for some offence that he had given, but Mr B. would not accept the apology. Mr B. fired first and missed, whereupon Mr H. promptly fired into the air. The duel was, however, allowed to continue. Mr B. fired again, and the ball passed through his opponent's hat, who again responded by firing into the air. The seconds then intervened to ask if Mr B. was satisfied, but he declared that he was not and insisted upon a further shot. He missed his opponent at the third shot, who again fired into the sky. Finally, the seconds intervened to terminate the meeting, but both parties left the ground without being reconciled.[88]

March 1804: Capt. Best and Lord Camelford behind Holland House, Kensington

A Mrs Symons, described by Millingen as 'an abandoned woman', had at one time been under the protection of Capt. Best but had subsequently placed herself under the protection of Lord Camelford. Millingen reports that she met Best at the opera one day and asked something improper of him. When he refused, she complained to Camelford that Best had been disrespectful towards her. Camelford then used the expressions 'scoundrel' and 'liar' in speaking to Best at his hotel. Best assured Camelford that he had been deceived and urged that if he, Camelford, retracted his expressions they could be reconciled. According to several accounts, Camelford admitted privately to his seconds that he knew he was in the wrong, but he could not bring himself to retract his remarks. In part this was because Best was a renowned shot and Camelford was afraid a retraction would be taken as an indication of cowardice. They met at fifteen paces, and Camelford was shot through the

---

87 *The Times*, 3 Jul. 1804, p. 3, col. c.

88 *The Times,* 31 Oct. 1803, p. 3, col. a.

lungs at the first fire. He lingered some time and forbade his friends and relatives from seeking to prosecute Best. Although all of society knew who his adversary had been, Camelford refused to name him. The result was that at the coroner's inquest it could not be established who had fired the fatal shot and the jury returned the verdict of 'wilful murder, or felonious homicide, by some person or persons unknown'.

The true cause of the duel remains a mystery. Truman, writing much later, alleges that the cause of the affair was Mrs Symons's husband, a gambler whom Best had assaulted after catching him cheating at cards. The complaint to Camelford, then, was an attempt to be revenged upon Best. Millingen was clearly not aware of this version of the affair. Nikolai Tolstoy, in his biography *The Half-Mad Lord*, has suggested that perhaps the woman was in fact involved in a plot against Camelford himself, possibly encouraged by the French. This too, however, remains but speculation.[89]

March 1804: Mr Grayson and Mr Sparling at Liverpool

Sparling had been engaged to marry Grayson's niece, but declined to go through with the marriage. Grayson then intervened to attempt to compel him to carry out the marriage contract and was promptly challenged. Grayson was killed in the duel, and the coroner's inquest charged Sparling, his second and the attending surgeon with murder. The grand jury at Lancaster Assizes found a true bill against them, but at trial on 4 April 1804 all parties were acquitted.[90]

June 1804: Mr H. and Mr W. of the 3rd West Yorkshire Regiment at Colchester

The regiment had recently held a court of inquiry upon the conduct of a Lieutenant F. Mr H. had given evidence at the inquiry and had thereafter been accosted and abused by Lieutenant F., who had accused him of having lied. In response, Mr H. had reported the accusation to the inquiry. However, Mr W., who was a personal friend of F., had then spread the rumour that Mr H. had suffered himself to be insulted and had not resented the insult as a gentleman should. In response, Mr H. challenged Mr W. and killed him at the first fire. A coroner's jury brought in a verdict of wilful murder, but Mr H. and all the seconds absconded before trial.[91]

---

89 See Millingen, *History of Duelling*, op. cit., vol. ii, pp. 171–9; Truman, *Field of Honor*, op. cit., pp. 186–198; *The Times* 13 Mar. 1804 p. 3, col. d.

90 See the report of the trial in *The Times*, 9 Apr. 1804, p. 6, col. e.

91 *The Times*, 18 Jun. 1804, p. 2, col. d.

January 1805: Capt. G. and Lt R., both Royal Navy, near Plymouth

A duel known only from *The Times* but included as an illustration of the petty quarrels that sometimes led to meetings. Lt R. had had a dream upon three successive nights that a particular number would come up in a forthcoming lottery. He had told Capt. G. of his dream, only to discover later that the captain had gone and purchased that ticket. The ensuing quarrel led to a single exchange of shots, after which the parties were reconciled.[92]

October 1805: Capt. B. and Mr P. at Worthing

The duel was caused by indecorous remarks made by Capt. B. about a young lady at a public function. Mr P. was acquainted with the lady and when he met the captain upon Worthing Sands he struck him. Capt. B. challenged, and both parties were wounded in two exchanges of fire.[93]

December 1805: Col. Bolton and Maj. Brookes in Liverpool

A year previously a quarrel had erupted between Maj. Brookes and Col. Bolton, and they were bound over to keep the peace for twelve months. Twelve months to the day however, they agreed to a meeting, and the major was killed at first fire. The colonel absconded.[94]

January 1806: Ensign Browne and Lt Butler near Basford, Notts

Browne was only seventeen. He quarrelled with Butler while they were both serving in the 36th Regiment and was killed at the first fire. The coroner's jury returned a verdict of murder, but Butler had absconded.[95]

March 1806: Mr Fisher and Lt Torrence on Galleywood Common near Chelmsford

Both duellists were officers of the 6th Regiment of Foot, and Lt Torrence was killed in the encounter. Mr Fisher and the seconds, Mr Campbell and Mr Blakeman, were arraigned at Essex Assizes on 27 July 1806, and a fellow officer gave evidence.

---

92 *The Times*, 8 Jan. 1805, p. 3, col. d.

93 *The Times*, 10 Oct. 1805, p. 4, col. a.

94 *The Times*, 24 Dec. 1805, p. 2, col. d.

95 Millingen, *History of Duelling*, op. cit., vol. ii, pp. 179–180.

He stated that on the evening before the duel Torrence had admitted to him that he had struck Fisher on the parade ground and had called him a coward. Thereafter, Torrence had ordered pistols, declared his intention to shoot Fisher should he meet him and left his rooms. Torrence's servant corroborated this evidence. However, although Torrence was found dying on the common the following morning, the only evidence that there had in fact been a duel was circumstantial. The only potential witness, the assistant surgeon to the regiment, refused to give evidence, claiming, 'I am myself so deeply implicated that I cannot give evidence consistently with my own safety.' The judge accordingly instructed the jury that there was no evidence whatsoever against the prisoners and instructed them to acquit.[96]

September 1806: Mr Tytheh and Mr Tyseen at Twyford House, Buckinghamshire

Mr Tythen, a Hamburg merchant, was killed in a duel caused by a dog. Both men were on shooting parties in the same neighbourhood, and the quarrel was occasioned when the dog of one of them disturbed the game in the area allotted to the other.[97]

September 1806: Baron Hompesch and Mr Richardson at Blackheath

A duel that illustrates the particular significance ascribed to a violation of bodily integrity, even one occasioned by a purely symbolic act. The baron was near-sighted and one day he bumped into Mr Richardson, who at the time was accompanied by two female companions. Richardson took this at once for a deliberate insult and responded by knocking Hompesch down. A challenge resulted, but both parties missed at the first exchange of fire on Blackheath. At this point Mr Richardson proposed a reconciliation, but the baron would not accept this – unless, that is, Richardson would permit him to lay a cane gently upon his shoulder. Richardson refused, and at the second exchange of shots, he was hit in the body.[98] It seems that although he was seriously injured, his wound did not prove mortal. Hompesch was never tried, and on 10 November 1806 Richardson's surgeons made an affidavit at Bow Street to the effect that they believed he would recover.[99]

---

96 See the account of the trial in *The Times*, 28 Jul. 1806, p. 3, col. b.

97 *The Times*, 18 Sep. 1806, p. 2, col. b.

98 *The Times*, 22 Sep. 1806, p. 2, col. d; 23 Sep. 1806, p. 2, col. b.

99 *The Times*, 10 Nov. 1806, p. 3, col. d.

1807: Lt Heazle and Lt Delmont at
Stroud in Gloucestershire

Little is known of this duel except that *The Times* advertised a forty-pound reward for the apprehension of a Lt Benjamin Heazle and Lit John Serjeant of 61st Foot, both of whom were charged at the coroner's inquest with the wilful murder of Francis Delmont of the 82nd Regiment in a duel. It seems that the men never came to trial.[100]

May 1807: Sir Francis Burdett and Mr Paull on
Wimbledon Common

Sabine says that this duel was 'in consequence of a misunderstanding about the former being chairman of a dinner to be given to the latter'.[101] Both parties were wounded in the meeting. Paull committed suicide in 1808.[102]

June 1807: Capt. Boyd and Maj. Campbell, both 21st
Regiment, in Armagh, Ireland

Although the duel took place in Ireland, it is included here since, in consequence of the death of Boyd, Campbell became the only British duellist of the nineteenth century to be executed for killing in the course of a duel. The dispute began when Gen. Kerr inspected the regiment and told Campbell that he had given a particular command incorrectly. In the officer's mess Campbell contended that his mode of giving the command had in fact been the correct one, but Boyd contradicted him. Campbell then left the mess, and Boyd followed shortly after. Sometime later two shots were heard, and Boyd was found wounded in a room close by, no seconds having been employed to witness the encounter. Boyd lived for some eighteen hours, and at trial in August 1808 a Lt MacPherson gave evidence that the following conversation passed between Campbell and Boyd: Campbell had asked him, 'on the word of a dying man, is everything fair?' To which Boyd was said to have replied, 'Campbell you hurried me, you are a bad man!' Campbell had then called upon Boyd again to say that the duel had been fair, 'Boyd before this stranger and Lt Hall was everything fair?' To which the dying Boyd was said to have responded, 'O my Campbell, you know I wanted you to wait and to have friends.'

Campbell's defence rested solely on his character, but he had attempted to evade justice by hiding for several months in Chelsea under a false name before surrendering

100 *The Times*, 27 Aug. 1807, p. 3, col. c.

101 Sabine, *Notes on Duels and Duelling*, op. cit., p. 80.

102 See Millingen, *History of Duelling*, op. cit., vol. ii, pp. 183–188.

for trial in Dublin. According to Millingen, this failure to surrender himself promptly counted against him, together with the arrogance of his witnesses. Sabine believes that the direction of the judge was crucial: 'You must recall to your minds the words of the deceased Captain Boyd, namely: "You have hurried me; I wanted to wait and have friends. Campbell you are a bad man." These words are very important; and if you deem them sufficiently proved, the prisoner is most clearly guilty of murder, the deceased will then have been hurried into the field; the contract of opposing life to life could not have been perfect.' The jury convicted Campbell of murder but recommended clemency on the grounds of character. This, however, was refused, and he was executed in Armagh on 24 August 1808. Sabine puts it succinctly: 'His offence was not that he killed Boyd, but that he killed him contrary to established rules.'[103]

February 1808: Lt Murchison and Lt Ogilvie, both 43rd Regiment, at Danbury, Essex

The duel was caused by an unknown dispute in the mess. Ogilvie was killed, and Murchison and the seconds indicted. During the trial at Chelmsford Assizes on 10 March, the regimental surgeon, Mr Lind, gave evidence. He claimed that having heard of the quarrel, he had headed towards Danbury 'in the hopes of preventing any mischief taking place'. He testified that he had happened upon the principal and the two seconds but that he had not seen the fatal encounter itself, merely being informed about it by 'a farmer's boy'. The jury acquitted all parties.[104]

March 1809: Lord Falkland and Mr Powell at Chalk Farm

A jocular remark caused the quarrel. Lord Falkland had addressed Powell at a London hotel by the name 'Pogey', which Powell found unduly familiar. When he had informed his lordship to this effect, Falkland, who was drunk, had replied with sarcasm and threats. Powell had responded by promising to defend himself with his stick if necessary, whereupon Falkland had snatched up another stick and attacked him with it. According to *The Times*, they were actually friends who had dined together the previous night. After the incident Falkland went to Powell's house and apologised for his drunken conduct, but Powell would not accept his apology unless it was made in public before the persons who had witnessed the event. Falkland

---

103 See Sabine, *Notes on Duels and Duelling*, op. cit., p. 72; Millingen, *History of Duelling*, op. cit., vol. ii, 188–199. For a full account of the trial see the British Library, Add. 29,736 *A Correct and Impartial Account of the Trail of Major Alexander Campbell*, Anon.

104 *The Times*, 11 Mar. 1808, p. 3, col. c.

refused, and Powell challenged. On the field, Falkland did not aim at his adversary but was nevertheless fatally wounded in the kidney himself.[105]

June 1809: Ensign Mahon and Assistant Surgeon O'Hara at Maldon, Essex

Little is known about the cause of this duel, but O'Hara was fatally wounded in the encounter. According to *The Times*, he urged his opponent to flee, but Mahon was taken into custody by the local constable. Afterwards, however, Mahon escaped and was seemingly never tried.[106]

September 1809: Lord Castlereagh and Mr Canning on Putney Heath

Both men had held positions in the Duke of Portland's cabinet, Castlereagh as the secretary for war and Canning as foreign minister. The cabinet had long been divided by personality and policy, and in September 1809 *The Times* spoke of 'the animosity which some Members of the present Administration have long been known to entertain towards each other.'[107] For his part, Castlereagh believed that Canning had tried to get him removed from office by means of a clandestine agreement with Portland to replace him with the Marquis of Wellesley. In addition, although publicly Canning had supported the plan to send the ill-fated Walcheren expedition to the Scheldt once the expedition had gone awry Canning had laid the blame for its failure at Castlereagh's door. Canning's refusal to shoulder any proportion of the blame led Castlereagh to send a challenge accompanied by a letter outlining his grievances. They met on Putney Heath on 21 September at six o'clock in the morning, Castlereagh attended by Lord Yarmouth and Canning by Mr Charles Ellis. The distance was set at ten paces, and at the second fire Canning was hit in the thigh. However, the wound was not serious. On 5 October Castlereagh's friends placed a statement in *The Times*, itemising his reasons for challenging Canning and including a detailed expose of Canning's plan to replace him.[108]

September 1810: Mr Cahill and Capt. Rutherford at Hadgton in Scotland

Both were members of the same regiment, Cahill being the regimental surgeon. While convalescing from an illness, Cahill took some newspapers from the regimental mess

---

105 *The Times*, 2 Mar. 1809, p. 3, col. a; 3 Mar. 1809, p. 3, col. a; 6 Mar. 1809, p. 3, col. c (the inquest).

106 *The Times*, 21 Jun. 1809, p. 3, col. d.

107 *The Times*, 22 Sep. 1809, p. 2, col. b. 23 Sep. 1809, p. 3, col. c.

108 *The Times*, 5 Oct. 1809, p. 4, col. a.

into his private room. This was against the mess rules, and Rutherford complained. Cahill alleged that the complaint was occasioned by a personal pique against him, and this suggestion offended Rutherford. They met in a local quarry, and Rutherford was killed. Cahill was subsequently tried but acquitted.[109]

September 1810: Capt. Clark and Mr Payne on Wimbledon Common

The duel was caused by an alleged attachment that had formed between Capt. Clark's sister and Mr Payne. Miss Clark had been a friend of Mrs Payne and had often visited the family home. Eventually, Clark grew suspicious of her frequent visits there and accused Payne of having an affair with her. Payne was killed at the first fire, and Clark subsequently fled.[110]

October 1812: Lt Bagnall and Lt Stuart, both Marines, on Southsea Common

Bagnall was killed in this duel, and Stuart gave his own account of its cause at the coroner's inquest in Portsmouth. He and Bagnall had been at Bagnall's lodgings when Stuart had observed that he would visit a particular young lady. Bagnall, who had had an attachment to the young lady, had told him that the lady would not receive him. Stuart admitted that he had replied that Bagnall could not know that and had accused him of trying to bully Stuart into not calling upon her. At that point Bagnall had ordered him out of his house and had gestured towards him, whereupon, Stuart recalled, he had replied, 'Don't touch me Bagnall for that never can be made up!' Stuart had then challenged when Bagnall continued to gesture at him.[111]

November 1812: Monsieur Le Courbe and another French officer at Leek, Staffordshire

This is one of a number of duels allegedly fought between French prisoners of war. Some of the accounts are clearly fanciful; the combatants are sometimes said to duel with scissors, for example, and the parties are rarely named. This, however, may have been an authentic duel. Le Courbe was a French naval officer given parole during the day but obliged to return to his lodging at night. One day he was late returning to his lodging and was pelted with stones by the local boys. According to *The Times*, this caused a fellow officer to observe that 'he was soft, that he would faint at the sight of

---

109 Sabine, *Notes on Duels and Duelling*, op. cit., pp. 271–272; *The Times*, 7 Sep. 1810, p. 4, col. c.

110 Millingen, *History of Duelling*, op. cit., vol. ii, p. 204; *The Times*, 8 Sep. 1811, p. 2, col. e.

111 *The Times*, 20 Oct. 1812, p. 3, col. d.

his own blood'. Le Courbe responded by calling him a liar, and the officer struck him. Le Courbe challenged, but together they could only acquire one pistol, so they cast lots as to who would fire first. Le Courbe was given first fire and hit his opponent in the thighs. His wounded opponent then received the pistol and shot Le Courbe dead. According to *The Times*, the coroner's jury, 'strange as it may appear', brought in a verdict of 'Died by the visitation of God.'[112]

July 1813: Lt Blundell and Ensign McGuire at Carisbrooke Castle on the Isle of Wight

The two men quarrelled because Blundell had allegedly spread a rumour that he supplied Mr McGuire with clothes. Angry communications passed between them. Hearing that McGuire might challenge Blundell in consequence of this, the local magistrate attempted to bind him to keep the peace, but McGuire would only give his word of honour that he would not challenge Blundell; he would not bind himself not to respond to a challenge. The magistrate then visited Blundell, who informed him that in certain situations men in the army were obliged to fight and that he would only promise not to fight in the magistrate's particular district. The men then met outside his jurisdiction, and Blundell was mortally wounded. On his deathbed Blundell told a captain of his regiment that he would have made up his dispute with McGuire had it not been for a number of visits from officers seeking to compel him to duel. Two of these, Mr O'Brien and Mr Dillon, eventually acted as seconds and they had 'told him, that if he did not meet M'Guire he should be discarded'.

McGuire, O'Brien, Dillon and a further second, Mr Gilchrist, were indicted for murder and convicted at Hampshire Assizes. They were sentenced to death, and the execution was respited until 21 August.[113] However, all parties were subsequently pardoned. The army's commander-in-chief concluded, 'the unfortunate officer who lost his life, and the officer by whose hand he fell (Ensign McGuire) are the least guilty, but no such palliation appearing on the part of Lt Dillon 101st, Ensign O'Brien 101st, or Ensign Gilchrist 6th West India Regt, those three are dismissed his Majesty's service; Lt Dillon being declared incapable of serving his Majesty again.'[114]

December 1817: Mr Cochrane and Maj. Lockyer at West Cowes, Isle of Wight

Both men were intending to go out to South America to start new lives. While dining with a number of other adventurers at an inn, Cochrane remarked that all the parties

---

112 *The Times*, 6 No. 1812 p. 3, col. e.

113 *The Times*, 4 Aug. 1813, p. 2, col. c.

114 *The Times*, 15 Sep. 1813, p. 3, col. e.

present were in debt and seeking their fortune. The major denied that such was the case with him and, objecting to the remark, issued a challenge. Cochrane was killed at the first fire the following day. Lockyer and the seconds fled. Lockyer and one second, Mr Hand, were subsequently arrested and tried at Winchester Assizes on 7 March 1818. They were convicted of manslaughter and sentenced to three months' imprisonment.[115]

January 1818: Lt Bailey and Mr O'Callaghan near Chalk Farm

Both men quarrelled while acting as the seconds for other parties intending to meet on the same day. The exact cause of the quarrel is unknown. Bailey was mortally wounded at the second exchange of shots. O'Callaghan was confined in Newgate and tried at the Old Bailey on 14 January 1818, where both he and the seconds were convicted of manslaughter and sentenced to three months' imprisonment.[116]

February 1821: Mr Christie and Mr Scott near Chalk Farm

Scott was the editor of the *London Magazine*, and Christie a friend of John Lockhart, the editor of *Blackwood's Magazine*. The quarrel arose after the *London Magazine* published a series of articles critical of the management of *Blackwood's*. Christie demanded that Scott apologise for the articles, and an acrimonious correspondence followed, which Scott published. Statement and counterstatement followed until Scott issued a challenge. Scott was mortally wounded at the second fire, but lived long enough to give a detailed account of events to witnesses. This was repeated at the coroner's inquest on 3 March 1821.[117] He described Christie as having behaved well, insofar as he had called out to Scott before the exchange of fire to shift his position as he was providing an easy target. The first exchange of fire missed, whereupon Christie's second, Mr Trail, called out to him to take proper aim at his target next time, since it appeared that he had fired deliberately wide of the target. Hearing this, Scott turned to his own second, Mr Patmore, exclaiming, 'What! Did not Mr Christie fire at me?' Presumably he intended to end the duel there, but Patmore responded, 'You must not speak, tis now of no use to talk, you have nothing now for it but firing.' Both men resumed their positions, and Scott was hit in the groin.

The coroner's jury brought in a verdict of wilful murder against Christie and the two seconds, Mr Patmore and Mr Trail. The grand jury found a true bill, and the three were tried at the Old Bailey on 13 April 1821. The chief presiding judge, Lord Chief Justice Abbott, seems to have summed up most favourably for the defence.

---

115 Millingen, *History of Duelling*, op. cit., vol. ii, pp. 222–223; *The Times*, 11 Mar. 1818, p. 3, col. e.

116 Millingen, *History of Duelling*, op. cit., vol. ii, pp. 324–334; *The Times*, 17 Jan. 1818, p. 3, col. c.

117 *The Times*, 3 Mar. 1821, p. 4, col. e.

He noted that no evidence had been given as to the feeling under which the duel had taken place, the defendants having only produced witnesses as to their character. He speculated that it was possible that since Christie had not apparently aimed at Scott during the first salvo, he might have been angered by the way in which his peaceable conduct had been ignored. If he fired the second shot in anger, under provocation as it were, then the jury might only convict him of manslaughter. Finally, the judge noted that in cases of doubt the jury should take the side of mercy, whereupon he spoke of the excellent character of the defendants. The jury, after an interval of twenty-five minutes, found all the defendants 'not guilty'.[118]

May 1821: Mr Brittlebank and Mr Cuddie, a former naval surgeon, at Winster, Derbyshire

Mr Cuddie, a practising doctor, attended a Miss Brittlebank, the daughter of an eminent solicitor. Both became enamoured of each other, but the family did not approve. Miss Brittlebank's brother, William Brittlebank, discovered the two out walking together one day, and an altercation with Mr Cuddie followed. The following day William Brittlebank challenged, but Cuddie did not respond. A second challenge followed, which Cuddie again declined. William then recruited the services of both of his brothers, Andrew and Francis, and of another surgeon, a Mr Spencer, who was acquainted with the parties. These four men then visited Cuddie's house and told him that he must either issue an apology or fight. Reluctantly, Cuddie consented to fight, and the duellists met at fifteen paces in his garden, the pistols being supplied by Spencer. Cuddie was mortally wounded and William Brittlebank absconded, but the other three were committed to Derby Jail. They were tried at Derby Assizes before Mr Justice Park, and the prosecution noted that the dying Cuddie had declined invitations to agree that the duel had been a fair one. Furthermore, he had received a great deal of provocation. According to Millingen, however, it seemed to count heavily with the jury that the defendants had rendered every possible assistance to the dying man. Nevertheless, there was an unusually long period of deliberation, some one hour and twenty minutes, before they found the defendants 'not guilty'.[119]

March 1822: Sir Alexander Boswell and Mr Stuart at Auchtertool near Fife

Alexander was the oldest son of James Boswell, and the root of the duel was a political difference between the parties. More specifically, though, it was occasioned by a song

118 *The Times*, 14 Apr. 1821, p. 3, col. f; Millingen, *History of Duelling*, op. cit., vol. ii, pp. 244–252.
119 Millingen, *History of Duelling*, op. cit., vol. ii, pp. 259–264; *The Times*, 2 Jun. 1821, p. 4, col. b.

published anonymously in the *Glasgow Sentinel* on 26 December 1821 but written in fact by Boswell. The song contained two imputations of cowardice against Stuart. Stuart had thereafter demanded to know whether he, Boswell, was indeed the author, but Boswell had declined to answer. They met at twelve paces, and Boswell was mortally wounded at the first fire. Both parties had privately expressed a desire to resolve the dispute, and on the field Boswell seems to have fired wide, although this does not appear to have been observed by Stuart. Both surgeons present subsequently testified that they had turned their backs at the moment of firing, so as not to be incriminated.

Stuart was tried before the High Court of Justiciary in Edinburgh on 10 June 1822. Summing up, the Lord Justice Clerk advised to jury to bear in mind, 'Mr Stuart's conduct on the field, and his conduct after that fatal event – the contrition which he had expressed for the fatal blow and the total absence of all vindictive feelings on his part'. He stated that 'in the whole course of his practice he had never heard higher or more distinct and discriminate praise bestowed on any character'. The jury, without retiring, promptly returned a verdict of 'not guilty'.[120] On 19 June 1822 *The Times* made some telling observations about the propriety of the affair, noting that two deputies of the Lord Advocate had previously signed a paper describing Stuart as cowardly for having refused a challenge to a duel, and then one of them had gone on to sign the indictment trying Stuart for having indeed now fought one.[121]

May 1824: Ensign Battier and the Marquis of Londonderry in Hyde Park

Londonderry was colonel of the 10th Royal Hussars, and on 24 November 1823 he instructed the ensign to leave the regimental mess and not to dine with the other officers. The reasons for the instruction are unclear, but it was given in the presence of a number of visiting ladies. Battier took grave exception and published a letter about the conduct of Londonderry, which, among other things, alleged that he was sheltering under his rank. The dispute rumbled on, Battier bombarding Londonderry with letters, which the marquis ignored, and at the same time appealing to the public via the press. Eventually Londonderry appointed Sir Henry Hardinge, who was later to argue passionately against duelling, as his second to deal with the matter. On 5 May 1824 a second appointed by Battier, Lt Col. Western, delivered a letter demanding an explanation of Londonderry's conduct on that day or else offering a challenge. Western assured Sir Henry that a statement from the marquis that when ordering the ensign from the mess he had had no intention of questioning his character as a gentleman would suffice to resolve the dispute. Initially, Londonderry would neither

---

120   *The Times*, 14 Jun. 1822, p. 3, col. b; 15 Jun. 1822, p. 4, col. a.
121   *The Times*, 19 Jun. 1822, p. 2, col. e.

offer an explanation, upon the grounds that Battier's appeal to the press had vitiated his right as a gentleman to receive one, nor would he meet him. Yet by the evening of the same day he had assented to a meeting, and the two met at ten paces in Hyde Park on 6 May. After a shot apiece, Battier declared himself satisfied.

Although the affair was bloodless, there was consternation that so senior an officer had been induced to hazard himself with a junior, seemingly over the exercise of military discipline. A general order was issued from the Horse Guards' commander-in-chief on 13 May to express his displeasure:

> The Commander-in-Chief having received a report from Lt-Gen the Marquis of Londonderry that his Lordship had accepted a challenge to fight a duel with Ensign Battier, late a cornet of the 10th Royal Hussars, upon a point which his Lordship considered to be one of military duty, his Royal Highness has felt it incumbent upon him to submit to the King a transaction at variance with the principles of subordination, and therefore of a tendency injurious to the discipline of the army. The King has consequently conveyed to his Royal Highness his Majesty's commands, to express his Majesty's concern and displeasure, that an officer of Lord Londonderry's high rank and military reputation should have committed himself in personal collision with an inferior officer, by accepting a challenge for any supposed aggression proceeding from the exercise of his authority as Colonel.[122]

On 18 May the *London Gazette* announced that Battier had been erased from the army's half-pay list.[123] The matter was not quite settled; Battier subsequently approached Henry Hardinge on his way to the House of Commons, shook a whip at him and declared that he should consider himself horsewhipped. Although Hardinge gave his card to the young man, it seems there was never a meeting.[124]

November 1824: Capt. Gourlay and Mr Westall outside Edinburgh

The dispute arose after the Doncaster races. Mr Westall had lost a bet with the captain and owed him seventy guineas. However, the captain for his part had also lost a bet with a friend of Westall's, and that debt had not yet been paid either. Upon meeting Westall at an inn in Edinburgh, the captain asked for payment of the debt, but Westall told him that his friend had told him that he could subtract the money that the captain owed to his friend from the amount that he, Westall, owed to the captain. In the dispute that followed the captain called Westall a 'swindler' and Westall

---

122 *The Times* 10 May 1824, p. 3, col. a; 17 May 1824 p. 3, col. c; 19 May 1824 p. 4, col. a.

123 *The Times*, 17 May 1824, p. 3, col. c; Millingen, *History of Duelling*, op. cit., vol. ii, pp. 281–283.

124 *The Times*, 20 May 1824, p. 3, col. a.

retaliated with 'liar'. The captain then struck Westall with a poker. They met outside Edinburgh near South Queens Ferry, and Gourlay was killed at first fire.[125]

August 1826: Mr D. Landale and Mr G. Morgan near Kirkcaldy, Fifeshire

Landale was a merchant, and Morgan his banker. Morgan gave out some confidential information as to Landale's creditworthiness to others, which resulted in some of Landale's debts being called in. He complained to the bank in the strongest possible terms, which led Morgan to consider a challenge. Morgan then took legal advice to the effect that the challenger was likely to be banished, so he determined to provoke Landale into issuing a challenge by launching an unprovoked attack with an umbrella. They met at twelve paces, and Morgan was killed at first fire. Landale was tried in Perth on 22 September 1826 and found not guilty.[126]

June 1828: Sir Jacob Astley and Capt. Garth in Osterley Park

The duel was caused by the alleged 'criminal conversation' between Garth and Astley's wife. Astley not only initiated a prosecution but also challenged Garth. Garth initially declined to accept the challenge, but according to *The Times*, 'On the seventh he was constrained, to avoid consequences more fearful than even the chains of death itself, to consent to the desired meeting.' He received fire from Astley but declined to return it. This, however, was not acceptable to Astley; he, or his seconds, determined that the affair must go to a second round but sought a pledge from Garth's seconds that Garth would return fire at Astley. Police intervened and prevented the affair from proceeding further, but the duel serves to illustrate the desire of a man of honour to hazard himself in order to rehabilitate his reputation.[127]

March 1829: The Duke of Wellington and Lord Winchilsea on Battersea Fields

Wellington was prime minister between January 1828 and November 1830, during which time he introduced the Catholic Relief Act 1829, which allowed Catholics to sit in Parliament. Introduced to appease sentiment in Ireland, the act nevertheless split the Tory Party. At the same time, Wellington was also giving his support to the founding of King's College London, intended to be an Anglican institution and a rival to University College London – which had been established as a secular institution

---

125 Millingen, *History of Duelling*, op. cit., vol. ii, pp. 283–284; *The Times*, 6 Nov. 1824, p. 2, col. e.

126 For a detailed discussion of this duel see Landale, *Duel*, op. cit.

127 *The Times*, 16 Jun. 1828, p. 6, col. g; 23 Jun 1828 p. 5, col. c.

in 1826. The irony of the duke promoting an Anglican foundation at the same time as he was supporting the emancipation of Catholics was not lost on his detractors. On 14 March 1829 Lord Winchilsea wrote to the secretary of the committee formed to establish King's College. He withdrew his own support for the college, and questioned Wellington's motives in supporting the foundation.

> Late political events have convinced me that the whole transaction was intended as a blind to the Protestant and the high-church party; that the noble Duke, who had, for some time previous to that period, determined upon breaking in on the constitution of 1688, might the more effectually, under the cloak of some outward show of zeal for the Protestant religion, carry on his insidious designs for the infringement of our liberties, and the introduction of Popery into every department of the state.[128]

The letter was circulated to the press, and Wellington demanded a written apology, which Winchilsea refused, or a meeting. They met at eight o'clock in the morning on 21 March 1829 on the Battersea Fields, then a large and uncultivated plain. The distance was set at twelve paces, and when the order to fire was given, Wellington aimed at Winchilsea's legs, fired and missed. In response, however, Winchilsea deliberately fired into the sky. Winchilsea then authorised his second, Lord Falmouth, to deliver to Wellington's second, Lord Hardinge, a letter admitting that he, Winchilsea, had been in the wrong in the affair and that he 'did not hesitate to declare of his own accord, that he regretted having unadvisedly published an opinion which had given offence to the Duke of Wellington'.[129]

Wellington's opponents in the Lords briefly considered trying him under the Ellenborough Act 1803, which made it a capital offence to 'shoot at, stab or cut' anyone regardless of whether any injury was inflicted.[130] This act, however, had never been applied in cases of duelling, and the peers recoiled from the enormity of the action. In part, they thought better of the proposal because the duke acquired a sudden popularity. John Russell wrote to Henry Brougham, 'All the Ladies are in Heaven about the Duke's duel – such flummery you never heard.'[131] According to the Earl of Auckland, George VI commented wistfully upon Wellington's new fame, 'The Duke is King of England, O'Connell King of Ireland and I am Dean of Windsor.'[132] Auckland concluded, 'The fight was a silly business which ended well – the King told the Duke

---

128 Millingen, *The History of Duelling*, op. cit., vol. ii, pp. 290–291.

129 See the published correspondence between them in *The Times* 23 Mar. 1829 p. 5, col. c.

130 43 Geo. III, c. 58.

131 The Brougham Papers, Henry Brougham 1st Baron Brougham and Vaux, Brougham HB/38138, University, college London. Letter of John Russell to Henry Brougham, 25 Mar. 1829.

132 The Brougham Papers:, Brougham HB/34247, University, college London. Letter from George Eden, Earl of Auckland to Henry Brougham, 25 Mar. 1829.

that if he had read the letter he would have called upon the Duke to resent it – probably by this time he thinks that he has been out himself or was second at least!' Nevertheless, within Parliament and within the public at large there was much disquiet that a man of Wellington's reputation, position and particular importance to the country during troubled times should have been provoked into hazarding himself.

April 1829: Capt. Helsham and Lt Crowther at Boulogne

Although this duel took place at Boulogne, I have included it here because the survivor, Helsham, was tried by a special commission at the Old Bailey. Crowther had applied to join a pigeon shooting club at Boulogne, but Helsham had objected to his membership. Helsham claimed that he had seen the lieutenant horsewhipped in England and that the lieutenant had not resented it as a gentleman should. Crowther demanded an apology; Helsham refused and declared he would fight. He seems to have suspected that some subterfuge might be used to make the duel a mere sham. He assured Crowther's second, 'I am ready to meet Mr Crowther, but I will make it an affair of business.' On the field, he insisted upon personally watching the seconds charge the pistols, contrary to normal duelling practice and despite being rebuked for this by the seconds themselves. The parties met at twelve paces and fired upon a signal. Crowther fired immediately, as was the custom, and missed, whereupon Helsham took a very slow and deliberate aim and fatally wounded Crowther in the neck.[133] The trial at the Old Bailey was unusually long, taking some ten hours, but in the end the jury took just twenty minutes to find Helsham not guilty of murder.[134]

January 1830: Mr Clayton and Mr Lambrecht on Battersea Fields

Mr Lambrecht had formerly been a lieutenant in the 43rd Regiment and had served at Waterloo. Oliver Clayton was a minor Irish writer who had converted to Protestantism. They quarrelled during a discussion over Catholic emancipation at a London hotel. Lambrecht was in favour of emancipation and described Clayton as a hypocrite. He furthermore alleged that Clayton had once been horsewhipped by another gentleman and had acted dishonourably by failing to challenge his assailant. The following day Clayton dispatched a letter demanding an apology, but Lambrecht refused; this refusal occasioned the challenge by Clayton.

The two men met at six o'clock in the morning in Battersea Fields on 8 January, and at the first volley Clayton was shot through the abdomen.[135] After procuring Clayton

---

133 *The Times*, 28 Apr. 1839, p. 3, col. b.
134 *The Times*, 9 Oct. 1830, p. 3, col. f; Millingen, *History of Duelling*, op. cit., vol. ii, pp. 304–309.
135 *The Times*, 11 Jan. 1830, p. 3, col. c.; 12 Jan. 1830 p. 2, col. f.

a doctor, Lambrecht fled. Clayton died some hours later. Indicted by a coroner's jury, Clayton surrendered himself and was tried for murder at Kingston Assizes on 2 April 1830, together with his second, Mr Bigley. The attending doctor testified that the dying Clayton had declared that the duel had been conducted fairly and that he forgave his opponent. The trial was most notable, though, for the fact that the jury defied the clear direction of the judge, Mr Justice Bayley. Bayley directed that the fairness of the proceedings in no way diminished the legal culpability of the defendants, and that if the jury were satisfied that it had been Mr Lambrecht's shot which had killed Mr Clayton, then they must return a verdict of murder. Some time after retiring the jury returned and asked if they could return a verdict of manslaughter, but the judge insisted that they could not. After deliberating for three hours, the jury acquitted both defendants.[136]

February 1832: Maj. Gen. Lorenzo Moore and Mr Miles Stapleton on Wimbledon Common

Moore's daughter and Stapleton had been engaged, but she had broken off the engagement. In revenge, Stapleton had written a satirical poem about her, which had fallen into the general's hands. The general challenged and in the duel dangerously wounded Stapleton in the chest. Moore was arrested and remanded in custody for nine days. However, by the end of that time it looked as though the wounded man would recover. Stapleton's friends and family interceded to say that no proceedings should be instituted against the general. He was therefore bailed on sureties of £4000 to appear at Surrey Assizes or to take his trial at the Old Bailey should Stapleton die of his wound.[137]

May 1833: Dr Hennis and Sir John Jeffcot near Exeter

Sir John had recently been appointed chief justice and judge of the Vice-Admiralty Court of Sierra Leone. There are various accounts of the quarrel, but it seems it began when Sir John proposed matrimony to the daughter of a leading Exeter family. Dr Hennis, a friend of that family, had received from a friend a letter containing some remarks detrimental to Sir John's reputation; in particular, it alleged that Sir John had falsely claimed to have a vote for the University of Dublin. Hennis showed the letter to the family of the intended bride with the result that the wedding was cancelled. The day before taking ship to Africa, Sir John discovered the cause of the cancellation and wrote to Hennis, accusing him of traducing his character. Hennis took offence at the tone of the letter and refused to make any apology. They met about six miles

---

136 Millingen, *History of Duelling*, op. cit., vol. i, p. 308. *The Times*, 3 Apr. 1830, p. 5, col. d.

137 *The Times*, 15 Feb. 1832, p. 3, col. a; 16 Feb. 1832, p. 5, col. e; Millingen, *History of Duelling*, op. cit., vol. ii, pp. 321–323.

outside of the city, on the Plymouth Road. Hennis was mortally wounded. Sir John promptly took ship for Africa, but three seconds were arrested. The coroner's jury returned a verdict of wilful murder, and the three were tried at Exeter Assizes on 26 July 1833. Mr Justice Patteson seems to have directed straightforwardly and in particular emphasised that since the duel was clearly premeditated, a manslaughter verdict could scarcely be appropriate. However, after only a few minutes' deliberation the jury returned a verdict of 'not guilty'.[138]

May 1837: Mr Harring and a polish officer on Hampstead Heath

Harring was Danish, and the reasons for his quarrel with the officer are unknown. Both parties, however, timed their meeting in accordance with the departure time of the steamer for Boulogne. They met at ten paces, and Harring was mortally wounded. The officer saw him conveyed on the way to the North London hospital, then rode to London Bridge to catch the steamer.[139]

August 1838: Mr Eliot and Mr Mirfin on Wimbledon Common

The duel arose out of a collision between coaches driven by the two parties. Mirfin was thrown out of his gig and suffered fractured ribs. An altercation ensued, and Eliot struck Mirfin then left the scene of the accident without leaving his card. Sometime later Mirfin chanced to see him in cigar shop and, after learning his identity, promptly engaged a second to issue a challenge. Eliot at first objected to meeting Mirfin, but under pressure from Mirfin's seconds and the seconds he himself had appointed to represent him, he relented. They met at twelve paces, and Mirfin was mortally wounded at the second fire.

An inquest was held at the Tankard Inn in Lambeth and it was here that the shocking details of the conduct of the affair began to be made public. It was said that Eliot had come to the field casually whistling and declaring that he was used to duelling and little bothered by the prospect of another one. A mill owner who chanced upon the scene testified that Eliot, far from being concerned for the dying Mirfin, had declared to him, 'I have done for the ***** [presumably swine].' According to *The Times,* at this point, 'a thrill of horror ran through the persons present at the unfeeling conduct of the individual'.[140] All the parties immediately fled the field save for a

---

138 For the somewhat differing versions of the quarrel see *The Times,* 14 May 1833, p. 6, col. g; 21 May 1833, p. 3, col. f.; 23 May 1833, p. 3, col. f; 24 May 1833, p. 5, col. g. For the trial see *The Times,* 29 Jul. 1833, p. 6, col. b and Millingen, *History of Duelling,* op. cit., vol. ii, pp. 327–334.

139 Millingen, *History of Duelling,* op. cit., vol. ii, pp. 341–342.

140 *The Times,* 25 Aug. 1838, p.5, col. f; 27 Aug. 1838, p. 6, col. c. For the subsequent stages of the inquest see *The Times,* 30 Aug. 1838, p. 7, col. a; 5 Sep. 1838, p. 6, col. f.

surgeon, Mr Scott, who had been engaged to attend to Mirfin. One person indeed assaulted a cab driver, who had tried to prevent him from fleeing. The coroner's jury returned a verdict of wilful murder, and Frances Eliot, three named seconds and two unnamed seconds were indicted for the murder.

Eliot, however, had already fled to Dieppe. Only two of the seconds surrendered themselves for trial at the Old Bailey on 21 September 1838: Mr Young and Mr Webber.[141] It had by this time emerged in the press that Eliot was indeed an experienced duellist, having survived a number of encounters in Spain. Mirfin, by contrast, had had no experience of firearms and appeared the aggrieved party.[142] The jury took twenty minutes to find the men guilty of murder. In addition, they expressed the opinion that Mr Scott, the surgeon who had attended the duel, should have been tried as well. At this point the prosecuting barrister intervened and said that the brother of the deceased had urged him to ask the court for mercy on account of the good character of the two men on trial. A sentence of death was recorded against them, but the judge, Mr Justice Vaughan, hastened to assure them that it would not be carried out. In the event, the sentence was communicated to twelve months in Guildford Prison.

In his account of the affair, Millingen says that the parties could claim only a doubtful gentility. Eliot was the nephew of an innkeeper and he had recently been an officer in the British Auxiliary Legion in Spain, whereas Mirfin was said to be the son of a mercer who 'had kept a linen shop in London'. The Times, however, presented a rather more detailed account of the status of the parties which reveals that as well as having connections in trade, the parties were also connected to the Bar and in one case to a baronet.[143] Millingen's final judgment on the matter is probably correct: 'The disgusting exhibition at Wimbledon in this case is believed to have done much to bring the practice of duelling into ridicule and detestation.'[144]

February 1839: Lord Powerscourt and Mr Roebuck at Combe Wood

The duel was occasioned by remarks made by Roebuck at a political speech in Bath. Powerscourt demanded an apology for the remarks, but Roebuck declined. On the field, Roebuck received Powerscourt's fire first and responded by firing into the air. He then made the desired apology. The duel is chiefly of interest for its illustration of the changing public attitudes to duelling. Although the encounter was bloodless, the archdeacon and clergy of Bath attacked Powerscourt's conduct in the press and

---

141   *The Times*, 22 Sep. 1838, p. 6, col. a.

142   *The Times*, 13 Sep. 1838, p. 7, col. c.

143   *The Times*, 10 Sep. 1838, p. 6, col. f.

144   Millingen, *The History of Duelling*, op. cit., vol. ii, pp. 349–355

elicited a published response admitting that it was lack of moral courage that had induced him to issue the challenge.[145]

January 1839: Mr Henry Grattan and the Marquis of Londonderry on Wimbledon Common

This was a political duel occasioned by reports that Daniel O'Connell had said in a speech he had made in Dublin that Mr Grattan had claimed that the Queen's life would not be safe if the Tory Party came to power in England. O'Connell went on to affirm his own belief that if the Tories formed the next government, the Queen would not live six months. Londonderry, a Tory, read these remarks and described them as 'base and infamous'. Grattan, for his part, denied his responsibility for comments upon his own views made by Daniel O'Connell and inquired whether the pejorative terms were meant to apply to himself? Londonderry replied in a letter suggesting that they were. On the field, Londonderry received Grattan's fire unharmed and himself fired into the air. Grattan's seconds declared the matter satisfactorily concluded.

Sometime later, perhaps encouraged by the success of the clergy of Bath in eliciting an apology for his conduct from Lord Powercourt, the clergy of Ripon and Thirsk placed an advertisement in the Durham Advertiser, which was duplicated by *The Times*, reproving Londonderry for duelling.[146] Londonderry replied, however, with a withering counterblast, pointing out that there was no connection between himself and the clergy of Ripon whereas this had been the case between the clergy of Bath and Lord Powerscourt, who sat as Bath's member of Parliament. He suggested that the clergy seemed to 'wish for publicity' and declared, 'you must leave to the British soldier the unfettered right of being the best judge and arbiter of his honour.'[147]

September 1840: The Earl of Cardigan and Capt. Harvey Tuckett on Wimbledon Common

The duel was occasioned by Cardigan's mismanagement of his 11th Light Dragoons after his appointment in 1837. A large number of his officers voluntarily left the regiment, and he was strongly criticised in the *Morning Herald* in August 1838.[148] The controversy over his conduct continued, and in 1839 he challenged the *Herald's* editor.[149] The 'Black Bottle' affair further alienated the public in the following year,

---

145 *The Times*, 22 May 1839, p. 5, col. f.

146 *The Times*, 30 Aug. 1839, p. 5, col. c.

147 *The Times*, 10 Sep. 1839, p. 4, col. d.

148 *Morning Herald*, 14 Aug. 1838.

149 *Morning Chronicle*, 16 Aug. 1839.

and in 1840 Tuckett, himself formerly of the 11th Dragoons, published letters in the *Morning Chronicle* traducing Cardigan's character. Cardigan promptly challenged.

The duel occurred on the 12 September and at the second fire, Tuckett was shot in the ribs, but was subsequently to recover. Given that fact, it was surprising that Lord Cardigan was ever tried, but Wandsworth magistrates charged him under 1 Vic. c. 85 s. 2, wherein wounding with intent to commit murder was a capital felony.[150] The prosecution before his peers famously failed, because Sir John Campbell neglected to call Tuckett into court and to ask witnesses to identify him as the man seen upon the field. Instead he relied upon the wounded man's card, which he had surrendered after the duel. Unfortunately, the indictment against Cardigan specified his opponent as Harvey Garnet Phipps Tuckett, whereas the card identified the bearer merely as Capt. Harvey Tuckett. Failure to prove that these were one and the same led to the judge, Lord Denman, declaring that in an ordinary court such a defect would have led to an acquittal. The peers duly followed, with only the Duke of Cleveland declaring, 'not guilty, legally, upon my honour'.[151]

The trial of Cardigan's second, Capt. William Douglas, similarly failed after the physician present at the duel, Sir James Eglinton Anderson, refused to give evidence and after Mr Justice Williams conceded that he might not be questioned to his own incrimination.[152] The verdict upon Cardigan was greeted with great cynicism by the press, but in his biography of Cardigan, Saul David points out that Cardigan himself had transferred his estate to a nephew (at considerable cost) to avoid the danger of confiscation upon conviction.[153] One consequence of the duel was that benefit of clergy for peers was abolished under 4 and 5 Vic., c. 22, having been already abolished for commoners under 7 and 8 Geo. IV., c. 28. A further consequence was still further cynicism about the conduct of men of honour when it was revealed in the press that whereas Captain Tuckett's pistols were of the simple smooth-bored variety, those of Cardigan were, in contradiction of convention, rifled inside and therefore deadly accurate.[154]

July 1843: Col. Fawcett and Mr Munro near the Brecknock Arms in Camden

Col. Fawcett was married to Munro's sister, and the dispute was alleged to have arisen as a result of an insulting remark Munro made to her at a party. Fawcett was

---

150 *The Times*, 17 Sep. 1840, p. 4, col. e; 21 Sep. 1840, p. 3, col. b; 22 Sep. 1840, p. 5, col. b.

151 Millingen, *History of Duelling*, op. cit., vol. ii, pp. 361–402 at p. 402. *The Times*, 17 Feb. 1841. p. 5., col. b.

152 See *R. v Douglas* 1841, Carrington and Moody 193, 174 ER 468.

153 David, *The Homicidal Earl*, op. cit., p. 208.

154 *The Times*, 20 Oct. 1840, p. 4, col. f.

killed at the first fire. *The Times*, reporting the inquest, remarked upon the 'singular circumstance' that 'notwithstanding there were so many military gentlemen and personal friends of the deceased present at the inquest, of there being no one who volunteered to speak to the identity of the body'.[155] The close familial connection between the parties caused much condemnation in the press and led *The Times* to call for the institution of a public prosecutor to deal with duellists.[156] Munro absconded, but two seconds, Mr Cuddy and Mr Gulliver, were tried for murder at the Old Bailey on 25 August 1843 and both were found 'not guilty'.[157] The government, in what some have seen as a significant step in the campaign against duelling, refused a pension to Fawcett's widow. This was a decision that caused much debate in Parliament, with some asserting that his widow was being unduly victimised and that an army officer had, under the provocation that Fawcett had received, no choice but to fight.[158] Munro surrendered himself to justice four years later, and this interval seems to have counted against him. Tried for murder at the Old Bailey on 18 August 1847, he was found guilty, although the jury recommended him for mercy.[159] In an editorial the following day, *The Times* strongly supported a plea for clemency, and the sentence was eventually commuted to twelve months' imprisonment.[160]

May 1845: Lt Hawkey and Lt Seton at Gosport

The duel was caused by a quarrel in the card room of the King's Room at Gosport. Seton had been directing inappropriate attentions to Mrs Hawkey, which led to Hawkey describing him as a 'blackguard' and a 'villain' and threatening to horsewhip him. Seton was mortally wounded, and it was said that Hawkey – without inquiring after the condition of his antagonist – fled at once, declaring, 'I am going to France.' In addition to this conduct, his reputation was also damaged by the revelation that he had practised at a shooting gallery an hour before the duel. He eventually surrendered himself and he was tried for murder at Winchester Assizes on 16 July 1846. The jury, though, returned a verdict of not guilty without retiring and after only a few seconds' deliberation.[161]

---

155 *The Times*, 5 Jul. 1843, p. 6, col. d.

156 *The Times*, 20 Jul. 1843, p. 4, col. b.

157 *The Times*, 26 Aug. 1843, p. 4, col. d; 26 Aug. 1843, p. 6, col. a.

158 *The Times*, 29 Feb. 1844, p. 4, col. a; 9 Mar. 1844, p. 3, col. f.

159 *The Times*, 19 Aug. 1847, p. 6, col. f.

160 *The Times*, 19 Aug. 1847, p. 4., col. c; 21 Sep. 1847, p. 5., col. f.

161 *The Times*, 17 Jul. 1846, p. 7, col. b.

October 1852: Monsieur Emmanuel Barthelemy and
Lt Fredric Cournet at Englefield Green, Surrey

The last fatal duel in England was in fact fought by two Frenchmen. One of them, Barthelemy, had already killed twice, and he shot Cournet dead at the first fire.[162] He is said to have taken offense at some remarks of Cournet's about a lady of his acquaintance. In reality, the duel may have been politically inspired; both men were part of the exiled French community in England, but Barthelemy supported the side led by Louis Blanc, while Cournet was a supporter of Blanc's opponent, Alexandre Ledru-Rollin. After the duel, three of the seconds, Allain, Baronnet and Mourney, were subsequently indicted for murder. They were found guilty of manslaughter and sentenced to a mere two months' imprisonment on the basis that they had already been imprisoned for five months and were ignorant of the law.[163]

---

162 *The Times*, 22 Oct. 1852, p. 8, col. e.

163 *The Times*, 22 Mar. 1853, p. 7, col. d.

Bibliography

Manuscript sources

Royal Archives

RA QVJ: 31 Jan. 1841.

British Library

Add. 29,736 A Correct and Impartial Report of the Trial of Major Alexander Campbell.
Add. 74087 The Walpole Papers vol. ccxxviii f. 17.
The Dropmore Papers (series ii) vol. cxxxxvii.
Add. 34,613 The MacVey-Napier Papers. ff. 36–67.
Francis Place Papers, BL Add. MS 27826 fo.144.

Essex Record Office (Chelmsford)

E.R.O Q/J 1/11.

Hansard

Hansard XIX March 29, 1811 cols 637–638.

India Records Office (London)

IOR/f/4/292/635.
Mss Eur D/888/7/ ff. 1–8. Papers of Sir Edward West Recorder and Chief Justice of Bombay 1823–1828.
IOR F/4/406/10143/ ff. 1–133.
IOR f/4/666/18569/ ff. 23–95.
IOR/H/532.
IOR/H.75/ ff. 118–148.
Pratt Manuscripts U840 0217/1/5.

Centre for Kentish Studies (Maidstone)

Queensborough Borough Records Qb/JP/1 1814–28.

London Metropolitan Archives

Miscellaneous Papers of 5th Countess of Jersey. Papers relating to Napoleon, Wellington and the Duke of York LMA ACC/1128/220–223.

Norfolk County Records Office (Norwich)

Walshingham Merton Collection:
WLS/XIV/8–12/425.
WLS/XXVII/9/415.
WLS/XLVI/8–12/425x4.
Bulwer of Heydon Family Papers:
4 Bul 16/13/1–17/705x2.
5 Bul 16/28/ 3–7.
5 Bul 16/28/18/3–6.
Ferrier of Great Yarmouth and Hemsby Family Papers:
MC 268/117/694x2.
Kretton-Cremer of Felbrigg Family Papers:
WKC 7/58.

Parliamentary Papers

The Report of The Select Committee on the Police of the Metropolis 1835.
Parliamentary Papers 1835, 2nd Rep., p. 339.
Cobbett's Parliamentary History XXXV. (18 April 1800).

National Archives: Public Records Office

W.O. 71/71.
W.O. 81/111.
H.O. 17/76 *Rules and Articles for the Better Government of His Majesty's Horse and Foot Guards* (London, 1778), sec. xvi. art. xxii.

University College London

Brougham Papers: Henry Brougham 1st Baron Brougham and Vaux.
Brougham HB/34247.
Brougham HB/10459.
Brougham HB/38138.
Brougham HB/26364.

Cases cited

Christie, R. v 1821, *The Times* 14 Apr 1821 p. 3, col. f.
Davies William and Charles, R. v 1818, *The Times* 30 Apr 1818 p. 3, col. f.
Dormer, R. v 1805 , *The Times* 29 Nov. 1805 p. 3, col. b.
Douglas, R. v 1841, Carrington and Moody 193, 174 ER 468.
England, R. v 1796, 2 Leach 767, 168 ER 483.
Fisher, R. v 1806, *The Times* 28 Jul. 1806 p. 3, col. b.
Richard Franklin, Howell State Trials XVII, 671–672.
Halstead, Holland and Melford, R. v 1833, *The Times* 29 Jul. 1833 p. 6, col. b.
Helsham, R. v 1829, 4 Carrington and Payne 394, 172 ER 754.

Hayward, R. v 1833, (1833) 6 C & P. 157.
Hynes 1860, *The Times* 17 Jul. 1860.
Lambrecht, R. v 1830, *The Times* 3 Apr. 1830 p. 5, cols d–f.
Lord Morley's Case 1666, 6. St. Tr. 770
MacNamara, R. v 1803, *The Times* 23 Apr. 1803 p. 2, col. d.
Maloney 1861 , 9 Cox CC 6.
Mawgridge, v *R.* v 1707, Kelyng J 119, 130–131, 84 ER 1107.
Merest v *Harvey* 1814, 5 Taunton 442, 128 ER 761.
Noon, R. v 1852, 6 Cox CC 137.
O'Callaghan, R. v 1818, *The Times* 17 Jan. 1818 p. 3, cols c–d.
Peel and Dawson, R. v 1818, *The Times* 16 Nov. 1818 p. 3, col. b
Phillips, R. v 1805, 6 East 464, 102 ER 1365.
Purefoy, R. v 1794, *The Times* 16 Aug. 1794 p. 3, col. b.
Rea, R. v 1802), *The Times* 22 Sep. 1802 p. 3, cols a–c.
Rice, R. v 1803, 3 East 581, 102 ER 719.
Smith, R. v 1866, 176 ER 910.
Taverner's Case, 3 Bulstr. 171.
Watson, R. v 1796, *The Times* 25 Mar 1796 p. 2, col. d.
Welsh 1869 , 11 Cox CC 336.
Woolcombe, R. v 1833, *The Times* 18 Nov. 1833 p. 3, col. e.
Young and Webber, R. v, 8 Carrington and Payne 644, 173 ER 655.

Newspapers and Journals

Annual Register
Bengal Hurkaru
Bristol Gazette
Calcutta Journal
Cobbett's Parliamentary History
Durham County Advertiser
Edinburgh Review
European Magazine
Female Tatler
Gentleman's Magazine
Gleaner
Hampshire Telegraph
Hull Advertiser
Le Temps
London Chronicle
London Magazine
Maidstone Journal
Manchester Guardian
Manchester Mercury
Morning Chronicle
Morning Herald
Notes and Queries
Oxford Magazine

Spectator
Tatler
The Times
Universal Register

Books and Articles Cited

Abbott, E. A. D., *Francis Bacon: An Account Of His Life and Works* (London, 1881).

Allen, John Taylor, *Duelling, An Essay Read In The Theatre, At Oxford, 10 June 1807* (Oxford: Brasenose College, 1807).

Andrew, Donna T., 'The code of honour and its critics: the opposition to duelling in England 1700–1850', *Social History*, 5 (1980), pp. 409–434.

Anon., *A true account of what passed at the Old Bailey, May the 18th, 1711, relating to the trial of Richard Thornhill, esq. indicted for the murder of Sir Cholmley Deering, Bart.* (London, 1711).

Anon., *The life and noble character of Richard Thornhill, esq. who had the misfortune to kill Sir Cholmley Deering, Bart, in a duel in Tuttle Fields on Wednesday 9th of May, 1711* (London, 1711).

Anon., *A Particular Account of the Trial of John Hamilton, esq.: for the Murder of Charles Lord Mohun and James, Duke of Hamilton and Brandon* (London, 1712).

Anon., *A Letter to the Gentlemen of the Army* (London: R. Griffiths, 1757).

Anon., *Index to the Durham County Advertiser* (Durham: Durham City Reference Library, 1978).

Anon., *A Short Treatise On The Propriety And Necessity of Duelling* (Bath, 1779).

Anon., *The Trial between William Fawkener, Esq (Clerk of the Privy-Council) Plaintiff, and The Honourable John Townshend (Son of Lord Viscount Townshend) Defendant; for Criminal Conversation with the Plaintiff's Wife, (Late Miss Poyntz;) Before the Honourable Francis Buller, Esq; one of the Judges of His Majesty's Court of King's Bench, in Westminster Hall, on Wednesday the 12th July 1786, with some interesting Particulars relative to The Duel between the Plaintiff and Defendant* (London: M. Smith, 1786).

Anon., *An Answer To The Letter Of Theophilus Swift, Esq. On The Subject Of The Royal Duel* (London: C. Stalker and J. Walter, 1789).

Anon., *Reflections upon Duelling and on the most Effectual Means for Preventing It* (Edinburgh: W. Creech, 1790).

Anon., *Advice to seconds: general rules and instructions for all seconds In duels by a late captain In the army* (Whitehaven, 1793).

Anon., *The British Code of Duel: A Reference to the Laws of Honour, and the Character of Gentlemen* (London, 1824).

Anon., 'Jonah Barrington's Recollections'recollections', *American Historical Review*, 32:2 (1828), pp. 498–514.

Anon., 'The life of Lord Kenyon', *Law Mag. Quart. Rev. Juris.*, 17 (1837), pp. 252–297.

Anon., 'The life of Lord Erskine', *Law Mag. Quart. Rev. Juris.*, 22 (1839), pp. 121–147.

Anon., 'Defects of the criminal law', *Law Mag. Quart. Rev. Juris.* (1842), p. 28.

Anon., *1st Report of the Association for the Discouragement of Duelling* (London: Alvey, 1844).

Anon., *2nd Report of the Association for the Discouragement of Duelling* (London: Alvey, 1845).

Anon., *3rd Report of the Association for the Discouragement of Duelling* (London: Alvey, 1846).

Anon., 'The English law of defamation: with especial reference to the distinction between libel and slander', *Law Quarterly Review*, 255 (1902).

Anon., *The Thunderer In The Making 1785–1841* (London: The Times, 1935).

Baldick, Robert, *The Duel: A History of Duelling* (London: Chapman and Hall, 1965).

Banks, Stephen, 'Dangerous friends: the second and the later English duel', *Journal for Eighteenth Century Studies*, 32:1 (2009), pp. 87–106.

Banks, Stephen, 'Killing with courtesy: the English duelist, 1785–1845', *Journal of British Studies*, 47 (2008), pp. 528–558.

Banks, Stephen, 'Punishment, performance and the perception of London's public space 1780–1840', *Law and Critique*, 16:2 (2005), pp. 231–254.

Banks, Stephen, 'Very little law in the case: contests of honour and the subversion of the English criminal courts, 1780–1845', *King's Law Journal*, 19:3 (2008), pp. 575–594.

Barnes, Thomas G., ed., *List and Index to the proceedings in Star Chamber for the reign of James I (1603–1625) in the Public Record Office, London, Class STAC8* (Chicago: The Foundation, 1975).

Barrington, Jonah, *Personal Sketches of His Own Times* (New York: Redfield, 1858).

Barrow J., *A Private Memoir of the Life and Services of the late William Barrow* (London: privately printed, 1850).

Barry, M., *An Affair of Honour: Irish Duels and Duellists* (Fermoy: Eigse Books, 1981).

Bayley, Col., *Diary of Colonel Bayley 12th Regiment 1796–1803* (London: Army and Navy Cooperative Society, 1896).

Beattie, J. M., *Crime and the Courts in England 1660–1800* (Oxford: Clarendon Press, 1986).

Berkeley, Grantley, *My Life and Recollections*, 4 vols (London: Hurst & Blackett, 1865).

Berry, Helen, 'Rethinking politeness in eighteenth century England: Moll King's coffee house and the significance of flash talk', *Royal Hist. Soc. Transactions*, 11 (2001), pp. 65–81.

Billacois, Francois, *The Duel: Its Rise and Fall in Early Modern France*, ed. and trans. Tristan Selous (New Haven: Yale University Press, 1990).

Binhammer, Karen, 'The sex panic of the 1790's', *Journal of the History of Sexuality*, 6:3 (1996), pp. 409–434.

Blackstone, Sir William, *Commentaries* IV.

Bosquett, Abraham, 'A treatise on duelling, together with the annals of chivalry, the ordeal trial and judicial combat from the earliest times', in A. J. Valpy, ed., *The Pamphleteer* (London, 1818), pp. 79–125.

Boswell, James, *The Life of Samuel Johnson 1791*, 3 vols, ed. A. Glover (London: J. M. Dent and Sons, 1925).

Bourdieu, Pierre, *Language and Symbolic Power*, ed. J. B. Thompson, trans. G. Raymond and M. Adamson (Cambridge: Polity Press, 1992).

Bowen, Huw V., *War and British Society 1688–1815* (Cambridge: Cambridge University Press, 1998).

Brailsford, H. N., *The Levellers and the English Revolution* (London: Cresset Press, 1961).

Brewer, J. S., Gairdner J. and Brodie, R. H., eds, *Letters and Papers, Foreign and Domestic, of the Reign of Henry VIII*, 23 vols (London: Longman, 1862–1910).

Brooks, C. W., 'Professions, ideology and the middling sort in the late sixteenth and early seventeenth centuries', in J. Barry and C. W. Brooks, eds, *The Middling Sort of People; Culture, Society and Politics in England 1550–1800* (Basingstoke and London: Macmillan and St. Martin's Press, 1994), pp. 113–140.

Bryskett, L., *A Discourse of Civill Life* (London: 1606).

Bryson, Anna, 'The rhetoric of status: gesture, demeanour and the image of the gentleman in sixteenth- and seventeenth-century England', in L. Gent and N. Llewellyn, eds, *Renaissance Bodies: The Human Figure in English Culture c. 1540–1660* (London: Reaktion Books, 1990), pp. 136–153.

Burnett, T. A. J, *The Rise and Fall of a Regency Dandy: The Life and Times of Scrope Berdmore Davies* (London: John Murray, 1981).

Cairns, D. J. A., *Advocacy and the Making of the Adversarial Criminal Trial 1800–1865* (Oxford: Clarendon, 1998).

Cameron, Charles. H., *Two Essays On The Sublime And Beautiful, And On Duelling* (London: Ibbotson and Palmer, 1834).

Carlyle, Thomas, *The French Revolution: A History*, 3 vols (London: Chapman and Hall, 1837.

Carter, Philip, 'James Boswell's Manliness', in T. Hitchcock and M. Cohen, eds, *English Masculinities 1660–1800* (London: Longman, 1999), pp. 111–130.

Carter, Philip, *Men and the Emergence of Polite Society, Britain 1660–1800* (London: Longman, 2001).

Charnock, John, *Biographa Navalis: Or Impartial Memoirs of the Lives and Characters of Officers of the Navy of Great Britain, from the Year 1660 to the Present Time* (London: R. Faulder, 1798).

Cockburn, J. S., 'Patterns of violence in English society: homicide in Kent 1560–1985', *Past and Present*, 130 (1991), pp. 70–106.

Cockburn, J., *The History and Examination of Duels, Shewing their Heinous Nature and the Necessity of Suppressing them*, 2 vols (Edinburgh, privately printed, 1888).

Cohen, Michele, *Fashioning Masculinity: National Identity and Language in the Eighteenth Century* (London: Routledge, 1996).

Cohen, Michele, Manliness, effeminacy and the French: gender and the construction of national character in eighteenth-century England', in T. Hitchcock and M. Cohen, eds, *English Masculinities 1660–1800* (London: Addison Wesley, 1999), pp. 44–62.

Cohen, Michele, 'Manners make the man: politeness, chivalry and the construction of masculinity, 1750–1830', *Journal of British Studies*, 44:2 (2005), pp. 312–329.

Colley, Linda, *Britons: Forging the Nation 1707–1837* (Yale: Yale University Press, 1992).

Comber, Thomas, *A discourse of Duels* (London, 1687).

Connell Robert W., *Masculinities* (Cambridge: Polity, 1995).

Connell, Robert W., 'The Big Picture: Masculinities in Recent World History', *Theory and Society*, 22 (1993), pp. 597–623.

Cook, J., ed., *William Hazlitt: Selected Writings* (Oxford: Oxford University Press, 1991).

Corfield, Penelope J., *Power and the Professions in Britain 1700–1850* (London: Routledge, 1995).

Cover, Robert, 'Violence and the word', *Yale Law Journal*, 95 (1986), pp. 1601–1629.

Crawford A., *Reminiscences of a Naval Officer, 1788–1869*, 2 vols (London: H. Colburn, 1851).

Critchley, T. A., *The Conquest of Violence* (London: Constable, 1970).

Crompton, R., *L'Office et Aucthoritie de Justices de Peace* (London, 1606).

Cross, A. L., 'The English criminal law and benefit of clergy during the eighteenth and early nineteenth century', *American Historical Review*, 22:3 (1917), pp. 544–565.

Cruickshank, I. R., *The Irish Duel; Or, The Loves Of Paddy Wackmacruck and Mackirkcroft The Tailor* (London, 1816).

Darnton, R., *The Great Cat Massacre* (Harmondsworth: Penguin, 1991).

David, Laurent Olivier, *Les Patriotes de 1837–1839* (Montreal: Senécalm 1884).

David, Saul, *The Homicidal Earl: The Life of Lord Cardigan* (London: Abacus, 1997).

Davies, C., ed., *The Private Correspondence of Lord MacCartney, Governor of Madras (1781–1785)*, vol. LXXVII (London: Royal Historical Society, 1950).

Davis, S. G., *Parades and Power: Street Theater in Nineteenth Century Philadelphia* (Philadelphia: Temple University Press, 1986).

Dawkins, D., *The Life and Times of Capt. John Pilford RN* (Horsham: Horsham Museum Society, 1988).

Dawson, Graham, 'The blond Bedouin: Lawrence of Arabia, imperial adventure and the imagery of English-British masculinity', in J. Tosh and M. Roper, eds, *Manful Assertions*, (London: Routledge, 1991), pp. 113–144.

Demeter, Karl, *Das Deutsche Offizerkorps in Gesellschaft und Staat*, 1650–1945 (Frankfurt: Bernard Graefe, 1962).

Dobree, B., ed., *Letters of Philip Dormer Stanhope, 4th Earl of Chesterfield*, 6 vols, ed. B. Dobree (London, Eyre and Spottiswoode: Viking Press, 1932).

Dogherty, T., *The Crown Circuit Assistant: Being A Collection Of Precedents, Of Indictments, Informations, Convictions By Justices, Inquisitions, Pleas and other Entries In Criminal and Penal Proceedings. Together With An Alphabetical Table To The Statutes relating to Felony, Brought Down To The Twenty-Sixth Year of his present Majesty King George the Third* (London: P. Uriel and E. Brooke, 1787).

Domash, Mona, 'Those gorgeous incongruities: polite society and public space on the streets of nineteenth century New York City', *Annals of the Association of American Geographers*, 88: 2 (1998), pp. 209–226.

Douglas, Mary, *Purity and Danger: An Analysis of the Concepts of Pollution and Taboo* (London and Melbourne: Ark, 1984).

Douglas, William, *Duelling Days In The Army* (London: Ward and Downey, 1887).

Downs, M. H., *Pugilistica: The History of British Boxing*, 3 vols (Edinburgh: John Grant, 1906).

Duman, Daniel, *The Judicial Bench in England 1727–1875* (London: Royal Historical Society, 1982).

Egan, Pierce, *Life in London or the Day and Night Scenes of Jerry Hawthorn Esq. and his elegant friend Corinthian Tom, accompanied by Bob Logic, the Oxonian, in their Rambles and Sprees through the Metropolis* (London, 1820).

Emsley, Clive, *British Society and the French Wars 1793–1815* (London: Macmillan, 1979).

Erskine, David and Kimber, William, eds, *Augustus Hervey's Journal: Being The Intimate Account Of The Life Of A Captain In The Royal Navy Ashore and Afloat 1746–1759* (London: William Kimber, 1953).

Fambri, Paolo, 'The free press and duelling in Italy, a lecture delivered before the Tribunal of Honour by Paolo Fambri, Questor of Deputies of the Kingdom of Italy', *North American Review*, Jan. (1869), p. 300.

Fauteux, A., *Le Duel Au Canada* (Montreal: Éditions de Zodiaque, 1934).

Firth, C. H., *Cromwell's Army* (London: Methuen, 1902).

Firth, Edith G., *The Town of York, 1793-1815: A Collection of Documents of Early Toronto* (Toronto: Champlain Society, 1962).

Ford, D., *Admiral Vernon and the Navy* (London: Fisher Unwin, 1907).

Fordyce, D., *Dialogues Concerning Education*, 2 vols (London, 1748).

Foster, Sir Michael, *A Report of Some Proceedings on the Commission for the Trial of the Rebels in the Year 1746, in the County of Surry; And of Other Crown Cases: to which are Added*

Discourses Upon a Few Branches of the Crown Law, 3rd edn (London: E. and R. Brooke, 1792)

Fraser, S. E., ed., *Ludvig Holberg's Memoirs: An Eighteenth Century Danish Contribution to International Understanding* (Leiden: Brill, 1970).

Freeman, Joanna B., 'Dueling as politics: reinterpreting the Burr–Hamilton duel', *William and Mary Quarterly*, 3rd series, 53:2 (1996), pp. 289–318.

Frevert, Ute, 'Honour and middle class culture: the history of the duel in England and Germany', in J. Kocka and A. Mitchell, eds, *Bourgeois Society in Nineteenth Century Europe* (Oxford: Berg, 1993), pp. 207–240.

Frevert, Ute, *Men of Honour: A Social and Cultural History of the Duel* (Cambridge: Polity Press, 1995).

Frevert, Ute, 'The taming of the noble ruffian: male violence and dueling in early modern and modern Germany', in P. Spierenburg, ed., *Men and Violence: Gender, Honor, and Rituals in Modern Europe and America* (Columbus: Ohio State University Press, 1998), pp. 37–64.

Gask, D., *Cm. John Mundell R.N. 1776–1833* (Cawsand: privately printed, 2001).

Gatrell, V. A. C., *The Hanging Tree: Execution and the English People* (Oxford: Oxford University Press, 1994).

George, M. D., *Catalogue of Political and Personal Satires Preserved in the Department of Prints and Drawings in the British Museum*, vols x–xi, ed. F. G. Stephenson and D. George (London: British Museum, 1952).

Gilbert, Arthur N., 'Law and honour amongst eighteenth century British army officers', *Historical Journal*, 19 (1976), pp. 75–87.

Gilchrist, J. P., *A Brief Display Of The Origin and History of Ordeals, Trials by Battle, Courts Of Chivalry Or Honour; And The Decision Of Private Quarrels By Single Combat: Also A Chronological Register Of The Principal Duels Fought From The Accession Of His Late Majesty To The Present Time* (London, 1821).

Goodley, A. D., ed., *Herodotus: The Histories* (London: Loeb, 1921).

Goffman, Erving, *Interaction Rituals: Essays in Face to Face Behaviour* (New York: Pantheon, 1983).

Goldsmith, M. M., 'Public virtue and private vice: Bernard Mandeville and English political ideologies in the early eighteenth century', *Eighteenth Century Studies*, 9:4 (1976), pp. 477–510.

Gottlieb Goede, C. A., *A Foreigner's Opinion of England, Englishmen, Englishwomen ... and a variety of other interesting subjects, including memorials of art and nature*, 3 vols, trans. Thomas Horne (London, 1821).

Greenberg, Kenneth S., 'The nose, the lie and the duel in the Antibellum South', *American Historical Review*, 95:1 (1990), pp. 57–74.

Gronow, Capt., *The Reminiscences and Recollections of Captain Gronow: Being Anecdotes of the Camp, Court and Society 1810–1860* (London: Bodley Head, 1964).

Hale, Sir Matthew, *Pleas of the Crown* (London, 1678)

Hall, Edward T., *The Hidden Dimension* (New York: Doubleday, 1966).

Halliday, Hugh, *Murder Among Gentlemen: A History of Duelling in Canada* (Toronto: Robin Brass, 1999).

Hamilton, J., *The Royal Code of Honor, For the Regulation of Duelling: As it was Respectfully Submitted To The European Sovereigns* (Dublin: Alexander Thom, 1805).

Harvey, Karen, 'The history of masculinity, circa 1650–1800', *Journal of British Studies*, 44 (2005), pp. 296–311.

Harvey, K. and Shephard, A., 'What have historians done with masculinity? Reflections on five centuries of British history, circa 1500–1950', *Journal of British Studies*, 44:2 (2005), pp. 274–280.

Hay Douglas, 'Property, authority and the criminal law', in D. Hay et al., eds, *Albion's Fatal Tree: Crime and Society in 18th C England* (London: Allen Lane, 1975), pp. 17–63.

Herr, Richard, 'Honor versus absolutism: Richelieu's fight against duelling', *Journal of Modern History*, 27:3 (1955), pp. 281–285.

Hey, Richard, *A Dissertation on Duelling* (Cambridge: Magdalen College, 1784).

Hilton, J., *Index to the Maidstone Journal* (Orkney: Kirkwall Press, n.d.).

Hobbes, Thomas, *The Elements of Law, Natural and Politic,* ed. F. Tonnies (London: Frank Cass, 1969).

Hobsbawm, E., 'The example of the English middle class', in J. Kocka and A. Mitchell, eds., *Bourgeois Society in Nineteenth Century Europe* (Oxford: Berg, 1993).

Hoffman, Piotr, *The Quest for Power: Hobbes, Descartes and the Emergence of Modernity* (Atlantic Highlands, New Jersey: Prometheus, 1996).

Hollis, Christopher, *Eton: A History* (London: Hollis and Carter, 1960).

Horder, Jeremy, 'The duel and the English law of homicide', *Oxford Journal of Legal Studies*, 12 (1992), pp. 419–430.

Horder, Jeremy, *Provocation and Responsibility* (Oxford: Clarendon Press, 1992).

Hough, William, *A Casebook of European And Native General Courts Martial Held From the Years 1801–1821, On Officers, Non Commissioned Officers And Privates in His Majesty's And The Honorable East India Company's Armies. To Which is Annexed The Forms And Precedents Observed At Courts Martial* (Calcutta, 1821).

Howell T. B., ed., *A Complete Collection of State Trials*, 33 vols (London: R. Bagshaw, 1809–1826).

Howitt, William, *Rural Life* (London: Longman, 1840).

Hughes, Steven, 'Men of steel: dueling, honour and politics in liberal Italy', in P. Spierenburg, ed., *Men and Violence: Gender, Honor and Rituals in Modern Europe and America,* (Columbus: Ohio State Press, 1989), pp. 64–81.

Ignatieff, M., *A Just Measure of Pain: The Penitentiary in the Industrial Revolution 1750–1850* (London: Peregrine, 1989).

Ingram, Rowland, *Reflections upon Duelling* (London: J. Hatchard, 1804).

Innwood, Stephen, *A History of London* (London: Macmillan, 1998).

Johnson, Christopher, 'British championism: early pugilism and the works of Fielding', *The Review of English Studies*, 47 (1996), pp. 331–351.

Joy, Henry, 'Letter of 1842', *Law Magazine Quarterly Review of Jurisprudence*, 28 (1842).

Kelly, James, *That Damn'd Thing Called Honour: Duelling in Ireland 1570–1860* (Cork: Cork University Press, 1995).

Kiernan, Victor G., *The Duel in European History: Honour and the Reign of Aristocracy* (Oxford: Oxford University Press, 1988).

King, Peter, 'Decision makers and decision making in the English criminal law', *Historical Journal*, 27:1 (1984), pp. 5–58.

King, Peter, 'Punishing assault: the transformation of attitudes in the English courts', *Journal of Interdisciplinary History*, 27 (1996), pp. 43–74.

Klein, Lawrence, *Shaftesbury and the Culture of Politeness: Moral Discourse and Cultural Politics in Early Eighteenth Century England* (Cambridge: Cambridge University Press, 1994).

Kohut, Adolph, *Das Buch berühmter Duelle* (Berlin: Alfred Fried, 1888).

Kriegal, A. D., 'Liberty and Whiggery in early nineteenth-century England', *Journal of Modern History*, 52:2 (1980), pp. 253–278.

Kropf, C. R., 'Libel and satire in the eighteenth century', *Eighteenth Century Studies*, 8:2 (1974–1975), pp. 153–168.

Landale, James, *Duel: A True Story of Death and Honour* (Edinburgh: Cannongate, 2005).

Langford, Paul, 'The uses of eighteenth century politeness', *Transactions of the Royal Historical Society*, 12 (2002), pp. 311–331.

Langford, Paul, *A Polite and Commercial People* (Oxford: Oxford University Press, 1992).

Langford, Paul, *Public Life and the Propertied Englishman 1689–1798* (Oxford: Clarendon Press, 1991).

Larkin J. F. and Hughes, P. L., *Stuart Royal Proclamations*, 2 vols. (Oxford: Clarendon Press, 1973).

Lawrence, Henry W., 'The greening of the squares of London: transformation of urban landscapes and ideals', *Annals of the Association of American Geographers*, 83 (1993), pp. 90–118.

Lennox, Lord William Pitt, *Fashion Then and Now: Illustrated By Anecdotes, Social, Political, Military, Dramatic and Sporting*, 2 vols (London: Chapman and Hall, 1878).

Loose, Jacqueline, *Duels and Duelling: Affairs of Honour around the Wandsworth Area* (London: Wandsworth Borough Council, 1983).

Low, Jennifer, *Manhood and the Duel: Masculinity in Early Modern Drama* (New York: Palgrave Macmillan, 2003).

Lucas, William, *The Duellist; Or, Men of Honour: A Story Calculated to Shew The Folly and Extravagance, And Sin of Duelling* (London: J. Cundee, 1805).

Macartney, Lord, *The Private Correspondence of Lord Macartney, Governor or Madras 1781–1785*, ed. C. Davies (London: Royal Historical Society, 1950).

Mackay, Charles, *Extraordinary Popular Delusions and The Madness of Crowds* (London: Wordsworth, 1995).

Madden, Samuel, *Reflections and Resolution Proper for the Gentlemen of Ireland* (Dublin, 1738).

Mahon, K. A., *An Index to the More Important Historical Information Contained in the Files of the* Hull Advertiser and Exchange Gazette *1794–1825* (Hull: University of Hull, 1955).

Mandeville, John, *The Fable Of The Bees Or Private Vices Public Benefits*, ed. E. J. Hundert (Indianapolis: Hackett, 1997).

Mann, Patricia S., *Micro-Politics: Agency in a Postfeminist Era* (Minneapolis: University of Minneapolis Press, 1994).

Manning, Roger B., *Swordsmen: The Martial Ethos in the Three Kingdoms* (Oxford: Oxford University Press, 2003).

Maxwell, Sir Herbert, ed., *The Creevey Papers: A Selection from the Correspondence and Diaries of the Late Thomas Creevey M.P.* (London: John Murray, 1912).

McAleer, Kevin, *Dueling: The Cult of Honor in Fin-de-Siècle Germany* (Princeton: Princeton University Press, 1994).

Millingen, J. G., *The History of Duelling Including Narratives Of The Most Remarkable Personal Encounters That Have Taken Place From the Earliest Period To The Present Time*, 2 vols (London: Richard Bentley, 1841).

Misson, Henri, *Memoirs and Observations of his Travels over England* (London, 1719).

Mitchell, Don, 'The end of public space? People's park, definitions of the public and democracy', *Annals of the American Association of American Geographers*, 85:1 (1985), pp. 108–133.

Moore, C., *A Full Inquiry into the subject of suicide: to which are added two treatise on duelling and gaming*, 2 vols (London, 1790).

Morgan, C., 'In search of the phantom misnamed honour: duelling in Upper Canada', *Canadian Historical Review*, 76:4 (1995), pp. 519–562.

Mosse, W., 'Nobility and bourgeoisie in nineteenth century Europe: a comparative view', in J. Kocka and A. Mitchell, eds, *Bourgeois Society in Nineteenth Century Europe* (Oxford: Berg, 1993), pp. 70–102.

Napier, P., *Part One of the Life of Captain Henry Napier RN 1789–1853*, 2 vols (London: Michael Russell, 1997).

Nichols, D. B., 'The devil's own article', *Military Law Review*, 12 (1963), pp. 116–117.

Nye, Robert A., 'Fencing, the duel and Republican manhood in the Third Republic', *Journal of Contemporary History*, 25 (1990), pp. 365–377.

Nye, Robert A., 'The end of the modern French duel', in P. Spierenburg, ed., *Men and Violence: Gender, Honour and Rituals in Modern Europe and America* (Columbus: Ohio State Press, 1998), pp. 82–101.

Odell, W. B., *Essay on Duelling, In Which The Subject Is Morally And Historically Considered; And The Practice Deduced From The Earliest Times* (Cork: Odell and Laurent, 1814).

Oldham, J., 'Law Reporting in the London Newspapers', *American Journal of Legal History*, 31 (1987), pp. 177–206.

Pacificus, Philo, *Two Extracts from a Pamphlet Entitled, The Friend of Peace: Containing A Special Interview Between The President of the United States and Omar, An Officer Dismissed for Duelling; With Six Letters From Omar to the President; And Omar's Solitary Reflections. The Whole Reported By Philo Pacificus* (Stockport: J. Lomax, 1816).

Parker, G., *A View of Society and Manners in High and Low Life*, X vols (London, 1781).

Parry, D., *The Meadley Index to the* Hull Advertiser *1826–1845* (Humberside: Humberside College, 1987).

Patterson, G., *More Studies in Nova Scotia History* (Halifax: Imperial Publishing Company, 1941).

Peltonen, Markku, 'Civilised with death: civility, duelling and honour in Elizabethan England,' in J. Richards, ed., *Early Modern Civil Discourses* (Basingstoke: Palgrave Macmillan 2003), pp. 51–67.

Peltonen, Markku, 'Francis Bacon, the earl of Northampton, and the Jacobean anti-duelling campaign', *Historical Journal*, 44:1 (2001), pp. 1–28.

Peltonen, Markku, *The Duel in Early Modern England: Civility, Politeness and Honour* (Cambridge: Cambridge University Press, 2003).

Pepys S., *The Diary*, eds. Robert Latham, William Matthews, et al., 11 vols. (London: Bell & Hyman, and Berkeley: University of California Press, 1970–1983).

Peterson, M. J., 'Victorian periodicals and the professions: medicine', in J. D. Vann ad R. T. Van Arsdel, eds, *Victorian Periodicals and Victorian Society* (Aldershot: Scolar, 1994) pp. 22–44.

Prest, W. R., *The Inns of Court under Elizabeth I and the Early Stuarts, 1590–1640* (London: Longman, 1972).

Prest, W. R., *The Professions in Early Modern England* (London: Croom Helm, 1987).

Priestly, Philip, *Victorian Prison Lives* (London: Pimlico Press, 1999).

Radford, P., *The Celebrated Captain Barclay: Sport, Money and Fame in Regency Britain* (London: Headline, 2001).

Reid, J. C., *Bucks and Bruisers: Pierce Egan and Regency England* (London: Routledge & Kegan Paul, 1971).

Reyfman, I., 'The emergence of the duel in Russia: corporal punishment and the honor code', *Russian Review*, 54:1 (1995), pp. 26–43.

Rhodes, Deborah L., 'Moral character as a professional credential', *Yale Law Journal*, 94 (1985), pp. 491–585.

Riddell, William Renwick, *Upper Canada Sketches: Incidents in the Early Times of the Province* (Toronto: Carswell, 1922).

Roots, Roger, 'When lawyers were serial killers: nineteenth century visions of good moral character', *Northern Illinois University Law Review*, 22 (2001), pp. 19–35.

Roper, Michael and Tosh, John, 'Introduction: historians and the politics of masculinity', in M. Roper and J. Tosh, eds, *Manful Assertions: Masculinities in Britain since 1800* (London: Routledge, 1991), pp. 1–24.

Russell, Gillian, *The Theatres of War: Performance, Politics and Society 1793–1815* (Oxford: Oxford University Press, 1995).

Sabine, Lorenzo, *Notes On Duels And Duelling, Alphabetically Arranged, With A Preliminary Historical Essay* (Boston: Crosby and Nichols, 1859).

Sainsbury, John, '"Cool courage should always mark me": John Wilkes and duelling', *Journal of the Canadian Historical Association*, 7 (1996), pp. 19–33.

Sassure, C. de, *A Foreign View of England in 1725–1729*, trans. Madame van Muyden 1902 (London: Caliban, 1995).

Schivelbusch, W., 'The policing of street lighting', *Yale French Studies*, 73 (1987), pp. 61–74.

Scott, W., *The Duellist, A Bravo to God and a Coward to Man* (London, 1774).

Selden, J., *The Duello, or Single Combat from antiquitie derived into this Kingdome of England, with kindes and ceremonious formes thereof, from good authoritie described* (London: J. Helme, 1610. Reprinted, London: William Bray, 1711).

Sennett, R., *Flesh and Stone: The Body and the City in Western Civilisation* (London: Faber and Faber, 1994).

Sharp, G., *Remarks On the Opinions of some of the most celebrated Writers on Crown Law Respecting the Due Distinction between Manslaughter and Murder* (London, 1773).

Shephard, Alexandra, 'From anxious patriarchs to refined gentlemen? Manhood in Britain, circa 1500–1700', *Journal of British Studies*, 44 (2005), pp. 281–295.

Shoemaker, Robert B., 'Male honour and the decline of public violence in eighteenth-century London', *Social History*, 26:2 (2001), pp. 190–208.

Shoemaker, Robert B., 'Reforming male manners: public insult and the decline of violence in London, 1660–1740' in T. Hitchcock and M. Cohen, eds, *English Masculinities*, 1660–1800 (London: Addison Wesley, 1999), pp. 133–150.

Shoemaker, Robert B., *The London Mob: Violence and Disorder in Eighteenth Century England* (London: Hambledon and London, 2004).

Shoemaker, Robert B., 'The taming of the duel: masculinity, honour and ritual violence in London 1660–1800', *Historical Journal*, 45 (2002), pp. 525–545.

Sieveking, A. Forbes, 'Duelling and militarism', *Transactions of the Royal Historical Society*, 3rd series, 11 (1917), pp. 165–184.

Silver, George, *Parades of defense* (London, 1599).

Simpson, Antony E., 'Dandelions on the field of honor: duelling the middle classes and the law in nineteenth century England', *Criminal Justice History*, 9 (1988), pp. 99–155.

Smith, Adam, *Lectures on Jurisprudence*, ed. R. L. Meek, D. Raphael and P. G. Stein (Oxford: Clarendon, 1979).

Smith, Adam, *Lectures on Justice, Police, Revenue and Arms* (1753; New York: Kelley, 1964).

Smith, Sir Rupert, *The Utility of Force: The Art of War in the Modern World* (London: Allen Lane, 2005).

Solkin, D. H., *Painting for Money: The Visual Arts and the Public Sphere in Eighteenth Century England* (New Haven: Yale University Press, 1993).

Spring, D., 'Some reflections on social history in the nineteenth century', *Victorian Studies*, 4 (1960), p. 58.

Stanton, S., *The Principles of Duelling with Rules to be Observed In Every Particular Respecting it* (London: Hookham, 1790).

Steinmetz, A., *The Romance of Duelling, in all Times and in all Countries*, 2 vols (London: Chapman and Hall, 1868).

Stephens, J. F., *A General View of the Criminal Law of England* (London: Macmillan, 1863).

Stephenson, F. G. and George, D., *Catalogue of Political and Personal Satires Preserved in the Department of Prints and Drawings in the British Museum*, vols iii–ix (London: British Museum, 1877).

Stewart, Alan, 'Purging troubled humours: Bacon, Northampton and the anti-duelling campaign of 1613–14' in S. Clucas and R. Davis, eds, *The Crisis of 1614 and the Addled Parliament: Literary and Historical Perspectives* (Aldershot: Ashgate, 2002), pp. 81–91.

Stockdale, P., *The Memoirs of the Life and Writing of Percival Stockdale*, 2 vols (London, 1809).

Stone, Lawrence, 'Interpersonal violence In English society 1300–1980', *Past and Present*, 101 (1983), pp. 23–33.

Stone, Lawrence, *The Crisis of the Aristocracy, 1558–1641* (Oxford: Clarendon Press, 1965).

Stone, Lawrence, 'A History of Violence in England: A Rejoinder', *Past and Present*, 108, (1985) pp. 216–224.

Stone, Lawrence, *The Road to Divorce: England 1530–1987* (Oxford: Oxford University Press, 1990).

Storch, Robert D., 'The policeman as domestic missionary: urban discipline and popular culture in Northern England 1850–1880', *Journal of Social History*, IX (1976), pp. 481–509.

Talbott, J. E., *The Pen and Ink Sailor, Charles Middleton and the King's Navy 1778–1813* (London: Frank Cass, 1998).

Thompson, Edward P., 'Eighteenth century English society: class struggle without class', *Social History*, 3 (1978), pp. 133–165.

Thompson, Edward P., 'Time, work-discipline and industrial capitalism', *Past and Present*, 38 (1967), pp. 56–97.

Tolstoy, Nikolai, *The Half-Mad Lord: Thomas Pitt, 2nd Baron Camelford* (New York: Holt, Rinehart and Winston, 1978).

Tosh, John, 'Masculinities in an industrializing society: Britain, 1800–1914', *Journal of British Studies*, 44 (2005), pp. 330–342.

Tosh, John, 'The old Adam and the new man: emerging themes in the history of English masculinities 1750–1850', in T. Hitchcock and M. Cohen, eds, *English Masculinities 1660–1800* (London: Addison Wesley Longman, 1999), pp. 217–238.

Trenchard, J., *An Argument, Shewing that a Standing Army is Inconsistent with a Free Government and Absolutely Destructive of the English Monarchy* (London, 1687).

Truman, B. C., *The Field of Honour: Being A Complete And Comprehensive History Of Duelling In All Countries* (New York: Ford, Howard and Hulbert, 1884).

Twain, M., *A Tramp Abroad*, 2 vols (Hartford: American Publishing Company, 1880).

Vagts, Alfred, *A History of Militarism* (New York: Meridian, 1959).

Verney, Margaret, ed. *Verney Letters of the Eighteenth Century*, 2 vols (London: Benn, 1930).

Vernier, Lt Col. Willoughby, *A British Rifleman: The Journals and Correspondence of Maj. George Simmons, Rifle Brigade, During the Peninsula War and the Campaign of Waterloo* (London: A&C Black, 1899).

Wahrman, D., 'Middle class domesticity goes public: gender, class and politics from Queen Caroline to Queen Victoria', *Journal of British Studies,* 32:4 (1993), pp. 396–432.

Walsh, J. E., *Ireland Sixty Years Ago* (Dublin, 1840).

Webb, B. and Webb, S., *English Local Government*, 4 vols (London: Longman, 1906–1922).

Weinstein, D., 'Fighting or flyting? Verbal duelling in mid-sixteenth century Italy', in T. Dean and K. J. P. Lowe, eds, *Crime, Society and Law in Renaissance Italy* (Cambridge: Cambridge University Press, 1994).

Wetherley, Edward, ed., *The Correspondence of John Wilkes and Charles Churchill* (New York: Columbia Press, 1954).

Wiener, Martin J., 'Judges v jurors: courtroom tensions in murder trials and the law of criminal responsibility in nineteenth century England', *Law and History Review*, 17 (1999), pp. 467–506.

Wiener, Martin J., 'The Victorian criminalization of men', in P. Spierenburg, ed., *Men and Violence: Gender, Honor and Rituals in Modern Europe and America* (Columbus: Ohio State University Press, 1998), pp. 197–212.

Wiener, Martin J., *Reconstructing the Criminal: Culture, Law and Policy in England 1830–1914* (Cambridge: Cambridge University Press, 1990).

Wrigley, E. A., *People, Cities and Wealth: The Transformation of Traditional Society* (Oxford: Blackwell, 1987).

Ziegler, *Philip, Addington: A Life of Henry Addington, First Viscount Sidmouth* (London: Collins, 1965).

Internet Resources

Literature Online (http://chadwyck.co.uk, 2 Jul. 2009), Mary Shelley, *Falkner* (London, 1838).

Old Bailey Proceedings Online (www.oldbaileyonline.org, 1 Oct. 2009), 5 June 1782, trial of Bennet Allen (ref. t17820605-1).

Old Bailey Proceedings Online (www.oldbaileyonline.org, 1 Oct. 09), 17 February 1796, trial of Richard England (ref. t17960217-27).

Index